PUBLICATIONS IN ARCHAEOLOGY
David P. Braun, General Editor

Also in this series

The Star Lake Archaeological Project:
Anthropology of a Headwaters Area
of Chaco Wash, New Mexico
edited by Walter K. Wait and Ben A. Nelson

Mobility and Adaptation:
The Anasazi of Black Mesa,
Arizona
by Shirley Powell

Papers on the Archaeology of Black Mesa,
Arizona, Volume II
edited by Stephen Plog and Shirley Powell

Decoding Prehistoric Ceramics
edited by Ben A. Nelson

Contributions to the Archaeology and
Ethnohistory of Greater Mesoamerica
edited by William J. Folan

Center for Archaeological Investigations
Southern Illinois University at Carbondale

Ripples in the Chichimec Sea

New Considerations of Southwestern-Mesoamerican Interactions

Edited by
Frances Joan Mathien and
Randall H. McGuire

Southern Illinois University Press
Carbondale and Edwardsville

E
78
.S7
R54
1986

Edited by Barbara E. Cohen
Designed by John K. DeBacher
Production supervised by Loretta Vincent

Library of Congress Cataloging-in-Publication Data

Main entry under title:

Ripples in the Chichimec Sea.

   (Publications in archaeology)
   At head of title: Center for Archaeological
Investigations, Southern Illinois University at
Carbondale.
   Includes bibliographies.
   1. Indians of North America—Southwest, New—Commerce—
Addresses, essays, lectures.   2. Indians of Mexico—
Commerce—Addresses, essays, lectures.   3. Indians of
North America—Southwest, New—Antiquities—Addresses,
essays, lectures.   4. Indians of Mexico—Antiquities—Ad-
dresses, essays, lectures.   5. Southwest, New—Antiquities
Addresses, essays, lectures.   6. Mexico—Antiquities
Addresses, essays, lectures.   I. Mathien, Frances Joan.
II. McGuire, Randall H. III. Southern Illinois
University at Carbondale. Center for Archaeological
Investigations. IV. Series: Publications in archaeology
(Southern Illinois University at Carbondale. Center for
Archaeological Investigations)
E78.S7R54   1986   979.01   85-27862
ISBN 0-8093-1247-6

89 88 87 86 4 3 2 1

12947672

5-28-91
AC

**To the memory of
Charles C. Di Peso**

a colleague whose warmth, friendliness, and cheerful discussions of all aspects of anthropology are treasured by those who knew him. He was one of the first to chart the Chichimec sea, beginning with his earliest work in southern Arizona and culminating in his monumental excavation at Casas Grandes. More importantly his creative ideas and theories have structured the debates concerning southwestern-mesoamerican interactions for the last quarter of a century. Without Charles Di Peso most of the insight and discussion in this volume would not have been possible. American archaeology has suffered a great loss with his passing.

Contents

Tables

Figures

Acknowledgments

The editors would like to thank the people who assisted us in the assembly and preparation of this volume. George Gumerman and David Braun helped us greatly in making contacts with SIU Press. Kenney Withers and his staff at SIU Press were extremely responsive to our needs while we were putting this volume together. The Division of Cultural Research of the National Park Service in Albuquerque provided Frances Joan Mathien with institutional support; Jennifer Bjork and Milford Fletcher of the Division of Natural Resources provided other help. The Department of Anthropology at the State University of New York at Binghamton assisted us with xeroxing and phone calls and, most importantly, allowed the departmental secretary, Peg Roe, to enter five of the papers on the department's word processor. We would like to give special thanks to Al Dekin and the department for this support. Finally, thanks to all of the authors for their prompt attention to revisions and deadlines.

Contributors

BEATRIZ BRANIFF C. is an archaeologist with the Instituto Nacional de Antropologia e História, Dirección de Monumentos Prehispanicos. She has conducted most of her fieldwork in northern Mexico, principally in Guanajuato and Sonora. She currently is directing a project to inventory all known archaeological sites in northern Mexico.

MICHAEL S. FOSTER, co-owner of Jornada Anthropological Research Association, has conducted research in and published numerous articles on northwest and west Mesoamerica, including a coedited book, *The Archaeology of West and Northwest Mesoamerica*. He is currently working on several projects including lithic materials from La Quemada, reevaluation of the dendrochronological dates from Casas Grandes, and chronological sequences from the West Coast of Mexico.

J. CHARLES KELLEY is Professor Emeritus, Department of Anthropology, Southern Illinois University at Carbondale, and Adjunct Professor at Sul Ross State University at Alpine, Texas. He has published many articles in journals, primarily concerned with his research in northwestern Mexico and its relation to southwestern U.S. archaeology. He is coeditor of three books published by the Southern Illinois University Press and one published by the University of Texas Press. In 1978 the Southern Illinois University Press published *Across the Chichimec Sea, Papers in Honor of J. Charles Kelley* (Carroll L. Riley and Basil C. Hedrick, editors).

STEVEN A. LeBLANC, Curator of Archaeology, Southwest Museum, directs a long-term research project in the Mimbres area. He has also directed research in the Zuni area. He authored *The Mimbes People*, and is coauthor of *The Galaz Ruin: A Mimbres Village in Southwestern New Mexico* and *Archaeological Explanation*.

RANDALL H. McGUIRE is an assistant professor at the State University of New York, University Center at Binghamton. He has carried out extensive archaeological research on both the history and prehistory of the Greater Southwest. He is currently conducting archaeological research in the Altar Valley of Sonora and on gravestones in the Binghamton, New York area. He is coauthor with Michael Schiffer of *Hohokam and Patayan: The Prehistory of Southwestern Arizona.*

FRANCES JOAN MATHIEN is an archaeologist with the Division of Cultural Research of the National Park Service in Albuquerque and Adjunct Assistant Professor in the Department of Anthropology at the University of New Mexico. She is the editor of *Environment and Subsistence in the Chaco Area, New Mexico.*

RICHARD S. NELSON is a research associate in the Department of Anthropology, New York University. His dissertation deals with the role of spheres of exchange in the regional and long-distance exchange systems of the Hohokam.

RICHARD A. PAILES, Associate Professor, Department of Anthropology, University of Oklahoma, has conducted research in Arizona and northern Mexico, with most of his field research in Sonora, Mexico. He has published several papers on the prehistory of Sonora, and with Joseph Whitecotton has coauthored several papers dealing with Mesoamerica and world systems.

STEPHEN PLOG is an associate professor of anthropology at the University of Virginia. His research interests include exchange systems, stylistic analysis, and cultural change in the American Southwest.

CARROLL L. RILEY is Professor of Anthropology at Southern Illinois University at Carbondale. He has done field research in the Greater Southwest, the Northwest Coast, Mexico, Venezuela, western Europe, and the Mediterranean region. Riley is coeditor of the multivolume *Southwestern Journals of Adolph F. Bandelier* and has edited and authored a number of other books.

BARBARA L. STARK, Associate Professor, Department of Anthropology, Arizona State University, has published settlement patterns and economic analyses of complex societies on the Gulf and Pacific coasts of Mesoamerica. Recently, she has been concerned with the analysis of economic ceramics.

STEADMAN UPHAM is Assistant Professor and Chief Archaeologist in the Department of Sociology and Anthropology, New Mexico State University. His research and publications deal with the archaeology and ethnohistory of the American Southwest. He authored *Politics and Power: An Economic and Political History of the Western Pueblo.*

JOSEPH W. WHITECOTTON is Professor, Department of Anthropology, University of Oklahoma. His research and publications deal with the ethnohistory of Mesoamerica—particularly Oaxaca—and northern New Mexico. He is author of *The Zapotecs: Princes, Priests, and Peasants* and co-editor of *Native American Ethnohistory*.

DAVID R. WILCOX is an anthropologist for the Museum of Northern Arizona, and Visiting Associate Professor, Northern Arizona University, Flagstaff. His research and publications deal with Hohokam site structure, regional systems, and social and political organization. He is coauthor of *Hohokam Ballcourts and Their Interpretation* and coeditor of *The Protohistoric Period in the North American Southwest, A.D. 1450–1700*.

Ripples in the Chichimec Sea

Adrift in the Chichimec Sea

Frances Joan Mathien and Randall H. McGuire

To the north of the painted pyramids and grand cities of Mesoamerica stretched a great sea of Chichimecs—descendants of dogs, the barbarian counterpoint to mesoamerican civilization. The archaeological region that we parochially call the Southwest lies adrift in this sea. In the eyes of some it was a peninsula of Mesoamerica, the northernmost and rudest outpost of the great civilizations; changes in the prehistory of the Southwest were simply the furthest eddies of the ebb and flow of mesoameriocan history. To others it was an island isolated in the sea that developed in its own right, taking on only those things of Mesoamerica that were tossed up on its shore like driftwood or brought by infrequent and sporadic voyagers across the sea.

Commentators have variously opposed these positions as isolationist vs. imperialist, progressive vs. conservative, or ecological vs. historical. Everyone who works in the Southwest must deal with this debate because it affects our basic perception of the Southwest and how to account for its prehistory. If the Southwest was a peninsula, our accounts of prehistory must reach far to the south, and our theory must be capable of integrating events across great distances, environments, and cultures. If the Southwest was an island, we may seek our explanations in regional ecological and cultural relations, with external contacts and influences relegated to a secondary status.

The debate engendered by the isolationist vs. imperialist positions creates ripples in the Chichimec sea. It is an overly polarized debate often characterized by "kill and overkill" (Frisbie 1983:215). The polarization springs from differences in personalities, the training of individuals, and the theoretical positions individuals bring to the debate. The majority of southwestern archaeologists, poorly trained in the prehistory of Mesoamerica, take for granted the obvious mesoamerican donations (pottery, agriculture) but see little need to consider Mesoamerica further. Archaeologists trained in mesoamerican prehistory and working on the northern frontiers of Mesoamerica, in contrast, find obvious and major connections between the two regions.

Perhaps more important than training and regional perspective is theoretical position. The ecological functionalism of the New Archaeology has dominated southwestern archaeology for more than a decade. This perspective oriented archaeologists toward the investigation of environmentally defined regions, such as basins or river valleys, and to seek explanations in the human-environmental relations of these units. In this milieu the advocates of a mesoamerican presence appeared, at best, wedded to an archaic historical form of explanation and, at worst, as diffusionists. The mesoamerican advocates for their part dismissed the ecological functionalism and overly formalized method of the New Archaeology.

The ripples in the Chichimec sea are also the actual connections, interactions, and influences that linked the two regions. The consideration of these forces raises theoretical issues beyond our concern with southwestern prehistory. What role do long-range connections play in cultural change? How do we integrate these long-range connections with local environmental and cultural relations to account for the unique development of any given region or site? Answering these questions requires the development and use of theory applicable to the study of prehistory anywhere in the world.

It was with the hope of establishing a dialogue between the two groups and of exploring the theoretical issues involved that we organized a symposium on the topic of mesoamerican-southwestern interaction at the 1983 Society for American Archaeology meetings in Pittsburgh. We felt the time was right for bringing together all the major participants in this debate. The publication in the last decade of Di Peso's work at Casas Grandes and Kelley's research in the Chalchihuites had provided a wealth of new data that stimulated many investigators to reevaluate older concepts, undertake new research, and reconstruct culture history for many of the prehistoric groups who lived both in Mesoamerica and the greater Southwest. Equally important, we sensed an increasing dissatisfaction in the Southwest and world archaeology in general for the narrow ecological functionalism of recent times and a growing concern for broad intra- and interregional interactions. Both these trends suggested we might be able to get beyond the simplistic dichotomy of the recent debates to a more sophisticated and elaborate understanding of the issue.

Were we successful? Not entirely. But we had a chance to meet one another in public, we aired our views, and we commented on one another's positions. Perhaps the most successful aspect of the session was that it revealed a variety of viewpoints. Most of us came prepared to do battle along the traditional line, but as we listened to each other that line appeared increasingly blurred. Although a few still chose to couch their arguments in terms of the dichotomy, we did see many investigators using the same or similar models to evaluate the data in a less biased manner than a kill/over-kill position. We also found that the presentations addressed theoretical issues of concern beyond our narrower interest in southwestern prehistory.

When the symposium ended we felt that the diversity of viewpoints expressed did represent new perspectives on the issue of southwestern-mesoamerican interaction, theoretically informed perspectives potentially of broad interest and worthy of broader dissemination. We therefore asked the participants in the session and other investigators who had been unable to attend the session to prepare and submit papers for this volume. We offer this volume as an attempt to evaluate the nature and extent of southwestern-mesoamerican interaction and as an exploration of the broader theoretical issues implied by this evaluation.

The contributions to this volume were not written based on an outline devised by the editors because we did not wish to impose narrow constraints on our colleagues. In some ways this made the task of organizing the volume more difficult because the papers did not fit into neat categories. We have included here a total of 12 papers and 2 commentaries on those papers.

David Wilcox ably reviews the historical background for our current discussions of southwestern-mesoamerican interactions. He summarizes the work of many scholars under three major topics; frontier theories, mechanisms of contact, and world systems models. He considers both the contributions made by investigators associated with each of the topics and evaluates the strength and weakness of their work. Wilcox concludes that a world systems model, while not always applicable as originally described by Wallerstein, has considerable potential for future inquiries.

In the second paper Carroll L. Riley uses a combination of archaeological and ethnohistorical data to reconstruct the protohistoric interaction between northwestern Mexico and the Southwest. He proposes a protohistoric "third wave" of mesoamerican influence into the Southwest and documents trade routes and goods. Major population shifts in the Southwest prior to the protohistoric make it impossible to transpose Riley's trade routes onto the prehistoric case, but they do provide a valuable starting point in a direct historical approach.

Michael S. Foster reviews the archaeological data from northern and western Mexico to demonstrate the existence of numerous prehistoric cultures in the area between the mesoamerican heartland and the Southwest. In particular, he sees the northern mesoamerican culture of Chalchihuites and the southwestern culture of Casas Grandes as prominent middlemen linking the two regions and assigns them a semiperipheral status. He does not propose that the cultures of the Southwest resulted directly from mesoamerican economic interaction but that they were substantially affected by such interaction.

Beatriz Braniff provides data from one of the least known parts of the Southwest, Sonora, Mexico. She compares her data from a recently excavated site in northeastern Sonora to both San Jose Baviácora to the south and Casas Grandes to the east. All three sites yielded similar ceramic types, yet absolute dates from the two Sonoran sites place these types at a later time than Di Peso's Medio chronology suggests. This leads Braniff to question Di Peso's inference of Toltec influence at Casas Grandes and to ask what foreign culture is represented at Casas Grandes.

Braniff's brief report provides us with a glimpse of the archaeology of Sonora. More important, it draws the attention of U.S. researchers to the archaeological programs of the Instituto Nacional de Antropología e Historia in northern Mexico. Those of us working north of the border have too often failed to seek out information about these excavations or recognized their significance.

J. Charles Kelley seeks to clarify the exact series of connections that would have linked the Southwest to Mesoamerica along the west coast of Mexico in the Early Post-Classic (circa A.D. 900–1200). Mixteca-Puebla style traits link Aztatlán sites to the Valley of Mexico as well as across the Sierra Madre Occidental into the highlands of Durango. New data from Cañón de Molino in Durango represent a combination of Chalchihuites, Loma San Gabriel, and Aztatlán cultural traits. Kelley postulates that the site was a trading outpost where mobile merchants lived and worked. Kelley suggests that the site was a link in a chain of trading centers that stretched from the Valley of Mexico through the Chalchihuites culture to Casas Grandes. The system did not exist with any one mobile trader spanning the entire system, yet cultural traits from the Valley of Mexico could easily have reached the Southwest through numerous connections.

Steven LeBlanc uses the concept of interaction spheres in his far-ranging consideration of southwestern prehistory. He proposes that three large interaction spheres dominated the prehistoric Southwest at different times and that these spheres interacted with mesoamerican traders. He dates the earliest sphere, the Chaco, between A.D. 900–1150. The second centering around Casas Grandes succeeded the Chaco from A.D. 1130–1300. Finally, the smallest of the three, the Hohokam, developed slowly from A.D. 1150–1300 and existed until 1450. LeBlanc's model, like many others in this volume, depends on a host of conflicting interpretations concerning the dating of events in the Southwest.

In his second contribution to the volume David R. Wilcox proposes a new model based on linguistic relationships to account for the meso-american traits found among the Hohokam. He suggests that the distribution of Tepiman speakers through modern Arizona and Sonora provided a corridor of cultures speaking mutually intelligible languages along which meso-american features such as ballcourts could have reached the Hohokam. Changes in the distribution of this language group through time would have affected the spread of mesoamerican features and account for some of the temporal and spatial variability we see in mesoamerican features among the Hohokam.

Richard S. Nelson also examines the Hohokam data in his evaluation of shifts in the distribution of prestige goods between the Sedentary and Classic periods. In the former he identifies a clustering of prestige items with rich burials and burial areas. In the Classic, however, Nelson is unable to find such distinct clusters. Nelson infers that a prestige sphere of exchange existed among the Hohokam with no direct intervention from Mesoamerica. The data reviewed and conclusions reached compare well with Wilcox's linguistic separation, as well as his expected changes in structure of interaction and communication through time.

Joseph W. Whitecotton and Richard A. Pailes discuss the application of Wallerstein's world systems model to Mesoamerica and its peripheries, primarily the Southwest. They identify Mesoamerica as a "world economy with core states competing for access to economic goods." One problem in applying Wallerstein's model to Mesoamerica is that Wallerstein dismisses trade in preciosities as providing an adequate basis for a world economy. Whitecotton and Pailes recognize that the majority of mesoamerican trade items, especially those linking Mesoamerica and the Southwest, were such items; but they argue that preciosities may be more important to the functioning and continuance of social groups than Wallerstein allows. It is not clear why Whitecotton and Pailes terminate a mesoamerican presence in the Southwest with the collapse of Casas Grandes, circa A.D. 1340, when Riley's third wave occurs after A.D. 1340.

Steadman Upham argues that the world systems model is a useful heuristic device but not when used as a spatial model of political and economic systems. He suggests that we should focus our efforts more on the distribution of status and prestige than on the distribution of material culture items. Upham suggests that our examinations should center on three topics: (1) population centers, (2) commodity exchange and information flow, and (3) cultural and ethnic diversity. Upham concludes that it is not wise to limit our analysis to the exchange of goods alone; we must also consider the coexistence of numerous regional systems which could have created world system linkages. Upham postulates a mesoamerican world system including the Southwest which moved information as well as goods and which was a flexible and connected diverse cultural group linked through a variety of networks.

Frances Joan Mathien accepts the Wallerstein model, not because it is perfect but because it does allow some parameters that can be used in an attempt to determine whether one area, the Chaco Anasazi, should be considered part of the periphery of a mesoamerican world system or external to it. Based on an evaluation of available data, she concludes it is not peripheral, but external. Mathien then suggests that some type of prestige exchange or down-the-line trade model might better explain how material items as well as ideas moved among various culture groups to reach the Chaco area.

Randall H. McGuire sees the world systems model as a useful heuristic device that has directed southwestern and mesoamerican archaeologists toward many of the right questions. The model is limited in its usefulness, however, because it puts too much emphasis on the action of cores and fails to consider how peripheries develop, how they interact with one another, or how they affect core areas. These limitations are especially debilitating when studying a periphery such as the Southwest. He proposes that any attempt to discuss southwestern-mesoamerican interactions must integrate both long-range connections of exchange and local productive relationships. He finds the concept of modes of production as discussed by Wolf a useful device for discussing relations of production and the concept of a prestige goods economy useful for demonstrating how different modes of production and societies in the Southwest and Mesoamerica were linked. He analyzes the great pueblo fall at the end of the Pueblo III period and the appearance of the Anasazi Katsina cult at the beginning of the Pueblo IV period to show how this model links local productive relations and long-range exchange to account for events in prehistory.

    With the exception of Joseph Whitecotton all of the contributors to this volume work in the Southwest or west Mexico. We therefore felt it would be useful to have a "real mesoamerican archaeologist," one more involved with the research and issues of core Mesoamerica, comment on these papers. Barbara Stark graciously agreed to fill this role.

    Stark examines the papers presented here in terms of two issues: (1) how the history of archaeology and cultures of the Southwest and west Mexico contrast with those of the south of Mesoamerica and (2) the overall organization of Mesoamerica. She notes that investigators working in the Southwest and west Mexico tend to be more ecologically oriented than those working on Mesoamerica's southern frontier. She also contrasts the types of cultures found in the two areas: chiefdoms or tribes and hunter-gatherers to the north and more complex chiefdoms to the south of Mesoamerica. She notes that in the south discussions of interaction have met with less debate and polarization of positions than in the north.

    In her discussion of the organization of Mesoamerica she contrasts a geographic concept with a structural concept and examines the processes that affect interaction. Stark's discussion points out how emphasis on an elite versus entrepreneurial exchange between the diverse groups that made up Mesoamerica affects discussions of the interactions between Mesoamerica and its peripheries. She feels that an understanding of the varying importance of prestige and entrepreneurial exchange in these relations requires a clear picture of the structural dependencies among the groups involved.

    We felt it would also be useful to have a southwestern archaeologist who did not have a published position on these debates examine and comment on the papers. Stephen Plog provides such commentary in the last paper of the volume. Plog reviews the positions presented in the papers and notes the declining polarization of the debate. He pays particular attention to the application of world systems theory to the prehistoric Southwest and Mesoamerica. He concludes his discussion by indicating some of the future empirical and theoretical research which these papers suggest.

After reviewing the papers contained here, various points of agreement and disagreement become apparent. It is obvious from these discussions that several different models and theoretical perspectives can be used to account for the data. The basic problem facing all of the researchers is agreement on just what the data are. On a theoretical level the issue remains, What role do we assign long-range interactions in the explanation of the prehistory of a given region?

Dating provides a good example of a lack of agreement on basic data. All the authors would agree that the Medio period at Casas Grandes was a crucial phenomena in southwestern-mesoamerican interactions. Despite this agreement, as LeBlanc, Braniff, Wilcox, and others note, we still do not agree on the dating of this key period. Interpretations for the beginning date vary by as much as 300 years and interpretations for the end date vary by at least 200 years. The dating of events in west Mexico at the northern edge of Mesoamerica are equally controversial. This leaves most of the explanatory scenarios dependent on unproven assumptions concerning the contemporaneity of events within and between the Southwest and Mesoamerica.

In these papers we also see a variety of theoretical perspectives on how to deal with long-range interactions in prehistory. These range from LeBlanc's invocation of the well-used concept of the interaction sphere to models of prestige economies utilized by Nelson and McGuire to Whitecotton and Pailes', Upham's, Wilcox's and Mathien's application of Wallerstein's world systems theory. These perspectives are by no means mutually exclusive; they overlap in various ways, but they do vary in their degree of sophistication and specificity. Prestige goods economies can exist in world economies and the term *interaction sphere* is vague enough to encompass either of these phenomena. The concept of a world economy does have the advantage of drawing our attention to the dynamics inherent in unequal relations in wide-ranging economic systems, while considerations of a prestige goods economy discuss more specifically the exact relations which would have made such systems work in the Southwest and Mesoamerica. McGuire's wedding of exchange and production theory attempts to go beyond the discussion of long-range interactions and integrate the effects of such interactions with local factors of production in our accounts of prehistory.

Deciding among these theoretical perspectives is not a simple matter of rejecting one or the other. Indeed, approaching the problem in this way leads us to discount the shared insights of all the positions and possibly overemphasize the differences. Each of these perspectives results from a complex process of synthesis and is a complex statement of relations. As such, none can be rejected out of hand and each can be evaluated only in terms of an equally sophisticated alternative.

Despite the rhetoric in a few of the discussions, these papers do appear to represent a significant movement away from the overly polarized debates of the past. None takes the simple position that southwestern prehistory resulted from the domination of the area by Mesoamericans nor that interactions with Mesoamerica were inconsequential to southwestern prehistory. We would be quick to point out, however, that both these positions still exist outside this volume. Our efforts replace the extreme polarization with a continuum of views ranging from those of Kelley to those of Mathien.

Instead of the arguments of kill and overkill, we seek to raise a series of more sophisticated issues which are at once both theoretical and empirical. Can we use models such as Wallerstein formulated to account for the rise of capitalism to study the prehistory of the Southwest and Mesoamerica and by implication other prehistoric economic systems? How do we draw boundaries around large-scale economic systems? When is a region peripheral and when is it external? Is any region ever truly external to larger scale processes? How do we integrate local productive processes with the effects of these larger economic forces in our understandings of prehistory?

The greater sophistication of these questions and the declining polarization of our debates does not, however, herald a final answer to the question of southwestern-mesoamerican interactions. The issues raised by this question are both substantively and theoretically so basic that such a resolution may not be possible. We will probably always be adrift in a Chichimec sea. This prospect should not be viewed with alarm because the ripples we study and create in this sea form the basis for creative new insights into theory and prehistory.

References Cited

Frisbie, Theodore R.
    1983 Anasazi-Mesoamerican Relationships: From the Bowels of the Earth and Beyond. In *Proceedings of the Anasazi Symposium 1981*, edited by Jack E. Smith, pp. 215–227. Mesa Verde Museum Association, Mesa Verde National Park.

2

A Historical Analysis of the Problem of Southwestern-Mesoamerican Connections

David R. Wilcox

The American Southwest and Mesoamerica are two of the most intensively studied archaeological zones in the New World. Between them lies north-western Mexico, where large areas remain archaeologically unknown and where much of the work that has been done addresses problems on a pan-regional scale, involving connections with the adjacent areas rather than in-digenous local or regional processes. Thus, it was in northwestern Mexico that scholars sought the southern boundaries of the southwestern culture area (Beals 1932; Brand 1935, 1939; Sauer and Brand 1931) or the northern boundary of Mesoamerica (Kirchhoff 1943). When excavations at Snake-town (Gladwin et al. 1937) produced data that convinced many anthropolo-gists that cultural interactions between the Southwest and Mesoamerica were much more frequent and significant than previously thought (see Wilcox and Sternberg 1983), the search began for mechanisms and routes of diffusion that could have transcended the intervening cultural boundaries.

As data accumulated and the discipline of anthropology matured, new approaches were brought to bear on the problem of southwestern-mesoamerican connections. But still northwestern Mexico remained a way-station between other objectives. It was a place to study the dynamics of Mesoamerica's northern frontier where factors influencing the rise and fall of the metropolitan polities could be elucidated (Armillas 1964, 1969; Braniff 1975; Palerm and Wolf 1957). Or it was identified as a rare-resource zone that was exploited by agents of mesoamerican states which extended their extractive operations even into the American Southwest (Di Peso 1968, 1974; Kelley 1974; Kelley and Kelley 1975; Pailes 1980; Weigand 1978, 1979; Weigand et al. 1977).

Gradually, however, in the course of this work, the outlines of local cultural sequences and regional systems have begun to emerge (Braniff 1975; Brown 1980; Kelley 1971; Kelley and Kelley 1980; Pailes 1980; Weigand 1978, 1979). It is now possible to begin an evaluation of the reconstructions of panregional systemic processes in terms of local and regional systems that also existed in northwestern Mexico. Many basic questions of chronology, the structure of settlement systems, exchange systems, and so on, remain unanswered or even unasked. Nevertheless, a critical evaluation of the data may reveal a series of facts or plausible assumptions on the basis of which alternative models of the nature of cultural connections between Mesoamerica and the American Southwest may be formulated.

This paper critically reviews the current state of the problem of mesoamerican connections. Debate in recent years has been polarized by an overemphasis on so-called isolationist and imperialist (*pochteca*) positions (Plog et al. 1982). Many of the isolationist or *pochteca* models have already been ably criticized by others (for example, see McGuire 1980; Nelson 1981; Pailes 1980). The objective here is to separate the facts at issue from the web of inference and assumption made in alternative models and to document the plausibility of the assumptions required for a new model. I begin with a review of the theories of Angel Palerm and Eric Wolf (1957) and of Pedro Armillas (1964, 1969). These authors have posited a grand series of frontier processes to explain the rise and fall of the central Mexican states. In their systems approach, regional perspective, and concept of temporal process, these innovative theorists profoundly influenced subsequent attempts to construct general explanations of mesoamerican prehistory (Blanton et al. 1981; Flannery et al. 1967; Sanders and Price 1968). Their theories continue to provide the most comprehensive theoretical framework for studying Mesoamerica's northern frontier (Braniff 1975; Brown 1980), and they are a primary intellectual datum in the effort to chart the articulation of cultural systems in the American Southwest with those of Mesoamerica.

The next step is the examination of the history of research concerned directly with mechanisms of contact between the Southwest and Mesoamerica. Three stages are apparent: (1) the search for boundaries and routes of diffusion undertaken both before and after the Snaketown excavations; this work culminated in the Mesa Redonda meetings of 1943 and in a famous paper by Emil Haury (1945); (2) the construction of cultural sequences in northwestern Mexico begun in the 1950s by J. Charles Kelley and Charles C. Di Peso, each of whom has contributed a great wealth of new empirical data and has adopted a *pochteca* model to explain the perceived patterns; and (3) the construction of "world system" models inaugurated by Joseph Whitecotton and two former students of J. Charles Kelley, Phil Weigand and Richard Pailes.

Each of these stages has significantly affected later work and several of the scholars involved in earlier stages have also contributed to later ones. J. Charles Kelley, in particular, has freely changed his approach to his models as new data have become available and as new ideas have evolved. Attention must be given to the historical evolution of the controversy over southwestern-mesoamerican connections if the current status of fact and supposition is to be clearly understood. In the end, I argue that world systems thinking offers a suitably broad and neutral framework for a united effort to resolve the issues encompassed by this problem.

Mesoamerica's Northern Frontier

The Palerm and Wolf Theory

A core-periphery paradigm was applied by Palerm and Wolf (1957) to interpret the changing structure of mesoamerican polities. Such theories were widely employed after World War II to explain national economic development (Brookfield 1975). An elegant synopsis of the theory is provided by J. Friedmann: "Major centers of innovative change will be called *core* regions: all other areas within a given spatial system will be defined as peripheral. More precisely, core regions are territorially organized subsystems of society that have a high capacity for innovative change; peripheral regions are subsystems whose development path is determined chiefly by core region institutions with respect to which they stand in a relation of substantial dependency. Peripheral regions can be defined by their relations of dependency to a core area" (1972:93; cited in Brookfield 1975:120). The later "world-systems" theory of Immanuel Wallerstein (1974, 1976) is a more recent development of this intellectual tradition (see also Wolf 1982).

Palerm and Wolf's version of this paradigm emphasizes ecological factors, but innovation is also important. They call the dominant core regions "key areas": "we may visualize a key area as the center of an economic network, with ties to other areas that depend on it. This complex of a key area and its dependent areas has been called a 'symbiotic region'" (Palerm and Wolf 1957:29).

Key areas build symbiotic regions and "each such center with its particular satellite system represents an adaptation—on a regional scale and through sociopolitical and economic means—to an environment which is internally diversified" (Palerm and Wolf 1957:30). In key areas, new agricultural innovations are readily adopted and it is possible within them to apply the full spectrum of techniques found in the symbiotic region. Palerm and Wolf also suggest that "symbiosis was favored most where regions contain a large variety of ecological types within easy reach and communication did not encounter great difficulties" (1957:31–32). Not all areas contiguous to the key area became satellites; some remained "internally marginal," having nothing to contribute to the symbiosis. Under certain conditions, however, they too were incorporated: "the symbiotic process implemented by military means could force production by demands for tribute. It could also integrate the depend[ent] areas more completely and efficiently, while imposing desired changes at the same time. Areas which came under the influence of a system of this type quickly lost their "internal[ly] marginal" characteristics, especially since the process was often supported by outright colonization" (Palerm and Wolf 1957:33).

The Basin of Mexico was a key area and the agricultural populations surrounding the successive metropolitan centers of Teotihuacan and Tula were its satellites. On some frontiers other metropolitan centers competed with Teotihuacan or Tula for satellites, while on the northern frontier, the hunter-gatherers called "Chichimecs" (centered in the Chihuahuan desert) continually raided the satellite farming settlements to their south and west. "Annual Chichimec raids could destroy the margin of safety in agriculture in an arid or marginal zone, and force the farmers to emigrate or become predatory hunters and gatherers themselves, thus setting off a kind of chain reaction all along the weakened frontier" (Palerm and Wolf 1957 : 5). On the other hand, ecological factors in the ambient environment also favored hunting and gathering in some zones, "like the Great Tunal of San Luis Potosi and the mesquite belt of Zacatecas-Durango [where] hunting and gathering may actually have produced higher yields than an unstable agriculture operating under the strain of Chichimec raiders" (Palerm and Wolf 1957 : 5). In general, then, the location of a frontier depended "on the ever-changing balance in sociopolitical integration and military power between the Mesoamerican cities, the marginal farmers and the Chichimecs" (Palerm and Wolf 1957 : 5).

Palerm and Wolf argue that the fall of Tula and Teotihuacan resulted from a shift in the balance of forces that maintained the frontiers: "the basic cause of the disaster was a struggle for political hegemony which brought with it the destruction of many civilized centers as well as general enfeeblement" (1957 : 4). The people of Teotihuacan, and later Tula, were unable to hold back the Chichimecs, and a domino effect of inward collapse is inferred. In fact, following the collapse of Tula, and probably El Tajin (Wilkerson 1979), hunters and gatherers did replace farmers in a huge zone from the Huastec area on the east to San Luis Potosi, Queretaro, and Guanajuato on the west (Braniff 1975), though farming may have ceased in portions of this area even earlier (Brown 1980).

The Armillas Theory

Though basically in agreement with the theory of Palerm and Wolf, Armillas (1964 : 316–317; 1969) emphasizes the role played by the environmental structure of the frontier and the determinate effect of environmental stress. Contrasting the distribution of Chichimecs in A.D. 1500 and A.D. 1000, Armillas (1969 : 697–701) shows that the A.D. 1500 boundary is correlated with the modern boundary between steppe and desert on the north side and temperate mountain forest on the south, while the A.D. 1000 boundary was shifted far to the north, adding another 40,000 square miles to the agricultural domain. Across the A.D. 1500 boundary hunter-gatherers directly confronted the Aztec and Tarascan states, whereas the earlier one was less pronounced and more permeable. Armillas infers that the frontier "reflects the fluidity of economic commitment characteristic of marginal conditions, which has a definite survival value—the least committed is the most adaptable to shifts in the precarious ecological balance. Also it may indicate the existence of some degree of peaceful symbiotic relationships, based on economic interdependence, between the settled people and the nomads [in the Chihuahuan desert]," (1969:698–700; see also Weigand 1979).

The presence of such "castle-towns" as La Quemada along the edge of this sphere of interdependence is noted (Armillas 1969), but the potential theoretical implications of this fact are not developed. Like Pecos, Taos, and Gran Quivira farther north at a later time (Kessell 1979; Spielmann 1982), La Quemada, Alta Vista, Schroeder, and Zape may have been entrepots generating their wealth by exploiting exchange relations with hunter-gatherers to their east (see Kelley 1980; Wilcox, Chapter 8 this volume).

To explain the changing location and character of Mesoamerica's northern frontier, Armillas proposes a general theory "founded on general principles of dynamic and synoptic climatology that relate changes in world weather patterns to changes in the general circulation of the atmosphere, and upon current understanding of the causative factors of aridity in subtropical latitudes in terms of the general circulation" (1969:702–703).

Starting with the public fact that winter temperatures in northern latitudes are well correlated with the amount of summer rainfall over central Mexico, he argues that changes in these variables are produced by "cyclical displacement of the locations of the Bermuda-Azores High and the related shiftings in the position of the summer cell over the Caribbean Sea that directs the influence of the trades" (Armillas 1969:702). Changes in this high system also presumably affected the amount of summer rainfall in the American Southwest and the Chihuahuan desert. Secular trends in these may have significantly affected the conditions for both farming and hunting and gathering in a domain that extended from the Anasazi area in the north to central Mexico in the south. Applying this theory, Armillas infers that "the well-known warming up of northern climates throughout the first millennium after Christ would correlate with the strengthening of the summer easterlies and gradual improvement of the environmental conditions in the margins of the arid zone of north-central Mexico; the onset of a cooling trend in the northern latitudes about A.D. 1200 must have entailed opposite effects" (1969:702). The lag in the spread of sedentary farming into northern Mexico compared to areas south of the Bajio is thus explained as a function of environmental conditions, as is the retraction of the agricultural frontier.

These processes may also have had devastating effects on central Mexican polities.

> The effects of the weakening of the summer easterlies after the 12th century would have also been gradual on the landscape, but must have been catastrophic from the onset on the delicate balance between population and resources. In marginal farming situations, any increase in the frequency of recurrence of drought conditions will

rapidly raise the subsistence risk above the level tolerance peculiar to the ecosystem. The movement of disaster-struck farmers away from the most exposed areas would have sufficed to set the whole unstable system in turmoil. Harassment of the weakened frontier settlements by bands of plundering Chichimecs and the influx of refugees into the zone to the south produced total collapse by a kind of tenpins effect—*even in areas that were only mildly affected by the climatic reversions* (Armillas 1969:703; emphasis added).

Environmental stress is thus held to be primarily responsible for the fall of Tula when "many farming nations retraced the tracks of the pioneers of earlier times, to fall as locust masses upon the fertile lands that laid behind the frontier belt. On the eve of these invasions, drought, famine, plague and internal unrest had weakened the structure of the bulwark of civilization constituted by the Toltec state. . . . It is highly probably that the same physical causes—drought and its consequences—triggered the migration of the frontier peoples" (Armillas 1969:701).

El Tajin was abandoned about the same time, perhaps in a related process (Wilkerson 1979). In the American Southwest, A.D. 1100–1150 is the time of the collapse of the Sedentary period Hohokam regional system, the collapse also of the Chacoan and Mimbres systems, and the abandonment of many areas on the Colorado Plateau, including the Grand Canyon, the Virgin area, and higher portions of Black Mesa and the Mesa Verde (Euler et al. 1979; LeBlanc 1980). The Schroeder and Zape centers in Durango were also abandoned about this time (Kelley 1971). By Armillas's theory, all of these historical events may be systemically related to the same environmental process (see also Euler et al. 1979).

To what degree each of the local changes in human settlement systems was due solely to the local expression of a general climatic process remains unclear. Quite possibly, however, social linkages and interdependencies such as Palerm and Wolf (1957) and Armillas (1969) have postulated for northern Mesoamerica may have existed in the American Southwest and northwest Mexico as well and may have had a systemic effect on the processes of collapse, abandonment, and reorganization in those regions. These possibilities bring us face to face with world-systems thinking, which is discussed below. First, however, we shall examine in more detail the history of efforts to understand southwestern-mesoamerican relationships.

Southwestern-Mesoamerican Relationships

The Early Stage: Before and After Snaketown

Starting in southeastern Arizona, the geographers Sauer and Brand (1930) traced southwestern culture southward in Sonora to the Fuerte River

(Sauer and Brand 1931:114), and then documented the northernmost expression of a mesoamerican culture in coastal Sinaloa (Sauer and Brand 1932). Stimulated in part by the work at Snaketown, Gordon Ekholm (1939, 1940, 1942) conducted a new survey in Sonora, confirming the Fuerte as a boundary. In Chihuahua, Henry Carey (1931) showed that the Casas Grandes culture (which he took to be derivative from Mimbres culture on the basis of continuities in certain designs) extended southward to the Babicora valley. From there southward a gap in site distributions was thought to extend some 450 km to Zape, Durango, where Mason (1937) discovered the northernmost ceremonial center of mesoamerican-related culture which he named "Chalchihuites" (Brand 1935, 1939). In fact, recent surveys (Brooks 1971; Kelley 1956) have revealed no villages and only a few scattered hamlets and farmsteads of the Loma San Gabriel culture between Zape and Babicora. Based on these data and his own findings in excavations at Guasave, Sinaloa, Ekholm summed up the situation as follows:

> How then were those traits which we have considered to be of Mexican origin transferred to the Southwest? The West Coast corridor does not seem a likely route, unless we are to suppose that such traits were transferred by travelers or traders who crossed great areas inhabited by peoples of relatively low culture. Approximately the same situation seems to have prevailed in the western highlands. A tongue of high culture of Central Mexican affiliation extended up through Zacatecas and into Durango and only at a late period did it come into close contact with Southwestern cultures—the spread southward of the Casas Grandes peoples. Those "later" contacts must, then, have occurred across great areas that were occupied by relatively primitive peoples, and it seems likely that it must have been accomplished in large part by small groups of travelers (1942:136).

Already the basic structure of Di Peso's (1974) later *pochteca* model is clear in this statement. Rather than a search for missing links to fill the gap, Ekholm recommended the reconstruction of cultural sequences in Durango and Zacatecas—a task begun by J. Charles Kelley a decade later.

The problem of southwestern-mesoamerican relationships was an important topic discussed by the scholars who gathered for the Mesa Redonda meetings in 1943. Several of them also focused on the Zacatecas-Durango area as crucial. Beals (1944b) included it in his specification of a "Greater Southwest" and called attention to the close linguistic connection between Piman and Tepehuan. Isabel Kelly was more specific:

> An examination of the temporal and spatial distribution of eight selected traits indicates that these culture elements reached West Mexico by various routes, from distinct culture hearths, and over a span of several centuries. When, therefore, we look to Mexico for the origin of certain Hohokam traits, we may expect a similarly complex

situation. . . . Before we can hope to recognize a cultural corridor . . . either by coast or highland—we must discover horizons much earlier than those known to date. It is suggestive that both ballcourts and paint cloisonné occur in the Western Highlands [but not in west Mexico or coastal Sinaloa]. This area should be examined for further Hohokam parallels, and its several ceramic complexes should be defined and placed chronologically, so that we may know whether or not the Western Highlands could have functioned in the transmittal of Mexican traits to the Hohokam (1944:216−217).

Other discussants, however, continued to favor a west coast route (Beals 1944b; Brand 1944).

Shortly after the Mesa Redonda meetings, Haury published a careful summary and evaluation of the data pertinent to the problem of contacts between the southwestern United States and Mexico. The traits traceable to Mexico were, Haury inferred, "borne by all methods of cultural transmission, from the diffusion of ideas from group to group to the importation of actual objects probably by traders" (1945:56). Recognizing the absence of support for a coastal route, Haury (1945:66, 69) nevertheless cautioned that material of an appropriately early age may not have been studied, and he argued that "some sort of relationship did exist and whether this was through the lowlands of the coast or through the sierras remains to be determined" (1945:57). Data on 19 traits from Mexico are presented, including corn, pottery, cotton, stone carving, ballcourts, copper bells, macaws, a variety of ceramic and lithic forms, and textile techniques (Haury 1945: 58−65). The different times of entry, routes, and source areas in Mexico imply that "we should not look for a fixed route of entry, pointing back to a single culture group, or . . . endeavor to find traces of a band of people which migrated wholesale from Mexico" (Haury 1945:65).

Like Ekholm (1942), Haury (1945:68) recognized two periods of Mexican influence. The first, bringing in corn, pottery and ceramic figurines, he argued occurred about A.D. 1. Following Beals (1932), he (1945: 66−67) suggested corn came in via the west coast along an arid-lands route. While the history of corn is now known to be more complex (see Ford 1981), Haury's discussion of pottery is no less incisive today (see LeBlanc 1982). "It is clear that early Mogollon and Hohokam pottery becomes more alike as one inspects older and older material. This refers to color, range of types, and design. The assumption of a common parentage for the pottery of these two groups is quite in line with the evidence. Further, what I consider of importance is the similarity of this earliest Southwestern ceramic fabric to the polished red, polished black, brown ware, and broad line red-painted types of the Middle Cultures [Preclassic] of the Mexican highlands . . . believed to date before the time of Christ" (1945:67). Figurines, too, appear related to Preclassic Mexican forms (Haury 1945:68).

The vast majority of the Mexican accretions identified by Haury

(1945:62–65) occur in Hohokam contexts during the late Colonial and Sedentary periods, A.D. 700–1100. Haury was uncertain about the route of entry for these traits, but "we may guess that the corridor lay well to the west in northwestern Mexico, either through Sinaloa and Sonora over routes similar to those followed by the early Spaniards, or somewhat farther to the east along the western foothills of the sierras. Here the river systems generally trend north and south, their heads leading directly to the upper drainages of the Santa Cruz and San Pedro Rivers, feeders of the Gila and the homeland of the Hohokam. *Connections with Durango, the northern outpost of high culture of Mexico[,] would not appear too difficult to establish*" (1945:68; emphasis added).

The Second Stage: Migrations, New Data, and Pochteca Models

Interest in the problem of southwestern-mesoamerican relationships in the decades after 1945 culminated in the middle 1950s with the publication of three different models proposing a migration from Mexico to account for Haury's (1945) "second wave" of traits (Di Peso 1956; Gladwin 1957; Schroeder 1956, 1960). Subsequent research has shown, however, that none of these models is tenable (Haury 1976; Kelley 1966:99; Wilcox and Sternberg 1983). Demonstration that the Mexican-like traits in Hohokam sites are not distributed in time or space as the migration models required clears the way for consideration of alternative possibilities. The most recent migration model, suggested by Haury (1976) to account for his "first wave" of Mexican traits, I have discussed in detail elsewhere (Wilcox and Shenk 1977; Wilcox and Sternberg 1983). Haury's migration model remains a viable possibility but so too is the hypothesis that indigenous Archaic populations became the Hohokam.

In this section I turn to work conducted in northwestern Mexico by J. Charles Kelley and Charles C. Di Peso. Both Kelley and Di Peso have been prolific in the expression of their views, making it possible to trace the evolution of their thought over several decades. Each has contributed a rich new corpus of data whose patterns they have attempted to explain by invoking *pochteca*-like merchant-priests engaged in directing culture change. Fundamental to their *pochteca* models are chronological frameworks that radically revised earlier temporal inferences. Recent work by Kelley and Kelley (1980) at Alta Vista, however, has yielded a correction of their chronology, which confirms the earlier "traditional" view. The calibration of Di Peso's (1974) Casas Grandes chronology has also been questioned (Doyel 1976; LeBlanc 1980; Wilcox and Shenk 1977:63–68; Wilcox and Sternberg 1983). Because the chronological issues fundamentally affect all efforts at model building, this discussion focuses on them, leaving aside many other considerations that are pertinent to a critique of the *pochteca* models (but see McGuire 1980 and Nelson 1981 for excellent discussions).

J. Charles Kelley's Evolving Model. The modern era of progress in understanding the nature of southwestern-mesoamerican relationships began in 1952 when J. Charles Kelley (1956) discovered the Loma San Gabriel sites near Villa Ocampo, Chihuahua. The presence of sedentary hamlets and farmsteads implied that the famous gap between Mesoamerica and the Southwest was a myth (Kelley 1956:139). Extending his surveys into Durango, Kelley soon conducted test excavations at the Schroeder site south of Durango City. His findings significantly confirmed the earlier suggestions of Ekholm (1942) and Kelly (1944) that the closest cultural connections between the American Southwest and northern Mesoamerica lay with the Chalchihuites culture in Durango and Zacatecas (Kelley 1966). Pursuing the matter further, Kelley (1971; Kelley and Abbott 1966; Kelley and Kelley 1971) and his associates began a systematic program of settlement system analysis in Durango and Zacatecas, culminating most recently in extensive excavations and other studies at the ceremonial center of Alta Vista, Chalchihuites (Aveni et al. 1982; Kelley and Kelley 1980).

At first, Kelley (1966) did not advocate a *pochteca* model. Impressed by the new data from Alta Vista and its vicinity and influenced by a flurry of *pochteca* theories published around 1970 (especially Di Peso 1968), Kelley (1974) finally began to argue in favor of a *pochteca* concept, though always with some qualifications. Its application to interpret southwestern data (for example Kelley and Kelley 1975) is deliberately polemical, intended to goad "card-carrying" southwestern isolationists to consider the evidence for mesoamerican connections. When the qualifications are examined, it is readily apparent that the argument varies little in substance from his earlier, more modest inferences (see Kelley 1966; Kelley and Kelley 1975:198). Yet no sooner had these *pochteca* models been proposed than a new series of C-14 dates from Alta Vista threw into question the chronological assumptions on which they were erected (Kelley 1978; Kelley and Kelley 1980). Nevertheless, citing fresh evidence for the sophistication of the Alta Vista site, Kelley (in Aveni et al. 1982) finds new ground for supporting a *pochteca* model.

Before Pochteca. The excavations at the Schroeder site had, by 1960, produced a local phase sequence and Kelley turned next to an assessment of cultural correlations with surrounding areas, first in a preliminary paper (Kelley 1960) and then in a more rigorous and critical one (Kelley and Winters 1960). Some of these correlations still appear valid today, while others have been or should be revised. Most of the difficulties center on the position of the Alta Vista phase. Interestingly, Kelley's initial conception of its correlation with central Mexico may yet prove to be sounder than its correlation with the Schroeder site sequence. Unlike the Ayala-Las Joyas-Rio Tunal phases, the Alta Vista phase was not present at the Schroeder site (see Figure 1). Its initial definition was based on ceramic comparisons (Kelley and Winters 1960:549; Marquina 1951; Noguera 1930) and it was not until later, when he shifted his operations southward into Zacatecas, that excava-

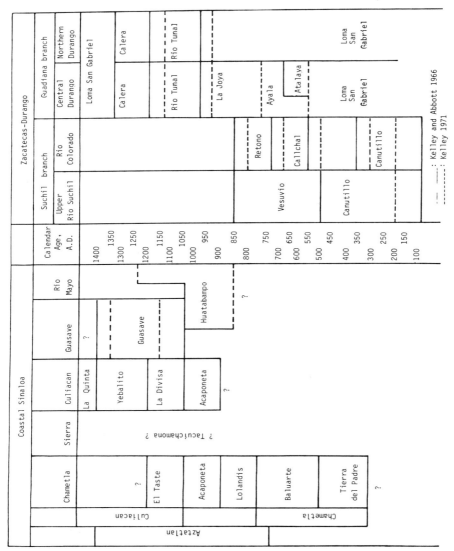

Figure 1. J. Charles Kelley's original phase sequence (after Kelley and Winters 1960 : 560)

tion data helped to refine its definition (Kelley and Kelley 1971). By then, however, hypotheses about its chronological position had hardened; only when a large series of C-14 dates did not confirm the chronological model did a basic reassessment begin (Kelley and Kelley 1980).

Kelley's preliminary view of "the leading Alta Vista [phase] pottery type, Suchil Red-on-brown, is [that it is] quite similar to Coyotlatelco ware from the Valley of Mexico" (1960:569) thus implying that it is correlated with the period following the fall of Teotihuacan, A.D. 750–900. These are precisely the dates most recently suggested for the Alta Vista phase (Kelley and Kelley 1980). Kelley and Winters (1960:549, 551), however, assumed that the Alta Vista phase was the oldest then known in the Chalchihuites culture, although at the Schroeder site it apparently overlapped the Ayala phase. They used the data from the Schroeder site excavations—based largely on ceramic cross-dating—to revise the coastal Sinaloa cultural sequences. The Durango Rio Tunal phase is thus correlated with the Sinaloan Acaponeta phase, Las Joyas with Lolandis, Ayala with Baluarte, and Alta Vista with Tierra de Padre (Early Chametla), though it is clearly stated that "no specific positive evidence" confirms the latter relationship (Kelley and Winters 1960:551, 554, 559–560). They also state that they "consider the appearance of Lolandis Red Rim Ware [Lolandis phase] to be related to the appearance of Coyotlatelco ware in Central Mexico, an opinion shared, more or less, by Kelly (1938:2n. 3; 1945: 8) and Ekholm (1942:48–49)" (1960:560). By this logic, the Alta Vista phase must be much earlier, and since the Tierra del Padre phase is correlated with the later two-thirds of Teotihuacan III, A.D. 250–300 to 500 (Kelley and Winters 1960:560), so too is the Alta Vista phase. All of this follows from the initial assumption that the Alta Vista phase antedates the Schroeder site sequence, an assumption that C-14 dates would later bring into question.

Preliminary correlations were also suggested with the Hohokam sequence (Kelley 1960). Rio Tunal is temporally equivalent to the Sedentary period, Las Joyas correlates with the Colonial, and Ayala-Alta Vista are seen as Pioneer period equivalents. Since copper bells occur both in Rio Tunal and Sedentary Hohokam contexts, but not in Acaponeta ones in Sinaloa, closer connections between the Chalchihuites and Hohokam than between the latter and coastal Sinaloa are postulated for that time (Kelley 1960:570; Kelley and Winters 1960:557, 558). The mechanism envisioned is indirect, explaining Kelley's (1956) early understanding of the importance of the Loma San Gabriel culture: "During the Las Joyas and Rio Tunal phases indirect contact between Chalchihuites and Hohokam Cultures may have been effected through [the] medium of the simple mountain culture, the Loma San Gabriel pattern, which had spread along the high Sierra Madre Occidental through much of the intervening area" (Kelley 1960:571). Immediately following the Sedentary period, however, when the Schroeder site was largely abandoned, "Mesoamerican contacts with the Classic Hohokam appear to have come directly from the Sinaloa cultures—specifically late Aztatlan [Guasave phase] (where Mixtec-Puebla type of ceremonialism had begun to flower) and Culiacan Cultures, probably owing in part to the coincident disappearance of the Chalchihuites Culture" (Kelley 1960:571; see also Haury 1945; Kelley and Winters 1960:560).

A more elaborate and carefully considered review of southwestern-mesoamerican relationships appeared a few years later (Kelley 1966). Though I would suggest somewhat different mechanisms, and would shift his emphasis, I too support much of what Kelley says here (Wilcox, Chapter 8 this volume). The underlying foundation for cultural interchange, he argued, was a dialect chain of Uto-Aztecan speakers: "perhaps by the time of Christ, if not before, there developed along the Sierra Madre occidental a chain of related cultures and peoples, characteristically simple agriculturalists, living in small fairly permanent hamlets, making simple pottery vessels, and in all probability speaking related dialects of Uto-Aztecan. One of these groups [was] the Loma San Gabriel culture" (Kelley 1966:99).

Along this communication net "trade items, descriptions, ideas, and wandering travelers must have moved with ease" (Kelley 1966:99–100). Coincident with the first appearance of ceramics, figurines, and sedentary farming villages in the Hohokam and Mogollon areas, the Preclassic frontier of Mesoamerica in the form of Chupicuaro culture moved northward into Zacatecas and Kelley notes numerous similarities between the two, suggesting that the former is a "trade diffusion" from the latter (1966:101–102). This similarity is especially evident in the quartered layout of nested triangles painted in broad lines on the earliest Hohokam and Mogollon painted ceramics. The same motif and quartered layouts are the principal decoration on the interior of bowls in the Chupicuaro-derived cultures of northern Jalisco, Zacatecas, and Durango (Kelley 1966:102). These designs in the latter areas are clearly related to cosmological concepts of the world quarters, as may be true in the Southwest as well (Kelley 1966:98, 102).

The effect of secondary linkages between the Hohokam and Chalchihuites cultures, Kelley argues, was the progressive acculturation of the Hohokam to Mesoamerica-derived ceremonial ideas (1966:102–104). A related process may have been the diffusion of Pima-Papago maize from the Chalchihuites area to the Hohokam "accompanied by the appropriate ceremonial techniques for growing it" (Kelley 1966:102). Late Pioneer and early Colonial Hohokam pottery shares numerous specific design resemblances with (what he took to be) contemporaneous or earlier Chalchihuites *ceremonial* ceramics (Kelley 1966:102–104). These are different traits than Haury (1945) considered, and *earlier* than his so-called second wave. Many other artifact classes are also shared between the two areas, including stone bowls and mortars, "medicine" stones, "doughnut" stones, mosaic mirrors, concho-shell trumpets, turquoise mosaics, and copper bells (Kelley 1966:103). By the Sedentary period, platform mounds also are present in several Hohokam sites (Wasley 1960) and "the large carefully made and oriented refuse mounds of the large Hohokam site at Snaketown . . . actually must be regarded as platform mounds or pseudo-pyramids of Mesoamerican inspiration" (Kelley 1966:103–104). Haury's (1976) work at Snaketown, as well as my own recent efforts there (Wilcox et al. 1981), confirm this view. Thus, Kelley concludes, by the late Sedentary period, the Hohokam had become "in fact a local and crude Mesoamerican image" derived from a "*weak* infiltration of Mesoamerican ceremonialism concerned with world quarters and the gods thereof, the fire god, the sun god, a twin war god concept associated with an early quetzalcoatl concept, and basic rain-fertility cult ideas" (1966:104, 109; emphasis added).

Several additional points are implicit in Kelley's discussion. No direct intervention by mesoamerican agents manipulating Hohokam society is postulated. To the contrary, like Beals (1944b) and Haury (1945), Kelley was arguing in 1966 that the Hohokam selected what they wanted from the mesoamerican-derived ideas that reached them, reinterpreting the concepts as they chose. The cultural capacity for significant local innovation is also apparent in the facts cited by Kelley: cremation ceremonialism, elaborate stone palettes, and specific house types, so characteristic of the Hohokam, are all but absent in the south (1966:104). Ballcourts, while present, are few in the south and are distinctly different in form from Hohokam courts (Kelley 1966:103); perhaps they too are a local Hohokam innovation (see Wilcox and Sternberg 1983).

Unnoticed by Kelley is the additional fact that the innovations of cremation ceremonialism and its related ritual paraphernalia (for example, stone palettes) cluster during the late Colonial period soon after ballcourts appear (Wilcox and Sternberg 1983). During the Sedentary period, when these innovations were elaborated and spread widely, palettes show up in Rio Tunal phase contexts in Durango. Otinapa Red-on-white, the characteristic painted ceramic of the latter phase, is also said to resemble a southwestern type, Three-Circle Red-on-white and, in general, "in many ways the Rio Tunal occupance represents a profound break with earlier [mesoamerican] traditions in ceramics and architecture" (Kelley 1971:796). Perhaps, then, by the tenth and eleventh centuries A.D., a reversal of the earlier cultural relationships was effected and southwestern culture began to acculturate a northern mesoamerican population.

New fieldwork in southern Durango and northern Zacatecas in the Alta Vista area resulted in a much more detailed picture of local cultural sequences (Kelley 1971; Kelley and Abbott 1966). A small series of C-14 dates seemed to confirm the previously constructed chronological models and Kelley and his associates were encouraged to begin formulating more elaborate interpretations of cultural processes. It was from these tentative processual hypotheses that the later *pochteca* model would emerge. Yet at the same time, they remained cautious about their reconstructions, noting that "many problems both of sequence and correlations remain unsolved or still reasonably muddled" (Kelley and Abbott 1966:326).

Four regional "cultures" were identified: the Bolanos-Juchipila in northern Jalisco and southern Zacatecas; the Malpaso (La Quemada) in east-central Zacatecas; the Chalchihuites, which was divided into the Suchil branch in northern Zacatecas and the Guardiana branch in Durango; and the Loma San Gabriel, the peasantry of the Chalchihuites centers, in Durango and southwestern Chihuahua (Kelley and Abbott 1966; Kelley 1971). The *Caxcana*, an early historic people in southern Zacatecas and adjacent Jalisco, are inferred to be descended from the Bolanos-Juchipila and Malpaso cultures, while the Tepehuan are thought to derive from Loma San Gabriel populations (Kelley and Abbott 1966 : 326—327; Kelley and Winters 1960 : 549; Riley and Winters 1963).

A quite detailed model of ceramic typology and developmental relationships together with stratigraphic data are the primary sources for these sequences (Kelley and Kelley 1971). Suchil Red-on-brown is now compared with Chupicuaro Red-on-brown rather than Coyotlatelco Red-on-brown (Kelley and Abbott 1966 : 334). The reasons for assuming that the Alta Vista phase is earlier than the phase sequence at the Schroeder site is also made clear. Such a conclusion follows logically from the equation of the Calichal and Ayala phases by virtue of their "almost identical" pottery types and the superposition of Calichal materials *above* Alta Vista ones (Kelley 1971 : 791). Now that C-14 dating has made it appear that the Alta Vista phase may be equivalent to Las Joyas (Kelley and Kelley 1980), a thorough reevaluation of the ceramic model and the stratigraphic reconstruction appears necessary.

Architecturally, Alta Vista during the Alta Vista phase is the most complex site in the Suchil branch. Its plazas, hall of columns, and pyramids placed it at the head of a regional hierarchy above lesser ceremonial centers, a chain of fortresses, and numerous villages and hamlets (Kelley 1971 : 783; Kelley and Abbott 1966 : 332). Also present was a large series of mines from which lime and valuable stones were extracted, probably beginning in the Canutillo phase (Kelley and Abbott 1966 : 332, 334; Weigand 1968). These mines presented a great stimulus to the archaeological imagination and from efforts to understand their cultural significance several *pochteca* models were derived. The initial evaluation was quite cautious, however.

> It may be that in constructing the new ceremonial centers at the beginning of the Alta Vista Phase, quarries were opened in the *portreros* to secure lime rock to burn for the making of lime plaster and mortar. When jewel stones (chalchihuitls) were discovered in the terrace gravels, renewed mining interest may have developed, perhaps even to the extent that contingents from the Valley of Mexico or from some closer new *Imperio* (such as the ancestral Tarascan political entity?), were sent into the area to exploit the resources there. Such groups might well have erected the fortress chain to protect the new interests

from the neighboring *Chichimecs*. If so, the population of the Alta
Vista Phase—and its geographic neighbors and immediate cultural
descendants—might well be regarded as an industrial or commercial
colony of the unknown *Imperio* to the south, accounting both for the
great increase in population and the accelerated cultural evolution of
the area (Kelley and Abbott 1966:334).

A later statement was less cautious, and the range of possibilities being considered was narrowed: "The appearance of the Alta Vista phase in the Rio
Colorado valley at circa A.D. 300 implanted a formalized Mesoamerican
Classic cultural pattern in that area; almost certainly this was a primitive
exploitative state inspired by and perhaps even controlled by Classic Teotihuacan, far to the south" (Kelley 1971:787). It was only a short step further
to a *pochteca* model (Kelley 1974).

Kelley's Pochteca Model. Before excavating at Alta Vista in the
middle 1970s, Kelley and Kelley (1980:66) had assumed that all of it was
constructed during the Alta Vista phase. They found, however, that the basic
layout and the hall of columns were built during the Canutillo phase, with
major expansion and remodelling occurring during the Alta Vista phase after
a brief period of Vesuvio phase occupation (Kelley and Kelley 1980:68).
Furthermore, a new series of C-14 dates caused them to recalibrate their
phase sequence (Figure 2), moving the beginning of the Alta Vista phase forward by 400 years (Kelley and Kelley 1980). What this means for the correlation of the Suchil and Guadiana branch sequences remains uncertain
(J. Charles Kelley, personal communication 1983). The C-14 dates seem to
indicate an equation of the Alta Vista and Las Joyas phases, thus confirming
earlier comparisons of their ceramics with Coyotlatelco Red-on-brown from
the Valley of Mexico, also dated A.D. 750–900. On the other hand, post–
Alta Vista, Calichal phase ceramics are thought to be nearly identical to
pre–Las Joyas, Ayala phase pottery (Kelley and Kelley 1971). A radical shift
of the Guadiana sequence upward in time would also affect correlations
with coastal Sinaloa and the American Southwest (Kelley and Winters
1960). The Pioneer period, for example, may have long been over before
the similar pottery of the Ayala or Alta Vista phases was made.

Now that it is apparent that Alta Vista was not created all at once but
was the outcome of an episodic progression of elaboration and remodeling
that was most vigorous *after* the fall of Teotihuacan, surely the original reasons (Kelley 1974; Kelley and Abbott 1966:334) for postulating outside
pochteca as the builders are weakened. A local Canutillo phase elite, participating in the regional culture of the Zacatecas-Jalisco-Guanajuato area,
could have conceived and executed these monuments by themselves. Why
is there any need to invoke outsiders who somehow were able to take over
control of the Suchil branch populations, exploiting them for the benefit of a
Teotihuacan or a west Mexican polity? Kelley (in Aveni et al. 1982) has
offered several arguments, each of which may be questioned:

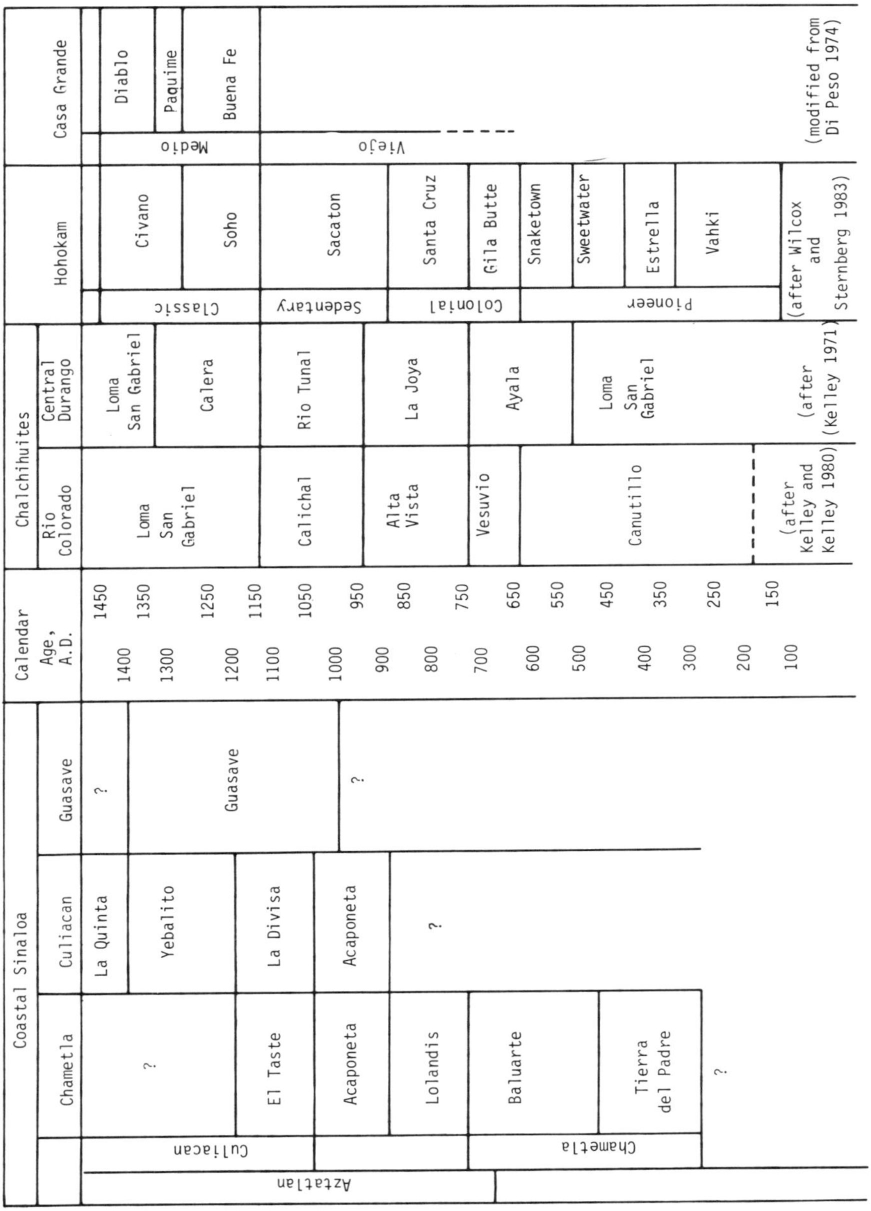

Casa Grande			Hohokam		Chalchihuites		Calendar Age, A.D.	Coastal Sinaloa		
					Central Durango	Rio Colorado		Guasave	Culiacan	Chametla
Diablo			Civano	Classic	Loma San Gabriel	Loma San Gabriel	1450 / 1400	?	La Quinta	?
Paquime							1350 / 1300		Yebalito	
Buena Fe			Soho		Calera		1250 / 1200	Guasave	La Divisa	El Taste
				Sedentary	Rio Tunal	Calichal	1150 / 1100		Acaponeta	Acaponeta
			Sacaton				1050 / 1000	?	?	Lolandis
					La Joya	Alta Vista	950 / 900			
			Santa Cruz	Colonial			850 / 800			Baluarte
			Gila Butte		Ayala	Vesuvio	750 / 700			
			Snaketown				650 / 600			Tierra del Padre
			Sweetwater	Pioneer	Loma San Gabriel	Canutillo	550 / 500			
			Estrella				450 / 400			?
			Vahki				350 / 300			
							250 / 200			
							150 / 100			

Casa Grande (modified from Di Peso 1974) — Medio / Viejo
Hohokam (after Wilcox and Sternberg 1983)
Chalchihuites: Central Durango (after Kelley 1971); Rio Colorado (after Kelley and Kelley 1980)
Coastal Sinaloa — Culiacan / Chametla / Aztatlan

Figure 2. Kelley's revised sequence and comparisons (after Kelley and Winters 1960 and Kelley 1974)

1. Vista Paint Cloisonné, a highly sophisticated ceramic ware with complex iconography attributed to the deity Tezcatlipoca, is found in Canutillo burials, principally in the ceremonial centers of Alta Vista and Cerro de Mochtehuma, and is widespread in similar contexts from Zacatecas to Michoacan (Kelley 1974; Holien and Pickering 1978). It may have been used in the ritual drinking of pulque (Kelley 1974:23). Kelley (in Aveni et al. 1982:331) hypothesizes that the makers of this pottery were itinerant *pochteca* who made it on demand, meanwhile trading for turquoise and other rare resources which they sent on to Teotihuacan or a subsidiary polity in west Mexico. More parsimonious would be an assumption that Vista Paint Cloisonné was exchanged through an elite network. Alternatively, it may have been made in a variety of local substyles by local specialists. Source-area and stylistic analyses are needed to resolve this issue.

2. Astronomical concepts have been shown to be embodied in the Alta Vista architecture, and at a nearby site pecked crosses similar to one found at Teotihuacan are present: "almost certainly the builders of Alta Vista were the makers of those petroglyphs. This conclusion associates them directly with Teotihuacan, and their involvement in widespread trade and regional exploitation points unmistakably in the same direction" (Aveni et al. 1982:331).

These data do certainly show a degree of intellectual sophistication previously unsuspected at Alta Vista. But *close* linkage with Teotihuacan remains uncertain. Pecked crosses are widespread in Mesoamerica and may have a variety of political-religious associations (Aveni et al. 1982:331). More significant may be the fact that the techniques used to express astronomical principles at Alta Vista are "unique in Mesoamerica." . . . "It is the corners, not the front of the building or its axes (such as doorway-stairway-court altar alignment), that point toward a celestial reference—the cardinal directions" (Aveni et al. 1982:319).

Alta Vista flourished after the fall of Teotihuacan when long-distance trade contacts between west Mexico and the Basin of Mexico were increased, and it was abandoned on the eve of Tula's rise to power (Bell 1971; Blanton et al. 1981). Intellectual specialists are clearly indicated, but I suggest it is more likely they were members of an intermarrying local or regional elite rather than Teotihuacan or west Mexican foreigners. There is thus reason to question the hypothesis accepted by Kelley that Teotihuacan dominated or extensively exploited west Mexico during the Classic period (see Wilcox and Sternberg 1983:80). *Pochteca* institutions may not have existed at that time (Weigand 1982; see also Diehl 1981:289; Millon 1981:226–227).

Charles C. Di Peso and Casas Grandes. Casas Grandes, the largest and most complex site in northwestern Chihuahua, was thought by early workers (Carey 1931; Sayles 1936) to represent a post–A.D. 1300 manifestation of southwestern culture. With the revival of interest in mesoamerican-southwestern relationships, new attention was paid to its mesoamerican flavor (for example, Kelley 1956:137), and in 1958–1961 Charles C. Di Peso (1966, 1968, 1974) directed an intensive program of field research by the Amerind Foundation at the site. A tremendous amount of new information was recovered (Di Peso et al. 1976) and Di Peso (1968, 1974) has constructed a unique model to account for it. While continuing to identify early occupation in the area with the Mogollon culture to the north, the occupation of the Casas Grandes site is assigned to the Medio period, the time when he infers mesoamerican merchant-priests (*pochteca*) began exploiting the Southwest for turquoise, slaves, and other goods they presumably sent southward to Mesoamerica (Di Peso 1974). The Medio period is divided into three phases: Buena Fé, Paquimé, and Diablo.

A crucial part of Di Peso's argument for mesoamerican *pochteca* domination is his chronological model for the Medio period (Di Peso 1968, 1974; but see also Di Peso 1966). By interpreting literally a small series of chronometric dates, he infers that the Buena Fé phase lies between A.D. 1060 and 1205. If so, it would be largely contemporaneous with the most expansive expression of the Chacoan, Mimbres, and Sedentary Hohokam regional systems, all of which collapsed circa A.D. 1100–1150. The Paquimé phase is said to fall between A.D. 1205 and 1261, while the succeeding Diablo phase is said to end about A.D. 1340, a century or so *before* the general regional abandonment of southern Arizona and southwestern New Mexico about A.D. 1400–1500. Even if his *pochteca* model is wrong, this Medio period chronology would have profound implications for the reconstruction of regional and panregional settlement systems in the American Southwest and northern Mexico. It is necessary, then, to discuss the problem of the Casas Grandes chronology and its correlations in some detail.

A Critique of Di Peso's Casas Grandes Chronology. I have argued above that *pochteca* models are implausible when viewed from the perspective of northern Mesoamerica. Haury (1976), McGuire (1980), Nelson (1981), and Plog et al. (1982) have attacked particular aspects of Di Peso's model. Their most important empirical point is that the quantities of exotic items, both at Casas Grandes from the south and in Mesoamerica from the north, evidence far too small a traffic in trade goods to sustain Di Peso's model.

More important for our purpose is a critical reevaluation of the Medio period chronology. Some time ago, Wilcox and Shenk (1977) showed that the empirical basis of Di Peso's Medio period chronology was weak and they argued that there were not sufficient data to prove that the traditional post−A.D. 1300 chronology was wrong. Of the 53 tree-ring dates recovered from Casas Grandes, for example, none are cutting dates, and since the beams from which they derive were artificially shaped, an unknown number of rings were removed (Di Peso et al. 1976, vol. 4). Di Peso arbitrarily assumes that only a few rings were removed and that the dates on the outermost rings are close to the cutting dates; one may equally well assume, however, that many rings were lost and that the construction dates were actually a century or more *later* than the dates on the outermost rings (Wilcox and Shenk 1977:65). The alternative possibilities can be tested by systematically reexamining the wood specimens for the number of sapwood rings (Wilcox and Shenk 1977:65); unfortunately, this has not yet been done.

More recently, Steven LeBlanc has argued against both extremes in favor of assigning the Medio period to the interval A.D. 1150–1300. His beginning date is supportable; but, I shall argue, his end date is not. LeBlanc shows that few of the tree-ring dates fall before A.D. 1130; those that do are usually in a construction context with later dates, implying that the building episodes occurred later than A.D. 1130. Thus, the Medio period probably began at the same time as the Hohokam Classic period (1980:801).

The only substantive question I have about the plausibility of LeBlanc's beginning date for the Medio period is Di Peso's report of Gila and Tonto Polychrome in a variety of Buena Fé phase contexts (De Peso et al. 1976:Fig 397–8). In all indisputedly-dated proveniences, Gila and Tonto Polychrome occur *after* A.D. 1300 (Doyel and Haury 1976; Wilcox and Shenk 1977:58–68). LeBlanc dismisses this problem, asserting that Gila Polychrome "is known from 1200s contexts other than Casas Grandes (LeBlanc and Nelson 1976)" (1980:802). In fact, however, LeBlanc and Nelson are far from definitive on this point: "Gila Polychrome has been recovered primarily from surface collections [from "Black Mountain" sites in the Mimbres area], but it has also been recovered in excavated contexts (Lekson and Klinger 1973). While there is evidence that points to a 1200s date for these occurrences, *the data are too scanty to reject a 1300s date*" (1976:73; emphasis added).

How certain, then, are the Buena Fé associations of Gila and Tonto Polychrome? Examining Di Peso's master chart of trade ceramics (Di Peso et al. 1976:Fig. 397–8), we discover that only 102 sherds and no whole vessels were found in "significant" Buena Fé contexts, while 2,091 and 4,533 sherds were found in Buena Fé/Paquimé and Paquimé/Diablo ones, respectively (Di Peso et al. 1976, vol. 4:32–33). Counting all Gila and Tonto Polychrome sherds, only 514 out of 26,585 were in pure Buena Fé contexts (Di Peso et al. 1976:Fig. 397–8). Pursuing the matter further, we find that the vast majority of those 514 sherds occurred in fill contexts and only a handful were found in contact with Buena Fé floors (Di Peso et al. 1976, vol. 4). It seems fair to conclude that although the association of Gila and Tonto Polychrome with the Buena Fé phase is weak (and may be spurious), they *are* strongly associated with the Paquimé and Diablo phases. Di Peso also came to this conclusion in a preliminary report (1966:21). On this basis, then, I conclude that the beginning date given by LeBlanc for the Medio period is highly plausible; it is not contradicted by the post–1300 dating of Salado polychromes.

The end date of the Medio period is another matter. Given the post–A.D. 1300 date of Gila Polychrome and its high frequencies in Paquimé and Diablo phase contexts at Casas Grandes, it seems likely that the Paquimé phase began about A.D. 1250–1300 and that the Diablo phase ended around A.D. 1400 (see Carlson 1981; Kidder et al. 1949:146). LeBlanc's (1980) argument against this view is based on a correlation between Medio period assemblages and material from southwestern New Mexico and the Mimbres area, which he assigns to the Black Mountain phase. The weakness of this argument is that it ignores the later Animas phase which has been cross-dated to the period A.D. 1300 to 1450.

The original concept of an "Animas phase" was formulated by the Gladwins and Kidder in the 1930s after excavations in the Pendleton ruin near Cloverdale, New Mexico (Kidder et al. 1949). This phase included assemblages that postdated the Classic Mimbres phase, and which contained high frequencies of Gila and Ramos Polychrome but little plain buff, polished red, or polished black pottery; these assemblages were thought to date after A.D. 1300 (Kidder et al. 1949:144–146).

Mixed in with the assemblage from the Pendleton ruin, however, were numerous sherds of St. Johns Polychrome and other tyes dating from the A.D. 1200s or earlier, and the ruin was found to be a coursed-adobe pueblo *superimposed on an earlier pueblo* (Kidder et al. 1949:125, 129, 137–138; emphasis added). Because Kidder could find no basis for assigning the earlier material to the older pueblo, he suggested that the occupation had been of short duration, following the Classic Mimbres phase *after a hiatus* of about 150 years (Kidder 1949:145–146). Contrary to this, obsidian hydration dates recently obtained from the site (see LeBlanc and Nelson 1976:73) suggest an occupation before A.D. 1300.

These data imply a multicomponent occupation at the Pendleton ruin. If so, the ceramic assemblage lumped together as Animas phase by Kidder should be partitioned into at least two separate phases, one before and one after the introduction of Gila Polychrome. The earlier phase should then correlate with the Black Mountain phase in the Mimbres area and the Buena Fé phase at Casas Grandes and the later one with the Paquimé and Diablo phases. We thus might speak of an "early" and "late Medio period," just as there is an early (Soho) and late (Civano) Hohokam Classic period. The tendency of some researchers (for example, Findlow and De Atley 1976) to lump everything in southwestern New Mexico that dates between A.D. 1175 and 1450 under the concept of the "Animas phase" has obscured this important distinction (see also LeBlanc 1975; LeBlanc and Nelson 1976).

The Third Stage: World Systems

The proponents of *pochteca* models have attempted to argue for two theses at once: (1) specific *pochteca* contact in the Southwest, and (2) general mesoamerican influence in the Southwest. They seek to show that the evolution of mesoamerican civilization significantly influenced the course of southwestern prehistory. If their specific argument—that *pochteca* merchant-priests from Mesoamerica entered the Southwest and directly affected southwestern populations—could be demonstrated, then so would the general thesis. However, the *pochteca* argument is so specific that it is questionable whether the archaeological record from the Southwest can be expected to provide the resolution necessary to test this concept. *Pochteca* burials have been sought (Reyman 1978), but even if elaborate burials were found, would it be possible to prove the skeletons derive from a non-southwestern and mesoamerican population? To claim simply that burials with exotic goods are *pochteca* would be tautological. The claim that abrupt organizational change is evidence of outside intervention is similarly weak, because local populations may have responded to different situations by rapidly evolving new organizational forms. What are the crucial tests in an objective choice between these alternatives? Parsimony is insufficient as a criterion because what is "simpler" to one observer may not appear so to another. The strong thesis of *pochteca* merchant-priests may, therefore, be untestable archaeologically.

It is important to recognize, however, that even if the *pochteca* models were shown to be wrong (though they have not been), the general thesis of significant mesoamerican influence on the Southwest may still be true. Direct intervention is not the only mechanism, nor even perhaps the most effective one, by which such influence could have been effected. The more basic problem, then, is how to test the general thesis without totally losing sight of the *pochteca* or isolationist extremes. The promise of the world system idea is that it may provide a framework for such a test.

The World-Systems Concept

The concept of a "world system" was popularized recently by Immanuel Wallerstein. The concept derives from the work of many scholars, especially European historians, who have attempted to explain the rise of capitalism (for example, Braudel 1972), though McNeill's (1963) concept of "*oikoumene*" is also a "world system" concept (see also Teggart 1939). Wallerstein begins with the concept of a social system, which he defines in terms of a division of labor: "We can regard a division of labor as a grid [network] which is substantially interdependent. . . . The smallest grid that would substantially meet the expectations of the overwhelming majority of actors within these boundaries constitutes a single division of labor" (Wallerstein 1976:397).

Applying this concept, he argues that only two classes of "social systems" can have existed: "those relatively small, highly autonomous subsistence economies not part of some regular tribute-demanding system and . . . world systems" (1974:348; 1976). World systems are social systems that integrate a set of different cultures into a coherent division of labor. Wallerstein identifies only two classes of world systems: world empires, which are politically as well as economically integrated; and world economies, which are not politically integrated. In his analysis of the European world-economy, which, he argues, became articulated as a single social system in the sixteenth century, Wallerstein employs a modified core-periphery paradigm to identify a set of competing "core" industrial states; dependent "peripheral" states that supplied raw materials to the core; and "semi-peripheral" states that are said to deflect political pressures away from the core states. The system was far from static because the different states competed to improve their positions. Wallerstein (1976:70−82) argues that the operation of this system led increasingly toward a concentration of industry in the core states of western Europe, toward monoculture in the peripheral states of eastern Europe and Spanish America, and toward relative self-sufficiency in agriculture in the semiperipheral Mediterranean states.

The basic idea that different cultures may be systemically connected into larger social systems, and that structural characteristics in those cultures may result from the nature of that systemic interaction, is already proving to be extraordinarily productive of new insights, as Wallerstein's (1976) work alone demonstrates (see also Brookfield 1975 for a comprehensive review of related theoretical applications and a critique of the core-periphery paradigm). The concept of a world system is especially intriguing in the present context because it allows the restating, in general terms, of the particular question of southwestern-mesoamerican relationships (Pailes 1980; Pailes and Whitecotton 1979; Weigand 1982; Weigand et al. 1977). Useful comparisons with other world systems will then be possible.

Several comments are in order at this point, however, on a number of shortcomings in Wallerstein's formulations (see also Blanton and Feinman 1984). While he rightly criticizes a historical approaches that "reify parts of the [social] totality into such [stage or ideal type] units and then . . . compare these reified structures" (Wallerstein 1974:389), his sharp contrast of world economies and small autonomous ones raises similar dangers. In fact, modern anthropological theory (Dennell 1983; Wobst 1976, 1978) makes it highly questionable whether the latter class of economies ever existed.

Blanton et al. (1981) have argued that all social systems can be described in terms of their scale, integration, and complexity, recognizing too that the political and economic subsystems must be treated separately. A huge variety of theoretical possibilities is thus describable. Following Wallerstein (1976), we might reserve the term "world system" for those social systems that encompass more than one culturally distinct regional population. A subclass of that set would be what Renfrew (1982) describes as "peer polity interaction" in which comparably organized chiefdoms or states interact with one another without any one being politically dominant. If that interaction is economic (and it is not clear that it must be), and if it involves a division of labor among the polities (which Wallerstein's definition of social system requires), then these systems would be "world economies." In such cases, however, it is by no means obvious that the concepts of core, periphery, or semiperiphery are applicable. The stress on *peer polity* interaction seems to imply that different structural arrangements may be involved. In

general, though it has been shown that core-periphery contrasts are appropriate in several precapitalist cases (for example, Palerm and Wolf 1957),
the structure of a world system should be treated as a separate empirical
problem in each case.

Another question has to do with the nature of the economic goods
flowing through the system. Wallerstein (1976) emphasizes bulk goods
(grain, cattle, woolens) and is skeptical that a trade in luxuries could create a
world economy. Jane Schneider has criticized this view, pointing out that
luxuries in precapitalist societies had potent economic effects: "Pitting some
[clients] against others, gift giving promotes the cooptation of class enemies,
making the patron-client relationship a forceful political adjunct to energy
capture" (1977 : 23). Citing Robert Adams, she suggests that "we assume for
the past as well as the present a model in which more complex societies
'dominate weaker neighbors, coalesce, experience predation, develop and
break off patterns of symbiosis and all in dizzying abrupt shifts.' The need to
adapt to such shifts is 'the single most overwhelming selective pressure to
which societies are exposed' (Adams 1974 : 249)" (Schneider 1977 : 23).

Societies that required shell, turquoise, argillite, or other materials exotic to their area would have periodically moved far afield to acquire those
resources or, if that were impossible, would have engaged foreign populations in an exchange arrangement. If those "foreign" populations were also
culturally distinct, then those exchanges would constitute a "world system"
subject to the kind of processes suggested by Adams and Schneider (see also
Blanton and Feinman 1984).

Mesoamerica, Blanton et al. (1981 : 245−250) have concluded, is
such a world system. Contrary to Wallerstein (1976), however, they deny
that it was either a world empire or a world economy in his sense. Rather,
they envision a system of elite, prestige exchanges involving marriages, visitation, competitive feasting, and war (Blanton et al. 1981 : 246). In a manner
similar to Schneider, they emphasize the economic importance of this
"world system" in the regulation of the participating societies (Blanton et al.
1981 : 248−250). For our purposes, then, it seems unnecessary to deny that
the mesoamerican world system was a "world economy," though we take
their point that the nature of the economic relations contrast with the case
analyzed by Wallerstein (1976; see also Blanton and Feinman 1984; Whitecotton and Pailes 1979).

Critique of Phil Weigand's World-Systems Model

The most detailed world-systems model yet developed that interprets
southwestern-mesoamerican relationships is presented in a series of recent
papers by Phil Weigand (Weigand 1978, 1979, 1982; Weigand et al. 1977).
His vantage point is Jalisco and Zacatecas where he has done extensive
fieldwork since the 1960s when he worked for Kelley excavating a rural
hamlet and studying the mines in the Chalchihuites area (Weigand 1968,
1978). When he first began formulating his world-systems model, the revi-

sions in the Alta Vista chronology were not yet available. A critical reevaluation that draws on those changes and other data is now in order.

To follow up his work in the Chalchihuites mines, Weigand, Harbottle, and Sayre began a long-term program of identifying the source areas of many rare resources found in Mesoamerica so that the structure of the exchange network could be reconstructed. "Our basic model is that of a world system in which the rare resource provinces play an active role side by side with more complex centers of civilization and consumption. In this view, cultures in rare resource areas have an economic/political interrelationship with zones that trade for their produce. *Since economics and politics are seldom separable,* there is an implicit direction required for such relationships—cultural influences from centers of consumption into rare resource zones and an ecological network of systematized demand, exploitation, trade, manufacture, distribution, and increased demand" (Weigand et al. 1977:23; emphasis added).

In particular, the distribution of turquoise is being closely examined. Preliminary results (Weigand et al. 1977; Weigand 1978:77−78) indicate that chemical turquoise from the Cerrillos and Azure mines in New Mexico and the Concepcion del Oro-Mazapil area of Zacatecas was acquired by populations of the Suchil branch of the Chalchihuites culture during the Alta Vista phase. Colonization of the Chalchihuites area by people directed from Teotihuacan is inferred during the Alta Vista phase (Weigand 1978:74; Weigand et al. 1977:18; see also Kelley 1971; Kelley and Abbott 1966). It is supposed that minerals from these mines and turquoise from the north were sent southeastward to Teotihuacan and later to Cholula (Weigand 1978:78; Weigand et al. 1977:18−21). Expeditions from Chalchihuites to the north and east are suggested as the principal means by which turquoise was obtained (Weigand 1978:78, 1979:23; Weigand et al. 1977:19). With the collapse of Alta Vista and the rise of La Quemada and Tula in the south and Chaco Canyon and Casas Grandes (Di Peso 1974) in the north, Weigand et al. infer that demand for blue-green stones "entered a new phase in the sense of both quantity and intensity of exploitation" (1977:21). Along the route to the north, Weigand envisions trade caravans serviced by colonies maintained and protected by the great fortress of La Quemada. The large Chaco Canyon sites are viewed as an urban emporium designed to produce rare resources for southern markets (Weigand 1979:24). Following the nearly coincident collapse of the Chaco and Tula centers, and the decline of La Quemada, the "trade route" into the American Southwest shifted to the coast and Casas Grandes, with Guasave and Culiacan, became the principal intermediaries (Weigand 1979; see also Kelley 1974, 1980).

The basic premises, as well as the empirical application of this model, may be questioned. Economics and politics are often *separate* systems with little in common (Blanton et al. 1981; Wallerstein 1974). The emphasis placed on colonization by Teotihuacan or upon domination by Tula may thus be theoretically unnecessary as well as empirically impossible—if the new Alta Vista chronology is correct (Kelley and Kelley 1980). By arguing for colonization, Weigand is in effect inferring a Teotihuacan "world empire" when some kind of "world economy" is more likely (see Blanton et al. 1981; Whitecotton and Pailes 1979). Interestingly, Weigand's (1980) recent use of Braudel's (1972) concept of a "trade structure" appears to be a move in this direction. But what kind of a world economy is indicated? How should we imagine it was structured? Although a "merchants' barrio" has been identified in Teotihuacan, just what it was is not clear. Rene Millon says, "I dubbed the area the 'merchants' barrio,' but the quotation marks are meant to indicate that this may be a misnomer. It does not appear to have been occupied by foreigners" (1981 : 226). More generally, little evidence is available on the role of merchants in Teotihuacan society (Millon 1981 : 226). The case of Tula is similar (Diehl 1981 : 289).

Expeditionary trade for turquoise (Weigand et al. 1977) also seems unlikely, particularly when social processes that are more parsimonious can account for the data. Moving the Alta Vista chronology forward in time to A.D. 750–900 affects this argument, but more important is the role of the Chihuahuan desert dwellers and the nature of their desert economy. Weigand, on the one hand, has argued that people from Chalchihuites must have gone to the Concepcion del Oro-Mazapil mines to get turquoises because "this zone has almost no agricultural potential [and] there were no groups capable of being 'Mesoamericanized'" (1978 : 78). Yet, he has also eloquently described the interaction that probably existed between the Chihuahuan desert dwellers and their sedentary neighbors (see also Armillas 1969):

> There were always two types of Chichimecas. The most important type from the Mesoamerican perspective were the "external proletariat," or those groups on or just beyond the frontier, in areas near colonies, or astride trade routes. Often they symbiotically lived with their civilized neighbors—even raiding is a form of symbiosis. While they were dedicated hunters and gatherers, they also were partly dependent on agriculture where there were favorable areas. *They traded with Mesoamericans the raw produce of their lands* for finished products, usually status markers. The raw material for which there is some evidence are peyote, animal hides, *blue-green stones,* and perhaps slaves. In return, they most likely received finished feathers, and *copper artifacts.* There is little evidence, however, for these Mesoamerican items. . . . In addition, many of these Chichimecas must have had some direct experience within the borders of civilization as traders, workers, or perhaps slaves, or knew a group who had. At least superficially, these Chichimecas were part of the ancient Mesoamerican world system as they contributed to its economy and shared many of its cultural and symbolic traits (Weigand 1979 : 30; emphasis added).

Why, we may ask, could not the Chichimecas of the Chihuahuan desert have always been the principal transfer agents for chemical turquoise from the American Southwest to the Chalchihuites area? Great mobility by these hunters and gatherers is well attested (Kelley 1955) and it is known that they did use turquoise in the early historic period (for an excellent discussion of the economy of these people see Kelley 1952, 1953). As we have suggested above, the ceremonial centers of Alta Vista, La Quemada, and even Schroeder and Zape may have been designed in part to attract the Chichimecan "trade." New research is needed to explore this possibility further. While the system that such a structural arrangement implies would not be a "world empire," it nevertheless would be some kind of "world system," which is, after all, Weigand's (1979) fundamental point.

The Larger Value of World Systems Thinking

The value of a world-systems approach was immediately recognized by Joseph Whitecotton and two scholars who were once students of J. Charles Kelley—Phil Weigand and Richard Pailes. Both Kelley and C. C. Di Peso began to employ the concept in their most recent work. Weigand has also succeeded in attracting the attention of several southwestern "isolationists" (Plog et al. 1982), including the present author.

That a world-systems framework is broad enough to incorporate many conflicting viewpoints into what may become a more fruitful dialogue is suggested also by the goals Richard Pailes (1980; see also Pailes and Whitecotton 1979) has set for his research in Sonora: "The continued uncovering of Mesoamerican traits and/or trade items within the Southwest itself, while serving to reinforce our conclusion that the Southwest was indeed a peripheral area in a larger world system, does not alone define the nature of the system. *By examining the intervening areas we hope to uncover evidence that will at least allow us to identify the kind of trade systems that were active*" (1980:24; emphasis added).

To implement this research, he advocates two approaches. The first is to construct a typology of trade systems, each of which is characterized by a different kind of trade goods, transmission techniques, and concomitant social relations. Secondly, "It is postulated that each of the . . . types of economic exchange would result in distinctive spatial distributions of trade goods relative to community settlement patterns. Undoubtedly the actual situation was more complicated than the four types suggest. For one thing, *there is no logical reason why more than one type could not have been operative at the same time*" (Pailes 1980:24; emphasis added).

Pailes's approach involves an effort to construct alternative expectations about the structure of settlement systems for each type of trade system. Together, these approaches specify a program that is a good step forward. Only the most recalcitrant isolationists can afford to ignore it. My own response has been to construct a model that emphasizes Pailes's types 1 and 2 trade systems (Chapter 8, this volume; Wilcox and Sternberg 1983). Others would begin from very different assumptions, but all contribute toward the larger goal of an objective understanding. New fieldwork and more innovative analyses are needed to test the alternatives.

Acknowledgments

This paper grew out of a study of Hohokam ballcourts and their interpretation that was funded by the Western Archeological Center, National Park Service, in a contract with the Arizona State Museum, University of Arizona. I thank all parties involved for teaching me the limits of contract work. Enormous assistance in my struggle to understand the problems of cultural contacts between Mesoamerica and the Southwest was provided in numerous letters and papers sent to me by J. Charles Kelley, Richard Pailes, Phil Weigand, Wick Miller, and Catherine Fowler. A seminar on the archaeology of west and northwest Mexico given by Phil Weigand at Arizona State University in the spring of 1979 was of inestimable value in the researching of this paper. The helpfulness and kindness of all of these scholars is greatly appreciated. I am also especially grateful to Edwin Ferdon, Emil Haury, David Gregory, Beatriz Baniff, Gary Feinman, R. Ben Brown, Barney Burns, Thomas Naylor, Steven LeBlanc, Vernon Scarborough, and the late Charles Di Peso for their help and support. For initial typing and editorial assistance, thanks go to Maria Abdin and Ben Smith, respectively. For support in preparing a revision for publication, special thanks go to Philip Thompson, Donald E. Weaver, Jr., and Lilia Scott, Museum of Northern Arizona, Flagstaff. Finally, without the perseverance and enthusiasm of my wife, Susan, this paper would not have been possible. I alone am responsible for any errors or misconceptions.

References Cited

Adams, Robert McC.
  1974 Anthropological Reflections on Ancient Trade. *Current Anthropology* 15:239–258.
Armillas, Pedro
  1964 Northern Mesoamerica. In *Prehistoric Man in the New World*, edited by Jesse D. Jennings and Edward Norbeck, pp. 291–330. University of Chicago Press, Chicago.
  1969 The Arid Frontier of Mexican Civilization. *New York Academy of Science Bulletin* 2(316):697–704.
Aveni, Anthony F., Horst Hartung, and J. Charles Kelley
  1982 Alta Vista (Chalchihuites): Astronomical Implications of a Meso-

american Ceremonial Outpost at the Tropic of Cancer. *American Antiquity* 47:316−335.

Beals, Ralph
1932 The comparative Ethnology of Northern Mexico Before 1750. *Ibero-Americana* 2:93−225. Berkeley.
1944b Relations Between Mesoamerica and the Southwest. In *El Norte de México y el Sur de Estados Unidos*, pp. 245−252. Tercera Reunion de Mesa Redonda sobre Problemas Antropologicos de México y Centro America, vol. 3. Sociedad Mexicana de Antropología, Mexico City.

Bell, Betty
1971 Archaeology of Nayarit, Jalisco, and Colima. In *Archaeology of Northern Mesoamerica, Part 2*, edited by Gordon F. Ekholm and Ignacio Bernal, pp. 694−753. Handbook of Middle American Indians, vol. 2, Robert Wauchope, general editor. University of Texas Press, Austin.

Blanton, Richard, and Gary Feinman
1984 The Mesoamerican World System. *American Anthropologist* 86: 703−705.

Blanton, Richard E., Stephen A. Kowalewski, Gary Feinman, and Jill Appel
1981 *Ancient Mesoamerica, A Comparison of Change in Three Regions.* Cambridge University Press, Cambridge.

Brand, Donald D.
1935 The Distribution of Pottery Types in Northwest Mexico. *American Anthropologist* 37:287−305.
1939 Notes on the Geography and Archaeology of Zape, Durango. In *So Live the Works of Men*, edited by Donald D. Brand and Fred E. Harvey, pp. 75−106. University of New Mexico Press, Albuquerque.
1944 Archaeological Relations Between Northern Mexico and the Southwest. In *El Norte de México y el Sur de Estados Unidos*, pp. 199−203. Tercera Reunion de Mesa Redonda sobre Problemas Antropologicos de México y Centro America, vol. 3. Sociedad Mexicana de Antropología, Mexico City.

Braniff, Beatriz
1975 Arqueologia del Norte de México. In *Los pueblos y senorios teocraticos*, El periodo de las ciudades urbanas, Primera parte. Instituto Nacional de Antropología e Historia, Mexico.

Braudel, Fernand
1972 *The Mediterranean and the Mediterranean World in the Age of Philip II*, 2 vols. Harper and Row, New York.

Brookfield, Harold C.
1975 *Interdependent Development.* University of Pittsburgh Press, Pittsburgh.

Brooks, Richard H.
1971 Lithic Traditions in Northwestern Mexico, Paleo-Indian to Chal-

chihuites. Ph.D. dissertation, University of Colorado, Boulder. University Microfilms, Ann Arbor.

Brown, Roy Bernard
1980 A Preparatory Statement to a Paleoecological Study on the Northern Frontier of Mesoamerica. Ms. on file, Arizona State Museum Library, University of Arizona, Tucson.

Carlson, Roy L.
1981 The Polychrome Complexes. In *Southwestern Ceramics, A Comparative Review*, edited by Albert H. Schroeder, pp. 201–234. Arizona Archaeologist No. 15. Phoenix.

Carey, Henry A.
1931 An Analysis of the Northwestern Chihuahua Culture. *American Anthropologist* 33:325–374.

Dennell, Robin
1983 *European Economic Prehistory, A New Approach*. Academic Press, New York.

Diehl, Richard A.
1981 Tula. In *Archaeology*, edited by Jeremy A. Sabloff, pp. 277–295. Supplement to the Handbook of Middle American Indians, vol. 1, Victoria Reifler Bricker, general editor. University of Texas Press, Austin.

Di Peso, Charles C.
1956 *The Upper Pima of San Cayetano del Tuamacacori: An Archaeo-Historical Reconstruction of the Ootam of Pimeria Alta*. Amerind Foundation Publications No. 7. Dragoon, Arizona.
1966 Archaeology and Ethnohistory of the Northern Sierra. In *Archaeological Frontiers and External Connections*, edited by Gordon F. Ekholm and Gordon R. Willey, pp. 3–25. Handbook of Middle American Indians, vol. 4, Robert Wauchope, general editor. University of Texas Press, Austin.
1968 Casas Grandes, a Fallen Trading Center of the Gran Chichimeca. *Masterkey* 42(1):20–37.
1974 *Casas Grandes, A Fallen Trading Center of the Gran Chichimeca*, vol. 3. Northland Press, Flagstaff.

Di Peso, Charles C., John B. Rinaldo, and Gloria J. Fenner
1976 *Casas Grandes, A Fallen Trading Center of Gran Chichimeca*, vols. 4–8. Northland Press, Flagstaff.

Doyel, David E.
1976 Classic Period Hohokam in the Gila River Basin, Arizona. *Kiva* 42(1):27–38.

Doyel, David E., and Emil Haury (editors)
1976 *The 1976 Salado Conference*. Kiva 42(1).

Ekholm, Gordon F.
1939 Results of an Archaeological Survey of Sonora and Northern Sinaloa. *Revista Mexicana de Estudios Antropologicos* 3(1):7–10.
1940 The Archaeology of Northern and Western Mexico. In *The Maya*

and their Neighbors, edited by Clarence L. Hay et al. pp. 320–330. Appleton-Century-Crofts, New York.

1942 *Excavations at Guasave, Sinaloa, Mexico.* Anthropological Papers of the American Museum of Natural History No. 38: 4.

Euler, Robert C., George J. Gumerman, Thor N. V. Karlstrom, Jeffrey S. Dean, and Richard H. Hevly

1979 The Colorado Plateau: Cultural Dynamics and Paleoenvironment. *Science* 205(4411): 1089–1101.

Findlow, Frank J., and Susan P. De Atley

1976 Prehistoric Land Use Patterns in the Animas Valley: A First Approximation. *Anthropology UCLA* 6(2): 1–57.

Flannery, Kent V., Anne V. T. Kirby, Michael J. Kirby, and Aubrey W. Williams, Jr.

1967 Farming Systems and Political Growth in Ancient Oaxaca. *Science* 158(3800): 445–454.

Ford, Richard I.

1981 Gardening and Farming Before A.D. 1000: Patterns of Prehistoric Cultivation North of Mexico. *Journal of Ethnobiology* 1(1): 6–27.

Friedmann, N. John

1972 The Spatial Organization of Power in the Development of Urban Systems. *Comparative Urban Research* 1: 5–42.

Gladwin, Harold S.

1957 *A History of the Ancient Southwest.* Bond, Wheelwright, Portland, Maine.

Gladwin, Harold S., Emil W. Haury, E. B. Sayles, and Nora Gladwin

1937 *Excavations at Snaketown I: Material Culture.* Medallion Papers No. 25. Globe, Arizona.

Haury, Emil W.

1945 The Problem of Contacts Between the Southwestern United States and Mexico. *Southwestern Journal of Anthropology* 1: 55–74.

1976 *The Hohokam: Desert Farmers and Craftsmen.* University of Arizona Press, Tucson.

Holien, Thomas, and Robert Pickering

1978 Analogues in Classic Period Chalchihuites Culture to Late Mesoamerican Ceremonialism. In *Middle Classic Mesoamerica: A.D. 400–700,* edited by Esther Paztory, pp. 145–147. Columbia University Press, New York.

Kelley, Ellen Abbott

1978 The Temple of the Skulls at Alta Vista, Chalchihuites. In *Across the Chichimec Sea: Papers in Honor of J. Charles Kelley,* edited by Carroll L. Riley and Basil C. Hedrick, pp. 102–126. Southern Illinois University Press, Carbondale.

Kelley, Ellen Abbott, and J. Charles Kelley

1980 Sipapu and Pyramid Too: The Temple of the Crypt at Alta Vista, Chalchichuites. In *New Frontiers in the Archaeology and Ethnohistory of the Greater Southwest*, edited by Carroll L. Riley and Basil C. Hedrick, pp. 62–80. Transactions of the Illinois State Academy of Science No. 72(4).

Kelley, J. Charles

1952 Factors Involved in the Abandonment of Certain Peripheral Southwestern Settlements. *American Anthropologist* 54:356–387.

1953 Some Geographic and Cultural Factors Involved in Mexican-Southwestern Contacts. In *Indian Tribes of 29th International Congress of Americanists*, edited by Sol Tax, pp. 139–144. University of Chicago Press, Chicago.

1955 Juan Sabeata and Diffusion in Aboriginal Texas. *American Anthropologist* 57:981–995.

1956 Settlement Patterns in North-Central Mexico. In *Settlement Patterns of the New World*, edited by Gordon R. Willey, pp. 128–139. Viking Fund Publications in Anthropology No. 23.

1960 North Mexico and the Correlation of Mesoamerican and Southwestern Cultural Sequences. In *Selected Papers of Anthropological and Ethnological Sciences*, edited by Sol Tax, pp. 566–573. University of Pennsylvania Press, Philadelphia.

1966 Mesoamerica and the Southwestern United States. In *Archaeological Frontiers and External Connections*, edited by Gordon F. Ekholm and Gordon R. Willey, pp. 95–110. Handbook of Middle American Indians, vol. 4, Robert Wauchope, general editor. University of Texas Press, Austin.

1971 Archaeology of the Northern Frontier: Pochtecas and Durango. In *Archaeology of Northern Mesoamerica*, edited by Ignacio Bernal and Gordon F. Ekholm, pp. 768–801. Handbook of Middle American Indians, vol. 11, Robert Wauchope, general editor. University of Texas Press, Austin.

1974 Speculations on the Culture History of Northwestern Mexico. In *The Archaeology of West Mexico*, edited by Betty Bell, pp. 19–39. Sociedad de Estudios Aranzados del Occidente de Mexico, A.C., Ajijic, Jalisco, Mexico.

1980 Alta Vista, Chalchihuites: "Port of Entry" on the Northwestern Frontier. In *Rutas de Intercambio en Mesoamerica y Norte de México*, vol. 1, pp. 53–64. 16th Reunion de Mesa Redonda, Saltillo, Mexico.

Kelley, J. Charles, and Ellen Abbott

1966 *The Cultural Sequence on the North Central Frontier of Mesoamerica*. 36 Congreso Internacional de Americanistas, Espana, 1964, vol. 1.

Kelley, J. Charles, and Ellen Abbott Kelley

1971 *An Introduction to the Ceramics of the Chalchihuites Culture of Zacatecas and Durango, Mexico. Part I: The Decorated Wares*. Mesoamerican Studies No. 5, Research Records of the University Museum. Southern Illinois University, Carbondale.

1975 An Alternative Hypothesis for the Explanation of Anasazi Culture History. In *Collected Papers in Honor of Florence Hawley Ellis*, edited by Theodore R. Frisbie, pp. 178–223. Papers of the Archaeological Society of New Mexico No. 2. Hooper Publishing, Norman.

Kelley, J. Charles, and Howard D. Winters
1960 A Revision of the Archaeological Sequence in Sinaloa, Mexico. *American Antiquity* 25:547–561.

Kelly, Isabel T.
1944 West Mexico and the Hohokam. In *El Norte de México y el Sur de Estados Unidos*, pp. 206–222. 3rd Reunion de Mesa Redonda sobre Problemas Antropologicos de México y Centro America, vol. 3. Sociedad Mexicana de Antropología, Mexico City.

Kessell, John L.
1979 *Kiva, Cross, and Crown: The Pecos Indians and New Mexico 1540–1840*. National Park Service, U.S. Department of the Interior, Washington, D.C.

Kidder, A. V., H. S. Cosgrove, and C. B. Cosgrove
1949 *The Pendleton Ruin, Hidalgo County, New Mexico*. Carnegie Institution of Washington Publication No. 585: Contributions to American Anthropology and History No. 50.

Kirchhoff, Paul
1943 Mesoamerica: Sus Limites Geograficas, Composition Ethnica y Caracteres Culturales. *Acta Americana* 1:92–107.

LeBlanc, Steven A.
1975 *Preliminary Report of the First Season of Excavation, 1974*. Mimbres Archaeological Center, Institute of Archaeology, University of California, Los Angeles.
1980 The Dating of Casas Grandes. *American Antiquity* 45:799–806.
1982 The Advent of Pottery in the Southwest. In *Southwestern Ceramics: A Comparative Review*, edited by Albert H. Schroeder, pp. 27–52. The Arizona Archaeologist, No. 15. Tempe.

LeBlanc, Steven A., and Ben Nelson
1976 The Salado in Southwestern New Mexico. *Kiva* 42(1):71–79.

Lekson, Stephen, and Timothy C. Klinger
1973 Villareal II: Preliminary Notes on an Animas Phase Site in Southwestern New Mexico. *Awanyu, The Journal of the Archaeological Society of New Mexico*, 1(2):33–38. Albuquerque.

McGuire, Randall H.
1980 The Mesoamerican Connection in the Southwest. *Kiva* 46(1–2):3–38.

McNeill, William Hardy
1963 *The Rise of the West: A History of the Human Community*. University of Chicago Press, Chicago.

Marquina, Ignacio
    1951 *Arquitectura Prehispanica*. Memorias del Instituto Nacional de An-
    tropología e Historia No. 1. Mexico.
Mason, J. Alden
    1937 Late Archaeological Sites in Durango, Mexico from Chalchihuites to
    Zape. In *Twenty-fifth Anniversary Studies, Publications of the Phila-
    delphia Anthropological Society*, vol. 1. Philadelphia.
Millon, Rene
    1981 Teotihuacan: City, State, and Civilization. In *Archaeology*, edited
    by Jeremy A. Sabloff, pp. 198–243. Supplement to the Handbook of
    Middle American Indians, vol. 1, Victoria Reifler Bricker, general edi-
    tor. University of Texas Press, Austin.
Nelson, Richard S.
    1981 The Role of a *Pochteca* System in Hohokam Exchange. Ph.D. disser-
    tation, New York University. University Microfilms, Ann Arbor.
Noguera, Eduardo
    1930 *Ruina Arqueologicas del Norte de México, Casas Grandes (Chihua-
    hua), La Quemada, Chalchihuites (Zacatecas)*. Publicaciones de la Sec-
    retarias de Educación Publica, Mexico City.
Pailes, Richard A.
    1980 The Upper Rio Sonora Valley in Prehistoric Trade. In *New Frontiers
    in the Archaeology and Ethnohistory of the Greater Southwest*, edited
    by Carroll L. Riley and Basil C. Hedrick, pp. 20–39. Transactions of the
    Illinois State Academy of Science No. 72(4).
Pailes, Richard A., and Joseph W. Whitecotton
    1979 The Greater Southwest and the Mesoamerican "World" System: An
    Exploratory Model of Frontier Relationships. In *The Frontier: Com-
    parative Studies*, vol. 2, edited by William W. Savage, Jr. and Stephen I.
    Thompson, pp. 105–121. University of Oklahoma Press, Norman.
Palerm, Angel, and Eric Wolf
    1957 Ecological Potential and Cultural Development. In Mesoamerica. In
    Studies in Human Ecology, pp. 1–37. Anthropological Society of Wash-
    ington and Pan American Union Social Science Monograph No. 3.
Plog, Fred, Steadman Upham, and Phil C. Weigand
    1982 A Perspective on Mogollon-Mesoamerican Interaction. In *Mogollon
    Archaeology, Proceedings of the 1980 Mogollon Conference*, edited by
    Patrick H. Beckett and Kim Silverbird, pp. 227–238. Acoma Books,
    Ramona, California.
Renfrew, Colin
    1982 Peer Polity Interaction as an Analytical Frame. Paper presented at
    the 47th annual meeting of the Society for American Archaeology, Min-
    neapolis, Minnesota.
Reyman, Jonathan E.
    1978 *Pochteca* Burials at Anasazi Sites? In *Across the Chichimec Sea:*

Papers in Honor of J. Charles Kelley, edited by Carroll L. Riley and Basil C. Hedrick, pp. 242–262. Southern Illinois University Press, Carbondale.

Riley, Carroll L., and Howard D. Winters
1963 The Prehistoric Tepehuan of Northern Mexico. *Southwestern Journal of Anthropology* 19:177–185.

Sanders, William T. and Barbara J. Price
1968 *Mesoamerica: The Evolution of a Civilization.* Random House, New York.

Sauer, Carl, and Donald Brand
1930 Pueblo Sites in Southeastern Arizona. *University of California Publications in Geography* 3(7):415–458. Berkeley.
1931 Prehistoric Settlements of Sonora with Special Reference to *Cerro de Trincheras*. *University of California Publications in Geography* 5(3): 67–148. Berkeley.
1932 *Aztatlán, Prehistoric Mexican Frontier on the Pacific Coast.* Ibero-Americana No. 1. Berkeley.

Sayles, E. B.
1936 *An Archaeological Survey of Chihuahua.* Medallion Papers No. 22. Gila Pueblo, Globe.

Schneider, Jane
1977 Was There a Pre-Capitalist World-System? *Peasant Studies* 6(2): 20–29.

Schroeder, Albert H.
1956 Comments on "A Trial Survey of Mexican-Southwestern Architectural Parallels." *El Palacio* 63(9–10):299–309.
1960 *The Hohokam, Sinagua, and the Hakataya.* Society for American Archaeology, Archives of Archaeology No. 5.

Spielmann, Katherine Ann
1982 Inter-Societal Food Acquisition among Egalitarian Societies: An Ecological Study of Plains/Pueblo Interaction in the American Southwest. Ph.D. dissertation, University of Michigan, Ann Arbor. University Microfilms, Ann Arbor.

Teggart, Frederick John
1939 *Rome and China: A Study of Correlations in Historical Events.* University of California Press, Berkeley.

Wallerstein, Immanuel
1974 *The Modern World System.* Academic Press, New York.
1976 *The Modern World-System (text edition); Capitalist Agriculture and the Origins of the European World-Economy in the Sixteenth Century.* Academic Press, New York.

Wasley, William W.
1960 A Hohokam Platform Mound at the Gatlin Site, Gila Bend, Arizona. *American Antiquity* 262:244–262.

Weigand, Phil C.
  1968 The Mines and Mining Techniques of the Chalchihuites Culture. *American Antiquity* 33:45–61.
  1978 The Prehistory of the State of Zacatecas: An Interpretation, Part 1. *Anthropology* 2(1):67–87.
  1979 The Prehistory of the State of Zacatecas: An Interpretation, Part 2. *Anthropology* 2(2):22–41.
  1982 Mining and Mineral Trade in Prehistoric Zacatecas. In Mining and Mining Techniques in Ancient Mesoamerica, edited by Phil C. Weigand and Gretchen Gwynne, pp. 87–134. *Anthropology* 6(1 and 2).
Weigand, Phil C., Garman Harbottle, and Edward V. Sayre
  1977 Turquoise Sources and Source Analysis: Mesoamerica and the Southwestern U.S.A. In *Exchange Systems in Prehistory*, edited by Timothy K. Earle and Jonathan E. Ericson, pp. 15–34. Academic Press, New York.
Whitecotton, Joseph W. and Richard A. Pailes
  1979 Mesoamerica as an Historical Unit: A World-System Model. Paper presented to the 43rd International Congress of Americanists, Vancouver, B.C., Canada, August 1979.
Wilcox, David R., Thomas R. McGuire, and Charles Sternberg
  1981 *Snaketown Revisited*. Arizona State Museum Archaeological Series No. 155. University of Arizona, Tucson.
Wilcox, David R., and Lynette O. Shenk
  1977 *The Architecture of the Casa Grande and its Interpretation*. Arizona State Museum Archaeological Series No. 115. University of Arizona, Tucson.
Wilcox, David R., and Charles Sternberg
  1983 *Hohokam Ballcourts and Their Interpretation*. Arizona State Museum Archaeological Series No. 160. University of Arizona, Tucson.
Wilkerson, S. Jeffrey K.
  1979 Huastec Presence and Cultural Chronology in North-Central Veracruz, Mexico. In *Actes du 42 Congrés International des Americanistes*. Musee de l'Homme, Paris.
Wobst, H. Martin
  1976 Locational Relationships in Paleolithic Society. *Journal of Human Evolution* 5:49–58.
  1978 The Archaeo-Ethnology of Hunter-Gatherers or the Tyranny of the Ethnographic Record in Archaeology. *American Antiquity* 43:303–309.
Wolf, Eric R.
  1982 *Europe and the People Without History*. University of California Press, Berkeley.

3

An Overview of the Greater Southwest in the Protohistoric Period

Carroll L. Riley

The central question of this volume involves the nature and extent of contacts between the sophisticated urbanized states of central and western Mexico and the Greater Southwest. How one views these ripples in the Chichimec sea will inevitably affect his or her interpretation of the pre-Colonial Southwest. Since people stand at different positions on this question, let me start by briefly considering how we got that way. For those wishing a more detailed analysis I recommend Wilcox and Masse (1981).

When the first group of anthropologists reached the Southwest in the latter part of the nineteenth century, they found it desirable to work simultaneously in various subbranches of the discipline and beyond it into history and the biological sciences. To use just one example, Adolph F. Bandelier, who labored in the Southwest from 1880 to 1892, was an archaeologist, ethnologist, ethnohistorian, historian, linguist, and botanist. With this ability to utilize a very broad prospective within the Southwest, and being intimately aware of the contemporary studies going on in Mexico and other parts of the New World, Bandelier and his pioneering colleagues generally considered the Southwest to be—historically and culturally—an integral part of Mesoamerica. Bandelier was so imbued with this concept of unity that he had no methodological difficulties whatsoever shifting his field and archival research between the Southwest and Mesoamerica and, finally, to the Central Andes. To Bandelier, the vast area stretching from the American Southwest to· Bolivia was part of one interrelated culture (White 1940, 1 : 197−198).

However, as various southwestern archaeological traditions became more sharply defined in the generation or two following the pioneers, archaeologists began to look on the Southwest as having a largely autochthonous development. This "isolationist" school began well before World War I but reached its peak in the 1920s and 1930s. For all practical purposes archaeologists of this period assumed that the Southwest stopped at the international boundary. Occasionally a researcher would take note of the ties between the Southwest and the high cultures to the south. One such was Edgar L. Hewett (1865–1946) who in his early years was much influenced by Bandelier. Hewett, writing near the end of his long career, uses words that might have been penned by Bandelier: "When one begins to write of the ancient Pueblos and cliff-dwellers, the real work on Mexico and Central America, to some extent also on the Andean people has commenced . . . one cannot travel the Mexican plateau or the Guatemalan and Andean Highlands without being conscious on every hand of shadows from the great Southwest. The Pueblo region proper ends in southern Chihuahua, roughly with the Conchos Valley" (Hewett 1936:51).

And yet Hewett by the 1930s was strongly isolationist. In his discussion of Chaco Canyon (Hewett 1968:279–301) he seems to be saying that the Pueblo III Chaco phenomenon was *totally* a matter of autonomous development, the result of some kind of internally kindled cultural evolution. In the same work, Hewett (1968:155–156) suggested that even southwestern pottery evolved in situ from pre-Pueblo sundried clay archetypes. In this he followed a suggestion previously made by Morris (1927:198) and, indeed, both men were airing ideas that had been widely circulated for a number of years.

The period following World War II saw a swing back to a belief in strong mesoamerican-southwestern involvement, with Mesoamerica largely functioning as a donor and the Southwest largely as a recipient. This line of thought, which is popular today, has been most highly developed by J. Charles Kelley and the late Charles C. Di Peso, both of whom see the Southwest as a source area for raw materials obtained by some organized group or groups. Kelley and Di Peso refer to these groups as *pochteca* or *puchteca* by analogy with that trading sodality of the Aztecs (Di Peso 1974; Kelley 1966).

Another approach, basically post–World War II and also currently popular, is a version of the between-the-wars isolationism but set in a processual mode. Here, changes in southwestern social and economic institutions, religion, technology, and art are seen as the result of interactive internal processes, or the interaction of various cultural subsystems with the environment. And, in very recent times, there has been a great deal of interest in a model of southwestern-mesoamerican interaction based on Immanuel Wallerstein's world system concept, a model which could—but would not have to—embrace the *pochteca* mechanisms of Kelley and Di Peso. Several points of view on Wallerstein are being presented in this volume.

The task I set myself with this paper is not to explain the presumed southwestern-mesoamerican connection, but, rather, to document it at least for the protohistoric period. Until we know just what were the level of contacts, and how such contacts modified the lives of southwesterners, it is difficult for us to properly apply ourselves to explanatory levels of discussion.

One problem with the study of southwestern-mesoamerican interaction at the various prehistoric levels is that our data are uneven and sometimes conflicting. It does look, however, as if there were two major periods of mesoamerican influence into the Southwest before protohistoric times (see Riley 1980b:15–16). The first corresponds to the rise of the macrotraditions: Anasazi, Mogollon, and Hohokam. This was pointed out a number of years ago by Schroeder (1965:299–301; 1966:683), who postulated an introduction of a superior race of Chapalote maize into the Southwest, perhaps in late B.C. times. Working from this augmented economic base southwestern cultures in subsequent centuries received ceremonial architecture, pottery (or at least new ceramic techniques), irrigation, new art motifs, a taste for shell ornamentation, cotton, and cremation among other habits. Not all of these traits, of course, reached all parts of the Southwest. More recently Haury (1976:351–353) stated that the early Hohokam tradition itself came from Mexico, the movement perhaps linked to an apparent expansion of mesoamerican culture in the late Preclassic.

The second wave of mesoamerican traits appears in the Great Pueblo period at Chaco Canyon, the Sedentary Hohokam, the expansionist Medio period at Casas Grandes, and perhaps also Classic Mimbres. Unfortunately, evidence for these contacts points in several directions and the *nature* of the connection is disputed. Some researchers, Kelley and Kelley for example, see clear penetration of a Mexican trading group or *pochteca* into Chaco Canyon during the Pueblo III period at Chaco (Kelley and Kelley 1975:201–206). Kelley and Kelley consider that the *pochteca* were middlemen in a trade network which served to funnel turquoise to Mesoamerica while copper ornaments, feathers, and shell were traded northward. They also believe that a number of architectural features at Chaco Canyon were of mesoamerican origin; for example, they feel that the great kivas were *pochteca* headquarters (Kelley and Kelley 1975:205). The model presented by Kelley and Kelley, in fact, necessitates a widespread *pochteca* network, and Frisbie (1978:210–216) and Reyman (1978:251–259) have reported high status burials of possible *pochteca* type in a number of southwestern sites in Pueblo III times.

All this, of course, has been challenged. Mathien (1983:204) seriously questions the impact on the Southwest in Chacoan times of mobile traders, *pochteca* or otherwise.

There is, however, no question about the third wave of mesoamerican influences, the protohistoric wave, which began sometime around or a bit after A.D. 1400, and for this period we *do* have rich data. An overview of these events will take up the balance of this paper.

My own study of the protohistoric Southwest has been predicated on the following model: "The Greater Southwest, at the time of first Spanish contact formed an interaction sphere in which the major linkages were those of trade but which included other kinds of sociopolitical and religious contacts" (Riley 1982:1). In order to test a series of hypotheses derived from this model I utilized various kinds of data but with a major concentration on the complementary use of archaeology and sixteenth and seventeenth century documentary sources.

The period from about A.D. 1250 to A.D. 1450 (that is, the period between the second and third waves of mesoamerican contact) was one of considerable shrinkage in the Greater Southwest. This time span saw the desertion of the San Juan basin and of large areas of central and northern Arizona. During this time there was the final breakup of Mogollon and Mimbres, disappearance of Classic Hohokam, and collapse of Casas Grandes. The reasons for the decline are still disputed, and I shall not speculate on them here. Not all portions of the Southwest shared in the decline during this "time of troubles." The northern Sonoran region seems to have been building up to a climax that, in the sixteenth century, would show itself as a series of active polities that controlled the middle and upper valleys of the Sonora and Yaqui rivers. Some years ago, I suggested the term "Sonoran Statelets" for this area, mainly on the basis of ethnohistorical evidence (see Figure 3). The archaeological reality of these statelets has been questioned (see Mathien, Chapter 12 this volume). Kelley especially stressed what he considers to be archaeological lacunae in that Sonoran area. "Perhaps the strongest case that Riley makes is his treatment of the Sonoran 'statelets' which he has described even more fully in an [earlier] paper. . . . The descriptions of socio-religious organization, Mesoamerican level architecture and ceremonialism in various localities are exciting but puzzling. Despite the efforts of earlier archaeologists, the most recent work of DiPeso, and the current work of Richard Pailes in the area concerned, *known* archaeological remains simply do not approach the cultural levels described in the ethnohistorical record cited by Riley" (Kelley 1980 : 65).

I had some problems with this statement even in 1980 for Pailes (1978 : 140) had already reported architectural complexity at the very large San José site in the central Sonora valley. In any case more recent work by Doolittle would seem to clear up the matter. Doolittle made an extensive demographic survey of the central valley of the Sonora river and demonstrated a sharp rise in population in late prehistoric times. Each segment of the Sonora valley had a large primary town associated with a linear distribution of villages and hamlets on the river plain. These central primary sites are quite large, for example San José covers more than 50 acres. They show indications of public architecture and strongly hint at a stratified society (Doolittle 1984b : 22–23). Population in the Serrana by the early sixteenth century may have reached 100,000 (Doolittle 1984a : 246; William E. Doolittle, personal communication, 1984). Doolittle sums up his findings in this way: "The data provided by the surveys indicate that a settlement pattern not unlike that suggested by Riley did exist in eastern Sonora during late prehistoric times. Kelley's critique of the statelet evidence appears to be no longer appropriate" (1984b : 19).

Not only was there an exuberant cultural development in the Serrana but also a renaissance in certain areas to the north. Along the central 'Rio

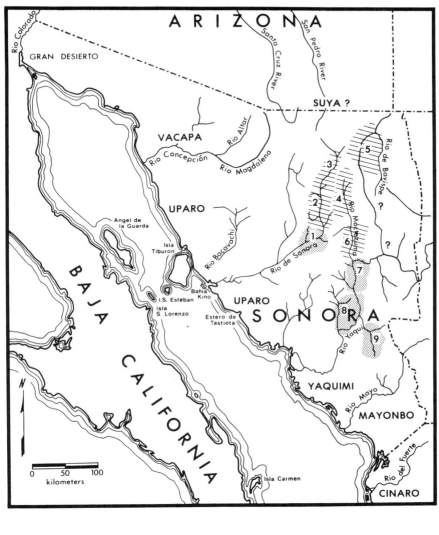

STATELETS *

1 Corazones   4 Cumupa   7 Pinebaroca
2 Señora   5 Sahuaripa   8 Paibatuco
3 Guaraspi   6 Batuco   9 Oera

* boundaries arbitrary
◻ Opata speaking
▦ mixed Opata-Pima
   or Pima speaking

Figure 3. Possible locations of the Sonoran statelets, ca. A.D. 1500

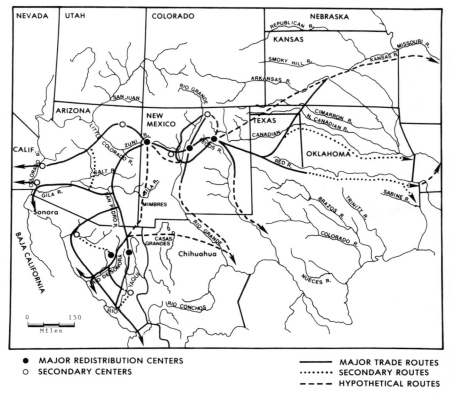

● MAJOR REDISTRIBUTION CENTERS   ——— MAJOR TRADE ROUTES
○ SECONDARY CENTERS   ········ SECONDARY ROUTES
                                                      – – – HYPOTHETICAL ROUTES

Figure 4. Trade routes in the Greater Southwest, ca. A.D. 1500

Grande and at Zuni and Hopi the Pueblo world was entering what Brew once referred to as a "golden age" (1944:242), with large towns and a brilliant development of art and religion. The golden age was underway by A.D. 1300; but its major development came after A.D. 1400, very likely stimulated by the reopening of the trade routes from Mexico.

Beginning sometime in the period A.D. 1400–1450, through mechanisms that are still unclear, a major trading route from west Mexico through the emerging Sonoran statelets was opening in the upper Southwest (see Figure 4). The collapse of Casas Grandes surely was a factor in the shift westward of the new route (Riley 1980a:46–48) although the relationship of Casas Grandes to the Sonoran statelets is anything but clear (Riley 1985). This great trunk route, called the "Camino Real" by Sauer (1932), quickly began to feed Mexican goods into the Southwest. What is even more important, it stimulated a whole series of trade relationships throughout the Southwest, not only to and from Mexico but in various other directions. This quickly developed into an exchange network with well-marked routes, trading centers, and an economic and political protocol throughout the area (Riley and Manson 1983 : 350–353).

The Yuman tribes on the lower Colorado River, at least by the early sixteenth century, had been caught up in the network. By that time major trade routes ran from the Sonoran statelets and from the northern Sonoran coast to the Zuni towns. From Zuni a trade route extended to Hopi and then to the Verde valley mining region and to the lower Colorado River. Eastward from Zuni was a major route—still followed by modern highways—that ran to Acoma with branches to Zia and to the Rio Grande Tiguex towns. From Tiguex a route extended north and south along the Rio Grande. Another major trail went eastward over Glorieta Pass to Pecos, and from that important trading center on to eastern Texas and Oklahoma, and central Kansas (Riley and Manson 1983 : 351, 353–354).

Traffic coming northward from Mexico included parrots and macaws, copper, shells, and surely other goods (peyote is one possibility). The Hopi country supplied pottery, cotton, and cotton cloth, trading it widely in the upper Southwest; and there is some reason to think the Sonoran statelets were also involved in the cotton trade. From the Rio Grande area came turquoise and pottery, from the Great Plains bison products, and from Pecos, fibrolite. Zuni supplied salt and probably olivene, and from the Gulf of California coast came floods of shell. The Sonoran statelets had a vigorous trade in slaves. Major transshipment centers for these diverse materials included Pecos, Hawikuh and perhaps other Zuni towns, one or more towns in Tiguex, and probably several of the urbanized centers in northern Sonora.

From this time period there is archaeological evidence for Cerrillos New Mexico turquoise in eastern Oklahoma, Gulf of California shell in central Kansas, Hopi pottery on the California coast, Rio Grande glazed sherds in northern Jalisco, and shell from places as far apart as eastern Texas, the Gulf of Mexico, the Gulf of California, and coastal southern California at Pecos (Riley 1976 : 40–41; 1982 : 143–144).

It is clear that at least by Spanish conquest times, southwestern Indians were acquainted with the entire Greater Southwest and travelled widely within it. Melchior Díaz, in northern Sonora in the winter of 1539–1540 heard detailed and correct descriptions of Cibola-Zuni, and Coronado in 1540 at Zuni was visited almost immediately by a trading party from Pecos. Just about that same time, Alarcón, on the lower Colorado River, was listening to elaborate stories of Cibola-Zuni and details of the Marcos-Esteban expedition of the previous year. In August 1542 Cabrillo, off the southern California coast, received accurate descriptions of Spaniards and southwestern Indians to the east (Riley 1982 : 77).

With this kind of wide-ranging contact, it makes sense to think that significant amounts of new sociopolitical and religious ideas would have washed over the Southwest, and indeed were in the process of doing so when the Spaniards came. We do not know what contributions western

Mexico might have made to the Southwest but considering what happened in earlier centuries, it could have been extremely important in terms of religion, technology, art, and perhaps even political organization (Riley 1982 : 143–146).

The reality, however, was that Spanish religious and political imperialism combined with the monstrous effect of Spanish disease simply destroyed the unity of the Greater Southwest. The exchange network, except for limited underground trade, was broken up and native institutions of all kind were modified or forbidden. By A.D. 1700 the Greater Southwest was either part of the Spanish polity or lay in cultural wreckage on the fringes of Spanish rule.

References Cited

Brew, J. O.
  1944 On the Pueblo IV and the Katchina-Tlaloc Relations. In *El Norte de Mexico y el Sur de Estados Unidos*. Tercera Reunion de Mesa Redonda, pp. 241–244.
Di Peso, Charles C.
  1974 *Casas Grandes: A Fallen Trading Center of the Gran Chichimeca*, vols. 1–3. Amerind Foundation Series No. 9. Dragoon, Ariz.
Doolittle, William E.
  1984a Cabeza de Vaca's Land of Maize: An Assessment of its Agriculture. *Journal of Historical Geography* 10(3) : 246–262.
  1984b Settlements and the Development of "Statelets" in Sonora, Mexico. *Journal of Field Archaeology* 11 : 13–24.
Frisbie, Theodore R.
  1978 High Status Burials in the Greater Southwest. In *Across the Chichimec Sea*, edited by Carroll L. Riley and Basil C. Hedrick, pp. 202–227. Southern Illinois University Press, Carbondale.
Haury, Emil W.
  1976 *The Hohokam: Desert Farmers and Craftsmen*. The University of Arizona Press, Tucson.
Hewett, Edgar L.
  1936 *Ancient Life in Mexico and Central America*. Bobbs-Merrill, Indianapolis.
  1968 *Ancient Life in the American Southwest*. Biblio and Tannen, New York. Originally published 1930.
Kelley, J. Charles
  1966 Mesoamerica and the Southwestern United States. In *Archaeological Frontiers and External Connections*, edited by Gordon F. Ekholm and Gordon R. Willey, pp. 95–110. Handbook of Middle American Indians, vol. 4, Robert Wauchope, general editor. University of Texas Press, Austin.

1980 Discussion of Papers by Plog, Doyel and Riley. In *Current Issues in Hohokam Prehistory*, edited by David E. Doyel and Fred Plog, pp. 49–66. Arizona State University Anthropological Research Papers No. 23. Tempe.

Kelley, J. Charles, and Ellen Abbott Kelley
1975 An Alternative Hypothesis for the Explanation of Anasazi Culture History. In *Collected Papers in Honor of Florence Hawley Ellis*, edited by Theodore R. Frisbie, pp. 178–223. Papers of the Archaeological Society of New Mexico No. 2.

Mathien, Frances Joan
1983 The Mobile Trader and the Chacoan Anasazi. In *Proceedings of the Anasazi Symposium, 1981*, compiled and edited by Jack E. Smith, pp. 197–206. Mesa Verde Museum Association, Mesa Verde National Park.

Morris, Earl H.
1927 *The Beginnings of Pottery Making in the San Juan Area*. Anthropological Papers of the American Museum of Natural History, vol. 28, pt. 2, New York.

Pailes, Richard A.
1978 The Río Sonora Culture in Prehistoric Trade Systems. In *Across the Chichimec Sea*, edited by Carroll L. Riley and Basil C. Hedrick, pp. 134–143. Southern Illinois University Press, Carbondale.

Reyman, Jonathan E.
1978 Pochteca Burials at Anasazi Sites? In *Across the Chichimec Sea*, edited by Carroll L. Riley and Basil C. Hedrick, pp. 242–262. Southern Illinois University Press, Carbondale.

Riley, Carroll L.
1976 *Sixteenth Century Trade in the Greater Southwest*. Mesoamerican Studies No. 10, Research Records of the University Museum, Southern Illinois University, Carbondale.

1980a Mesoamerica and the Hohokam: A View from the 16th Century. In *Current Issues in Hohokam Prehistory*, edited by David E. Doyel and Fred Plog, pp. 41–48. Arizona State University Anthropological No. 23. Tempe.

1980b Trade and Contact in the Prehistoric Southwest. In *New Frontiers in the Archaeology and Ethnohistory of the Greater Southwest*, edited by Carroll L. Riley and Basil C. Hedrick, pp. 13–17. Transactions of the Illinois State Academy of Science No. 72(4).

1982 *The Frontier People: The Greater Southwest in the Protohistoric Period*. Center for Archaeological Investigation Occasional Paper No. 1. Southern Illinois University, Carbondale.

1985 Spanish Contact and the Collapse of the Sonoran Statelets. In *The Archaeology of West and Northwest Mesoamerica*, edited by Michael S. Foster and Phil C. Weigand. Westview Press, Boulder, Colorado, in press.

Riley, Carroll L., and Joni L. Manson
   1983 The Cibola-Tiguex Route: Continuity and Change in the Southwest. *New Mexico Historical Review* 58(4): 347–367.
Sauer, Carl O.
   1932 *The Road to Cibola.* Ibero-Americana No. 3.
Schroeder, Albert H.
   1965 Unregulated Diffusion from Mexico into the Southwest Prior to A.D. 700. *American Antiquity* 30: 297–309.
   1966 Pattern Diffusion from Mexico into the Southwest after A.D. 600. *American Antiquity* 31: 683–704.
White, Leslie A.
   1940 *Pioneers in American Anthropology: The Bandelier-Morgan Letters, 1873–1883,* 2 vols. The University of New Mexico Press, Albuquerque.
Wilcox, David R., and W. Bruce Masse
   1981 A History of Protohistoric Studies in the North American Southwest. In *The Protohistoric Period in the North American Southwest, A.D. 1450–1700,* pp. 1–27. Arizona State University Anthropological Research Paper No. 24. Tempe.

4

The Mesoamerican Connection: A View from the South

Michael S. Foster

The nature and scope of mesoamerican-southwestern interaction continues to be a topic of debate among archaeologists working in the two areas. In most instances southwestern archaeologists tend towards an isolationist view, rejecting the proposition that mesoamerican cultural developments influenced the development of southwestern society (e.g., Martin and Plog 1973:302). Southwesternists have relied upon local, ecologically based, explanations for the development of southwestern societies. Recently, some southwestern archeologists have begun to move away from this isolationist viewpoint and are at least discussing mesoamerican-southwestern interaction (McGuire 1980; Plog et al. 1982). However, their conclusions have been generally unchanged: mesoamerican cultures had little if any influence on the development and character of southwestern societies.

Those Mesoamericanists studying mesoamerican-southwestern contact have relied upon economic models to explain the integration of the northwestern hinterland, the Greater Southwest, into the mesoamerican sphere of influence. The most frequently used model is based on long distance trade and the presence of long distance traders (e.g., *pochteca*) who took with them culture and knowledge into the hinterlands (Di Peso 1974; Kelley 1966; Kelley and Kelley 1975). The culture and knowledge diffused to the various groups, resulting in the appearance of many material, iconographic, architectural, and religious traits which parallel their mesoamerican predecessors. These traits range from imported items, such as copper bells, to iconographic figures, such as the feathered serpent, and have been discussed in great detail (Di Peso 1974; Ellis 1976; Kelley 1966; Kelley and Kelley 1975; Lister 1978; Reyman 1971, 1978; Schroeder 1981). More recently, some individuals have employed Wallerstein's (1974) world systems model in an effort to discuss the integration of the Southwest into the mesoamerican sphere of influence (Di Peso 1980; Dirst and Pailes 1976; Kelley 1980; Pailes and Whitecotton 1975). However, the application of the world systems model archaeologically awaits some refinement, although it looks to be a useful approach to the problem of mesoamerican-southwestern interaction (see Whitecotton and Pailes, Chapter 10 this volume).

Mesoamerican-Southwestern Contact: The Archaeological Base

Most of the discussion regarding mesoamerican-southwestern contact focuses on relatively recent events, in particular, those beginning around and after A.D. 1000. Yet, it is generally accepted that a variety of cultigens and ceramic technology found in the Southwest were derived from Mexico beginning as early as 2000 B.C. These did not come hand-in-hand, nor did they greatly alter the existing lifeways. These innovations were likely passed from group to group as they became useful. These traits were transmitted via two possible routes, the eastern flanks of the Sierra Madre Occidental or the west coast of Mexico.

The point of this is that, first, there is a great deal of archaeology between the Rio Grande and the Valley of Mexico. Second, there is also great time depth to these remains. Paleoindian remains appear in central Durango, Chihuahua, and Sonora (Arroyo de Anda 1964). These materials have clear affinities to the Paleoindian traditions so well documented in the Southwest. Archaic materials are more widespread, particularly in the Mesa del Norte from Coahuila to the Pacific coast and from Chihuahua to Zacatecas. Again, strong similarities between these materials and those found in the Southwest have been noted (Hartfield 1975; Marrs 1949; Spence 1971), particularly those from the south of New Mexico and Arizona and west Texas.

Settled village life, in the form of the Loma San Gabriel culture (Foster 1978, 1982; Kelley 1971), appears to have been established prior to A.D. 1, possibly as early as 300 B.C., in western Zacatecas. Ceramic evidence indicates Loma villages were present in central Durango by at least A.D. 100–300. In general the Loma culture represents an adaptation that is much more like that of southwestern cultures. The adaptations in material culture, subsistence patterns, and settlement patterns prior to A.D. 1000 along the eastern foothills of the Sierra Madre Occidental from central Zacatecas into the central mountains of western New Mexico and eastern Arizona are quite similar. This has been referred to as the Loma San Gabriel-Mogollon continuum (Foster 1982; Kelley 1962; Kelley and Kelley 1975). To the south, Loma sites are contiguous to Preclassic cultures of western Mexico.

Between A.D. 100 and 300 a mesoamerican presence appears in western Zacatecas and Durango during the Canutillo phase. It is unclear whether this is an incipient mesoamerican development out of the existing Loma San Gabriel peoples or a mesoamerican intrusion into the area. This is soon followed by the development of the Chalchihuites culture, a fully mesoamerican adaptation which is likely associated with the expansion of the mesoamerican heartland. Alta Vista, the principal ceremonial center for the Chalchihuites culture, is a very complex site which also functioned as an observatory, mining center, and trading outpost (Aveni et al. 1982; Kelley 1976, 1980; Weigand 1978; Weigand et al. 1977). Around A.D. 1000 Durango became the center of Chalchihuites activities.

Also, at about this time, there was a great deal of activity in the Malpaso valley at La Quemada. There was new construction at La Quemada along with the building of road systems and satellite communities (Trombold 1976; Weigand 1978). Weigand (1978:223) believes the cohesive force at Alta Vista was ceremonial while at the later La Quemada it was military, although long-distance trade was very important.

Another important aspect of late Classic-Postclassic development in northwestern Mexico was the Aztatlán horizon (see Kelley, Chapter 6 this volume; 1983); Further, coastal peoples were clearly in contact with Chalchihuites groups (Ganot et al. 1983; Kelley and Winters 1960).

To the north, the initial developments at Casas Grandes were underway (Di Peso 1974). Trade items, although limited, show that there was contact with the west coast and Chalchihuites areas. Casas Grandes influence spread into Sonora (Pailes 1972, 1978) and the Animas (Ravesloot 1979) and Dona Ana/El Paso phases (Schaafsma 1979) of southern New Mexico and west Texas.

Along the west coast little is known of the Archaic period. Preclassic settlements are numerous, especially in Nayarit, Colima, and Jalisco (Bell 1971). Classic and Postclassic sites are common along the coast from Nayarit northward (Kelly 1938; Meighan 1976; Scott 1983). The coastal events are somewhat overshadowed by major cultural developments in the highlands of Jalisco (Weigand 1983). Again, there appears to be a great deal of exchange and movement during the Classic and Postclassic, particularly during the Aztatlán horizon (Kelley 1974). However, not much coastal material seems to have made its way into the Río Sonora culture's area (Pailes 1972) or to Casas Grandes (Di Peso 1974).

The Río Sonora culture's greatest affinities appear to be with the Mogollon and, to a lesser extent, Casas Grandes (Pailes 1972:371–388; 1978). There are few indications of ties to the Hohokam or Trincheras cultures. The prehistoric coastal adaptations of Sonora (Bowen 1976) seem to be fairly independent from other cultures of the area, although some figurines recently found at a site in southern Sonora are similar to Hohokam Santa Cruz phase types and others are similar to Chametla types from Sinaloa (Palma 1982).

As the southwestern United States was first explored by the Spanish, it appears that known, preexisting routes were followed up the west coast and along the eastern foothills of the Sierra Madre Occidental. Furthermore, a great variety of goods were being exchanged and the knowledge of other peoples and events in any given area was quite extensive. This early contact period activity has been been extensively discussed by Riley (1976, 1982).

This cursory overview of the archaeology of northwest Mexico demonstrates several important points. First, there was not a prehistoric cultural void between the mesoamerican heartland and the southwestern United States. In areas that have been studied, a fairly continuous occupation of the region is indicated. Limited excavations and fairly extensive surveys have allowed the construction of a cultural historical framework for the area, although most of the region is in need of more intensive research.

Second, the Greater Southwest is a cultural and geographic (ecological) unit that is contiguous to the mesoamerican heartland. The western portion of the Mesa del Norte, the uplands and basin-and-range country of western Zacatecas, Durango, Chihuahua, and Sonora are geographic and environmental extensions of similar lands in Arizona, New Mexico, west Texas, and the Colorado plateaus. This is a natural region in which numerous similar cultural adaptations occurred; it is a culture area (Kroeber 1939). It is bounded to the south by more intensive mesoamerican cultural adaptations which arose in more humid and resource diverse environs. A continuum exists through both time and space. It is a continuum in which there was substantial cultural homogeneity as well as diversity.

Long-Distance Trade and Traders

Most of the discussion of mesoamerican-southwestern interaction focuses on events beginning around A.D. 1000, with the appearance of larger, more economically and socially diverse settlements throughout the Southwest. At the same time, the mesoamerican boundary was approaching its maximum northern expansion. In many of the discussions, especially those of the southwesternists, it seems that there is a belief that mesoamerican trade and traders are Postclassic phenomena. Obviously, this is the result of the use of the *pochteca* model by mesoamericanists.

However, long-distance trade has a long history and an important role in the development of many mesoamerican societies as in many other prehistoric societies around the world. Olmec personages are depicted on boulders in western El Salvador, and Olmec influence reached into Guatemala and Honduras as well. At a minimum, these areas are 700 km from the Olmec heartland. Teotihuacan is another notable example, with its influence dominant or present in vast areas of Mesoamerica from western Zacatecas to Kaminaljuyu, Guatemala and into western Mexico. The maximum length of some of these routes was in excess of 1,200 km. These economic ventures were undoubtedly organized at the state level, and the routes were established not only to transport goods and materials from suppliers and resource areas but also to establish the presence of various societies in areas outside their homeland. Additionally, it is likely that most mesoamerican societies had their own versions of traveling traders. In other words, long-distance trade and traders are not an Aztec or Postclassic phenomenon.

It is likely that few, if any, trading expeditions from the Valley of Mexico reached the Southwest in order to directly obtain rare resources or other goods. However, trading groups from the Chalchihuites, Casas Grandes, and west coast of Mexico appear to have reached well into the Southwest at a relatively early date, possibly as early as A.D. 350 (Weigand et al. 1977). At this time the Southwest was still in the pithouse period and dominated by small, scattered villages. However, by A.D. 600 there were signs of increased social complexity and reorganization in some of these villages. For example, it has been suggested that during this period the development of local leadership took place among pithouse groups in the Mogollon area (Lightfoot and Feinman 1982). Lightfoot and Feinman note that there were greater quantities of nonlocal goods associated with the presumed leaders' larger houses. They associate this development with the transition to a more sedentary lifeway, increased population, intensification of subsistence patterns, and increased interregional exchanges. If such social organization did exist, it is possible that traders from northwestern Mexico interacted with, provided additional stimulation for the development of, and reinforced the status of such local leaders.

At the same time, to the west, the Hohokam were expanding during the Colonial period. There was an influx of Mexican traits and probably people as well (Gumerman and Haury 1979; Haury 1976). Mexican influence (Casas Grandes) may be strongly manifested in Classic period Hohokam architecture as well (Lekson 1983:188). Not only were the developing societies of the Southwest bounded to the south by mesoamerican cultures, there was a heavily mesoamericanized society—the Hohokam—in the heart of the Southwest.

It appears that there was systematic exploitation of the Southwest, beginning at an early date, by a series of "middlemen" who obtained goods not only for consumption by their own local elite, but also to pass surplus goods on into the heartland of Mesoamerica, as demand required. These middlemen acted as the mechanism for the diffusion, soft and hard (Schroeder 1965, 1966), of mesoamerican culture and knowledge. The traders introduced a variety of traits—everything from new cultigens and technology to ideology—to the elementary, evolving societies of the Southwest. Not all these traits were introduced at the same time, nor were they all of equal importance. It is also likely that many traits were introduced as a complex of traits. For example, when new cultigens were introduced, it was as important to know the religious complex associated with them as much as the technological aspects of raising the crop. This "advanced" technology and knowledge might have been passed on to the local leadership in exchange for goods and political/economic support of one kind or another. Local leadership then used this knowledge, after adapting it to local requirements, to further enhance their status within a group.

This may have been a mechanism by which the Southwest was integrated into the mesoamerican world system. It was an integration based on an economic exploitation of the Southwest, which is viewed as a periphery in the mesoamerican world system. Therefore, it was a zone of exploitation and not necessarily an equal trading partner. After A.D. 1000 this exploitation seems to have increased, resulting in the increase of mesoamerican traits. It appears that trade in the Greater Southwest was primarily in local hands and that there were few organized long-distance traders coming out of the mesoamerican heartland. However, it is quite likely that mesoamerican societies such as Chalchihuites and Casas Grandes were sending traders northward. In some respects, this may be viewed as intraregional rather than interregional exchange and exploitation. As previously stated, Chalchihuites and Casas Grandes traders may have acted as middlemen in the operation between the core areas of the south and the periphery to the north.

In sum, mesoamerican-southwestern interaction may be explained by looking within the Greater Southwest itself. In fact, after A.D. 700 the southern sector of the Greater Southwest was dominated by mesoamerican societies, first the Chalchihuites culture and then Casas Grandes. Although it is possible that long-distance traders from the mesoamerican heartland penetrated the northern sector of the Greater Southwest, they were not essential to the mesoamericanization of those societies.

Mesoamerican Derived Traits

Mesoamericanists have emphasized the occurrence of Mexican items, technology, and iconographic symbols in the Southwest as evidence for a mesoamerican presence in the Southwest. These traits not only represent tangible bits of material culture but also elements in a belief system. These traits of probable Mexican origins have recently been summarized by Kelley and Kelley (1975), Lister (1978: 236–239), and Schroeder (1981: 52–54). Again, some of these represent trade items, others borrowing of technology, and others may be imitations of Mexican items. Other Mexican traits can be seen in southwestern ceremonialism. The parallels in ceremonialism and symbolism have been discussed in great detail most recently by Reyman (1971), Ellis (1976), and Frisbie (1983).

Southwesternists tend to discount this Mexican influence for two reasons. The first is the general lack of mesoamerican trade goods in the Southwest and secondly, the lack of absolute similarity in form and context for the ceremonial iconography and associated ceremonialism (e.g., McGuire 1980: 7–10). Many Mexican items (bells, feathers) found in the Southwest are found in a ceremonial or status context, suggesting use by local leadership or elite. So the few items that appear in the Southwest were probably utilized in a fairly restricted manner. Again, the Southwest was a zone of exploitation, peripheral to a series of more complex mesoamerican societies. Goods and resources were moving southward with just enough materials moving northward to maintain and satisfy the northern "contacts" with whom the southern traders were dealing. It is reasonable to assume that local southwestern leadership depended far more heavily upon "local" symbols of authority and status than on rare mesoamerican items.

Mesoamerica and the Southwest also share numerous iconographic and ceremonial traits in their religions. Southwesternists (e.g., McGuire 1980:24–26) suggest these are mere coincidences and reject the possibility of mesoamerican origins for the southwestern versions because they vary in form and utilization from their mesoamerican analogs. Culture is an adaptive, evolving system; and diffusion is a mechanism for spreading traits, not an explanation of why traits are adopted. As stated earlier, it is likely that many traits were passed into the Southwest in complexes. Some of these traits had adaptive value and were thus incorporated into the evolving southwestern societies while others were not used at all. Southwestern societies did not become sedentary village dwellers simply because such lifeways had already evolved in Mesoamerica. These people were responding to various stimuli in their own environments and what they took from mesoamerican culture and knowledge had to have some adaptive value. Once adopted, traits were undoubtedly modified to local conditions and needs. Through time these traits were further elaborated upon and modified by these local cultures. Thus, although the various southwestern iconographic and ceremonial traits have their origins in mesoamerican mythology, they vary from their mesoamerican roots. These same processes can be seen in the evolution of mesoamerican mythology itself. Therefore, it seems inappropriate to argue for the totally independent parallel evolution of these particular traits.

Pochteca Outposts

One of the greatest debates between mesoamericanists and southwesterists focuses on the presence of mesoamerican trading outposts in the Southwest. The two most discussed examples are Chaco Canyon and Casas Grandes.

Chaco Canyon

A great deal of effort has been put into proving that the Chaco phenomenon was the result of adaptation to local environmental conditions and the need to pool and redistribute a wide variety of resources, primarily foodstuffs, from a vast area. More recently Judge (1984) has referred to Chaco as a central place which may have served as the integrative center for the socioeconomic and ritualistic activities of the 25,000 mi^2 Chacoan system. He even goes further and compares the Chacoan system to lowland Maya centers. There are clear parallels between similar systems so common in Mesoamerica and the Chacoan system, but, again this does not mean Mexican traders established themselves in Chaco Canyon and built the system. It has also been suggested that an incipient market system involved in the exchange of non-food commodities may have developed (Judge et al. 1981).

What is suggested here is that local leadership at Chaco was dealing with or had knowledge of markets to the south. Once local ecological factors had initiated the Chaco phenomenon, the development of a more ranging market system may have been stimulated by contact with mesoamerican traders. In other words, local Chacoan leadership saw political and economic advantage in their economic ventures with foreign traders and markets. Again, the emphasis was on the transportation of goods southward and entrenchment of leadership status in terms of local culture. Some of the proposed mesoamerican traits such as architectural features at Chaco may be nothing more than inspired by the mesoamerican visitors rather than being constructed at the request and under the direction of mesoamerican residents. Other items of probable Mexican origin appear to have been imported (Lister 1978). Again, the question is where exactly did they come from and who brought them. At some level, Chaco seems to have been integrated into the mesoamerican world system.

Casas Grandes

There can be little argument that Casas Grandes was a major trading and manufacturing center on the northern frontier (Di Peso 1974). The site is clearly mesoamerican, and the suggestion that it was a mere emulation of high cultures to the south (McGuire 1980:23) ignores a great deal of data. Interestingly, there are numerous parallels between the Chaco and Casas Grandes systems in terms of overall settlement system organization and economic activity, although they are separated by time and space. Much of Casas Grandes trading activities seem to be directed to the north (Di Peso et al. 1974, 8:143). Relatively few items from the Chalchihuites and west coast areas have been recovered from Casas Grandes. Again, it appears that the Casas Grandes merchants were acting as middlemen with importation of goods from the northern sector of the Southwest and then passing them southward, probably to various markets.

Di Peso (1974) argues the mesoamericanization of north-central Chihuahua resulted from the arrival of mesoamerican peoples into the area and their organization of the local population into what later became a complex social and economic regional urban center. The mesoamerican culture and technology these lords brought with them are manifested in various architectural, iconographic, and socioeconomic features at the site. Thus, with the presence of Casas Grandes in Chihuahua and the Chalchihuites culture in Durango and Zacatecas, much of the southern sector of the Greater Southwest was dominated by mesoamerican societies from as early as A.D. 300.

Summary

The discussion of mesoamerican-southwestern interaction is one that still eludes any satisfactory conclusion. There was a mesoamerican presence and influence in the Southwest, and yet we seem to lack any systematic approach to defining the extent and consequences of that interaction. Data are manipulated on both sides of the argument to support or reject the notion of interaction between the two areas. Southwesternists, despite veiled attempts to appear otherwise (e.g., McGuire 1980; Plog et al. 1982), generally reject the possibility of mesoamerican-southwestern interaction. They believe that the Southwest was a closed cultural system and that the type of inter- and intraregional interaction so often identified in the archaeological records of adjacent areas and elsewhere in the world are somehow beyond expectation in the Southwest.

There was a direct mesoamerican presence in the Greater Southwest. The Chalchihuites and Casas Grandes cultures are the two most notable examples. Others of importance include La Quemada and probably the Hohokam. The question is, What do sites like Alta Vista and Casas Grandes mean in terms of trade and economic exploitation of the Greater Southwest? It does not appear that these sites themselves represent state level societies, although they were likely tied to state level societies in the heartland of Mesoamerica (Kelley 1980). These sites would not be considered core areas in terms of Wallerstein's world system, although they may have approached such a level. Their locations are intermediate between the core areas and the periphery, in the semiperiphery. They were extensions of the economic systems in the core areas and as such functioned as devices for the exploitation of the periphery, the northern sector of the Greater Southwest. At times, these sites and cultures were highly integrated into the mesoamerican world system, probably colonial outposts, while at other times they were autonomous politically and economically while still interacting with their southern counterparts. No matter the circumstances, it is likely they served the same function, middlemen of the semiperiphery.

How then did these groups exploit and influence the Southwest? First, interaction within the Southwest has a long history extending well back into the Archaic. During early times contact took place group to group. However, as the mesoamerican heartland expanded northward, mesoamerican outposts were established in the southern sector of the Greater Southwest. These groups exploited the northern sector through group to group exchange as well as directly with their own version of long-distance traders. This was the mechanism by which mesoamerican traits were introduced into the northern sector of the Greater Southwest and how the northern periphery as a whole was incorporated into the mesoamerican sphere of influence.

This is not to say the Southwest was a consequence of mesoamerican civilization nor that economic interaction between the two areas was a prime mover in the development of southwestern societies. Southwestern societies were adapting and evolving as consequences of adjustment to the local environments in which they existed. Mesoamerican traits were primarily utilized only if they had adaptive value. But those traits and ideas that were used had substantial impact, at different times and places, upon the trajectory of southwestern societies. This type of developmental consequence resulting from economic interaction has been identified for a number of areas in Mesoamerica (Flannery 1972; Michels 1979; Sanders and Michels 1977) and these events parallel those suggested as explanations for the mesoamericanization of the Greater Southwest.

In sum, a mesoamerican presence in the Southwest cannot be ignored, nor can the consequences of that presence. This was a phenomenon of substantial time depth and a major, but secondary, force in the evolution and development of southwestern societies. The northern sector of the Greater Southwest cannot be viewed as an isolated cultural or ecological area impervious to external cultural developments.

References Cited

Arroyo de Anda, Luis Aveleyra
1964 The Primitive Hunters. In *Natural Environment and Early Cultures*, edited by Robert C. West, pp. 384–412. Handbook of Middle American Indians, vol 1, Robert Wauchope, general editor. University of Texas Press, Austin.

Aveni, Anthony, Horst Hortung, and J. Charles Kelley
1982 Alta Vista (Chalchihuites): Astronomical Implications of a Mesoamerican Ceremonial Outpost on the Tropic of Cancer. *American Antiquity* 47:316–335.

Bell, Betty
1971 Archaeology of Nayarit, Jalisco and Colima. In *Archaeology of Northern Mesoamerica*, edited by Gordon F. Ekholm and Ignacio Bernal, pp. 694–753. Handbook of Middle American Indians, vol. 11, Robert Wauchope, general editor. University of Texas Press, Austin.

Bowen, Thomas
1976 *Seri Prehistory: The Archaeology of the Central Coast of Sonora, Mexico*. Anthropological Papers of the University of Arizona No. 27. Tucson.

Di Peso, Charles C.
1974 *Casas Grandes, A Fallen Trading Center of the Gran Chichimeca*, vols. 1–3. Amerind Foundation Series No. 9, Dragoon, Ariz.

1980 The Northern Sector of the Mesoamerican World System. Paper presented at the 13th Annual Meeting of the Society of Historical Archaeology, Albuquerque.

Di Peso, Charles, John B. Rinaldo, and Gloria Fenner
1974 *Casas Grandes, A Fallen Trading Center of the Gran Chichimeca*, vols. 4–8. Amerind Foundation Series No. 9. Dragoon, Ariz.

Dirst, Victoria, and Richard A. Pailes
1976 Economic Networks: Mesoamerica and the Southwest. Paper presented at the 41st Annual Meeting of the Society for American Archaeology. St. Louis.

Ellis, Florence Hawley
1976 Datable Ritual Components Proclaiming Mexican Influence in the Upper Rio Grande of New Mexico. In *Collected Papers in Honor of Marjorie Ferguson Lambert*, edited by Albert H. Schroeder, pp. 85–108. Papers of the Archaeological Society of New Mexico No. 3, Albuquerque.

Flannery, Kent V.
1972 Summary Comments: Evolutionary Trends in Social Exchange and Interaction. In *Social Exchange and Interaction*, edited by E. Wilmson, pp. 129–135. Anthropological Papers No. 46. Museum of Anthropology, University of Michigan, Ann Arbor.

Foster, Michael S.
1978 *Loma San Gabriel: A Prehistoric Culture of Northwest Mexico*. Unpublished Ph.D. dissertation, Department of Anthropology, University of Colorado, Boulder.
1982 The Loma San Gabriel-Mogollon Continuum. In *Mogollon Archaeology: Proceedings of the 1980 Mogollon Conference*, edited by Patrick H. Beckett, pp. 251–262. Acoma Books, Ramona, Calif.

Frisbie, Theodore R.
1983 Anasazi-Mesoamerican Relationships: From the Bowels of the Earth and Beyond. In *Proceedings of the Anasazi Symposium 1981*, edited by Jack E. Smith, pp. 214–228. Mesa Verde Museum Association.

Ganot, Jaime, Alejandro Peschard, and Jesus Lazalde
1983 Relacíon Prehispanica Entre las Culturas del Noroeste de Mexico y el Sitio Arquelogical "El Cañón del Molino" en El Estado de Durango. Paper presented at the XVIII Mesa Redonda of the Sociedad Mexicana de Antropología, Taxco.

Gumerman, George J., and Emil W. Haury
1979 Prehistory: Hohokam. In *Southwest*, edited by Alfonso Ortiz, pp. 75–90. Handbook of North Amercian Indians, vol. 9, William G. Sturtevant, general editor. Smithsonian Institution, Washington.

Hartfield, Lorraine
1975 Archaeological Investigations of Four Sites in Southwestern Coahuila, Mexico. *Bulletin of the Texas Archaeological Society* 46:127–178. Austin.

Haury, Emil
  1976 *The Hohokam, Desert Farmers and Craftsmen: Excavations at Snaketown, 1964–1965*. University of Arizona Press, Tucson.
Judge, W. James
  1984 New Light on Chaco Canyon. In *New Light on Chaco Canyon*, edited by David Grant Noble, pp. 1–12. School of American Research Press, Santa Fe.
Judge, W. James, William B. Gillespie, Stephen H. Lekson, and H. Wolcott Toll
  1981 Tenth Century Developments in Chaco Canyon. In *Collected Papers in Honor of Erik Kellerman Reed*, edited by Albert Schroeder, pp. 65–98. Papers of the Archaeological Society of New Mexico No. 6, Albuquerque.
Kelley, J. Charles
  1962 Mesoamerican Colonization of Zacatecas-Durango: The Loma-San Gabriel and Chalchihuites Cultures. Unpublished manuscript in possession of author.
  1966 Mesoamerica and the Southwestern United States. In *Archaeological Frontiers and External Connections*, edited by Gordon F. Ekholm and Gordon R. Willey, pp. 95–110. Handbook of Middle American Indians, vol. 4, Robert Wauchope, general editor. University of Texas Press, Austin.
  1971 Archaeology of the Northern Frontier: Zacatecas and Durango. In *Archaeology of Northern Mesoamerica*, edited by Ignacio Bernal, and Gordon F. Ekholm, pp. 768–801. Handbook of Middle American Indians, vol. 11, Robert Wauchope, general editor. University of Texas Press, Austin.
  1974 Speculation on the Culture History of Northwestern Mexico. In *The Archaeology of West Mexico*, edited by Betty Bell, pp. 19–39. Ajijic, Jalisco, Mexico.
  1976 Alta Vista: An Outpost of Mesoamerican Empire on the Tropic of Cancer. In *Fronteras de Mesoamerica*, vol. 1, pp. 21–50. Sociedad Mexicana de Antropología, Mexico.
  1980 Alta Vista, Chalchihuites, "Port of Entry" on the Northern Frontier. In *Rutas de Intercambio*, vol. 1, pp. 53–64. Sociedad Mexicana de Antropología, Mexico.
  1983 Hypothetical Functioning of the Major Postclassic Trade System of West and Northwest Mexico. Paper presented at the XVIII Mesa Redonda of the Sociedad Mexicana de Antropología, Taxco, Mexico.
Kelley, J. Charles, and Ellen Abbott Kelley
  1975 An Alternative Hypothesis for the Explanation of Anasazi Culture History. In *Collected Papers in Honor of Florence Hawley Ellis*, edited by Theodore R. Frisbie, pp. 178–223. Papers of the Archeological Society of New Mexico No. 2, Albuquerque.

Kelley, J. Charles, and Howard C. Winters
  1960 A Revision of the Archaeological Sequence in Sinaloa, Mexico. *American Antiquity* 25 : 546−561.
Kelly, Isabel T.
  1938 *Excavations at Chametla, Sinaloa.* Ibero-Americana No. 14, Berkeley.
Kroeber, A. L.
  1939 *Cultural and Natural Areas of Native North America.* University of California Publications in American Archaeology and Ethnology No. 38. Berkeley.
Lekson, Stephen H.
  1983 Chaco Architecture in Continental Context. In *Proceedings of the Anasazi Symposium 1981*, edited by Jack E. Smith, pp. 183−196. Mesa Verde Museum Association.
Lightfoot, Kent G., and Gary M. Feinman
  1982 Social Differentiation and Leadership Development in Early Pit-house Villages in the Mogollon Region of the American Southwest. *American Antiquity* 47 : 64−86.
Lister, Robert
  1978 Mesoamerican Influences at Chaco Canyon, New Mexico. In *Across the Chichimec Sea: Papers in Honor of J. Charles Kelley*, edited by Carroll L. Riley and Basil C. Hedrick, pp. 233−241. Southern Illinois University Press, Carbondale.
Marrs, Garland J.
  1947 *Problems Arising from the Surface Occurrence of Archaeological Material in Southeastern Chihuahua, Mexico.* Unpublished M.A. thesis, Department of Anthropology, University of New Mexico, Albuquerque.
McGuire, Randall H.
  1980 The Mesoamerican Connection in the Southwest. *Kiva* 46(1−2): 3−38.
Martin, Paul S., and Fred Plog
  1973 *The Archaeology of Arizona.* Doubleday-Natural History Press. Garden City, N.Y.
Meighan, Clement W. (editor)
  1976 *The Archaeology of Amapa, Nayarit.* Monumenta Archaeologica, vol. 2. Institute of Archaeology, University of California, Los Angeles.
Michels, Joseph W.
  1979 *The Kaminaljuyu Chiefdom.* Pennsylvania State University Press, University Park.
Pailes, Richard A.
  1972 *An Archaeological Reconnaissance of Southern Sonora and Reconsideration of the Rio Sonora Culture.* Unpublished Ph.D. dissertation, Department of Anthropology, Southern Illinois University, Carbondale.
  1978 The Río Sonora Culture in Prehistoric Trade Systems. In *Across the*

Chichimec Sea: Papers in Honor of J. Charles Kelley, edited by Carroll
L. Riley and Basil C. Hedrick, pp. 134–143. Southern Illinois University Press, Carbondale.

Pailes, Richard A., and Joseph W. Whitecotton
1975 Greater Southwestern and Mesoamerican World Systems, an Exploratory Model. Paper presented at the Southwestern Anthropological Association Annual Meeting, Santa Fe.

Palma, Ana Maria Alvarez
1982 Archaeological Investigations at Huatabampo. In *Mogollon Archaeology: Proceeding of the 1980 Mogollon Conference*, edited by Patrick H. Beckett, pp. 239–250. Acoma Books, Ramona, Calif.

Plog, Fred, Steadman Upham, and Phil C. Weigand
1982 A Perspective on Mogollon-Mesoamerican Interaction. In *Mogollon Archaeology: Proceedings of the 1980 Mogollon Conference*, edited by Patrick H. Beckett, pp. 227–238. Acoma Books, Ramona, Calif.

Ravesloot, John C.
1979 *The Animas Phase: The Postclassic Mimbres Occupation of the Mimbres Valley, New Mexico*. Unpublished M.A. thesis, Department of Anthropology, Southern Illinois University, Carbondale.

Reyman, Jonathan E.
1971 *Mexican Influence on Southwestern Ceremonialism*. Unpublished Ph.D. dissertation, Department of Anthropology, Southern Illinois University, Carbondale.
1978 *Pochteca* Burials at Anasazi Sites? In *Across the Chichimec Sea: Papers in Honor of J. Charles Kelley*, edited by Carroll L. Riley and Basil C. Hedrick, pp. 242–262. Southern Illinois University Press, Carbondale.

Riley, Carroll L.
1976 *Sixteenth Century Trade in the Greater Southwest*. Mesoamerican Studies No. 10. Southern Illinois University, Carbondale.
1982 *The Frontier People: The Greater Southwest in the Protohistoric Period*. Center for Archeological Investigations, Occasional Paper No. 1. Southern Illinois University at Carbondale.

Sanders, William T., and Joseph W. Michels (editors)
1977 *Teotihuacan and Kaminaljuyu: A Study in Prehistoric Culture Contact*. Pennsylvania State University Press, University Park.

Schaafsma, Curtis
1979 The "El Paso Phase" and its Relationship to the Casas Grandes Phenomenon. In *Jornada Mogollon Archaeology*, edited by Patrick H. Beckett and Regge N. Wiseman, pp. 383–388. New Mexico State University, Las Cruces.

Schroeder, Albert H.
1965 Unregulated Diffusion from Mexico into the Southwest Prior to A.D. 700. *American Antiquity* 30:297–309.

1966 Pattern Diffusion from Mexico into the Southwest after A.D. 600. *American Antiquity* 31 : 683–704.

1981 How Far Can a Pochteca Leap Without Leaving Footprints? In *Collected Papers in Honor of Erik Kellerman Reed*, edited by Albert H. Schroeder, pp. 43–64. Papers of the Archaeological Society of New Mexico No. 6, Albuquerque.

Scott, Stuart D.

1983 Project Marismas: Reconstructing the Natural and Cultural Environment of a Northwest Coastal Settlement Area. Paper presented at the XVIII Mesa Redonda of the Sociedad Mexicana de Antropología, Taxco, Mexico.

Spence, Michael W.

1971 *Some Lithic Assemblages of Western Zacatecas and Durango, Mexico.* Mesoamerican Studies No. 8. Southern Illinois University, Carbondale.

Trombold, C. Dickson

1976 Spatial Distribution, Functional Hierarchies and Patterns of Interaction in Prehistoric Communities Around La Quemada, Zacatecas, Mexico. In *Archaeological Frontiers: Papers on New World High Cultures in Honor of J. Charles Kelley*, edited by Robert Pickering, pp. 149–182. University Museum Studies No. 4, Southern Illinois University, Carbondale.

Wallerstein, Immanuel

1974 *The Modern World System.* Studies in Political Discontinuity, Academic Press, New York.

Weigand, Phil C.

1978 La Prehistoria del Estado de Zacatecas: Una Interpretation. In *Zacatecas: Anuario de Historia.* Universidad Autonoma de Zacatecas, Zacatecas.

1983 El Caracter de la Civilizacion en El Clasico del Occidente. Paper presented at the XVIII Mesa Redonda de la Sociedad Mexicana de Antropología, Taxco, Mexico.

Weigand, Phil C., G. Harbottle, and E. Sayre

1977 Turquoise Sources and Source Analysis: Mesoamerica and the Southwest U.S.A. In *Exchange Systems in Prehistory*, edited by T. Earle and J. Ericson, pp. 15–34. Academic Press, New York.

5

Ojo de Agua, Sonora and Casas Grandes, Chihuahua: A Suggested Chronology

Beatriz Braniff C.

In 1977 the Centro Regional del Noroeste, Instituto Nacional de Antropología e Historia (INAH), was informed that engineers working on the new Nacozari-Agua Prieta, Sonora, road had "found" a few metates. When we investigated their origin and visited the site we were confronted with the sad evidence of the nearly complete destruction of an archaeological site. Sauer and Brand (1931 : 104) had recorded it as Tibidehuachi, No. 36, and it is now called Ojo de Agua de Santa Rosa Corodehuachi (Son H:2 : 2) after the spring which in colonial times provided water to the famous Presidio of Fronteras, located some 2 km to the north (Figure 5). Sauer and Brand identified the ceramics at the site as Casas Grandes types.

The site lies on the northern bank of the Cuquiarachi River and the western bank of the Fronteras River which flows into the Bavispe, within the "Serrana" area of eastern Sonora, close to the Chihuahua border. This region is higher than the Sonoran desert to the west and more conducive to agricultural endeavours.

This site, despite the recent destruction and previous leveling for cultivation, still contains interesting elements; adobe house mounds of different heights (up to 2 m) are distributed in the area, some of them organized along L— and I-shaped mounds. Metates and manos, pottery, and shell appear strewn about. The bulldozers exposed a partly destroyed burial, where we found a human skeleton together with a parrot and an incised jar, typical of Casas Grandes burial customs—as opposed to cremation, which is found toward the west.

We were able to make two small but interesting stratigraphic excavations: one within a series of cultural deposits filling a natural pit and another in what was left of a house. In addition we excavated a small mound, which turned out to be an adobe house with at least three contiguous rooms. The materials recovered in each of these pits were few, and they all belong to the same complex. For the sake of this paper we considered them together as one unit, ignoring their internal stratigraphy.

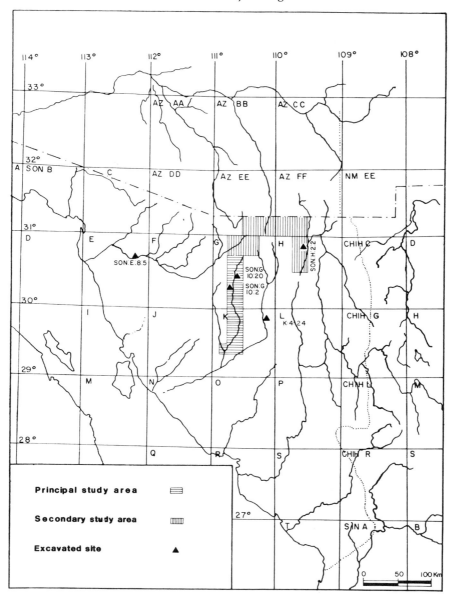

Figure 5. Archaeological investigations in Sonora, Mexico

TABLE 1. Pottery from Ojo de Agua (Son:H:2:2)

	Types	Number	%	Total
1.	Undecorated			
1.1	Ojo de Agua Plainware	10,005	77.76	10,005
2.	Textured			
2.1.1	Ojo de Agua Scored	10	0.07	
2.1.2	Ojo de Agua Rubbed Scored	20	0.11	
2.1.3	Ojo de Agua Pattern Scored	3	0.02	
2.2.1	Ojo de Agua Simple Corrugated	15	0.17	
2.2.2	Ojo de Agua Indented Corrugated	12	0.09	
2.2.3	Ojo de Agua Scored Corrugated	1	0.00	
2.2.4	Ojo de Agua Rubbed Corrugated	15	0.11	
2.2.5	Ojo de Agua Pattern Incised Corrugated	6	0.04	
2.2.6	Ojo de Agua Pattern Incised Indented Corrugated	2	0.01	
2.3.1	Ojo de Agua Decorated Incised and			
2.3.2	Ojo de Agua Grooved Incised	355	2.75	
2.3.3	Ojo de Agua Punched	1,234	9.59	1,801
3.	Unpainted			
3.1.1	Ojo de Agua Red (Playas Red)	565	4.38	
3.1.2	Ojo de Agua Black (Ramos Black)	19	0.14	584

3.1.1	Babícora Polychrome	55	0.42
3.3.2	Carretas Polychrome	82	0.63
3.3.3	Huérigos Polychrome	19	0.14
3.3.4	Ramos Polychrome	69	0.53
3.3.5	Villa Ahumado Polychrome	82	0.63
3.3.6	Casas Grandes various polychromes	68	0.52
		375	
4.	Intrusives		
4.1	Babocomari Polychrome	38	0.29
4.2	Chupadero Black-on-white	1	0.00
4.3	Cloverdale	1	0.00
4.4	Dragoon Red-on-brown	1	0.00
4.5	Gila Polychrome	4	0.03
4.6	Mesoamerican ?	1	0.00
4.7	Santa Cruz Polychrome	38	0.29
4.8	Tanque Verde Red-on-brown	8	0.06
4.9	Tonto Polychrome	3	0.02
4.10	Unidentified bichrome	1	0.00
4.11	Unidentified polychrome	3	0.02
		99	
5.	Figurine fragment ?	1	
	TOTAL	12,866	

TABLE 2. Pottery from Casas Grandes and Ojo de Agua

Types at H:2:2. See Table 1	Types at Casas Grandes	Medio*	Tardio*	Ojo de Agua
1.1	Casas Grandes Plainware	54.1%	64.21%	77.76%
2.1.1	Casas Grandes Scored	2.6	3.78	0.07
2.1.2	Casas Grandes Rubbed Scored	0.6	3.63	0.11
2.1.3	Casas Grandes Pattern Scored	0.0	—	0.02
2.2.1, 2.2.2 & 2.2.3	Casas Grandes Corrugated	0.2	0.58	0.27
2.2.4	Casas Grandes Rubbed Corrugated	0.2	0.07	0.11
2.2.4	Casas Grandes Pattern Incised Corrugated	0.1	5.45	0.04
	Casas Grandes Vertical Corrugated	—	0.07	—
2.3.1 & 2.3.2	Casas Grandes Incised	1.3	0.14	2.75
2.3.4 & 2.4.1	Casas Grandes Tool Punched	0.7	0.50	10.19
2.3.3	Casas Grandes Rubbed Incised	0.3	—	0.38
C.	Casas Grandes Broad Coil	0.2	—	—
3.1.1	Playas Red	9.3	4.14	4.38
3.1.2	Ramos Black	4.2	2.47	0.14
	Madera Black-on-red	1.1	—	—
3.1.1	Babícora Polychrome	1.5	0.07	0.42
3.3.2	Carretas Polychrome	0.8	0.21	0.63
	Corralitos Polychrome	0.6	—	—
	Dublán Polychrome	0.1	—	—
	Escondida Polychrome	0.8	0.7	—

	Col A	Col B	Col C
3.3.3 Huérigos Polychrome	0.2	5.96	0.14
3.3.4 Ramos Polychrome	11.5	1.45	0.53
3.3.5 Villa Ahumada Polychrome	1.3	3.5	0.63
Intrusives			
4.1.0 Babocomari Polychrome	—	—	x
4.2.0 Chupadero Black-on-white	x	—	x
4.3.0 Cloverdale Corrugated	x	—	x
4.4.0 Dragoon Red-on-black	—	—	x
4.5.0 Gila Polychrome	x	—	x
4.7.0 Santa Cruz Polychrome	—	—	x
4.8.0 Tanque Verde Red-on-brown	—	—	x
4.9.0 Tonto Polychrome	x	—	—
Tularosa Black-on-white	x	—	—
St. Johns Polychrome	x	—	—
Heshotauthla Polychrome	x	—	—
Pinto Polychrome	x	—	—
Tuscon Polychrome	x	—	—
El Paso Polychrome	x	—	—

x: Present

—: Not Present

*: Di Peso 1974: Figs. 653–6 and 654–6.

We found that the lithics and shell fit nicely within the Casas Grandes, Chihuahua, Medio period types as defined by Di Peso (1974), but pottery is much more eloquent in establishing such a relation (Tables 1 and 2). All the domestic ceramic types (plain and textured), as well as the polychromes, clearly correspond to the Medio period types of the Casas Grandes sequence, though they appear in different proportions. Such an identification is also obvious regarding the Tardio period (Table 2). Most of the intrusives at Ojo de Agua have been found throughout the Southwest in contexts dated from the thirteenth to the fifteenth centuries. The Casas Grandes polychromes, especially Ramos, are always found as intrusives associated with ceramics well dated by dendrochronology to the fourteenth century, plus or minus 100 years. This group includes Jeddito Black-on-yellow, Four Mile Polychrome, Heshota or Heshotauthla Polychrome, Gila and Tonto Polychromes, Casa Grande Red-on-black, Tanque Verde Red-on-brown, Tucson Polychrome, Chupadero Black-on-white, and El Paso Polychrome (Thompson 1961). Babocomari Polychrome and Santa Cruz Polychrome also are of this late period.

Based on this information we must conclude that our site dates closer to the fourteenth century and not earlier, as Di Peso's (1974) chronology places the Medio period (A.D. 1060–1340). Our date is tentatively confirmed by two C–14 dates: A.D. 1420±70 (samples A-No. 1911 and 1912, Laboratory of Isotope Geochemistry, University of Arizona). These dates correspond to the Tardio period, following the abandonment of Casas Grandes.

Let us now consider the published information regarding the archaeological investigations made by the University of Oklahoma along the río Sonora Valley, especially at the San José Baviácora site (Son K:4:24). As Table 3 shows, there are both textured and polychrome types similar or identical to those of Casas Grandes Medio period at the rió Sonora site. Again, the list of intrusives includes mainly types occurring within the fourteenth century.

The association of C–14 dates and pottery at San José Baviácora is not clear. Pailes (1980:29) mentions four architectural phases: (1) a house in a pit which yielded C–14 dates of A.D. 1075 and 1085; (2) the remodeling of this house in a pit with a raised floor dating A.D. 1305 and 1315; (3) a rectangular surface adobe structure; and (4) a large civil structure. Dirst (1979:93–94) seemingly completes this information relating C–14 dates and ceramics: on the raised floor of a pithouse (phase 2?) tentatively dated to A.D. 1310, the Oklahoma researchers found Casas Grandes Polychromes, as well as Santa Cruz Polychrome and Babocomari Polychrome. In a surface structure (phase 3?) they found Casas Grandes Polychromes, Santa Cruz and Babocomari polychromes together with Gila Polychrome and C–14 dates of A.D. 1500 ± 90, and A.D. 1840 ± 60. Dirst (1979:93–94) mentions that in the fill of a large rectangular structure (phase 4?) excavators found six Medio period polychromes together with two "Trincheras" types, Tanque Verde Red-on-brown, Babocomari Polychrome, Gila Polychrome, and Tula-

TABLE 3. Pottery Types at San Jose Babíacora (Son:K:4:24)

*	Plain Incised Identical to Viejo and Medio periods of Casas Grandes
*	Plain Incised and Polished Red: Playas Red
*	Plain Incised and Punctate: Casas Grandes Incised and Punctate
*	Babíacora Polychrome
*	Carretas Polychrome
*	Dublán Polychrome
*	Huérigos Polychrome
*	Ramos Polychrome
*	Villa Ahumada Polychrome
ox	Babocomari Polychrome
o	Dragoon Red-on-brown
o	El Paso Polychrome
o	Encinas Red-on-black
o*	Gila Polychrome
*	Guasave Red
o	St. Johns Polychrome
o*	Santa Cruz Polychrome
o	Tanque Verde Red-on-brown
x	Tucson Polychrome
x*	Tularosa Black-on-white
x	Trincheras

*   Pailes 1980
o   Dirst and Pailes 1976
x   Dirst 1979

rosa Black-on-white. Dirst tentatively dates the structure between A.D. 1300 and 1400.

From this information I conclude that these stuctures, pottery, and phases 2 through 4 date between A.D. 1310 and 1500, which is the same temporal range which we give to our Ojo de Agua (Son H:2:2) site.

Comparing these two sets of dates and material with those from Casas Grandes, Chichuahua, we believe there are two possible interpretations: one would suggest that the Medio and Tardio periods of the Casas Grandes sequence are contemporaneous and late—fourteenth century plus or minus 100 years (A.D. 1200–1500) and not A.D. 1060– 1345. Wilcox and Shenk (1977) working at Casa Grande on the Gila also suggest this late date for the Medio period. The other interpretation would be that this ceramic complex—including domestic, polychromes, and intrusive types—survived late in Sonora, without losing any one of its attributes. This seems difficult to support and would also mean that some intrusives at Casas Grandes occur earlier there than in the rest of the Southwest.

Di Peso (1974) has suggested that Casas Grandes was a trading center that interacted with Mesoamerica. We should therefore discuss this trading center as part of an economic mesoamerican (and southwestern) system.

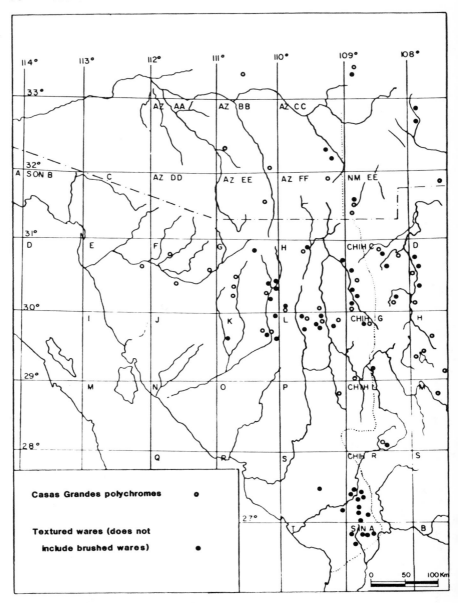

Figure 6. Locations of Casas Grandes polychromes and textured wares

Sadly such a system has never been defined, much less investigated, leaving us in the realm of speculation. Yet, the two sets of dates mentioned above (A.D. 1060–1345 and A.D. 1200–1500) suggest that Casas Grandes participated in two consecutive events in Mesoamerica, related, if such was the case, to two political systems: the first would correlate to Early Postclassic times, and the Toltec "empire"; and, the second to the Late Postclassic, Tepanec, and Aztec rules. Only the latter, and that after A.D. 1450, had the political structure to organize an "agency" of the importance of Casas Grandes. At this late date, the Tarascan "empire" existed between the Southwest and the Mesa Central. We have practically no archaeological information for this empire.

Given this series of options, I support a late date (A.D. 1200– 1500) for the intrusion of Casas Grandes into Sonora (Figure 6)—but if by this time Paquimé has ceased to exist, where was the political or trading center located? On the other hand, if these late dates apply to the economic domination of Paquimé itself (at least into Sonora), where was the mesoamerican "state" to which it is linked? Until we can locate this state, we are forced to argue that Casas Grandes belongs to the cultural developments of the Southwest corresponding to the Hohokam Classic period.

References Cited

Di Peso, Charles C.
  1974 *Casas Grandes, A Fallen Trading Center of the Gran Chichimeca*, 8
    vols. Amerind Foundation, Series No. 9. Dragoon, Ariz.
Dirst, Victoria A.
  1979 *A Prehistoric Frontier in Sonora*. Unpublished Ph.D. dissertation,
    Department of Anthropology, University of Arizona, Tucson.
Dirst, Victoria D., and Richard A. Pailes
  1976 Economic networks: Mesoamerica and the American Southwest.
    Paper presented at the 41st Annual Meeting of the Society for American
    Archaeology. St. Louis, Missouri.
Pailes, Richard A.
  1980 The Upper Rio Sonora Valley in Prehistoric Trade. *Transactions of
    the Illinois State Academy of Science* 72(4):20–39.
Sauer, Carl, and Donald Brand
  1931 *Prehistoric Settlements of Sonora, with Special Reference to Cerros
    de Trincheras*. The University of California Publications in Geography,
    Vol. 5, No. 3, Berkeley.
Thompson, Raymond H.
  1961 Rasgos diagnósticos de la cerámica del siglo XIV en el Suroeste de

los Estados Unidos y Noroeste de México. Paper presented at the IX Mesa Redonda, Sociedad Mexicana de Antropología, Chihuahua.

Wilcox, David R., and Lynette O. Shenk

1977 *The Architecture of the Casa Grande and Its Interpretation.* Arizona State Museum Archaeological Series No. 115 . The University of Arizona, Tucson.

6

The Mobile Merchants of Molino

J. Charles Kelley

During the last few years, perhaps beginning with Randall McGuire's "Mesoamerican Connection in the Southwest" (1980), we appear to have entered a new era in our discussions of the nature and importance of the relationships that may have existed between prehistoric southwestern cultures and those of Mesoamerica. Southwestern isolationism is not dead; Chaco Canyon is still fiercely defended against hypothetical Mexican invaders like another Texas Alamo. Southwestern archaeologists in general apparently remain biased against the hypothesis of prehistoric mesoamerican exploitation of the Southwest and in favor of indigenous cultural evolution conditioned by local/regional ecological factors. But now the controversy is out of the closet; and southwestern archaeologists obviously feel not only free to discuss such matters but also apparently have a strong drive to do so. Some of the resulting productions are poorly conceived but others are significant contributions. Many of the questions invoked are real ones; they require answers. Free and open discussion of the question of mesoamerican-southwestern interaction is in the interest of all of us, regardless of mutual biases.

But the discussion must be an informed one, and indications so far are that only a few southwestern researchers are really willing to invest the time and energy needed to acquire the requisite data base for the archaeology of western and northwestern Mesoamerica. The defenders of that Anasazi "Alamo," the Chaco, do not appear to be willing to counterattack farther than Casas Grandes, or perhaps Durango! Apparently most southwesterners have largely ignored the well-documented existence of an extensive mercantile system in west and northwest Mexico which served to integrate the remote trading outposts of Culiacán, Guasave, and Casas Grandes with the mesoamerican core area.[1]

Characteristic of this attitude perhaps is the reaction of an esteemed colleague who recently stated: "I find it hard to believe in a single well-organized long-distance trade route operating out of a central core area" (Frances Joan Mathien, personal communication, 1982). In fact, understanding of the inferential operation and the process of geographic extension of this so-called Mixteca-Puebla Postclassic mercantile system in western and northwestern Mexico is crucial to the entire problem of mesoamerican-southwestern interaction. There are other examples of long-distance organized trade structures operating out of the mesoamerican core area and these too should be brought into the discussion.

In this paper an attempt is made to summarize the evidence for the existence of this hypothetical northwestern mercantile system and to present new data from archaeological sites in Durango (Ganot et al. 1983; Kelley 1983; Lazalde et al. 1983; Peschard 1983) regarding its inferred functioning. In order to avoid use of overly loaded and controversial terms, "mobile merchant" will be substituted for *pochteca* and *trocadór*; and in place of "Mixteca-Puebla" or "West Coast route," the name "Greater Aztatlán horizon" will be used to identify the entire mercantile system. References will be made to "geographic corridors," "trade routes," and "mercantile systems"— concepts that should not be used interchangeably.

Development of the Trade System Concept

In 1932 the geographer Carl Sauer noted the existence of a remarkable cultural/geographic corridor which had both historical depth and environmental justification: "The land passage through northwestern New Spain was mostly by one great arterial highway. . . . From the densely peopled lands of central Mexico a road led by way of the coastal lowlands of the Mexican Northwest to the northern land of the Pueblo Indian. . . . It [is] here called the Road to Cibola" (1932:1). In the same year Sauer and Donald D. Brand (1932) published the results of their archaeological survey of Sinaloa, demonstrating that in this coastal section there was also archaeological depth to Sauer's cultural corridor; they called this prehistoric cultural frontier route by one of its ancient names "Aztatlán." In Sauer's 1932 map the road to Cibola is shown extending from the vicinity of Guadalajara (where it connected directly with another corridor running along the Río Lerma drainage from the area of the Valley of Mexico) through western Jalisco to and along the Nayarit-Sinaloa coastal strip and thence through Sonora to the American Southwest.

Subsequent work by other archaeologists including Kelly (1938, 1939, 1945), Ekholm (1939, 1942), Meighan (1959, 1971, 1976) and associates (Bell 1960, 1971; Bordaz 1964), Mountjoy (1970a, 1970b, 1974), Scott and associates (Gill 1974; Scott 1974; Sweetman 1974) established and correlated local sequences along the entire coastal strip from San Blas, Nayarit, to Guasave in northern Sinaloa. Mesoamerican cultures had appeared in the south during the Preclassic and had spread as far as Chametla on the Río Baluarte during the Classic. Most significantly the investigators identified a Nayarit-Sinaloa pancoastal culture, early Postclassic in age, which became known as the Aztatlán horizon. During the late Postclassic this culture had been replaced by local developments which continued into the Spanish contact period in the area from San Blas to Culiacán, but not in the extreme north at Guasave.

Quite early, investigators suspected an origin for the Aztatlán culture in the Jalisco highlands. Early work by Lister at Cojumatlán (1949), later work by Meighan and associates at Tizapan el Alto (Meighan and Foote 1968), investigations by Glassow (1967) and Weigand (1976, 1977, 1979) at Etzatlán, and research by Gifford at Ixtlán del Río (1950) confirmed that there were indeed upland local cultures that closely resembled those of the Aztatlán culture. These early Postclassic cultures extended from San Gregorio on the lower Río Lerma along the south side of Lake Chapala and through Etzatlán to coastal Nayarit where they were identifiable with the Aztatlán horizon. Astonishingly, from the lower Río Lerma to coastal Nayarit and northward to Guasave in northern Sinaloa there had developed a chain of closely related early Postclassic sites distributed along a natural corridor over 1000 km in length.

On the lower Río Lerma the Aztatlán trade route intersected an even older series of routes that followed the Río Lerma from the Valley of Toluca to Lake Chapala. Via this natural corridor trade between the Valley of Mexico and West Mexico, the Chupicuaro-Ticomán connection especially, had developed at least as early as the Preclassic. There is also strong evidence that this trade route continued in use through the Classic and Postclassic periods.

The Mixteca-Puebla Connection

Gordon Ekholm, working at Guasave, first noted that the Aztatlán component there had even more far-reaching relationships (1942). From his excavations he inferred the presence of a long list of traits, many highly specific, characteristic of the far-off Mixteca-Puebla culture of central Mesoamerica.[2] So clearcut was the archaeological relationship that he postulated that a small group migration had occurred beginning at Cholula or elsewhere in the Mixteca. Among the Guasave Mixteca-Puebla traits listed by Ekholm, in addition to ceramics and other artifacts, are specific forms of dental mutilation and cranial deformation. These traits are also found at virtually all of the greater Aztatlán cultural components, suggesting indeed the actual involvement of foreigners.

Ekholm's identification of Guasave traits as Mixteca-Puebla has not been seriously challenged,[3] but this explanation of them in terms of migration has been disregarded. Instead, the Guasave phenomena are now regarded as evidence for the existence of a major mercantile system. It would be difficult to characterize otherwise the existence of a long chain of closely related cultural components distributed along a major corridor of movement and communication. Virtually all known components of the Greater

Aztatlán trade system represent a stage or phase in which foreign stylistic elements were grafted onto a local ceramic development. These intrusive elements, stylistically and iconographically, are attributable to the Mixteca-Puebla complex and rather specifically to the ceramics known as Aztec I (see Figure 7). Aztec I ceramics apparently derive from Culhuacán and associated sites in the Valley of Mexico and from the Postclassic trade center of Cholula in Puebla.[4] Unfortunately the age of Aztec I is now subject to controversy; its influence on the Aztatlán sites certainly was a relatively late phenomenon, to be discussed later. Objects of copper, especially bells, are found consistently in Aztatlán components as are spindle whorls in quantity and, less frequently, smoking pipes. Copper artifacts, cotton and cotton goods, and tobacco probably represent major long-distance trade commodities in the mercantile structure.

The Aztatlán trade route and mercantile system, thus conceptu-

Figure 7. Stylized pottery designs: bird-serpent combinations? *Above:* Mixteca-Puebla complex, Guasave, Sinaloa. *Below:* Aztec I Pottery, Valley of Mexico

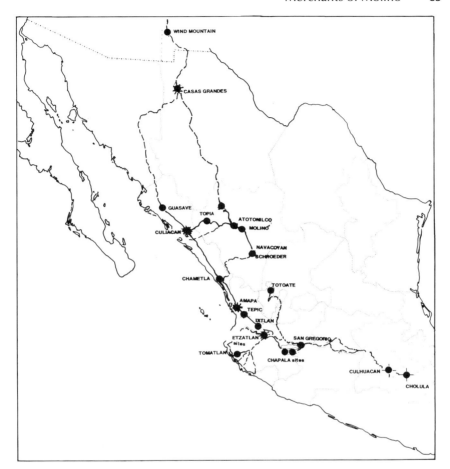

Figure 8. The greater Aztatlán trade route

alized, resembles in many ways other well-known long-distance mesoamerican trade systems, such as that postulated on an earlier time period for
Teotihuacan-Tikal or Teotihuacan-Kaminaljuyú commercial relations.[5] Including the Cholula to Lake Chapala segment (a series of braided trade
routes established in the Preclassic) the entire distance to Guasave is over
1,400 km (Ekholm says 1700 km); the overland distance between Teotihuacan and Kaminaljuyú was around 1,700 km. But Guasave/Culiacán was not
the end of the line; the Aztatlán system definitely extended across the Sierra
Madre Occidental into the interior highlands of Durango. (See Figure 8.)

It should be pointed out that the Aztatlán horizon is divisible into two major periods. The earlier period is characterized primarily by Lolandis Red-rimmed pottery (Kelley and Kelley 1971:124–127) and associated pottery (Kelley and Kelley 1971:125–127) and associated types which are widespread in the Nayarit-Sinaloa coastal strip and apparently indigenous there. During this earlier period the mercantile system represented appears to have been localized on the West Coast, with extensions eastward across the Sierra Madre Occidental; but at Amapa it connected with an early or basic "Toltec" system extending from the lower Río Lerma to Nayarit.

The later period represents the full Mixteca-Puebla development; the Nayarit-Sinaloa route and the Lerma-Nayarit route were combined into a major mercantile system anchored in the Valley of Mexico. During this period the Chalchihuites culture of Durango was incorporated into the Greater Aztatlán mercantile system (Ganot et al. 1983).

Extensions of the Aztatlán System in Durango

In Durango the mesoamerican tradition is represented primarily by the Guadiana branch of the Chalchihuites culture, known primarily from excavations carried out at the Schroeder site in 1954–1958. The antecedent Suchil branch apparently began early in the Christian era; but the Guadiana branch is later, inaugurated by colonization from the Suchil area (Kelley 1971; Kelley and Abbott 1966). The revised Chalchihuites chronology, based on a large series of radiocarbon dates from the Alta Vista ceremonial center, suggests that this colonization took place more or less following the fall of Alta Vista around A.D. 875–925; the earliest Ayala phase of the Guadiana branch cannot have begun much before A.D. 900, although radiocarbon dates from the Schroeder site suggest a much earlier dating.

During the Ayala phase, trade relations were established between the Schroeder site occupants and those of the Middle Chametla culture (Baluarte phase) of Sinaloa (Kelley and Winters 1960). Middle Chametla ceramics and spindle whorls appeared in the Schroeder site at this time (Figure 9). However, no reciprocal trade materials have been reported from Chametla, suggesting that expeditionary trade by Chametla mobile merchants is involved. Exchange of coastal products (shell, dried fish, fruits, cotton goods) for Durango hides, tallow, jerky (?), and perhaps obsidian, *chalchihuitl*, and peyote must be represented.

In the succeeding Las Joyas phase in Durango, probably dating after A.D. 950, there is abundant evidence for increased trade with Sinaloa, involving the earliest (Lolandis) phase of the Aztatlán horizon. This trade included actual transfer of a coastal pottery type—Lolandis Red-rimmed, derived from a West Coast ceramic tradition—to the Durango highlands and replaced decorated bowl forms of the Chalchihuites tradition at the

---

Figure 9. Codex Style depictions on pottery from Guasave, Sinaloa: Mixteca-Puebla complex. *Left:* the god Xochipilli. *Center and right:* the god Nanautzin. God identifications by J. Eric Thompson. Exterior design from a Sinaloa polychrome jar found at the Schroeder site, Durango.

Schroeder site and elsewhere in Durango. This change, inferentially representing an authentic small group migration,[6] was accompanied by other ceramic variations and by major changes in Durango ceramic iconography. The number of spindle whorls traded may be evidence of inauguration of cotton growing in the highlands, and the appearance of the pottery tripod *molcajete* suggests that chili had become part of the exchange system. Again, no reciprocal Chalchihuites artifacts have been identified in contemporary West Coast components and essentially expeditional trade by Sinaloa mobile merchants is probably represented. The Las Joyas phase at the Schroeder site was one of great building activity and regional expansion. Las Joyas components were established along another major ecological corridor extending northwestward to the Zape area. This appears to be an example of colonization extending along a previously established trade route. The course followed was duplicated centuries later by Spanish colonial settlement along this same route, a major Spanish *camino real*.

The final two phases of the Chalchihuites culture, Río Tunal and Calera, were very poorly represented at the Schroeder site, to the conclusion, now doubtful, that the culture was clearly on the wane. Exotic ceramic types appeared, terminating the long Chalchihuites tradition in decorated ceramics. Aztatlán trade items now included not only ceramics and spindle whorls but also smoking pipes and copper artifacts of specific Culiacán and Guasave origin, representing the climax of Aztatlán trade system. Notable was the discovery of a small tripod jar of Sinaloa Polychrome decorated on the exterior by depiction of Mixteca-Puebla gods in pure codex style. Again no reciprocal trade items are reported on the West Coast. Clearly, the trade route from the lowlands now followed up one and probably both branches of the Río Culiacán through the Topia gateway across the Sierra.[7] This was the route followed by Nuño Guzman's forces from coast to highlands in 1530–1531 (Sauer 1932:9–10) and by Francisco Ibarra from highlands to coast (and return) in 1563–1564 (Obregón 1924, see Chapters 7–9). Subsequently, it became a major corridor across the Sierra Madre, remaining so until well into the present century.

In the Guadiana Valley local archaeologists made collections from the hilltop site of Navacoyán throughout the early 1950s (Howard 1957), and in 1958 the Durango collector Federico Schroeder was responsible for large-scale looting of the site. With the cooperation of Schroeder much of his collection was photographed before it was smuggled into the United States and dispersed through sale. Apparently Navacoyán reached its climax during the late Chalchihuites phases when the Schroeder site was fast declining. The Schroeder collection included, in addition to Chalchihuites specimens, Aztatlán ceramic vessels (as well as unidentified exotic trade pieces) and a great number of West Coast spindle whorls, pipes, and copper objects. No thorough study of the collection could be made and internal associations had not been recorded.

The Cañón de Molino Collection

In 1982 another such large collection from the Cañón de Molino site, located in the Guatimapé valley northwest of the city of Durango, became available for study. The site was described in part by J. Alden Mason in 1932 (Mason 1937). Over a period of years the residents of an adjacent *ejido* had excavated in the lower part of this site, primarily in a cemetery area, and had retrieved several hundred artifacts, including many intact pottery vessels, spindle whorls, smoking pipes, copper artifacts in quantity, and other items. The collection was discovered in the *ejido* by Jaime Ganot, Jesus Lazalde, and Alejandro Peschard of the Escuela de Medicina of the Universidad de Juarez del Estado de Durango while they were engaged in photographing *arte rupestre* (Lazalde et al. 1983) near the site. The doctors, who are avocational archaeologists, rescued the collection and prepared a detailed catalog which they will subsequently use to register the specimens with the Instituto Nacional de Antropología e Historia, as required by law, after which the collection will be placed in the Museó de la Universidad de Juarez in Durango. Their report on the collection is complete (Ganot R. et al. 1983; Lazalde et al. 1983). J. Charles and Ellen Kelley served as advisors in this study and the doctors have generously allowed them to photograph most of the collection.

The Cañón de Molino site is located on a high spur of the eastern front ridge of the Sierra Madre Occidental projecting into the valley of Guatimapé, located northwest of the city of Durango. The Cañón de Molino, which bounds the site on the south, has a flowing stream and extensive farmlands; the canyon is one of numerous open passes leading from the Sierra into the interior valley of Guatimapé itself. These canyons offer passage to the Topia gateway through the Sierra. The Guatimapé valley itself is a lush well-watered plain heavily cultivated today.[8] There are numerous sites of both Chalchihuites (Guadiana Valley branch) and Loma San Gabriel cultural traditions located along the western foothill margin of the valley. Bounding the valley on the east is a mountain range beyond which lies the Chihuahuan desert and the true Chichimeca. The Molino site potentially dominated both a principal southeast to northwest corridor (the *camino real*) and the Topia gateway to the West Coast; in addition it was certainly an outpost for trade with the Chichimecs of the Mesa del Norte.

The principal site is situated on the top of the high ridge point. There are many court and platform assemblages in characteristic Chalchihuites stone masonry architecture, plus isolated structures in the Loma San Gabriel architectural tradition. Defensive walls, partially natural, surround the flanks of the upper site. Below, on the south, the lower section of the site is situated on a narrow flank of the hillside, actually an old alluvial terrace of the Cañón de Molino. In addition to innumerable looted burial pits there are remains of houses or house platforms of stone masonry in this terrace area.

The presence of these structures and the occurrence of many metates and manos indicate that the terrace was a living area as well as a cemetery. The hilltop site may have been an area of elite residence and a stronghold. There is no conspicuous ceremonial architecture so identification of the hill as a ceremonial center is not well supported.

Ceramics and other artifacts in the collection represent three major cultural traditions: Guadiana branch Chalchihuites; the sub-mesoamerican Loma San Gabriel culture (which was partially contemporary with the Chalchihuites tradition); and the Aztatlán-Culiacán tradition of the West Coast. The Chalchihuites tradition is represented by ceramic types of the Las Joyas, Río Tunal, and Calera phases, plus some early specimens representing the Ayala-Las Joyas phase transition; the site may have first been occupied around A.D. 935–950.

The Loma San Gabriel cultural tradition is represented by many plain wares and a few decorated ceramic vessels. Loma San Gabriel is an old Sierran culture whose people apparently lived in cultural symbiosis with the Chalchihuiteños (Foster 1978, 1980; Kelley 1971 : 799–801). Temporally it preceeded the earliest Chalchihuites occupation and survived the demise of that culture. It is believed that the Loma San Gabriel tradition is ancestral to that of the modern Tepehuan (Riley and Winters 1963); the Cañón de Molino site may be the historic Tepehuan site "Concepción de la Boca" (Lazalde et al. 1983 : 9), although no definite historic artifacts were recovered. It is fairly certain that this is the site of the village (presumably Tepehuan) conquered by Francisco Ibarra in the winter of 1563–1564, while he searched for the Topia gateway.[9] Notably, various Loma San Gabriel structures on the hilltop look much more recent than the Chalchihuites structures.

The Aztatlán cultural tradition is represented at the Molino site by a surprisingly large number of decorated and monochrome ceramic vessels and by many spindle whorls, copper artifacts, and smoking pipes. Identified Aztatlán ceramics are types from various West Coast sites: Amapa-Peñitas, Chametla, Culiacán, and Guasave. Especially interesting is a fragmentary vessel of Iguanas Polychrome, a ware probably made at Peñitas and widely traded both in Nayarit and Jalisco. Both early and late phases of the Aztatlán culture are represented, and surprisingly, types attributed to the putative Protohistoric Late Culiacán (La Divisa) phase are present; clearly the site survived later than other known Chalchihuites components.

The most interesting ceramics from the Molino site are decorated vessels on which attributes of West Coast and Chalchihuites types are "scrambled" in new combinations, including attributes of vessel form, legs, color combinations, design layout, and design elements. One can visualize a new ceramic type (Molino Red-on-cream) just on the point of stabilization. Late Chalchihuites ceramic types are involved in these recombinations. These Río Tunal and Calera types also tend to blend their characteristic attributes so that type diagnostics are blurred. A similar blending of the attributes of the monochrome wares of all three major ceramic traditions is visible. It seems clear that Aztatlán horizon and late Chalchihuites potters lived and worked together at the Molino site.

Spindle whorls conform to the pattern set by the ceramics. Amapa, Chametla, Culiacán, and Guasave types are present as are examples of the collar-button type found principally in the Chalchihuites Calera phase and Casas Grandes, where they are attributed to the Diablo phase.

Smoking pipes belong principally to the late phases of the Aztatlán horizon; many of them are identifiable with the Cocoyolitos type of late Chametla. As in the case of other artifact categories Amapa types also are well represented.

Copper artifacts are quite numerous; there are 81 copper bells and approximately 115 copper elements together. This quantity can be compared with some 684 copper elements including 115 bells at Casas Grandes; 134 copper elements including 111 bells at Guasave, and 198 copper objects including bells at Amapa. The Schroeder site, Culiacán, Cojumatlán, and Tizapan el Alto, for example, produced only a few copper objects, while some 450 copper bells have been found in the entire American Southwest. Evidence for smelting of copper artifacts is convincing for both Casas Grandes and Amapa. The Cañón de Molino bells have parallels in both Amapa and Casas Grandes but included some examples not known from other published sites. One specialized type is known elsewhere only from Cojumatlán, and Tarascan types are present.

A number of intact human skulls survived in the collection. Many of these skulls illustrate tabular-erect deformation, and dental mutilation is represented. Tabular erect deformation is rare in other Chalchihuites components and dental mutilation is unknown.[10] Both traits are present consistently in Greater Aztatlán components. This is valuable supplemental evidence that actual West Coast persons lived (and died) at Cañón de Molino.

The Source of Cañón de Molino Intrusives

The Cañón de Molino site accordingly appears to be a highland trading outpost in which mobile merchants from various Aztatlán centers lived and worked side-by-side with resident Chalchihuiteños. Culiacán-Guasave was clearly the staging area for the West Coast mobile merchants who used the Topia gateway, although the imported items come from a variety of Greater Aztatlán components, as far distant as Cojumatlán on Lake Chapala. Culiacán archaeology is poorly known but there is much Spanish documentary evidence. The Culiacán valley was the home of advanced mesoamerican culture. It was heavily populated; more than two hundred pueblos were subject to the lords of Culiacán (who were carried in hammocks/

litters). There were markets in the larger towns where cotton clothing, fish, and fruit could be purchased. Honey and beeswax, as well as "alligator" skin shields, are additions to the usual roster of trade commodities (Sauer and Brand 1932 : 49—55).

Topia itself was clearly an intermediate center on this trans-Sierran trade route and Spanish accounts suggest that in architectural and other features this Acaxee stronghold was mesoamerican in culture, perhaps a remnant of Chalchihuites culture surviving in the highlands. It has not been located archaeologically. While Ibarra was at San Juan del Rio in 1563 before going to the Guatimapé valley "some natives brought information of the town of Topia . . . from which they had brought and exhibited a feather shield of many colors . . . ; a feather crest of silver; and cotton clothing woven of twisted thread, which the natives [Tepehuan?] had acquired by exchange from the people of Topia" (Obregón 1924).

Beals provides us with a fascinating picture of the Acaxee traveling family (from the documentary sources, Beals 1933 : 33). The women carried a large conical burden basket, using a tumpline. In the basket, from which hung deer hooves strung on canes and tinkling deer foot bones, there was a bushel of soft corn topped by plates (comales) and spoons and above this a sleeping child wrapped in a mantle; at the basket's outer edge parrots and macaws were carried. The women carried their load up and down mountains apparently with great ease.

The case of Topia and the Acaxee can fairly be regarded as contact period analogues of the Cañón de Molino and its composite population. Cotton probably was grown in the Guatimapé valley and woven there, as well as desert fibers, while copper trinkets, cotton goods, tobacco, tropical fruits and vegetables, dried fish and shrimp, honey and beeswax, sea shells, parrots and macaws, feathers, and perhaps caymán skin shields were almost certainly commodities available for trade to both Chalchihuites people and Chichimecs. Reciprocal trade goods would have included hides, dried meat, desert fibers (and textiles made from them), and various minerals. Non-Chalchihuites practices in head deformation and dental mutilation indicate the presence of foreigners; the mingling of ceramic traits from lowland and highland indicates the same thing. Weaving (a female occupation) and pottery making (almost certainly a male activity in this mesoamerican context) are probably indicative of the presence of West Coast men and women in the local enclave. Interestingly enough, the skull with dental mutilation and tabular erect deformation described by Peschard from the Molino collection is that of a young adult, probably female. This might suggest marriage with West Coast females as the source of the trade items, but since mesoamerican pottery making was primarily a male occupation this could not explain the blend of ceramic traditions.

Functioning of the Mercantile System

From the data presented several inferences may be made, subject to testing, regarding the structure and operation of the Greater Aztatlán mercantile system. It may be described as a stratified dendritic system, one in which long-distance trade in highly desirable items (including luxury goods)[11] was superimposed on local trade systems dealing primarily in subsistence commodities. The long-distance trade itself was carried out by mobile merchants, primarily males in the initial stages of development of the system. This appears to be indicated by the appearance of central mesoamerican ceramic attributes in local pottery traditions, considering that mesoamerican ceramic production seems to have been primarily a male activity.[12] Inevitably, the mobile merchants married into the local populations and in subsequent generations their descendants (genetically mixed) continued the trade. Beyond the established trade centers the mobile merchants ventured farther; thereafter new centers became integrated into the system. In effect the mobile merchants in pursuing expeditionary trading formed the "cutting edge" of the mercantile operation, continually advancing the system into new territory, following principally natural corridors. Actual family units probably followed the paths blazed by the original mobile merchants and expeditionary trade was replaced by organized trade between adjacent centers. Although some exotic items undoubtedly travelled the entire length of the system, the major trade involved mercantile interaction between pairs of trading centers and between adjacent regions. By the time mobile merchants from the West Coast had established themselves at Cañón de Molino they probably carried very few genetic characters derived from central Mesoamerica, but even so brought a rich cultural tradition derived from the core area.

The conceptualization of this system by southwesterners as one in which mesoamerican individuals set out periodically to cover the entire road from the core area to far-flung outposts such as Culiacán and Cañón de Molino has no basis in reality nor in the thinking of most archaeologists working in the west and northwest of Mexico. Speculations as to how far a mobile merchant could profitably and practically travel are irrelevant to the discussion. The goods introduced by mobile merchants into the Chalchihuites culture (or into the Southwest!) did not come from the Valley of Mexico but rather from the West Coast of Mexico.

But the tradition of ancestral origins undoubtedly persisted as did a long-distance sense of belonging. When Nuño de Guzman was in Michoacan among the Tarascans he made inquiries regarding a distant place on his proposed *entrada* route known as "Techuculuacan" (Crane and Reindorp 1970:91). This is undoubtedly a reference to "huey Culhuacán," or "old Culhuacán," the original name for Culiacán in Sinaloa. Clearly he had received advance information in Tenochtitlán of the existence of a traditional outpost far away on the northwestern frontier. Certainly not coincidentally this outpost bore the name of "Culhuacán," the name of the probable Valley of Mexico staging center for the northwestern mercantile system. And there is evidence that actual persons during their lifetime traveled to remote outposts. Thus, Ekholm noted that specific pottery designs at Guasave were executed in "codex style" but probably by local artists. However, as previously noted, a jar of the type Sinaloa Polychrome, presumably made at Guasave, was recovered from late deposits at the Schroeder site. In the decoration of this vessel there are three circular medallions depicting mesoamerican gods. These god figures, easily identified by J. Erik Thompson (letter to Howard Winters, 1957), are executed in pure "codex style." Clearly an artist trained in central Mesoamerica painted them on locally made Guasave pottery. And someone at Guasave imported a dragonfly delicacy presumably made only in the Valley of Mexico. But such long-distance travels must have been the exception, not the rule.

Were the mobile merchants of Molino and the Aztatlán system institutionalized and state controlled like the Aztec *pochteca*? There is no simple answer to this question. The general inference would be that in hierocratic mesoamerican political entities the state (and the priesthood) had some involvement in everything, especially the trade in luxury goods. Even among the Tarascans where there is no evidence for an organized *pochteca* and trade appears to have been largely entrepreneurial, the documents state: "There was a supervisor over all the dealers who gather gold, plumages, and stones for the Cazonci [King] by exchange or barter" (Crane and Reindorp 1970:15). In the tightly class-structured Tarascan society all such luxury goods were the property of the nobility and for the most part were controlled by the king. There was even a chief treasurer with a staff of assistants. With regard to entrepreneurial activity it should be noted that even in the *pochteca* system some such activity was permitted.

Casas Grandes and Beyond

Adding the Culiacán to Cañón de Molino segment (estimated at over 325 km) to our estimated distance from Cholula brings the total to around 1575 km (subtracting the Culiacán to Guasave sector), still under the estimated 1700 km between Teotihuacan and Kaminaljuyú. But this was not the farthest extent of the Aztatlán system. From Cañón de Molino to Casas Grandes by the highland foothill route the distance was on the order of 500 km; the total from Cholula about 2,075, well over the Teotihuacan to Cholula distance but probably within the limits of the later trade route between Tula and Nicaragua-Costa Rica.

The late Charles Di Peso effectively demonstrated the developments in the Casas Grandes valley and surrounding area that clearly indicate a mesoamerican presence there (Di Peso 1974). His depiction of a stratified society with division of labor, an elaborate and varied mercantile economy, the presence of a production center for copper items, and the rebuilding of the city itself to incorporate mesoamerican ceremonial architecture remains virtually undisputed by southwestern archaeologists. The latter, however, have disputed Di Peso's chronology for Casas Grandes, the degree and nature of its mesoamericanization, and its influence on southwestern developments. In view of the demonstration in this paper of a strong mesoamerican mercantile presence in the highlands some 500 km to the south, a discussion of these points is in order.

Unfortunately, there are remarkably few ties between Chalchihuites cultural components and Casas Grandes. Significantly, however, the earliest contacts occurred during the Viejo period. Early in the period (Convento phase) widely distributed mesoamerican traits such as pottery drums and mirror plaques appeared. In the succeeding Perros Bravos phase, which Di Peso dated to circa A.D. 950-1060, trade sherds of the types Aguaruto Exterior Incised and Guasave-like polychrome were found. These types belong to the early phase of the Aztatlán (Mixteca-Puebla) horizon at Culiacán, which is heavily represented in Chalchihuites sites, especially at Cañón de Molino. Their presence in the Casas Grandes valley before the building of the city indicates that mobile traders of the Aztatlán horizon had already penetrated the area, possibly to engage in expeditionary trading. I remain somewhat dubious of the Totoate-like types that Di Peso describes (Di Peso 1974, 1:248–252). The Aztatlán traders could have entered the Casas Grandes valley directly across the Sierra Madre Occidental from Culiacán or Guasave as Di Peso apparently believed, but more probably they came through the Topia gateway to Molino and then northwest. The West Coast and Chalchihuites datings would more or less correspond with Di Peso's dates for the Perros Bravos phase.

Accordingly, the building and subsequent mesoamericanization of Casas Grandes would correspond with the second stage of the Greater Aztatlán horizon, that characterized by the Mixteca-Puebla connection with the Valley of Mexico. Unfortunately there are no specifically mesoamerican pottery types to identify the source of the foreign influences at Casas Grandes, understandable perhaps in view of the great distances involved and the extreme roughness of the intervening terrain. But there is a specific tie to late Chalchihuites culture through a trait well-represented at Cañón de Molino. This is the spindle whorl type "collar-button incised," which appears in Durango at the very end of the Río Tunal phase and is especially well-represented in the subsequent Calera phase when Mixteca-Puebla traits are best represented in Durango. At Casas Grandes the comparable specimens were attributed to the Medio period, Diablo phase (Di Peso 1974, 2:54, 624–625).[13] The evidence for the origin of the mesoamerican presence at

Casas Grandes in the final stage of the Greater Aztatlán horizon either directly from Culiacán-Guasave or indirectly through northern Chalchihuites sites such as Cañón de Molino seems to be quite strong. The preoccupation of the mercantile system with trade in copper artifacts is reflected in the presence of a copper producing facility at Casas Grandes, which supplied what is now called the Casas Grandes interaction sphere with copper artifacts. This metallurgical production center at Casas Grandes probably represents the migration there of members of a copper artisan guild from the West Coast, a familiar pattern in Mesoamerica.

However, there is another possibility. Phil C. Weigand has proposed that the great Postclassic site of La Quemada (which he considers basically Toltec) was the source of the Casas Grandes mesoamerican phenomena (Weigand 1978). Di Peso also attributed the mesoamerican presence at Casas Grandes to a Toltec source, whereas the evidence presented in this paper identifies the source as the Mixteca-Puebla of Culhuacán and Cholula. In effect Weigand presents no archaeological evidence for La Quemada-Casas Grandes relationships and to the best of my knowledge no La Quemada or Casas Grandes pottery types, or other specific diagnostic traits, have been found along the ancient trails from La Quemada, which in any event pass first through the Chalchihuites area. Nevertheless the possibility should be further investigated.

New interpretations of the Casas Grandes chronology would seem to indicate that the development of the city and its interaction sphere could have had little effect on southwestern developments such as those in the Chaco Canyon. Thus one new chronology (LeBlanc 1980) would date the Medio period at circa A.D. 1150–1300, while another (Wilcox and Sternberg 1983:74–75) would date the same period at circa A.D. 1150–1450. Neither chronology would be out of line with datings for the final phase of the Greater Aztatlán (Mixteca-Puebla) horizon mercantile system.

However, both chronologies would eliminate Casas Grandes as the source of mesoamerican influences on the Chaco development, beginning early in the eleventh century. But it should not be forgotten that the earlier (Lolandis) phase of the Greater Aztatlán horizon was represented in the Casas Grandes valley probably as early as the middle tenth century A.D. Finally, and most significantly, in his last excavations at the Mogollon Wind Mountain site, located in southwestern New Mexico, Di Peso found mesoamerican sherds also attributable to the Lolandis phase of the Greater Aztatlán horizon (personal communication, 1979). This strongly suggests that expeditionary trade had entered the great trade corridor extending northward (roughly along the Arizona-New Mexico state line) into the Anasazi heartland. And the Greater Aztatlán horizon mercantile system still remains the most probable source for the copper bells found in Chaco Canyon, not to mention the other remnants of a mesoamerican presence there.

Final Note

This paper has demonstrated that developments in the Casas Grandes valley and in the upland Chalchihuites culture sites to the south in Durango do not represent isolated phenomena. Rather they were part of a great mercantile system which existed from around A.D. 900 through A.D. 1400, if not later, and during its latest manifestation had ties directly to Mixteca-Puebla sites in the Valley of Mexico and Puebla. In evaluating the mesoamerican presence in the Southwest archaeologists must take these data into account. Perhaps when they do and when they read more extensively in the archaeological literature of Mesoamerica, especially that which concerns long-distance mercantile systems, we may reach a working concensus beneficial to all of us. It should be remembered that the defense of the Texas Alamo against the Mexicans finally ended in defeat. The same may hold true for its prehistoric New Mexico equivalent in the Chaco Canyon.

Notes

1. A summary of this evidence has been available in print for several years (Kelley 1980).
2. Ekholm's list includes elements derived from central Mexico in general, from the Vera Cruz coastal area, from central America, from Cholula and Oaxaca, and from the highland cultures of west Mexico. With regard to specifically Mixteca-Puebla traits he notes: "Most of the traits are on the religious-ceremonial plane; they consist of objects or designs on vessels which were found with burials, usually a focus of religious ceremonialism. . . . [T]he drawings of gods on the Guasave vessels are closely similar to those in the Mixteca codices, and other designs which resemble those of Cholula pottery are all of a symbolic nature. The resemblances are quite definitely with the Mixteca-Puebla style of ceremonial art rather than that which is usually called Aztec" (1942:128).

Ekholm defines the concept: "The term Mixteca-Puebla . . . is used as a general term to designate the Cholula and Mixtec cultures of Puebla and northern Oaxaca which were closely similar and which together formed a single highly important development. . . . This was apparently the source of the ceremonial elements, including the great pantheon of gods, the calendar, and picture writing which reached the Valley of Mexico and continuing from Aztec II were so important a part of Aztec culture" (1942:126).

3. Indeed, they have been confirmed by later studies (see Fahmel 1981:233), and by subsequent finds in Durango.
4. See Séjourné (1970) for descriptions and depictions of Aztec I pottery from Culhuacán. Aztec I is, of course, a misnomer. The pottery is Mixteca-Puebla and not ethnically Aztec.

5. Sanders and Price identify the Teotihuacan/Kaminaljuyú system as "a Cacao Route, analagous to the Amber Route of Bronze Age Europe" (1968:168). There is an extensive literature on the commercial relation between Teotihuacan/Kaminaljuyú and Teotihuacan/Tikal. Southwestern archaeologists in general seem to have ignored this literature (see for example Kidder et al. 1977; Michels 1979, Chapter 8; Parsons and Price 1971; Sanders and Michels 1977; Sanders and Price 1968).

6. The ceramic ware, Lolandis Red-rimmed, represents an abrupt break in the evolution of Chalchihuites ceramics but has developmental antecedents at Chametla (and probably at Amapa) on the West Coast. Specimens of Lolandis have a past composition different from other local Chalchihuites ceramics, but because the paste differs also from West Coast examples they cannot be trade wares. The picture that emerges is that of actual trade wares from the West Coast introduced during the preceding Ayala phase by Chametla mobile merchants, followed by small group colonization in the Las Joyas phase.

7. The drainage of the Río Grande de Santiago in Jalisco-Nayarit provides relatively easy passage from the highlands of the west Mexico to the coast. This was the route followed by the merchants of the Greater Aztatlán mercantile system and by the modern railway and road systems. At the extreme northern end of the Sierra Madre Occidental there is relatively easy passage across the northwestern end of the range just south of the Mexican border (Cananea-Agua Prieta-Janos). In between (a distance of some 1,200 km or 750 mi), the only relatively easy passage was that of the Topia gateway. Until the opening of the Durango to Mazatlan highway about 1950 there was no easy vehicular passage across the entire Sierra. In the present decade precarious passage for trucks or four-wheel drive vehicles has become possible through the Topia gateway during the dry season. Needless to say numerous Indian foottrails cross the Sierra in various localities.

8. This was largely the old bed of the ancient Lago de Santiaguilla.

9. Actually he searched for legendary Copala, perhaps Paquimé; see discussion in Lazalde et al. 1983:7–9.

10. Data regarding the Molino skulls are derived from the excellent report prepared by Alejandro Peschard (1983), and other data have been abstracted from the informative reports of Jesus Lazalde and Jaime Ganot (Ganot et al. 1983), supplemented by personal observations. Inferences drawn from these reports are my own and do not necessarily represent the views of Ganot, Lazalde, and Peschard.

11. Inasmuch as trade in turquoise between the Southwest and northwest Mexico is known from the Contact period and inferred for earlier periods as well, its relative rarity in the Molino collections comes as a surprise. But the Molino burials were excavated with pick and shovel, without screening, so that much turquoise present may not have been found. Also much of it actually found may have been retained by the finders when the main collection was rescued. Beyond this, however, there is not an abun-

dance of turquoise in collections from excavated components of the Greater Aztatlán horizon. Perhaps the turquoise actually found was just that which was in transit "down the line" and was not regularly utilized locally because of its high trade value.

12. This is a surprisingly difficult point to ascertain. It certainly holds for the Mexica (Dibble and Anderson 1961:83) but is not so certain for other mesoamerican groups. Although ample data are available demonstrating that weaving was customarily done by women, the question of which sex made pottery is rarely answered in the sources. Among the Tarascans a male official was in charge of potters and still another was in charge of those who made jars, plates, and bowls; but the sex of the potters is not stated (Crane and Reindorp 1970:12–15). Perhaps significantly a male was in charge of gourd lacquerware painters; in the late 1890s when lacquerwork utilized gourds, wooden plates, and plaques, the wooden items were made in one town (presumably by men, the wood workers) and the finished product was made in Uruapan. There men cut out the incised designs and women completed the painting and lacquer finish (Lumholtz 1973, 2:444–445). In the Sierra Madre Occidental among the sub-mesoamerican Huichol and Tepehuan pottery was made by women, sometimes aided by men.

13. The putative Mercado Red-on-cream sherds from Casas Grandes represent a misidentification on my part (first two sherds); Di Peso was later informed that these sherds were not Mercado; unfortunately that section of the report was already in press.

References Cited

Beals, Ralph L.
  1932 *The Comparative Ethnology of Northern Mexico Before 1750.* Ibero-Americana No. 2. Berkeley.
  1933 *The Acaxee, A Mountain Tribe of Durango and Sinaloa.* Ibero-Americana No. 6. Berkeley.
Bell, Betty B.
  1960 *Analysis of Ceramic Style: A West Mexican Collection.* Unpublished Ph.D. dissertation, Department of Anthropology, University of California, Los Angeles.
  1971 Archaeology of Nayarit, Jalisco, and Colima. In *The Archaeology of Northern Mesoamerica, Part 2,* edited by Gordon F. Ekholm and Ignacio Bernal, pp. 694–753. Handbook of Middle American Indians, vol. 11, Robert Wauchope, general editor. University of Texas Press, Austin.
Bordaz, Jacques
  1964 *Pre-Columbian Ceramic Kilns at Peñitas, A Post-Classic Site in Coastal Nayarit, Mexico.* Unpublished Ph.D. dissertation, Department of Anthropology, Columbia University, New York.

Crane, Eugene R., and Reginald C. Reindorp (translators and editors)
  1970 *The Chronicles of Michoacan*. University of Oklahoma Press, Norman.
Dibble, Charles E., and Arthur J. O. Anderson (translators)
  1961 *Florentine Codex: General History of the Things of New Spain by Fray Bernardino de Sahagún*, Book 10: The People. Monographs of the School of American Research and the Museum of New Mexico, No. 14, pt 11.
Di Peso, Charles C.
  1974 *Casas Grandes: A Fallen Trading Center of the Gran Chichimeca*, vols. 1–3. Amerind Foundation Series No. 9. Dragoon, Ariz.
Ekholm, Gordon F.
  1939 Results of an Archaelogical Survey of Sonora and Northern Sinaloa. *Revista Mexicana de Estudios Antropologicas* 3(1):7–10.
  1942 *Excavations at Guasave, Sinaloa, Mexico*. Anthropological Papers of the American Museum of Natural History No. 38(2).
Fahmel B., Bernd
  1981 *Dos Vajillas Toltecas de Comercio: Tohil Plumbate y Fine Orange*. Tesis professionál, Escuela Nacional de Antroplogía e Historia, Mexico, D. F.
Foster, Michael S.
  1978 *Loma San Gabriel: A Prehistoric Culture of Northwest Mexico*. Unpublished Ph.D. dissertation, Department of Anthropology, University of Colorado, Boulder.
  1980 *Loma San Gabriel: Una Cultura del Noroeste de Mesoamerica*. *Rutas de Intercambio en Mesoamerica y Norte de México* 2:175–182. XVI Mesa Redonda de Sociedad Mexicana de Antropología, Saltillo.
Ganot R., Jaime, Jesus F. Lazalde, and Alejandro Peschard F.
  1983 Relacíon Prehispanica Entre las Culturas del Noroeste de México y el Sitio Arqueologico El Cañón del Molino en el Estado de Durango. Paper presented at the XVIII Mesa Redonda of the Sociedad Mexicana de Antropología, Taxco.
Gifford, E. W.
  1950 *Surface Archaeology of Ixtlán del Río, Nayarit*. University of California Publications in American Archaeology and Ethnology No. 43(2). Berkeley.
Gill, George W.
  1974 Toltec-Period Burial Customs Within the Marismas Nacionales of Western Mexico. In *The Archaeology of West Mexico*, edited by Betty Bell, pp. 83–105. Sociedad de Estudios Avanzados del Occidente de Mexico, A.C. Guadalajara.
Glassow, Michael A.
  1967 The Ceramics of Huistla, A West Mexican Site in the Municipality of Etzatlan, Jalisco. *American Antiquity* 32:64–83.

Hedrick, Basil C., J. Charles Kelley, and Carroll L. Riley (editors)
  1971 *The North Mexican Frontier: Readings in Archaeology, Ethnology, and Ethnography*. Southern Illinois University Press, Carbondale.
Howard, Agnes M.
  1957 Navacoyan: A Preliminary Survey. *Bulletin of the Texas Archaeological Society* 28:181–189.
Kelley, J. Charles
  1971 Archaeology of the Northern Frontier: Zacateca and Durango. In *The Archaeology of Northern Mesoamerica, Part 2*, edited by Gordon F. Ekholm and Ignacio Bernal, pp. 768–801. Handbook of Middle American Indians, vol. 11, Robert Wauchope, general editor. University of Texas Press, Austin.
  1980 Discussion of Papers by Plog, Doyel, and Riley. In *Current Issues in Hohokam Prehistory*, edited by David E. Doyel and Fred Plog, pp. 49–71. Arizona State University Anthropological Research Paper No. 23. Tempe.
  1983 Hypothetical Functioning of the Major Post-Classic Trade System of West and Northwest Mexico. Paper presented at the XVIII Mesa Redonda of the Sociedad Mexicana de Antropología, Taxco.
Kelley, J. Charles, and Ellen Abbott
  1966 The Cultural Sequence on the North Central Frontier of Mesoamerica. *XXXVI Congreso Internacional de Americanistas, España, 1964, Actas y Memorias* 1:325–344. Seville.
Kelley, J. Charles, and Ellen Abbott Kelley
  1971 *An Introduction to the Ceramics of the Chalchihuites Culture of Zacatecas and Durango, Mexico. Part 1: The Decorated Wares*. Mesoamerican Studies No. 5, Research Records of the University Museum, Southern Illinois University at Carbondale.
Kelley, J. Charles, and Howard D. Winters
  1960 A Revision of the Archaeological Sequence in Sinaloa, Mexico. *American Antiquity* 25:547–561.
Kelly, Isabel T.
  1938 Excavation at Chametla, Sinaloa. *Ibero-Americana No. 14*. Berkeley.
  1939 An Archaeological Reconnaissance of the West Coast: Nayarit to Michoacan. *International Congress of Americanists* 2:74–77.
  1945 Excavations at Culiacán, Sinaloa. *Ibero-Americana No.25*. Berkeley.
Kidder, Alfred V., Jesse D. Jennings, and Edwin M. Shook
  1977 *Excavations at Kaminaljuyú, Guatemala*. The Pennsylvania State University Press, University Park.
Lazalde, Jesus F., Alejandro Peschard F., and Jaime Ganot R.
  1983 *Art Rupestre del Valle de Guatimapé, Durango*. Documentos Sobre Rocas, Durango.
LeBlanc, Steven A.

1980 The Dating of Casas Grandes. *American Antiquity* 45:799–806.
Lister, Robert H.
1949 *Excavations at Cojumatlán, Michoacan, Mexico.* University of New Mexico Publications in Anthropology No. 5, Albuquerque.
Lumholtz, Carl
1973 *Unknown Mexico.* The Rio Grande Press, Glorieta, New Mexico. Originally published 1902.
McGuire, Randall H.
1980 The Mesoamerican Connection in the Southwest. *Kiva* 46(1–2): 3–38.
Mason, J. Alden
1937 Late Archaeological Sites in Durango, Mexico, from Chalchihuites to Zape. *Twenty-fifth Anniversary Studies, Publications of the Philadelphia Anthropological Society* 1:117–126.
Meighan, Clement W.
1959 New Findings in West Mexican Archaeology. *Kiva* 25(1):1–7.
1971 Archaeology of Sinaloa. In *The Archaeology of Northern Mesoamerica, Part 2*, edited by Gordon F. Ekholm and Ignacio Bernal, pp. 754–767. Handbook of Middle American Indians, vol. 11, Robert Wauchope, general editor. University of Texas Press, Austin.
Meighan, Clement W. (editor)
1976 *The Archaeology of Amapa, Nayarit.* Monumenta Archaeologica No. 2. Institute of Archaeology, The University of California, Los Angeles.
Meighan, Clement W., and Leonard J. Foote
1968 *Excavations at Tizapan El Alto, Jalisco.* Latin American Studies No. 11. Latin American Center, University of California, Los Angeles.
Michels, Joseph W.
1979 *The Kaminaljuyú Chiefdom.* Pennsylvania State University Press, University Park.
Mountjoy, Joseph B.
1970a *Prehispanic Culture History and Culture Contact on the Southern Coast of Nayarit, Mexico.* Unpublished Ph.D. dissertation, Department of Anthropology, Southern Illinois University at Carbondale.
1970b *La Succession Cultural en San Blas.* INAH Boletin No. 39. Instituto Nacionál de Antropología e Historia, Mexico.
1974 San Blas Complex Ecology. In *The Archaeology of West Mexico*, edited by Betty Bell, pp. 106–119. Sociedad de Estudios Avanzados del Occidente de México, A. C., Guadalajara.
Obregón, Baltesar de
1924 *Historia de los Descubrimientos Antiquos y Modernos de la Nueve España, Escrito por el Conquistadór Baltesár de Obregón, Año de 1584.* Secretaría de Educación Publica, Mexico.
Parsons, Lee A., and Barbara J. Price
1971 Mesoamerican Trade and Its Role in the Emergence of Civilization in Mesoamerica. In *Observations on the Emergence of Civilization in*

Mesoamerica, edited by Robert F. Heizer and John A. Graham, pp. 165–195. Contributions of the University of California Archaelogical Research Facility No. 11. Berkeley.

Peschard F., Alejandro
1983 Restos Óseos del Cañón del Molino, Durango. Paper presented at the XVIII Mesa Redonda of the Sociedad Mexicana de Antropología, Taxco. Riley, Carroll L., and Howard D. Winters
1963 The Prehistoric Tepehuan of Northern Mexico. *Southwestern Journal of Anthropology* 19(2):177–185.

Sanders, William T., and Joseph W. Michels (editors)
1977 *Teotihuacan and Kaminaljuyú: A Study in Prehistoric Culture Contact.* Pennsylvania State University Press, University Park.

Sanders, William T., and Barbara J. Price
1968 *Mesoamerica: The Evolution of a Civilization.* Random House, New York.

Sauer, Carl
1932 *The Road to Cibola.* Ibero-Americana No. 3. Berkeley.

Sauer, Carl, and Donald Brand
1932 *Aztatlán: Prehistoric Mexican Frontier on the Pacific Coast.* Ibero-Americana No. 1. Berkeley.

Scott, Stuart D.
1974 Archaeology and the Estuary: Researching Prehistory and Paleo-ecology in the Marismas Nacionales, West Mexico. In *The Archaeology of West Mexico*, edited by Betty Bell, pp. 51–56. Sociedad de Estudios Avanzados del Occidente de México, A. C., Guadalajara.

Séjourné, Laurette
1970 *Arquelogía del Valle de México, vol. 1. Culhuacán.* Instituto Nacional de Antropología e Historia. Mexico, D.F.

Sweetman, Rosemary
1974 Prehistoric Pottery from Coastal Sinaloa and Nayarit. In *The Archaeology of West Mexico*, edited by Betty Bell, pp. 68–82. Sociedad de Estudios Avanzados del Occidente de México, A. C., Guadalajara.

Weigand, Phil C.
1976 Circular Ceremonial Structure Complexes in the Highlands of Western Mexico. In *Archaeological Frontiers: Papers on New World High Culture in Honor of J. Charles Kelley*, edited by Robert B. Pickering, pp. 183–227. University Museum Studies, Research Records No. 4. Southern Illinois University at Carbondale.
1977 Rio Grande Glaze Sherds in Western Mexico. *Pottery Southwest* 4(1):3. Albuquerque.
1978 La Prehistoria del Estado de Zacatecas: Una Interpretacíon. In *Zacatecas. Anuario de Historia*, pp. 203–248. Universidad Autonoma de Zacatecas.
1979 The Formative-Classic and Classic-Postclassic Transitions in the Teuchitlán-Etzatlán Zone of Jalisco. *Los Procesos de Cambio* 1:413–

423. XV Mesa Redonda de la Sociedad Mexicana de Antropología, Guanajuato.

Wilcox, David R., and Charles Sternberg

1983 *Hohokam Ballcourts and Their Interpretation.* Archaeological Series No. 160, Cultural Resource Management Division, Arizona State Museum, University of Arizona, Tucson.

7

Aspects of Southwestern Prehistory: A.D. 900–1400

Steven A. LeBlanc

Information accumulated in the last decade points to the existence of more complex prehistoric societies in the Southwest than previously recognized. Moreover, these complex organizations had considerably more impact on southwestern prehistory than has been suspected. There are some generalizations that can tentatively be made about the development, duration, and collapse of these complex organizations. The purpose of this paper is to discuss their development and impact in a general way. By necessity, the full documentation for such a discussion cannot be presented here. Equally important, when we try to model what happened prehistorically we cannot rely only on what is already demonstrated, but we must utilize expectations about what will be found. Of course, we must differentiate the "known" from the expected.

The thrust of the present argument is that various forms of complex society existed in the Southwest from circa A.D. 900 to 1400. Each of these organizations or systems consisted of populations that were sociopolitically linked at a more complex level than for the Southwest in general and are best considered as "chiefdoms" (Service 1962) or ranked societies, in contrast to the more prevalent "tribal" level of organization. In each of these cases, one can see evidence for a greater level of sociopolitical integration, and by inference less political autonomy, than the southwestern norm; hence, Altshul's (1978) "interaction sphere" seems to be a useful term by which to describe these phenomena.

There were three such interaction spheres in the prehistoric Southwest. There was probably only one in existence at any given time, with the three succeeding each other sequentially. The areas encompassed by each of these interaction spheres were large, about eighty thousand square kilometers, and they had considerable impact on the populations of their respective areas even after their demise. The three interaction spheres are the Chaco, the Casas Grandes and the Classic Hohokam.

In the past archaeologists have seen local southwestern areas in too much isolation, and the role of sociopolitical behavior has been too little considered, especially at the expense of environmental explanations of change. This type of error seems to be inherent in our work because it is easier to "see" or recover information on environmental change than it is to recover sociopolitical behavior.

A good case in point is the recently rediscovered system of Chaco roads (Obenauf 1980). As recently as 10 years ago only a few sites, such as Aztec (Morris 1919), Lowry (Martin 1936), and Village of the Great Kivas (Roberts 1932), had been perceived as being related to Chaco. While the similarity in architecture between these sites and those in the canyon had been recognized, the degree of political interrelatedness had not. Recently, roads have been found linking such outlying communities to Chaco. Even though there are other features of these sites that imply political integration, it has really been the roads that have forced the recognition of such integration on us. Even though a case could be made for a Chaco "system" prior to the rediscovery of the roads, it was not made. This case should remind us how hard it is to recognize, much less demonstrate, political integration in the Southwest.

The Cultural Baseline

The period between A.D. 700–900 provides a good baseline from which to contrast later events in the Southwest. The largest sites at this time ranged in size from perhaps 80 household structures at Snaketown (Wilcox et al. 1981) to 35–40 households at Galaz, one of the largest Mogollon sites (Anyon and LeBlanc 1984). Generally, larger sites were located adjacent to well-watered flood plains and smaller sites were in less productive areas. Except for the Hohokam, there is no evidence for irrigation at this time or any other agricultural intensification, although most groups seem to have been dependent on agriculture.

Cultural boundaries existed at several levels. The three major cultural divisions—Anasazi, Mogollon, and Hohokam—do seem to represent real cultural phenomena, not simply archaeological constructs. Within each of these three broad taxa there were regional variants (the taxonomic branches). Obviously at some level they represent ethnic, linguistic, and adaptive differences. It is almost inconceivable that there was any political integration between these three main taxa and almost as unlikely that there was political integration between the branches during this time interval (this does not imply that there was integration within branches).

Warfare, as evidenced by sites with a defensive posture, was extremely limited during the A.D. 700–900 interval. That is, few sites were situated in inaccessible locations; few sites had palisades; and few were built with high exterior walls. While the presence of such features does not automatically demonstrate the presence of warfare, their absence, especially in contrast to periods during which architecture had such features, argues for relatively less warfare. Trade seems to have been, for the most part, sparse with no controlling centers. With the exception of the Hohokam, craft specialization was at best rare. Social organization must have been exogamous. This argument is based on the fact that even the biggest sites were too small to be biologically self-sufficient (Wobst 1974). There is virtually no evidence for ranked individuals in terms of house size or burial practices (Lightfoot and Feinman 1982, not withstanding), implying rather egalitarian behavior.

Although some population growth rates have been proposed or implied for various areas, such as those by Zubrow (1971) and Hayes (1981), most rates are for areas too small to give us an idea about regional intrinsic growth. We can, however, use likely growth rates as a means of evaluating some aspects of cultural behavior. Based on the arguments of Cowgill (1975) and Hassan (1981), reasonable rates of intrinsic growth probably did not exceed 0.1%–0.3% annually for the time scales we are considering. Maximal upper limits most likely did not exceed 0.7%. A rate of 0.1%–0.3% is equivalent to population doubling every 230–700 years. It is hard to see how, with these rates of growth, population pressure could have been the driving force behind the events that followed.

Sites—or closely proximic sites considered communities in the sense used by Marshall et al. (1979), Powers et al. (1983), or Watson et al. (1980)—can be characterized as unplanned or minimally planned, with "public works" or corporate labor efforts restricted to great kivas in the Mogollon and Anasazi areas. There seems to have been slightly more village planning and corporate efforts in the Hohokam area, beginning with the production of platform mounds, ballcourts, and canals (Wilcox et al. 1981; Wilcox and Sternberg 1983). Impressionistically, the Hohokam had greater population densities and more trade than the rest of the Southwest at this time.

At about A.D. 900 a series of events radically restructured the Southwest. These changes revolve around the three interaction spheres mentioned above—Chaco, Casas Grandes, and the Classic Hohokam. The first two, the Chaco and Casas Grandes interaction spheres, seem quite similar at the structural level. The third, the Classic Hohokam, is more unique. This paper presents the the argument that all Southwest prehistory from A.D. 900 on must be considered in the context of these phenomena regardless of whether a particular area was or was not within any of these interaction spheres. Each of these three interaction spheres will be discussed separately: then generalizations about them will be made.

The Chaco Interaction Sphere

The Chaco interaction sphere is by far the best understood of the three, and several aspects can be discerned. It appears that this interaction sphere was dominated by a ranked or chiefdom level society in contrast to the previous more egalitarian societies in the area. The interaction sphere, which was much larger than has previously been recognized, came to an abrupt end about A.D. 1130—1140.

Chaco Communities

By current perception, the interaction sphere included the big towns and small villages in the canyon (Hayes 1981), as well as at least 40 and probably 80 or more outlying communities (Marshall et al. 1979; Powers et al. 1983). These latter communities, now generally referred to as "outliers," had a series of distinctive features, although not all were necessarily present at any given site. There was always a "big house" or "great house," which was a multistoried structure, usually with thin tabular sandstone masonry and core and veneer construction. This was in contrast to construction where large blocks were used, common in the late 1200s.

Chaco big houses had several distinctive features. For example, rooms were atypically large for the region, averaging about 40 percent larger than village rooms (Powers et al. 1983). This aspect is complex, however, as the larger the big house the larger the average room, and there were some very small cellular rooms in big houses which lower the average room size. Almost invariably, Chaco big houses had a distinctive shape; they faced to the south or east, and their back was multistoried while the front row of rooms was not. This gave them a tiered effect, and they frequently enclosed a courtyard on the low front side. The orientation and shape of Chaco big houses contrasted to multistoried structures in the Anasazi area dating to A.D. 1250—1300, which tend to be hollow centered with central plazas.

Some Chaco big houses also had "tower kivas" (e.g., Salmon Ruin, Chetro Ketl, La Ventana, and Lowry). These were large cylindrical rooms, several stories high, usually situated in the back row of the big house. The smallest big houses were sometimes referred to as McElmo style units, and these tend to be high on all sides and dominated by a circular "kiva" feature. It is interesting to note that the central or tower kiva portions of big sites like Salmon Ruin were configured very much like these smaller "McElmo" houses. Also distinctive were kivas (generally rather large) inside the room areas of the big houses. That is, these blocked-in kivas were not in front of the house but were integral parts of the structure. On occasion they were symmetrically placed and in some cases comprised a large portion of the total floor area of the big house.

Great kivas were another, almost universal, part of a Chaco outlier group. The term *great kiva* has various usages, some of which are too broad. In the Anasazi area prior to A.D. 1000 great kivas were generally 13 m in diameter or larger. These were slab-lined and had no formal ramp or stair entranceway. After A.D. 1000, great kivas were masonry-walled, usually had a bench, and often had standard features such as four central roof supports and a raised fire box. They frequently had a stair or stepped entranceway. All, or almost all, of the masonry-lined great kivas known archaeologically in the Anasazi area are associated with Chaco big houses. There are no known

examples of kivas with diameters of 13 m or larger that date to or are associated with sites that definitely post-date A.D. 1130. Many great kivas are on
sites that have a post-A.D. 1130 component, but in all such cases there is a
pre-A.D. 1130 component as well. Big kivas that definitely post-date A.D.
1130, such as Atsinna and Mirabal (Watson et al. 1980), are only in the 6–9
m diameter range. Thus, definitions such as that of Martin and Plog (1973)
which define great kivas as being at least 9 m in diameter combine two distinct phenomena. For present purposes, "great kiva" refers to kivas with
diameters in the 13 m or greater range and "Chaco great kivas" to the
masonry-walled versions.

Only a few of the largest Chaco sites had great kivas located in the
courtyards of the big houses; otherwise, the great kivas were separated, generally by about one hundred meters, but sometimes more, from the big house.
A far less common feature of these sites was the triwalled or biwalled structure. These existed only in Chaco Canyon and in a few sites to the north. They
were so rare that they may not be an important Chaco feature.

The two remaining aspects of Chaco outliers are hard to characterize
because of the state of our knowledge. Many, if not most, Chaco big houses
and great kivas were imbedded in communities of considerable size. These
communities consisted of many small roomblocks, either of jacal or masonry, but always single-storied and rarely over 30 rooms; the roomblocks
averaged about 10 rooms. Examples where good surveys have been conducted range from 13 to 34 units. This very important aspect of the outliers
is hard to deal with because in many cases no survey has been conducted
around big houses or, if so, the surveys are incomplete. Thus the size and
frequency of communities around big houses are poorly known. Also, we
have little idea about the numbers and the size of communities within the
Chaco sphere that were not actual outlier communities and did not contain
big houses or great kivas. This lack of knowledge is probably the biggest
limitation in modeling the nature of the Chaco interaction sphere. Some, but
apparently not all, of the outlier communities were in existence before
A.D. 1000. Several have early slab-lined great kivas within the communities.
Did the process of agglomeration into communities of many roomblocks begin much before the development of formal outliers? At the peak of the Chaco
interaction sphere, was most of the population within the sphere in these
outlier communities? Such critical questions are presently unanswerable.

The final aspect of the outliers to be considered is the roads (Kincaid
1983; Obenauf 1980). When a potential outlier is seen as being connected
by a road to the rest of the system, it has been assumed that it is a Chaco
outlier. As noted, these roads are only recently rediscovered and, in fact,
segments are being located so frequently that there is no currently comprehensive listing of them. The roads are exceptionally straight and undoubtedly required considerable effort to build. They seem to radiate from Chaco
Canyon in a dendritic fashion and do not seem to link outliers in an overall
lattice. In some instances there are two or more parallel or almost parallel

segments separated by only a few hundred meters. It is rather difficult to view these roads as primarily of economic concern considering their straightness and elaborate curbings. While they may have served an economic role in facilitating travel, they must also have served a sociopolitical function. Physically, they demonstrate that the communities were sociopolitically linked.

The biggest limitation to studying the roads is that they are difficult to detect. In some instances repeated ground searches and aerial photography have failed to detect them, only to have additional photography clearly reveal them. When this limitation is combined with the fact that no systematic search for roads has ever been undertaken, our data is really too limited to model the road system. In particular, little effort has been made to look for roads outside the general area of the central San Juan Basin. Published maps (e.g., Kincaid 1983) show roads extending some 100 km from the canyon. Suspected roads exist, however, near the Lowry and Goodman Point ruins in Colorado and at the Manuelito Canyon outlier and Cox Ranch Pueblo near Zuni Salt Lake in New Mexico. The furthest of these are about 180 km and 165 km north and south from the canyon proper. Thus, it seems the full extent of the system is not presently recognized.

Dating

The dating of the Chaco interaction sphere is surrounded by a considerable amount of confusion. This is not because there are no well-patterned dates, but because of differences in terminology and what is being discussed. The difficulty actually began with the original Pecos classification. While the orginal scheme was seen as developmental (and to some degree temporal), it was in fact classificatory. Chaco big houses were termed Pueblo III because they were big and multistoried. Thus they were conceptually combined with other big multistoried sites of the A.D. 1250–1300 span that, as it is now seen, are not temporally close nor developmentally equivalent.

Another terminological difficulty with the Chaco sequence is the use of the Bonito and Hosta Butte phases. They initially served a useful, descriptive function, but now we recognize that the two phases are contemporaneous and, in fact, represent different kinds of structures in the same community (the Bonito phase is characterized by the big house, the Hosta Butte phase is characterized by a smaller single-storied structure). This usage of the term *phase* is so at odds with general usage that it only results in confusion. The difficulty with the current terminology becomes clear when we consider the dating of the Chaco interaction sphere.

Construction of at least three big houses in the canyon began in the A.D. 900s (Judge et al. 1981), and possibly at some outliers as well. Major widespread construction began in the A.D. 1000s, much apparently after A.D. 1050 (Powers et al. 1983). Judge (1983) argues that most of the early outliers were south of the canyon, but it would appear that this conclusion is premature. If slab-lined great kivas are early in the Chaco sequence, then their presence in a Chacoan community implies the community is early. Such slab-lined great kivas are found north as well as south of the canyon. Judge fails to take these northerly sites into consideration because most fall outside his narrow interpretation of the Chaco sphere.

The dating of the end of construction of Chaco big houses is clearer than the beginning. Some tree-ring dates are available for 27 definite or possible outliers. The latest construction dates are A.D. 1132 from Pueblo Alto (with the possibility of some early A.D. 1140 dates from Bis sa'ani (Breternitz et al. 1982). Thus there is little doubt that construction of Chaco big houses virtually ceased in the interval A.D. 1130–1140. The latest use of big houses is far more nebulous. There is clear reoccupation of many big houses in the late 1200s, and there is evidence for continued use well into the late A.D. 1100s. Therefore, there may not be a time during the 150 years after A.D. 1130 when there was absolutely no use of some big houses. After A.D. 1140, however, use seems to have been only in portions of big houses; rooms are subdivided and new construction is sparse and of poor quality.

The more interesting question is whether A.D. 1130–1140 represents a major behavioral or processual change or simply the end of construction. It is argued here that it represents the end of Chaco as an interaction sphere and is one of the most critical dates in southwestern prehistory. Almost all of the sites with more than a handful of dates have some that are in the early 1100s. Therefore it appears that construction activity was almost universal in the early 1100s. It seems unlikely that construction stopped so abruptly without a major cultural restructuring; moreover, at La Ventana (Marshall et al. 1979) the great kiva was never completed, which is more in keeping with an abrupt social change than continued use of these sites for many years after all big house construction ceased. After A.D. 1130 use seems to represent far fewer people than before and, in some cases, it is almost as if people were "camping out" in virtually abandoned structures. All evidence points to a rapid and sudden collapse of the Chaco system. This was not accompanied by complete abandonment of the entire region, as there is some evidence of later occupation in and around the canyon and the outliers. The termination of the system and the late use of some buildings and areas are distinct phenomena and need to be kept conceptually separate.

Two more factors need to be considered. One is the apparent dates of unexcavated Chaco outliers. As noted, many if not most outliers seem to have been reoccupied in the A.D. 1200s. Rooms were frequently subdivided into smaller ones; kivas were built in old rooms or tower kivas remodeled into regular kivas. This activity almost invariably left an overlay of late Pueblo III ceramics on these sites, so that in the field one encounters a multi-storied structure with late Pueblo III sherds. Therefore, the initial survey report on most outliers describes them as late Pueblo III. Upon excavation or closer scrutiny, these sites invariably turn out not to be late Pueblo III, but to have construction dates between A.D. 1000 and 1130.

This problem exists because of a failure to realize that there were basically only two periods during which multistoried structures were built (in the area encompassed by the Chaco interaction sphere). One period was the time of the Chaco interaction sphere (A.D. 900-1130) and the other was after A.D. 1240. There was no continuum of building multistoried structures between these periods, but a real gap. Assigning a multistoried structure to Pueblo III does not clarify to which of these periods it belongs.

If one accepts the above propositions, the terminological problem becomes apparent. If one uses Pueblo III to equate with the time period A.D. 1050–1300, then one combines the latest part of the Chaco interaction sphere with the developments of the A.D. 1250–1300s, which were processually different. The use of A.D. 1100–1300 for Pueblo III does not solve the problem. The obvious solution is to abandon the Pecos classification and use actual temporal spans. If that is not realistic, and it probably is not, then the Pueblo II-Pueblo III division must be at A.D. 1130, as any other division point combines part of the span of the Chaco interaction sphere with the post-interaction sphere, leading to conceptual confusion. Regardless of what they are called, temporal divisions based on apparent processual changes would include: (1) early Chaco interaction sphere, early A.D. 900s to 1050; (2) late Chaco interaction sphere, A.D. 1050 to 1130; (3) initial post-Chaco collapse, A.D. 1130 to 1240; and (4) a period of population aggregation, A.D. 1240 to 1300. At a more general level, the first two periods can be combined into a Chaco interaction sphere period and the last two periods into a post-Chaco but pre-abandonment period.

Development and Dynamics

Having briefly described some characteristics of the Chaco interaction sphere and its temporal span, aspects of its development and dynamics can be considered. Sometime in the early A.D. 900s at least three Chaco towns were founded (Judge et al. 1981). They were radically different from any prior settlements in the region. They were large, planned, multistoried, and had large rooms. This period probably marks the beginning of a new level of organization in the canyon, but it is not clear whether it had a major effect outside the canyon proper. While many of the outliers were built in areas with preexisting communities, there are no convincing dates from outlying big houses before the A.D. 1000s, although Lowry and Guadalupe ruins may be such examples (see Powers et al. 1983, for a discussion of the developmental sequence of outliers). Apparently it was not until the early 1000s that there was a substantial spread of the Chaco sites. A subsequent burst of activity beginning about A.D. 1080 expanded the extent of the system and possibly added sites between existing ones. It is hard at this point to describe the development of the system; its maximal state can be more usefully considered.

Based on the previous discussion of what constitutes an outlier, the system ultimately extended about 185 km (115 mi) north, at least 130 km (80 mi) and possibly 195 km (120 mi) to the west, and at least 165 km (100 mi) and possibly 240 km (150 mi) to the south. Its extent to the east, of only 80 km (50 mi), is truncated compared to other directions. The current "farthest out" outliers include Chimney Rock, Escalante, and Cahone ruins in Colorado, and possibly the Montezuma Canyon Group in Utah. In Arizona the furthest west outliers are White House, Kinlechee, and Allantown, but there is the possibility of one near Holbrook and one near Lindon (Hough 1907), and the Forestdale Ruin also has some of the characteristics of an outlier. In general the situation is poorly understood in the south. La Ventana and Village of the Great Kivas are recognized as outliers, but there are also at least three possible outliers on the Zuni Reservation (Anyon, personal communication, 1983). Further south, Cox Ranch pueblo is now considered an outlier and has a road segment. The site complex sometimes referred to as the Dittert site (Site LV:4:14, Dittert 1959), some 30 km south of La Ventana, has a road and possibly represents the remains of an outlier. A bulldozed site near old Fort Tularosa on the San Francisco River was described as three stories high with cored masonry in roomblock kivas; it had a ceramic assemblage of the right time span. There is also reputed to be a nearby great kiva; the site is the farthest south candidate for an outlier.

These extensions of the perceived area of the interaction sphere significantly increase the area involved. In the south we have an area of about twenty thousand square kilometers that has never been seriously considered to contain outliers, yet has a good dozen possible outlier candidates. This is comparable to the area north of the New Mexico state line of 10,000 km^2 which is known to contain outliers but has never been conceptually integrated into models of Chaco, as is an area of some fifteen thousand square kilometers in Arizona. In particular, such an areal extent in Colorado would include the sites of Yellowjacket, Goodman Point, and Cahone, and there are sure to be other outliers between these and the San Juan and La Plata river outliers in northern New Mexico, such as Morris's site 33 (Morris 1939). Thus the usually conceptualized area of the Chaco interaction sphere, that of the central San Juan Basin, is about forty thousand square kilometers, yet an excellent case can be made that it encompassed over eighty thousand square kilometers. If this larger area is, in fact, correct, then most proposed models of the system are in considerable error (e.g., Tainter and Gillio 1980).

A most unexpected consequence of this distribution of Chaco outlier communities is that much of the Cibola or Reserve branch was included in the Chaco interaction sphere. There has been a long held feeling, as noted in ceramics (Reserve Black-on-white) and architecture, that there was a major Anasazi influence over this area, which was previously Mogollon. This Anasazi influence seems to begin about A.D. 1000 and is possibly explanable by the presence of the Chaco outliers. Demonstrating the presence of outliers, however, does not explicate the processes involved in the Reserve area or elsewhere. The unanswered question is, what was the nature of relationships within the interaction sphere? Was the entire region's population integrated around outlying communities? Or were there, in the areas between outliers, sites which remained politically autonomous? What was the nature of the political integration in the interaction sphere as a whole? It seems believable that some outliers served as outposts, conducting trade but otherwise not affecting the population removed from the outlier community itself. Some realistic models that can be tested are badly needed concerning the nature of political integration over the interaction sphere in general.

A strong case can be made that the overall system falls within a ranked society or a chiefdom (Service 1962). A full discussion of this topic is far beyond the present scope (see Schelberg 1982 for a review of some of the evidence and arguments). Briefly, the presence of corporate architecture in the form of big houses, canals, and roads, and the sumptuary nature of some of the construction are what we would expect for chiefdom level organization and not tribal society. Moreover, the absolute number of people living in close proximity (at least a few thousand according to Hayes 1981) in the canyon is also of the magnitude associated with chiefdoms. There seems to be evidence for craft specialists in terms of turquoise artifact production, ceramics, and architecture. The big houses can be seen as differential architecture for elites. Finally, there are good candidates for status or elite burials, both in terms of the grave goods placed with them and the preparation of crypts.

Inferences can be drawn about the population that comprised the Chaco interaction sphere. If we take A.D. 900 as a base year and assume a 0.3 percent growth rate (near the upper realistic limit), by A.D. 1130 the population could have at most been 2.3 times the A.D. 900 population level. By the big expansion period of A.D. 1080, it could have increased only 1.7 times over the A.D. 900 level. If the average outlying community contained 200 people (a conservative figure) and there were 60 such communities (also conservative) then there were at least 12,000 people resident in the outliers. Population estimates for the canyon vary considerably, ranging from 2,000 to 10,000 at its peak (Windes 1985). Therefore the majority, if not the bulk, of the population of the Chaco sphere lived outside the canyon.

Hayes (1981) provides relative population numbers for the canyon proper which imply population increases in excess of a 0.3 percent annual rate. These figures suggest that the canyon was more likely a recipient of immigration than an exporter of people. Looked at another way, even if there were 3,000 residents in the canyon at A.D. 1000, and all the subsequent population increase emigrated, these people could have represented less than 2,000 of the minimum 12,000 people in the outlying communities. Thus, the suggestion of Vivian (1983) that outliers are the result of excess population emigrating from the canyon can be rejected.

Most of the inhabitants of outlier communities must have represented primarily local populations and not emigrants from the canyon. If such local population comprised most of the inhabitants of Chacoan outlier communities, then even though they may have adopted some "Chacoan" traits they would appear broadly similar to the ancestral pre-Chacoan population and would not appear as a homogeneous group over the entire interaction sphere. Thus, it will always be easy to contend that an interaction sphere did not exist, except in some form of copying or influence. In reality, the continuity of local traditional traits is by no means incompatible with a model of regional integration. Of course such local variability does make it more difficult to demonstrate the model.

Given that there was a politically integrated interaction sphere with a chiefdom level of organization, what mechanisms might have lead to its development? What would have induced the outlying population to become participants. Three possible scenarios exist: (1) economic advantage—it may have been advantageous to become part of the system in spite of the increased effort required as a result of supporting the public works and an elite; (2) religious or messianic appeal—just as Chavin, Olmec, and Hopewell all seem to have cult aspects and all integrated previously diverse peoples, so a similar process may have occurred in the Chaco; (3) military force—groups could have been brought into the sphere by the threat of, or actual, force. There is evidence of sites beyond the edge of the canyon system in the Gallinas, the Flagstaff, and the Black Mesa areas for a defensive posture at this time, and some extreme edge outliers such as Chimney Rock and Escalante also look defensively located. Also, one can see the straight roads as being more useful in moving people rapidly (militarily useful) than for the efficient movement of goods. The Chaco sphere could have raided groups outside the sphere for slaves, thereby accounting for the defensive sites around the margin. The case for military force, however, is presently weak.

While a messianic or military explanation may seem farfetched at present, we must remember that many researchers do not even believe in the interaction sphere at all. A case can be made for a variety of developmental scenarios and few can obviously be rejected; thus we must keep an open mind and be prepared for the unexpected.

According to the chronology discussed above, big house construction came to an abrupt end by A.D. 1130. There were few dated structures of any type in the region during the next hundred years (until A.D. 1240) and no large multistoried structures. Those sites that did exist were small and exhibit evidence of being unplanned. Many of the Chaco communities continued to be occupied but without major new construction. Great kivas, as defined above, ceased to be built. In all, it appears that the Chaco interaction sphere, as a political or social organization, ceased abruptly and a retrograde period followed. It can be compared to a dark age during which the general level of integration and interaction was low. Only in late Pueblo III (A.D. 1240–1300) do we again see population aggregation and any semblance of planning in community design, which suggests a resurgence of cultural integration.

The Casas Grandes Interaction Sphere

In all probability the Casas Grandes interaction sphere was every bit as extensive as the Chaco interaction sphere. As to its extent, the nature of its communities, its dates, our information is considerably poorer; therefore, the discussion must be more brief. There seem to be broad similarities between Chaco and Casas Grandes. Each had a definite center, major outlying communities, chiefdom level organization, and sociopolitical integration over a large area that was not previously integrated.

The Casas Grandes interaction included parts of the former San Simon and Mimbres branches of the Mogollon and all of the former Viejo period area of northern Chihuahua (which was clearly another Mogollon branch). It probably also included part of the Jornada area. Unfortunately, we know little of the extent of the Casas Grandes system to the west, east, or south. It seems to have extended into Sonora on the west and to the mouth of the Conchos on the east. On the north it extended some 250 km (150 mi) from Casas Grandes. If this degree of extent occurred in other directions, then the interaction sphere would have encompassed almost two hundred thousand square kilometers. As it is unlikely it had such an extent in all directions, an overall extent of about a hundred thousand square kilometers, or an extent similar to the Chaco system, is likely.

Prior to the development of the Casas Grandes interaction sphere, the area had several distinctive local traditions. The ceramics in the four areas mentioned above—San Simon, Mimbres, northern Chihuahua, and Jornada—were distinctive, as were some architectural characteristics. In general, the populations were living in pithouses or single-storied pueblos, usually built of stone and adobe. Rectangular great kivas were the only public architecture, and maximal village size did not exceed 300 people. There is no evidence for elites (see, for example, Anyon and LeBlanc 1984).

Casas Grandes sites were built of adobe. Without excavation they appear far more nondescript than Chaco big houses and are hence harder to characterize. The well-known site of Casas Grandes was very large, multistoried, and had ballcourts, plazas, and platform mounds. Outlying sites were similarly constructed and had similar details in terms of posthole patterns and firepits, but it is unclear whether any were multistoried. Brand (1943) describes several sites in Mexico that had multiple roomblocks but he did not describe features such as ballcourts or platform mounds. Kivas in the old Mogollon style were absent.

In fact, none of the clear similarity found for the Chaco outliers is seen in the Casas Grandes outliers. The Casas Grandes outliers are so radically different from their precursors, contain such distinctive ceramics, and have such an overall similarity to Casas Grandes that one can accept them as being equivalent to Chaco outliers. That is, Chaco outliers are perceived as such by having a polythetic set of common architectural traits. Instead,

Casas Grandes outliers are much less distinctive but can be recognized by their different appearance from their local precursor. Examples in the southwestern U.S. include the Animas phase sites in Hidalgo County of New Mexico (Kidder et al. 1949; McCluney 1962), the Black Mountain phase sites in the Mimbres area (LeBlanc 1980; LeBlanc and Whalen 1980), the Ringo site (Johnson and Thompson 1963), and part of the Curtis site near Safford (Mills and Mills n.d.).

The dating of the Casas Grandes interaction sphere is based on far less information than for Chaco. Most of the relevant information is given by Di Peso (1974) and LeBlanc (1980), and various scenarios exist. The interpretation suggested by LeBlanc (1980) is that the interaction sphere began about A.D. 1130 and terminated by A.D. 1300. This is a minor, but important change from Di Peso's A.D. 1060–1344 range of dates. It is considerably different from the post-1300 beginning date of Casas Grandes as an interaction sphere proposed by Wilcox and Shenk (1977). It seems that there is a growing consensus that Casas Grandes began about A.D. 1130, but a number of workers feel that it persisted long after A.D. 1300, and that its nature changed after that date. The A.D. 1130–1300 range will be assumed to be correct for the following discussion.

Even though our knowledge of the Casas Grandes system is rather minimal, some differences and similarities with Chaco are notable. Like Chaco there was a center at which has been found evidence for craft specialization, considerable public works, and an elite. The evidence for an elite is perhaps stronger at Casas Grandes than it is at Chaco. Craft specialization was more developed, with macaw raising areas, groundstone workshops, a possible smelter, and a storeroom in which were found over a million shell beads. The House of the Serpent, the House of the Dead, and possibly the House of the Macaws were perhaps elite residence areas. They have areas of restricted access, ceremonial rooms that could have housed only a small fraction of the community's population, and semi-elite burials (e.g., burial 44–13 in the House of the Dead). Interestingly, these "houses" are single-storied while elsewhere most of the site is multistoried. The prehistorically-looted crypts in the Mound of the Offerings are very good candidates for elite burials. The burials were differentially interred—uncremated and placed in large jars—and the roomlike crypts were, in a way, parallel to the rooms turned into crypts for elite burials in Pueblo Bonito. In fact, in both cases the crypts may not have been filled in with soils after bodies were interred. This would have allowed for ritual visitation or other ritual behaviors with respect to these elite burials.

Arguments similar to those for Chaco population dynamics apply. That is, the apparent population of Casas Grandes itself was so much greater than for any conceivable precursor population that there must have been net immigration into the town. Consequently, because of this and because of the short temporal span involved, the outlying sites could not have been populated by emigrants from the site of Casas Grandes. Thus the interaction sphere must have grown through incorporating previously independent groups and not by means of intrinsic growth.

Potentially important differences between Casas Grandes and Chaco also exist. In particular, no extensive road networks have been described, although Di Peso notes some short segments and early Spanish accounts may refer to roads in northern Mexico. As no systematic search for roads has been undertaken, the possibility of their existence remains.

Also, there seems to have been a greater break with the past in the Casas Grandes sphere than in the Chaco. Casas Grandes outliers show a marked change in architecture, ceramics, and burial practices, and even in such minor aspects as hearth types, posthole patterns, and posthole construction. Such a degree of temporal change is not observed in the Chaco case, where local tradition seems to continue more strongly. The difference may imply that two different integrative processes were at work in the two areas.

Casas Grandes sites do not appear defensive in their configurations or locations. At least in New Mexico there does seem to be a broad area with few sites between the northernmost Casas Grandes outliers and the southernmost Tularosa phase sites. This may represent some form of frontier zone, although other explanations are possible. In northeastern Sonora there are both major and minor Casas Grandes outliers (Pailes 1984). To the west of these there are apparently contemporaneous Trincheras sites. This may again represent a frontier, although in this case it would appear that the people outside the interaction sphere had taken a defensive posture.

The Hohokam

A variety of models for the Hohokam development have been described in recent years (e.g., Doyel and Plog 1980; Grady 1976; Upham and Rice 1980; Wilcox 1979; Wilcox and Shenk 1977). The amount of new information becoming available is staggering, and any discussion may soon be obsolete. Little attention has been paid to the potential development of a chiefdom level of organization, and the following formulation does not follow any of the widely-held views. Some workers have felt that the peak of Hohokam social complexity was reached during the late Colonial and Sedentary periods (circa A.D. 900-1150); some felt that the Soho phase (circa A.D. 1150–1300) was a period of cultural retrograde or a dark age; and some argue that the Civano came to an abrupt end around A.D. 1450. While cognizant of these views, the model proposed here rejects all of these ideas.

A case can be made that Hohokam social complexity underwent a series of stages of increasing complexity which peaked in the early Civano period and that it was only then that the level of complexity was on a par with the other two interaction spheres. After about A.D. 1350–1400 there began a gradual decline in population and in the system's complexity. This decline was accelerated by the effects of the Spanish conquest and the system was essentially extinct by the time of Kino.

The late Colonial/Sedentary interval was marked by an extensive system of settlements showing a considerable level of similarity, but little evidence for complexity. This is best reflected in the wide distribution of ballcourts as shown by Wilcox and Sternberg (1983). Over 150 communities had one or two ballcourts. The courts did not take much effort to build, nor did the low platform mounds often found at these sites. These were the only forms of public architecture and did not appear to be of restricted access. Considerable corporate labor, however, was expended on the canal systems. There was some planning to these villages; Wilcox suggests that a central plaza was defined and surrounded by platform mounds, and crematoria were well demarcated and placed in standard locations. The large Sacaton houses seen at Snaketown might have been elite residences but more likely were sodality or council houses. Some craft specialization, as seen in the etched shell, seems to have been practiced.

Social organization at this time was probably more complex than that known for the historic Zuni and less complex than at Chaco. It might have taken the form of a big man type system with the big men being more priestly or ceremonially oriented than their New Guinea analogues. I suspect nonhereditary leaders used the production of others, especially craft specialists, to enhance their positions. Their ability to organize labor was not very great, although constructing and maintaining canals was being carried out. The Hohokam at this time were probably symbiotic or at least noncompetitive with Chaco. Both may have been interacting with groups to the south, one linkage through Chihuahua, the other through Sonora. In the case of the Hohokam there seems to be little evidence for a central place or for the level of political integration in existence at that time at Chaco.

At about A.D. 1150 there was a marked change in organization among the Hohokam. This is not surprising given the change that took place in adjacent areas. The Chaco system, which must have been the recipient for much of their shell exports, disintegrated. Casas Grandes began to flourish and was competitive in the shell trade and began to expand into Sonora, perhaps threatening the Hohokam linkages to the south. The most obvious change was reduction in the extent of the Hohokam area. Outlying areas such as the Verde and the San Pedro were either abandoned or the local population converted to a non-Hohokam behavior pattern.

Nevertheless, in the core area there was probably somewhat increased social complexity. If Gregory et al. (1982) and Wilcox and Sternberg (1983) are correct we have a shift in the focus of community ceremonialism away from ballcourts and toward restricted access platform mound complexes. During the Soho phase this took the form of developing low platform mound complexes in standard relationship to existing ballcourts (Gregory et al. 1982; Schroeder 1953).

These mounds were at first little more elaborated than their Sacaton precursors, except that they had one or two large houses associated with them, and these mounds eventually evolved into platform mound-compound complexes. They did have post enclosures around them, but not very elaborate ones. The mounds grew in size throughout the Soho phase through deliberate burning and rebuilding. Large sites may have contained several of these complexes; this may imply several competing elite groups in some villages. I believe these loci were evolving into residential-ceremonial centers for the emerging elite and that they supplanted the ballcourts as a community focus.

The Soho phase is difficult to explicate because two opposing trends were in existence. On the one hand, the areal extent of the Hohokam was considerably diminished and also the level of external trade was probably lessened. On the other hand, the emerging elite probably became more institutionalized with increased authority and control.

The final level of complexity was reached at the beginning of the Civano phase, around A.D. 1275–1300. The platform mound complexes were greatly enlarged and enclosed by massive adobe walls or compounds. At this time, structures were built on top of the mounds and these and the few rooms inside the compound walls were probably only for the elite and their craft specialists and retainers.

The classic Civano communities represent considerable evidence for a more complex society than previously. There are some sites with no compounds which mirror the smaller communities of earlier periods. There are also sites with compound-mound complexes. There were at least 38 sites in the Phoenix Basin (lower Gila and Salt rivers) that had one or more of these compound-mound complexes. These compounds are characterized as having areas of restricted access—some rooms and courtyards are only accessible by going through narrow passageways. These compounds mimic, on a very small scale, the elite restricted access of the residence compounds seen in Mesoamerica and Peru. In addition, there are frequently other "compounds" on these sites. These are perhaps better conceived of as roomblocks, sometimes with compound or enclosure walls along some margins. They have a greater density of rooms than compound-mound complexes and lack mounds or a thick enclosing wall that extends completely around the perimeter.

Wilcox and Sternberg (1983) suggest that the ballcourts were no longer made in the Classic period. Yet Gregory et al. (1982) point out that many of the sites with platform mound complexes had ballcourts and that there was a very regular pattern in the placement of these two features. Either Gregory et al. are incorrect or ballcourts continued to be an important feature during the Classic period. This argues for strong social continuity between the Sedentary and Classic periods.

The overall characterization of the Classic Hohokam interaction sphere is somewhat different from either the Chaco or Casas Grandes spheres.

Even if we see a site like Casa Grande as a primary Hohokam center, it is not much larger than other communities (Upham and Rice 1980), certainly not to the degree that Casas Grandes is larger than any other town in that sphere; however, there may be more of a parallel with Chaco. Even though Chaco Canyon held the most dense concentration of big houses, it did consist of separate structures spread out over several miles. Perhaps we need to view the Casa Grande and similar big sites like Los Colinas not as single sites but as including all those along their canals as well. There were four additional sites with compound-mound complexes along the Casa Grande canal (Midvale 1965).

Changes other than the platform mound-compound complex also took place in the Hohokam area at about this time. After the areal retraction at the beginning of the Soho, people just outside the new system boundary took up a defensive posture. This is seen to the north in the Verde area (Gumerman and Weed 1976) and in the Trincheras to the south along the Santa Cruz and adjacent areas (Wilcox 1979). It appears that during the Civano phase the Hohokam became expansive, as did the Chaco and Casas Grandes interaction spheres. In the case of Santa Cruz River area, the trincheras sites seem to be abandoned and platform mound complex-like facilities were constructed, as at University Ruin (Hayden 1957). These superficially mimic the Salt-Gila complexes but were produced by different construction techniques. To the north, a defensive posture continued and no Hohokam-like villages or platform mound complexes were found. In the Tonto Basin, according to Wood and McAllister (1982), we get a phenomenon like that for Santa Cruz drainage in that platform mound-like structures are found.

Defensive trincheras and other defensive sites were built by local populations in reaction to the expansion of the Classic Hohokam interaction sphere, but despite local defenses it successfully expanded into the Tucson area. In contrast, the defensive posture was more successful in the New River, Agua Fria, and Verde areas and such expansion did not take place.

One can argue that the Civano phase represents a final organizational shift that brought the Hohokam to a level of complexity rather like Chaco and Casas Grandes. Only the expansive aspect of the Hohokam interaction sphere was less successful; thus the system attained a size of only about thirty-five thousand square kilometers.

In the Phoenix Basin there is a good possibility that a signaling system could have existed between sites whereby the tops of the mounds were used as signaling points. The presence of major villages along the same canals implies a level of integration beyond the single site. In general, however, evidence for social complexity or chiefdom level organization is more scanty here than for the other interaction spheres. No really good candidates for elite burials are known, although there were reported adobe "sarcophagi" burials from Los Muertos (Haury 1945) that may be analogous to the crypt or room burials from Chaco and Casas Grandes. The Classic period is generally considered to have less well-made goods than the Colonial or Sedentary periods, negating the development of craft specialists during the Classic period. On the other hand, the presence of extended inhumations as contrasted with cremations may be evidence of social stratificaton. In Chaco the elite or elite-associated were the only individuals who were buried in an extended fashion (Schelberg 1982).

While the Hohokam interaction sphere took longer to develop and underwent a more complex evolution, it was perhaps more short lived. If, as is argued below, there was a substantial population decline over the rest of the Southwest beginning in the mid-1200s, then it probably included the Hohokam area. If it did, and if it took effect in the south later than in the north (see below), we would expect its impact to be seen only after A.D. 1350 in the Salt-Gila heartland. Substantial but gradual decline in population from that point on would have limited the ability of the system to support an elite and to expand. The system most likely did not rapidly decay after A.D. 1450 as has been suggested, but instead a gradual decline began a century earlier. By A.D. 1400 the decline had become marked enough that little new construction activity took place and progressively more, if not most, of the mound-compound complexes were abandoned as the elite no longer maintained itself. This gradual process was probably still underway in the mid-1500s when European diseases reached the Hohokam, still further reducing the population. I do not believe, in sum, that the same type of phenomenon which brought an abrupt end to the Chaco and Casas Grandes systems was at work in the Hohokam. Instead, the decay process was slow and was caused by an as yet not understood pan-southwestern phenomenon.

The Interaction Spheres and Southwestern Prehistory

Although to this point I have generally considered each of the three interaction systems in isolation, I feel that such an approach misses two important aspects. First, the development and collapse of any one was related to or affected the history of the others. Second, the subsequent history of each area was colored by the prior existence of the interaction spheres.

It is unlikely that the collapse of Chaco accidentally coincided with the rise of Casas Grandes. The changes in the Hohokam area around A.D. 1150 and the full development of the interaction sphere by A.D. 1300 were not likely divorced from the effect of the collapse of Casas Grandes at this same time. The idea that each of these events could be unrelated and a product of only local conditions, especially local climatic change, seems remote, and a model built on overall sociopolitical factors seems much more likely.

Before considering the interrelationships of the development of the three interaction spheres, a second concern, namely the post-collapse effects, will be considered. This will allow for the discussion of certain topics useful to the formulation of an interrelationship model.

The Post-Chaco Events

In the case of Chaco, which, it has been argued, comprised almost all of the Anasazi area as well as the Reserve or Cibola branch of the Mogollon, there were three major phases after the collapse. The period from A.D. 1130 to 1240 was characterized by a "dark age." No large communities were built and little construction took place. Organization appears to have been less complex than what came before or after. There is evidence for renewed population aggregation sometime in the mid-1200s which first took the form of pueblo clusters. Relatively small pueblos of between 10 and 40 rooms were built in close (100 m) proximity to each other. The remains of upwards of 20 pueblos were present in some of these clusters. In many ways they were similar to the Chaco outlier communities except that a big house and great kiva were absent. However, usually one or more pueblos in a cluster were situated on a high point with good visibility. This settlement pattern was widespread, but in particular it shows up in high elevations (above 7000 ft) where previously there had been relatively little habitation.

Sometime between A.D. 1240 and 1300 (generally earlier in the north) these communities of pueblo clusters were abandoned and the population moved into very defensible situations. These consisted of either defensible locations for sites, such as the Tsegi phase or Mesa Verde phase cliff dwellings, or large pueblos built with high, two-storied, unbroken outer defensive walls. Examples include the El Morro pueblos (Watson et al. 1980), Crumbled House in the Chuskas (Marshall et al. 1979), and Kinishba (Cummings 1940) in the White Mountains. A few other types of defensive sites, such as the Hovenweep towers, also date to this period. There is generally an inverse relationship between the size of these sites and their degree of fortification. Large communities appear to be less fortified, presumably because size alone constituted a defense. Small sites, on the other hand, seem to have needed more elaborate defenses to compensate for their smaller number of defenders.

After about A.D. 1270 almost the entire population of the old Chaco sphere and its peripheries (in other terms, the original Anasazi and northern Mogollon area) was aggregated. These aggregations were sometimes of considerable size, comprising 900 or more rooms. Even though there were sites which were considerably smaller than this, the smallest we have found archaeologically rarely have fewer than 50 rooms.

The most viable model for these events assumes that after the Chaco collapse the aggregated population dispersed to some degree. Some new small sites were founded and some Chaco period sites continued to be occupied. Beginning in late Pueblo III (circa A.D. 1230—1240), the deteriorating climate resulted in food stress and a reduction in usable land. Perhaps an isolated raid or two on various groups set off a wave of fear resulting in people moving together for protection. The process was gradual, but as one's neighbors became significantly more aggregated than oneself there was motivation to further agglomerate in response. This resulted in the establishment of loosely agglomerated settlements in locations with good visibility as additional protection. The problems did not disappear, however, because the climate continued to deteriorate and because agglomeration proved to be a poor solution to food provisioning under the circumstances of drought. Finally, a new wave of agglomeration took place resulting in recognizably defensible sites, including cliff dwellings, large multistoried inward-facing pueblos, and fortlike structures. This further agglomeration coincided with the worst of the drought and probably further reduced provisioning efficiency.

If this model is correct, it might appear that climatic change was the cause of the defensive, agglomerated settlement pattern. This, however, was not the case, because although environmental change was perhaps the trigger, it did not dictate the response. The most practical response to drought might have been to disperse over as much varied terrain as possible, to have large quantities of stored foods, to increase wild food procurement, and to trade extensively to alleviate local shortcomings. The agglomerated population response did not succeed in satisfying most of these needs and ultimately proved itself to be a cultural mistake, not preordained by an environmental shift.

Settlement distribution focused on two zones. Some tended, as we have seen, to settle at altituted around 7000–7200 ft, probably as a means of capitalizing on increased orographic rainfall; other sites were established at low altitudes where river irrigation could be employed. The former strategy was apparently no longer possible after the drought ended. As shorter growing seasons were accompanied by moister conditions, the higher areas were abandoned.

After A.D. 1300, when conditions improved, the situation might be expected to have reversed, and smaller, non-defensive sites to have spread more evenly over the area. This might be expected because areas that had previously been unproductive due to poor growing conditions would have become usable once again. However, once fortified and agglomerated, the population came under the control of a series of social patterns, such as war priests and sodalities, which precluded ready dispersal. By this time the population was declining at a significant rate. As it declined, groups seem to have been forced to recombine to keep their group size up, and the population decline is evident not in the reduction in the size of individual communities but in the reduction in the number of total communities. This process continued until near the Spanish entrada, but it may have been lessening at that time.

While this scenario seems to have been a poor response, attitudes and beliefs probably would have enhanced it. Once the warfare cycle began, institutional responses and their consequences probably enhanced the degree of warfare, and in this way it might have continued long after it had any potential adaptive value.

This scenario is a "local events" explanation, but the final shift to defensive sites coincides closely with the collapse of Casas Grandes. Perhaps the political instability over the entire region that resulted from that event triggered the move, in some localities, to defensive postures which then snowballed over the entire region. In sum, a process triggered by environmental change is not the only viable model, but at this point I see no means to choose between the two models. Of course, an interrelated combination of both may turn out to be the correct explanation.

Of final note is the prior existence of the Chaco interaction sphere, which resulted in a homogenization of the population within the former sphere. That is, one can see the concept of Western Pueblo (Reed 1948) as representing the post-Chaco people. While there was certainly variability within the post-Chaco area, the similarity of Acoma, Hopi, Zuni, and the big post-1300s sites in the White Mountains and Little Colorado area can be seen as reflecting the Chaco system heritage and their similar subsequent evolution into big communities.

Thus the initial Chaco area consisted of much of the Anasazi area, which had previously been divisible into several branches, and the northern part of the Mogollon. For the period following the Chaco collapse, most of this taxonomy is not applicable and we have evidence of clinal variation over the area, with sites being neither Anazasi nor Mogollon. This is the root of the long-felt need for new terminology. By A.D. 1400–1450 the area north of the Mogollon rim was either abandoned or fell into two categories: the Western Pueblo sites which historically relate to the Chaco system, or the Rio Grande province which was never within the Chaco sphere.

Post-Casas Grandes Events

A parallel series of events occurred to the south. After the collapse of the Casas Grandes system, we can no longer identify the local differences represented by the previous Mogollon branches. Instead we have a confused situation that has been termed, in part, Salado. Unfortunately this term has so many meanings and connotations that it is not really useful. (See Doyel and Haury [1976] for regional discussions and Nelson and LeBlanc [1985] for a synthetic treatment.) At this time the area was inhabited from the Tonto Basin to southwestern New Mexico by a series of populations which varied clinally in a number of traits but which broadly shared a number of attributes that were in contrast to what occurred in this area before Casas Grandes developed. These traits included adobe architecture, freestanding or compound walls, Gila polychrome pottery, a lack or paucity of communal structures, and large but generally non-interconnected rooms.

This collection of sites probably represents, in part, the region's population having first been relocated and restructured by having been part of the Casas Grandes interaction sphere and then left without an overriding political organization. Thus it is parallel to Western Pueblo sites in that the "Salado" represents a post-interaction sphere group of people; perhaps the term *Southern Pueblo* is appropriate. While warfare, or its threat, is less apparent than in the north, the population was also agglomerated and also declined in a very analogous way, so by A.D. 1400–1450 most of the area was abandoned. As in the case of the Chaco collapse, where the terms *Anasazi* and *northern Mogollon* lose their taxonomic utility, we have the southern Mogollon and the eastern periphery of the Hohokam so restructured that these taxons no longer have meaning.

The Salado concept has obscured several aspects in the study of these sites. First, they are distinct from the Classic Hohokam, which was in the past considered "taken over" by the Salado. This idea is now generally discredited, but the relationship between the two areas remains obscure. Moreover, the concept of a Salado "heartland" centered on the Tonto Basin, as presented, does not seem to have any validity. The density of "Salado-like" population in the San Pedro, along the Gila, in southeastern Arizona, and in southwestern New Mexico is much greater than generally perceived and must exceed by several times the population of the Tonto Basin. The rate of growth of populations precludes the possibility of people from the Tonto area having significantly populated any of these other areas. In sum, there is considerable misconception and lack of knowledge hindering our seeing the real patterning of the Salado or the Southern Pueblo.

There is an interesting, but highly speculative, model that explains both the post–Casas Grandes Southern Pueblo concept and the once suggested Salado take-over of the core Hohokam area. The interesting possibility is that the Tonto Basin was actually part of the Classic Hohokam interaction sphere. Some (for example, Wood and McAllister 1982) see several platform mound-compound complex sites in the basin. Haury and others see a level of similarity between the two areas not seen for all of the proposed Southern Pueblo area. While the old model had a take-over or invasion from the Tonto Basin of the Hohokam area, it makes more sense to see the reverse. In the Civano phase, the Hohokam converted to a more complex system and successfully expanded into the lower Santa Cruz and the Tonto Basin. The area to the east of the Tonto Basin, while sharing many traits with this system and being influenced by it, was politically independent. While such a model may not be correct, we need to consider this region in terms of such models.

In summary, we have a series of ranked or complex systems whose present or prior existence resulted in the development of four "cultural areas" in the Southwest by A.D. 1400: the Western and Southern Pueblo areas as a result of Chaco and Casas Grandes respectively, and the Rio Grande and Hohokam areas, one never becoming a ranked society and the other lasting as one late into the prehistoric period.

A significant population decline took place throughout the Southwest. Its affects on the northern area are clear, but it is harder to see on the southern area with our current data. Due to the decline, the extent and the nature of the organization in each area was rapidly changing and static models are not appropriate for them (e.g., Upham 1982).

The Development of the Interaction Spheres

An obvious question is, why did the three interaction spheres develop? In a sense it is premature to try to model the growth and decline of the interaction spheres because they are so poorly characterized. Most important, almost all the excavations on all outliers of both Chaco and Casas Grandes were done before they were recognized as outliers; thus, research has not been directed to the relation between outliers and the system as a whole. The model that I think is most viable includes a trade connection with Mexico, in part as a result of rejecting various alternative models. Population aggregations that existed just prior to the development of the Chaco and Casas Grandes interaction spheres were of a size far below what we expect for ranked societies; it is hard to build a viable model of development based on internal, unstimulated growth. Thus a mesoamerican connection remains an alternate possibility.

Not only does a mesoamerican connection provide a rationale for the development of these interaction spheres, it can also account for their collapse. The idea that the Chaco system collapsed because of environmental factors seems difficult to accept. In most parts of the interaction sphere, the areas and even the sites were not abandoned in A.D. 1130–1150. Also, the San Juan and other major tributaries, such as La Plata and Animas, seem quite impervious to drought or arroyo cutting. While there certainly were climatic difficulties in the mid- 1100s, it is far from clear that these were so severe and widespread as to destroy a system as large and buffered as the Chaco interaction sphere.

Similarly, it has been argued that the Casas Grandes collapse was a consequence of the drought of the late 1200s, but here again the substantial Salado or Southern Pueblo population that occupied the northern portion of the Casas Grandes territory immediately after the collapse implies that conditions were not bad at all in the A.D. 1300s. Why did the system fail to recover if it were simply a product of population pressure and a need for regional exchange?

Among the sociopolitical models suggested for the development and collapse of the interaction spheres, an important one has been the *pochteca* model. A considerable literature has built up over the concept of the *pochteca* model for a mesoamerican trade connection with the Southwest. (This literature has recently been reviewed by McGuire 1980.) The problem with most of the arguments for a *pochteca* model and with McGuire's critic of it, is that the model is always considered specifically and not generally or structurally.

In structural terms the *pochteca* argument is that long-distance trade did occur in Mesoamerica and that at sometime it was organized and structured from the core area and was not a "down-the-line" form of trade. The *pochteca* covered great distances and formed alliances to facilitate trade. The Aztec *pochteca* had a particular sociopolitical structure, special symbols, and distinctive burial practices. There is little reason to believe that the specific form of these traits existed in A.D. 900 or even A.D. 1300. However, mesoamerican trade was quite significant during the Toltec and earlier periods, so it is reasonable to suspect that mechanisms that functioned similarly to the *pochteca* existed at that time. That is, we should not argue by analogy for the presence of *pochteca* in the Southwest; but we can, because of our knowledge of the *pochteca*, reasonably hypothesize the existence of similar mechanisms to facilitate long-distance trade more structured than "down-the-line." Whether this took the form of itinerant traders with distinctive behaviors is undocumented. Such a structural model cannot be rejected because no traits isomorphic with known *pochteca* traits have been shown to exist in the Southwest.

An alternative model also exists. By analogy with fur trappers and traders, a "Hudson's Bay" analogy is equally appealing. By forming alliances with one group, frequently through marriage, according to this model the traders served as brokers of imports and exports. Such an analogy is not really at odds with the *pochteca* as a general analog, but it serves to remind us how few people it might have taken to organize a long-distance network under the right conditions.

Regardless of the model proposed for the emergence and maturation of a long-distance trade network, the point is that the level of social complexity was dependent upon it; if the trade collapsed then so would the system. It is a distinct possibility that the Chaco and Casas Grandes interaction spheres collapsed because they were dependent on the trade for their existence. While we do not have a good model for why this was the case, I see it as the most viable explanation we have to account for the information we currently have.

What is difficult to understand is, what commodity or commodities from the Southwest would have been scarce or valuable enough in Mesoamerica to warrant the development of such a system? It is hard to accept that turquoise alone was sufficient, as there does not seem to be the quantity of turquoise imports in Mexico one might expect (Mathien 1981). Nevertheless, we must be careful not to reject the overall model because we have not yet demonstrated the particulars. Even with its limitations, a long-distance trade model is as viable as any other that has been proposed to account for the rise and collapse of Chaco.

While the role of Chaco as a trading center is far from convincing, the case for Casas Grandes is much more substantial. The discovery of a room with several million shell beads can hardly be explained by any other means. The presence of a clear role for trade at Casas Grandes strengthens the case for Chaco being similarly organized. If the interaction spheres were structurally similar, and their development and collapses do appear related, it is reasonable to suspect that the underlying rationale for each was similar or related.

Rather than pursue what we do not seem to understand, we can look at the structural differences between these two systems. Operating under the assumption that Chaco was a trading center, what were its characteristics? First, it was 630 km (390 mi) farther than Casas Grandes from any southern depot for the traded items. Second, none of the imported exotic goods—macaws, macaw feathers, and copper bells—were produced in the Chaco system area. Third, it was also much further from any source of shell than Casas Grandes.

In contrast, Casas Grandes was a producer of macaws and copper artifacts, not just an importer, and was closer to Mesoamerica or peripheral mesoamerican groups. It is southerly enough that macaws could be raised and local sources of copper ore were available; all these features were lacking in the Chaco area, although copper may have been available within or near the interaction sphere. Thus one can see considerable advantage for Casas Grandes as a trading center over Chaco. The difference may be likened to a shift from a Hudson's Bay-like system to a frontier production town (like early St. Louis) system of extracting goods from a hinderland. Chaco might have played the role of an importer of finished goods and perhaps produced, or at least, accumulated goods for export. Casas Grandes, instead, may have itself produced most of the goods it traded north for the same goods that had previously been provided by Chaco. This represents a considerable increase in efficiency in the entire process. Also of importance, the relocation would have shortened the trip to the Mexican destination for whatever goods were being sent.

Given these considerations, it is plausible that Chaco was abandoned as a trading center and replaced by Casas Grandes because of its greater efficiency. How such a shift came about, whether as a decision made in Mesoamerica or simply as an evolution in the north, is beyond our present understanding. Such a shift seems to be the only model that accounts for the history of both Chaco and Casas Grandes. We can then see the climatic deterioration of the late A.D. 1200s as not resulting in the direct collapse of Casas Grandes, but instead having a major affect on the sites in the northern part of the Southwest. This would have reduced their participation in the trade system, thus eliminating the rationale for Casas Grandes being an outpost to articulate with them. As in the case of Chaco, once the rationale disappeared, the system rapidly collapsed. That is, warfare may have precluded the ability to trade at the level required. Alternatively, of course, the Casas Grandes collapse was unrelated to climatic change and its collapse might have served to precipitate the warfare.

One may look at the above scenario from the perspective of any given locale and not see convincing evidence for it, but that is not the issue. The question is, are we prepared to accept that Chaco was as large as described here, or the collapse as swift and complete? Similarly, do we accept the dating sequence suggested here? Furthermore, are we prepared to see the dissolution of both the Anasazi and Mogollon as a result of such factors as migrations from a "Salado heartland"? Or can we reject such explanations as being impossible from the standpoint of population dynamics?

We can model anything we want to, but if we model completely different sets of "facts" we go at cross purposes with little utility. Finally, we must remember that only one set of events actually happened, if we want to generalize about these events we must correctly perceive them, to do otherwise is to discuss fairy tales.

References Cited

Altshul, Jeffrey H.
   1978 The Development of the Chacoan Interaction Sphere. *Journal of Anthropological Research* 34(1):109–146.
Anyon, Roger, and Steven A. LeBlanc
   1984 *The Galaz Site: A Mimbres Village in Southwestern New Mexico.* University of New Mexico Press, Albuquerque.
Brand, Donald D.
   1943 The Chuhuahua Culture Area. *New Mexico Anthropologist* 6–7(3): 115–158.
Breternitz, David A., Cory Dale, David E. Doyel, and Michael P. Marshall (editors)
   1982 *Bis Sa'ani: A Late Bonito Phase Community on Escavada Wash, Northwest New Mexico.* Navajo Nation Papers in Anthropology No. 14. Window Rock.
Cowgill, George L.
   1975 On Causes and Consequences of Ancient and Modern Population Changes. *American Anthropologist* 77 : 505–525.
Cummings, Byron
   1940 *Kinishba, a Prehistoric Pueblo of the Great Pueblo Period.* Hohokam Museums Association, University of Arizona, Tucson.
Di Peso, Charles C.
   1974 *Casas Grandes: A Fallen Trading Center of the Gran Chichimeca,* vols. 1–3. Amerind Foundation Series No. 9. Dragoon, Ariz.
Dittert, Alfred E., Jr.
   1959 *Culture Change in the Cebolleta Mesa Region, Central Western New Mexico.* Unpublished Ph.D. dissertation, Department of Anthropology, University of Arizona, Tucson.
Doyel, David E., and Emil W. Haury
   1976 The 1976 Salado Conference. *Kiva* 42(1).

Doyel, David E., and Fred Plog (editors)
1980 *Current Issues in Hohokam Prehistory.* Anthropological Research Paper No. 23. Arizona State University, Tempe.

Grady, Mark A.
1976 *Aboriginal Agrarian Adaptation to the Sonoran Desert: A Regional Synthesis and Research Design.* Unpublished Ph.D. dissertation, Department of Anthropology, University of Arizona, Tucson.

Gregory, David A., Lynn S. Teague, Fred Nials, and Patricia L. Crown
1982 *Final Research Design: Archaeological Data Recovery at Las Colinas (AZ T:12:10, ASM and AZ T:12:38, ASM).* Cultural Resource Management Division, Arizona State Museum, The University of Arizona, Tucson.

Gumerman, George J., and Carol S. Weed
1976 The Question of Salado in Agua Fria and New River Drainages of Central Arizona. *Kiva* 42(1):105–112.

Hassan, Fekri A.
1981 *Demographic Archaeology.* Academic Press, New York.

Haury, Emil W.
1945 *The Excavations of Los Muertos and Neighboring Ruins in the Salt River Valley, Southern Arizona.* Papers of the Peabody Museum of American Archaeology and Ethnology No. 24(1). Harvard University, Cambridge, Mass.

Hayden, Julian D.
1957 *Excavation, 1940, at University Indian Ruin.* Southwestern Monuments Association Technical Series No. 5.

Hayes, Alden C.
1981 A Survey of Chaco Canyon Archeology. In *Archeological Surveys of Chaco Canyon, New Mexico,* by Alden C. Hayes, David M. Brugge, and W. James Judge, pp.1–68. National Park Service Publications in Archeology No. 17A. Chaco Canyon Studies. Washington, D.C.

Hough, Walter
1907 *Antiquities of the Upper Gila and Salt River Valleys in Arizona and New Mexico.* Bureau of American Ethnology Bulletin No. 35. Washington, D.C.

Johnson, A. E., and Raymond H. Thompson
1963 The Ringo Site: Southern Arizona. *American Antiquity* 28:465–481.

Judge, W. James
1983 Results of the Chaco Project: 1972–1983. Paper presented at the 82d Annual Meeting of the American Anthropological Association, Chicago.

Judge, W. James, William B. Gillespie, Stephen H. Lekson, and Henry W. Toll
1981 Tenth Century Developments in Chaco Canyon. In *Collected Papers in Honor of Erik Kellerman Reed,* edited by A. H. Schroeder, pp. 65–

98. Archaeological Society of New Mexico Anthropologial Papers No. 6.

Kidder, A. V., Harriet S. Cosgrove, and C. B. Cosgrove
1949 *The Pendleton Ruin, Hidalgo County, New Mexico.* Contributions to American Anthropology and History No. 50. Carnegie Institute of Washington Publication No. 585.

Kincaid, Chris (editor)
1983 *Chaco Roads Project-Phase I: A Reappraisal of Prehistoric Roads in the San Juan Basin.* U.S. Bureau of Land Management, Santa Fe.

LeBlanc, Steven A.
1980 The Dating of Casas Grandes. *American Antiquity* 45:799–806.

LeBlanc, Steven A., and Michael E. Whalen
1980 *An Archeological Synthesis of South Central and Southwestern New Mexico*, with contributions by R. Anyon, P. A. Gilman, P. E. Minnis, and M. Nelson. Office of Contract Archaeology, University of New Mexico, Albuquerque.

Lightfoot, Kent G., and Gary M. Feinman
1982 Social Differentiation and Leadership Development in Early Pithouse Villages in the Mogollon Region of the American Southwest. *American Antiquity* 47:64–86.

Marshall, Michael P., John R. Stein, Richard W. Loose, and Judith E. Novotny
1979 *Anasazi Communities in the San Juan Basin.* Public Service Company of New Mexico and the Historic Preservation Bureau, Planning Division, Department of Finance and Administration of the State of New Mexico.

Martin, Paul S.
1936 *Lowry Ruin in Southwestern Colorado.* Field Museum of Natural History Anthropological Series No. 23(2).

Martin, Paul Sidney, and Fred Plog
1973 *The Archaeology of Arizona.* Doubleday / Natural History Press. Garden City, New York.

Mathien, Frances Joan
1981 *Economic Exchange Systems in the San Juan Basin.* Unpublished Ph.D. dissertation, Department of Anthropology, University of New Mexico, Albuquerque.

McCluney, Eugene B.
1962 *Clanton Draw and Box Canyon: An Interim Report on Two Prehistoric Sites in Hidalgo County, New Mexico.* School of American Research Monograph No. 26. Santa Fe.

McGuire, Randall H.
1980 The Mesoamerican Connection in the Southwest. *Kiva* 46(1–2): 3–38

Midvale, Frank
1965 Prehistoric Irrigation of the Casa Grande Ruins Area. *Kiva* 30(3): 82–86.

Mills, Jack P., and Vera M. Mills
n.d. *The Curtis Site: A Prehistoric Village in the Safford Valley.* Privately printed.

Morris, Earl H.
1919 *The Aztec Ruin.* Anthropological Papers of the American Museum of Natural History No. 26(1).
1939 *Archaeological Studies in the La Plata District, Southwestern Colorado and Northwestern New Mexico.* Carnegie Institution Publication No. 519.

Nelson, Ben A., and Steven A. LeBlanc
1985 *Post-Mimbres Occupation in the Mimbres Valley: The Janss, Stailey and Disert Sites.* University of New Mexico Press, Albuquerque, in press.

Obenauf, Margaret S.
1980 *The Chaco Roadway System.* Unpublished M.A. thesis, Department of Anthropology, University of New Mexico.

Pailes, Richard A.
1984 Agricultural Development and Trade in the Rio Sonora Valley. In *Prehistoric Agricultural Strategies in the Southwest,* edited by Suzanne K. Fish and Paul R. Fish, pp. 309–325. Arizona State University Anthropological Research Paper No. 30.

Powers, Robert P., William B. Gillespie, and Stephen H. Lekson
1983 *The Outlier Survey: A Regional View of Settlement in the San Juan Basin.* Report of the Chaco Center No. 3. National Park Service, Albuquerque.

Reed, Erik K.
1948 The Western Pueblo Archaeological Complex. *El Palacio* 55 : 9–15.

Roberts, Frank H. H., Jr.
1932 *Village of the Great Kivas on the Zuni Reservation, New Mexico.* Bureau of American Ethnology Bulletin No. 111. Washington, D.C.

Schelberg, John D.
1982 *Economic and Social Development as an Adaptation to a Marginal Environment in Chaco Canyon, New Mexico.* Unpublished Ph.D. dissertation, Department of Anthropology, Northwestern University, Evanston, Illinois.

Schroeder, Albert H.
1953 The Bearing of Architecture on Developments in the Hohokam Classic Period. *Southwestern Journal of Anthropology* 9 : 174–194.

Service, Elman R.
1962 *Primitive Social Organization: An Evolutionary Perspective.* Random House, New York.

Tainter, Joseph A., and David Gillio
1980 *Cultural Resources Overview Mt. Taylor Area, New Mexico.* U.S.D.A. Forest Service, Southwestern Region, Albuquerque, New

Mexico and Bureau of Land Management, New Mexico State Office, Santa Fe, New Mexico.

Upham, Steadman
1982 *Polities and Power: An Economic and Political History of the Western Pueblo*. Academic Press, New York.

Upham, Steadman, and Glen Rice
1980 Up the Canal Without a Pattern: Modelling Hohokam Interaction and Exchange. In *Current Issues in Hohokam Prehistory: Proceedings of a Symposium*, edited by David Doyel, and Fred Plog, pp. 78–105. Arizona State University Anthropological Research Paper No. 23. Tempe.

Vivian, R. Gwinn
1983 The Chacoan Phenomenon: Cultural Growth in the San Juan Basin. Paper presented at the Second Anasazi Symposium, Salmon Ruin, New Mexico.

Watson, Patty Jo, Steven A. LeBlanc, and Charles L. Redman
1980 Aspects of Zuni Prehistory: Preliminary Report on Excavations and Survey in the El Morro Valley of New Mexico. *Journal of Field Archaeology* 7:201–218.

Wilcox, David R.
1979 Warfare Implications of Dry-laid Masonry Walls on Tumamoc Hill. *Kiva* 45(1–2):15–38.

Wilcox, David R., Thomas B. McGuire, and Charles Sternberg
1981 *Snaketown Revisited*. Arizona State Museum Archaeological Series No. 155. Tucson.

Wilcox, David R., and Lynette O. Shenk
1977 *The Architecture of the Casa Grande and its Interpretation*. Arizona State Museum, Archaeological Series No. 115. Tucson.

Wilcox, David R., and Charles Sternberg
1983 *Hohokam Ballcourts*. Arizona State Museum Archaeological Series No. 166. Tucson.

Windes, Thomas C.
1985 A New Look at Population in Chaco Canyon. *Kiva*, in press.

Wobst, H. Martin
1974 Boundary Conditions for Paleolithic Social Systems: A Simulation Approach. *American Antiquity* 39:147–178.

Wood, J. Scott, and Martin E. McAllister
1982 The Salado Tradition: An Alternative View. In *Cholla Project Archaeology*, vol. 1, edited by J. J. Reid. Archaeological Series No. 161. Arizona State Museum, University of Arizona, Tucson.

Zubrow, Ezra W.
1971 Carrying Capacity and Dynamic Equilibrium in the Prehistoric Southwest. *American Antiquity* 36:127–138.

8

The Tepiman Connection:
A model of Mesoamerican-
Southwestern Interaction

David R. Wilcox

The nature and significance of cultural connections linking the American Southwest and Mesoamerica has long been a conundrum in American archaeology—as this volume well illustrates. Nearly 60 years ago, in a famous passage, A. V. Kidder concluded that "the Southwest owes to outside sources little more than the germs of its culture and that its development from those germs has been a local and almost wholly independent one" (1962:326). Against this view, Herbert Spinden claimed that "later Southwest evolution is authochthonous until the end of Pueblo III when the concepts of the Plumed Serpent, the Eagle Man, Four-direction symbolism, etc., come from Mexico with Toltec trade" (1928:251; see also Brew 1944). Excavations at Snaketown (Gladwin et al. 1937), however, soon produced evidence for a much more continuous series of cultural interactions, though the concept of two main waves of influence persisted (Haury 1945). Copper bells, iron-pyrites plaques, shell trumpets, and scarlet macaws dating to the Colonial and Sedentary periods are physical evidence for such contacts. Many stylistic similarities, especially in Pioneer and Colonial period ceramics, further document the case. Four-directional symbolism, for example, is apparent in the earliest Hohokam designs (Gladwin et al. 1937:225).

Undoubtedly the most dramatic symbol of mesoamerican connections was Emil Haury's identification of a ballcourt at Snaketown. Prehistoric ballcourts had only recently been identified in the Mayan area (Blom 1932) and their presence 3000 km away in southern Arizona astounded nearly everyone (Brew 1940; Corbett 1939:ii; but see Brand 1939). Decades then passed during which new work by J. Charles Kelley (1956, 1966, 1971) and his colleagues (Johnson 1958; Kelley and Abbott 1966; Kelley and Winters 1960; Weigand 1968) in Durango and Zacatecas showed that Hohokam interactions with Mesoamerica were probably mediated by the Chalchihuites culture, a hypothesis others had suspected (Haury 1945; Kelley 1944) and later supported (Haury 1976). Nevertheless, because few new ballcourts were found in northern Mexico, and as morphological differences between the mesoamerican and Hohokam courts became more apparent, the stage was set for Edwin Ferdon's (1967) elegant comparison that clearly revealed the formal contrasts that exist between Hohokam and mesoamerican courts. His suggestion that Hohokam courts were dance plazas analogous to the Papago *wiikita* grounds was soon cited by Martin and Plog (1973) as support for an extreme isolationist position. After a generation of belief in meso-american connections, opinions shifted and the pendulum swung in a new direction.

Hidden below the surface of the superficial polemic expounded by Martin and Plog was a profound impatience with the logic of previous models. New kinds of models whose propositions are more readily testable using archaeological data were now required (see discussion in Pailes 1980; Plog et al. 1982). This paper suggests such a model.

Let us begin by looking again at Ferdon's (1967) critique of Haury's Hohokam ballcourt hypothesis. Ferdon assumed that ballcourts are a mono-thetic class when, in fact, like the mesoamerican ballgame, they are poly-thetic (see Needham 1975). This means that many features of the elements in the subsets of the class are not universal. Stern (1948), Borhegyi (1980), and others (Hellmuth 1975; Leyenaar 1978; Taladoire 1981) have shown how diverse were the rules and associated paraphernalia of the game. After stone ring goals were introduced in the Late Classic, for example, the game probably became much faster and less positional (Borhegyi 1980). No courts are required to play the game. Versions are still played today in Nayarit and Sinaloa on nothing more than a demarcated area of cleared ground (Leyenaar 1978). Early Preclassic figurines from Openo in West Mexico, Tlatilco in the Basin of Mexico, and San Lorenzo in the Olmec area (Grove 1981) afford evidence that versions of the game were nearly as wide-spread as the earliest mesoamerican villages half a millenium or more be-fore organizational changes in the Late Preclassic led to the construction of the first formal courts (Grove 1981; Lowe 1977; Scarborough et al. 1982; Wyshak et al. 1971).

What Linton Satterthwaite (1944) called the "stop-surfaces" of meso-american courts are far from identical to one another. It is difficult to agree with Ferdon (1967) that certain formal features are more basic than others. Formal differences with Hohokam courts certainly exist, but the crucial question is whether or not the courts are functionally comparable. Is there a historical continuity of thought and praxis that links the Hohokam courts with mesoamerican ones?

I infer that there was an essential continuity in the playing of the game, not in the building of ballcourts (Wilcox and Sternberg 1983). The ballgame diffused, not the ballcourt. This may have happened when pottery, figurines, and the earliest villages appeared in both southern Arizona and the Chalchihuites area during the early centuries A.D. The first Hohokam courts were built during the Gila Butte phase (Gladwin et al. 1937), prob-ably about A.D. 700, at a time of organizational change in Hohokam society

(Wilcox and Sternberg 1983). Several Hohokam figurines are inferred to represent ballplayers (Haury 1976 : 257–259, 262–264; Wilcox and Sternberg 1983 : 61). Most pertain to the Pioneer period. Hohokam courts may thus have been invented independently from mesoamerican ones, making explicable their formal differences. Functionally, however, their length-width indices, symmetry, and the smooth regularity of their stop-surfaces are closely comparable to mesoamerican courts (Wilcox and Sternberg 1983).

The perspective afforded by this argument clarifies important aspects of the larger problem of mesoamerican-southwestern connections. Diffusion of the ballgame suggests a kind of social interaction and communication more complex than previously imagined. It challenges the assumption that local groups were autonomous, observing the practices of others from afar and adopting for their own use only what suited them. On the contrary, interaction may have been much more continuous and direct, linking social groups into complex regional and panregional networks that constrained and channelled the innovations of their constituent local groups. What are required, then, are models of the structure and evolution of these regional and panregional systems. Happily, this perspective converges with recent theoretical developments in archaeology, making model formation somewhat easier (see Dennell 1983; Friedel 1979; Moore 1983; Plog 1980; Wobst 1977, 1978).

Basic Structural Features

North of the Bajio in central Mexico, hunter-gatherer adaptations persisted for a millenium or more after a network of sedentary villages first appeared in many parts of Mesoamerica. The historical distribution of Uto-Aztecan languages (Steele 1979) and the closeness of their linguistic features are evidence that supports the theoretical inference that these hunter-gatherer groups were open systems, freely communicating with one another and fluidly exchanging members in a vast human network linking Oregon to Guanajuato (see Miller 1983; Wobst 1976). If it is recognized that Uto-Aztecan was a polythetic class of dialects, the unity once postulated for a "Desert Culture" may yet prove to have more meaning than is presently believed (Jennings 1973; see also Zingg 1939). The spread of corn agriculture and then the adoption of sedentism transformed and restructured communication within this huge human reservoir, ultimately shrinking the area occupied by hunter-gatherers to the Great Basin and the Chihuahuan Desert (Kirchoff 1954).

Even in the latter areas, structural changes are implied by new patterns of interaction between the hunter-gatherers and sedentary groups living along the peripheries of their domains. Along the western rim of the Chihuahuan Desert, for example, a complex symbiosis has been proposed (Armillas 1964, 1969; Kelley 1952, 1953; Palerm and Wolf 1957; Weigand

1979) in which populations switched back and forth from one strategy to another. The large ceremonial centers, such as La Quemada, Alta Vista, Schroeder, and Casas Grandes, which flourished in the agricultural zone, like Taos, Pecos, and Gran Quivira at a later time in New Mexico (Spielmann 1982; Wilcox 1984), may have been entrepots designed in part to attract hunter-gatherers from the desert.

Highly mobile and fluidly connected to like groups from New Mexico to San Luis Potosi, those hunter-gatherers may have been the principal transfer agents of turquoise, macaws, and other exotics to these ceremonial centers (Wilcox and Sternberg 1983). Sherds have been found on Chihuahuan Desert sites that derive from the agricultural zones surrounding it, thus indicating interaction of some kind (Heartfield 1975). Turquoise was exchanged between the farmers and hunter-gatherers historically (Hammond and Rey 1953:400; Weigand 1979:30) and the fact that one of the earliest source areas for turquoise found in Alta Vista phase contexts is in the Concepcion del Oro-Mazapil area of Zacatecas, well into the Chihuahuan Desert, may mean that the historic pattern is very old (but see Weigand 1978:78). The natural range of the scarlet macaw is along the Gulf Coast from about Tamaulipas south (Olsen and Olsen 1974). To reach Chalchihuites or Malpaso sites, or those in the American Southwest where the scarlet macaw is the most frequent species of macaw found (Nelson 1981), they either had to cross or bypass the Chihuahuan Desert. Whether significant quantities of subsistence goods were also exchanged in a mutualistic system similar to the one between dog nomads and protohistoric Pueblos (Speilmann 1982) is even more uncertain. New research is needed on these possibilities.

Structural change in regional exchange arrangements is indicated by the macaw-breeding pens at Casas Grandes sites (Di Peso 1974). Similarly, the rise and fall of the ceremonial centers occurred at different times and these too are relations that bear significantly on the changing structure of the panregional system. Environmental change could also have brought about structural change in social arrangements, particularly if the distribution and abundance of bison, antelope, or other game was affected (Hester 1975). Before considering further the implications such relations have for model building, let us skip back a millenium or so and begin again.

The Tepiman Connection

The florescence of the Chupicuaro phenomenon (McBride 1969) circa 500 to 100 B.C. in the Late Preclassic facilitated the penetration of the ecological boundary marked by the Bajio, and village life began to spread northward. Explanations for this change are still extremely sketchy (Armillas 1964, 1969; Braniff 1975; Brown 1980; Palerm and Wolf 1957). Remarkably, however, the earliest villages known in the Chalchihuites, Hohokam, and Mogollon areas appear to date to the early centuries A.D., and the earliest pottery in the intervening area of central Sonora is also said to date to that time (Kelley and Kelley 1980; LeBlanc 1982; Pailes 1972, 1976; Whalen 1981; Wilcox 1979). These data seem to define a geographic corridor, suggesting that the spread of sedentism or pottery into these areas was a unified systemic process. By A.D. 450 to 650, sedentary villages were common in zones adjacent to this "corridor," a structural transformation that brought new cultural systems into existence (see Di Peso 1974; LeBlanc 1982; Wilcox 1979).

The reality of the corridor I have sketched remains to be tested archaeologically. In particular, the presence of appropriately early villages in central Sonora or northern Durango has yet to be demonstrated. Recent work in Matty Canyon near Tucson, Arizona, suggests that a form of sedentary village with corn agriculture may have been well established in certain microenvironments well before pottery arrived (Bruce Huckell, personal communication 1983). The Hohokam and Chalchihuites chronologies also remain controversial. However, the fact that the same geographical structure is indicated by the distribution of the Tepiman dialect chain circa A.D. 1550 (Sauer 1934; see Figure 10) is a sufficient basis for postulating a general model to account for these data, if only as a guide to future research. The claim here is not that this assumption is true; only new data can permit a decision about that. The claim is that the model specifies worthwhile directions for future research.

Upper and Lower Piman, Northern and Southern Tepehuan, and Tepecano are all dialects of a single language called Tepiman by linguists (Miller 1983). The northern boundary of the Tepehuan in A.D. 1600 was the Rio Verde, a river that has cut a deep pathway across the Sierras, easing human access between northern Durango and central Sonora (Pennington 1969). The Rio Verde joins the Rio Fuerte, whose lower course marks the boundary between southwestern culture and that of Mesoamerica (Ekholm 1942; Sauer and Brand 1931). From the junction of the Chinipas Valley with the Rio Fuerte, northward 440 km to southeastern Arizona, the Spaniards found communities that were organized into multivillage polities that practiced irrigation agriculture (Riley 1982; Sauer 1934). This is the same geographical zone of "oases of high quality and large size" to which Sauer and Brand (1930:448) pointed when discussing the entry of corn agriculture into Arizona (see also Ford 1981; Haury 1945). That a communication corridor occupied this zone prehistorically is also implied by Richard Pailes's (1972, 1980) concept of a Rio Sonora culture, though it may pertain to Taracahitan rather than Tepiman populations. Separating the Lower Pima and Northern Tepehuan in the late sixteenth century was a gap filled by Varohio and Tarahumaran speakers. Explaining how that gap came about is a task for both archaeological and linguistic models.

Most historical linguistics proceeds from the theoretical assumption that a diverse set of related languages must have evolved from a single protolanguage (Haas 1969). The age-area method (Sapir 1918), however,

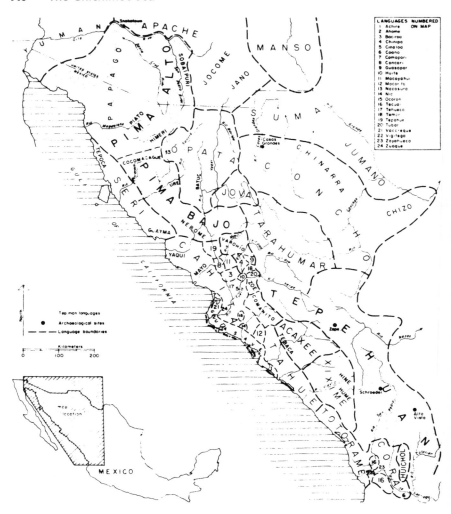

Figure 10. Language distributions in northern Mexico, ca. A.D. 1600

which is still often used to construct historical models, is biased by the further assumption that protolanguages were monothetic classes. In fact, the dialect geography of a polythetic protolanguage may have been as complex and extensive, or more so, as the modern distribution. The fact that linguistic change is not inherent to language (Barth 1972; Greenberg 1963:

64—65) means that indices of linguistic diversity are a function of variables other than time alone. These variables are parameters of what I shall call the "structure of communication" that characterizes networks of human populations at any one time. Changes in those structures shape the evolution of languages. Identification of both the structural parameters of communication systems and their changes are a necessary prerequisite to model formation. Only an illustration of this position can be offered in the Tepiman model that follows.

The Model

Local groups of hunter-gatherers often consisted of only about 25 people, whereas early villages apparently had four to six times that many (Flannery 1972; Martin 1973). Life in villages also affected the annual schedules of interaction with other groups. Both of these changes illustrate changes that transformed the structure of communication within and among local groups. As one set of groups switched to sedentism, previous linkages with neighboring hunter-gatherers in the regional network were broken. Those hunter-gatherers that could not adjust to those changes may then have also switched to a more sedentary strategy, thereby forming a new set of social linkages with their sedentary and hunter-gatherer neighbors (see Dennell 1983; Moore 1981; Wobst 1976). A domino effect could thus be produced that would be visible archaeologically as a rapid spread of village life. In light of these theoretical expectations, I propose that (1) a corridor of early villages from the Chalchihuites area through central Sonora to southern Arizona developed as a result of such a domino process, and (2) Tepiman then differentiated from the rest of Uto-Aztecan.

These hypotheses are consistent with linguistic facts, though not with certain glottochronological models based on those facts. Wick Miller (1983 : 118), for example, infers that proto-Tepiman became a separate language about 3,500 years ago, while the proto-Taracahitan languages became distinct a millenium later. Even rates of linguistic change are assumed, and it is this premise that the changing structure of communication inferrable from archaeological data may be used to test. I am arguing that differential rates will be found. Differentiation in place of a Tepiman corridor from a polythetic Uto-Aztecan dialect network of hunter-gatherers would have geographically isolated the proto-Cahitan from proto-Opatan-Tarahumaran populations. Maintenance of communication along this corridor may have been due to (1) a more rapid rate in that zone of the evolution of agricultural economies compared to adjacent zones, and (2) sociological parallels in the development of village populations from Alta Vista to Zape and from the Chinipas Valley to southern Arizona. On the other hand, centers of cultural innovation (such as Chalchihuites and Hohokam) existed at each end of this Tepiman corridor, a condition that could have increased the linguistic change within this polythetic class more rapidly than among Taracahitans. The Taracahitans seem to have developed agricultural economies more slowly, were differently structured sociologically, and occupied mountainous habitats that encouraged the formation of separate social identities and dialects.

The Tepiman connection I envision was an evolving system. Not only did it begin and end, but the nature of its social linkages changed as the social organization on community, local, regional, and panregional scales evolved. The most detailed picture of these processes has been reconstructed from Hohokam data (Wilcox and Sternberg 1983). Patterns in assemblages of ritual paraphernalia and their associations indicate fundamental changes in Hohokam ceremonial systems. The Pioneer period is marked by the production of hundreds of clay figurines that presumably reflect the importance of households and of ancestor worship in the agricultural economy (Haury 1976; see also Dennell 1983:167). This stylistic tradition of clay figurines disappears just as the first ballcourts were built and just after irrigation agriculture was adopted in the Phoenix Basin. Complex cremation ceremonialism involving newly formalized exchanges among a small series of intracommunity social formations is apparently present by the late Colonial period. The widespread adoption of these beliefs and rituals of death served to incorporate neighboring local systems into a Hohokam regional system. A structure of ceremonial exchanges was created that apparently served to strengthen the continuity and integration within a regional mating network. Work requirements and associated social organization in the component local systems were not identical, but for many generations their structure was kept sufficiently comparable to maintain regional communication and exchange. This may not have been possible with more distant, less developed groups.

By the Sedentary period, the data on site structure and ballcourt distribution and orientation indicate the presence of a more complex, functionally differentiated ceremonial system. Like that of the later protohistoric Pueblos, this system may have been calendrically structured (see Titiev 1960).

Evidence for such systems is apparent in the Basin of Mexico by the late Middle Classic, A.D. 550 to 700 (Pasztory 1978:130–135), and in the Alta Vista and other Chalchihuites sites by A.D. 750 to 950 (Aveni et al. 1982; Kelley and Kelley 1980). Adoption of some version of these ideas by Hohokam and other Southwestern societies apparently served to choreograph exchange flows on several scales of social interaction. It is at this time that many of the exotic Mexican items (such as iron-pyrites plaques and copper bells) entered the Southwest (that is, before A.D. 1150). I infer that the principal mechanism for this transfer was ceremonial exchange along the Tepiman corridor, though it is also possible that hunter-gatherers in the Chihuahuan Desert were transfer agents for some items, especially scarlet macaws and feathers (Nelson 1981; Olsen and Olsen 1974). The concept of prestige exchange postulated by Plog et al. (1982; see also McGuire 1980;

Nelson 1981) is a compatible hypothesis. Unlike most *pochteca* and related models (Kelley and Kelley 1975; Pailes 1980; Weigand 1979), which postulate long-distance transfers between a few nodal points, the present model requires a continuous chain or network of short-distance transfers that passed a few exotic items over long distances. If it could be shown that such connections did not exist, the class of *pochteca* models would become more probable.

The gap or break in the Tepiman dialect chain may have been created circa A.D. 1000 or so, if glottochronological reckoning is to be believed (Miller 1983). The fact that Tepehuans and Lower Pimans could still understand one another circa A.D. 1550 (Sauer 1934) does suggest that the gap had not long existed. It is also significant that by A.D. 1150 vast changes had occurred in regional systems throughout the American Southwest and northern Mexico. Coastal Sinaloan culture expanded northward circa A.D. 1000 to Guasave where it absorbed the local Huatabampo folk (Ekholm 1942; Kelley 1980). The Río Tunal phase ended about A.D. 1150 with the demise of Chalchihuites ceremonial centers like the Schroeder site and Zape; local peasants apparently took them over during the later Calera phase (Kelley 1971). In the American Southwest, the Sedentary-period Hohokam, the Mimbres, and the Chacoan regional systems all collapsed and were reorganized by A.D. 1100 to 1150 (LeBlanc 1980; Powers et al. 1983; Wilcox and Sternberg 1983). Concurrently, in central Mexico, barbarians invaded the civilized centers and Tula and other polities collapsed (Armillas 1964, 1969; Palerm and Wolf 1957).

A fundamental restructuring of exchange and communication systems on a vast panregional scale is indicated by the conjunction of these processes. I infer that one effect of these unsettled times was the severing of the Tepiman dialect chain by Varohio and Tarahumaran mountain folk. Evidence for warfare is widespread at this time (Weigand 1979; Wilcox and Sternberg 1983) and it was endemic in the Sierras in the early historic period (Sauer 1934). Violence may thus have been involved in this ecological displacement.

The severing of the Tepiman connection may be correlated with the beginning of a period of vigorous cultural innovation of Taracahitan populations. The rise of Casas Grandes, which filled the power vacuum on the edge of the Chihuahuan Desert created by the demise of the Durango ceremonial centers, apparently led to the formation of an exchange structure linking coastal Sinaloa and Guasave to northeastern Chihuahua (see Kelley 1971, 1980; Riley 1982; Wilcox and Sternberg 1983). The expansion of Opatan speakers at the expense of Pimans (Sauer 1934) may have moved forward at this time. If so, it seems possible that the Guasave-Casas Grandes axis may have bypassed or hopped over the intervening Pimans. Much more archaeological work in Sonora is necessary before such possibilities can be explored further (see Dirst 1979; Pailes 1980).

One fact is clear, however. The concentration at Casas Grandes of shells and the specialist production there of copper bells, macaws and feathers, and polychrome pottery, all of which were highly valuable exchange items in these societies, are evidence for the emergence of a panregional system whose structure was very different from its predecessors. Casas Grandes is located at the southern end of both the Salado and the Rio Grande regional systems. It held a monopoly on these systems' access to Mexican exotics. The previous role I have inferred for the Chihuahuan Desert dwellers was apparently eliminated, and the growth of sedentary villages in the Big Bend area (Kelley 1956) may be indicative of their response to new circumstances (see also Hester 1975). More importantly, the operation of regional mating networks must have been fundamentally changed. The general southwestern pattern of aggregation into large communities and related organizational changes may have been as much a response to these changes in the social environment (mating networks) as it was to variability or risk in the natural environment.

Access to mates is a fundamental prerequisite of social reproduction (Meillassoux 1981; Root 1983). The monopoly control of valuables exercised by Casas Grandes may have so disrupted the equilibrium of the southwestern mating networks that many communities and local systems began to go to extinction, while others grew larger and more complex (see Salisbury 1962; Wilcox 1984). The emergence of multicommunity alliances within Pueblo ethnic groups that became endogamous, thus reducing the net flow of spouses to adjacent areas while continuing to receive spouses from them, may have been one response to this situation (Wilcox 1984). In the end, widespread regional abandonment ensued particularly in areas apparently lacking multicommunity endogamous alliances. The Casas Grandes system, too, failed to survive. Warfare may have been a proximate cause of this (Di Peso 1974), but the ultimate causes remain to be determined.

Conclusion

In conclusion, a few of the anomalies in my argument must be noted. The concept of a Tepiman corridor implies the successive articulation of the Hohokam with Mogollon in southeastern Arizona (Sayles 1945), the Rio Sonora culture (or an earlier culture) in Sonora (Pailes 1972, 1980), the Loma San Gabriel culture in Durango (Kelley 1971), and the Chalchihuites culture in Zacatecas-Durango (Kelley 1971). The nature of this articulation is supposed to have changed through time. How such "articulation" may be identified or tested is a crucial problem that requires new data and new methods (see Freidel 1979; Root 1983; Wobst 1978). Not all of these populations may in fact have spoken Tepiman. The Chalchihuites, for example, may have spoken an early dialect of Cazcana or some other Uto-Aztecan language. Even the Hohokam may have spoken a Taracahitan dialect or some other non-Tepiman language (Crosswhite 1981; Wick Miller, personal communication 1983).

Historic analogies (Pennington 1969) suggest that it is unlikely that villages existed in the rugged territory south of the Rio Verde between Zape and the Chinipas. The Northern Tepehuan, who occupied this area historically, may be descendants of Loma San Gabriel populations who were driven westward into the Sierras during the protohistoric period (Riley and Winters 1963). Other scholars dispute a Loma San Gabriel derivation, suggesting that the Tepehuan migrated southward about the time Casas Grandes collapsed (Fowler 1980; Wigberto Jimenez Moreno, personal communication 1983). Yet the fundamental difficulty plaguing my Tepiman or any other model is the nearly total absence of archaeological data in most of the 775 km zone from Zape via the Rio Verde and Chinipas to the international border. The call over 40 years ago at the third Mesa Redonda meetings for research in the Chinipas Valley (Beals and Haury 1944:355) went unheeded. If this paper has contributed nothing else, I hope it may awaken a renewed interest in the archaeology of this important area.

Acknowledgments

This paper grew out of a study of Hohokam ballcourts and their interpretation that was funded by the Western Archeological Center, National Park Service, in a contract with the Arizona State Museum, University of Arizona. I thank all parties involved for teaching me the limits of contract work. Joan Mathien and Randall McGuire graciously invited me to prepare this paper for their symposium. Enormous assistance in my struggle to understand the problems of cultural contacts between Mesoamerica and the Southwest was provided in numerous letters and papers sent to me by J. Charles Kelley, Richard Pailes, Phil Weigand, Wick Miller, and Catherine Fowler. I am also especially grateful to Edwin Ferdon, Emil Haury, David Gregory, Gary Feinman, R. Ben Brown, Barney Burns, Thomas Naylor, Vernon Scarborough, and the late Charles Di Peso for their help and support. A version of this paper was read at the 18th Mesa Redonda meetings in Taxco, Guerrero, Mexico, where I benefitted greatly from the comments of Beatriz Braniff and Wigberto Jimenez Moreno. I alone am responsible for any errors or misconceptions.

For initial typing and editorial assistance, thanks go to Maria Abdin and Ben Smith, respectively. For support in preparing a version for publication, special thanks go to Philip Thompson, Donald Weaver, and Lilia Scott, Museum of Northern Arizona. Finally, without the perseverance and enthusiasm of my wife Susan this paper would not have been possible.

References Cited

Armillas, Pedro
  1964 Northern Mesoamerica. In *Prehistoric Man in the New World*, edited by Jesse D. Jennings and Edward Norbeck, pp. 291–330. University of Chicago Press.
  1969 The Arid Frontier of Mexica Civilization. *New York Academy of Sciences Bulletin* 2(316):697–704.
Aveni, Anthony F., Horst Hartung, and J. Charles Kelley
  1982 Alta Vista (Chalchihuites): Astronomical Implications of a Mesoamerican Ceremonial Outpost at the Tropic of Cancer. *American Antiquity* 47:316–335.
Barth, Fredrik
  1972 Ethnic Processes on the Pathan-Baluch Boundary. In *Directions in Sociolinguistics, The Ethnography of Communication*, edited by John J. Gumperz and Dell Hymes, pp. 454–464. Holt, Rinehart and Winston, New York.
Beals, Ralph, and Emil Haury
  1944 Summary of Sections Dealing with Mesoamerica and the Southwest. In *El Norte de México y el Sur de Estados Unidos*, pp. 351–355. Tercera Reunion de Mesa Redonda sobre Problemas Antropologicos de Mexico y Centro America, vol. 3. Sociedad Mexicana de Antropología, Mexico City.
Blom, Frans
  1932 *The Maya Ball-Game "Pok-Ta-Pok" (Called "Tlachtli" by the Aztec)*. Middle American Research Institute, Tulane University, Publication No. 4, 485–530.
Borhegyi, Stephan F. de
  1980 *The Pre-Columbian Ballgames: A Pan-Mesoamerican Tradition*. Milwaukee Public Museum Contributions in Anthropology and History No. 1.
Brand, Donald D.
  1939 Notes on the Geography and Archaeology of Zape, Durango. In *So Live the Works of Men*, edited by Donald D. Brand and Fred E. Harvey, pp. 75–106. University of New Mexico Press, Albuquerque.
Braniff, Beatriz
  1975 Arqueologia del Norte de México. In *Los Pueblos y Senorios Teocraticos*, pp. 217–278. El periodo de los ciudades urbanas No. 1. Instituto Nacional de Antropología e Historia, Mexico City.
Brew, J. O.
  1940 Introduction. *Papers of the Excavators Club* 1(2):3–5. Boston.
  1944 On the Pueblo IV and on the Katchina-Tlaloc Relations. In *El Norte de Mexico y el Sur de Estados Unidos*, pp. 241–245. Tercera Reunion de Mesa Redonda sobre Problemas Antropologicos de Mexico y Centre America, vol. 3. Sociedad Mexicana de Antropologia, Mexico City.

Brown, Roy Bernard
  1980 A Preparatory Statement to a Paleoecological Study on the Northern Frontier of Mesoamerica. Ms. on file, Arizona State Museum Library, University of Arizona, Tucson.
Corbett, John M.
  1939 *Ball Courts and Ball Games of the Ancient American Indians.* Unpublished M.A. Thesis, Department of Anthropology, University of Southern California, Los Angeles.
Crosswhite, Frank S.
  1981 Desert Plants, Habitat and Agriculture in Relation to the Major Pattern of Cultural Differentiation in the O'odham People of the Sonoran Desert. *Desert Plants* 3(2):47−76.
Dennell, Robin
  1983 *European Economic Prehistory, A New Approach.* Academic Press, New York.
Di Peso, Charles C.
  1974 *Casas Grandes: A Fallen Trading Center of the Gran Chichimeca,* 3 vols. Northland Press, Flagstaff.
Dirst, Victoria Ann
  1979 *A Prehistoric Frontier in Sonora.* Ph.D. dissertation, University of Arizona, Tucson. University Microfilms, Ann Arbor.
Ekholm, Gordon F.
  1942 *Excavations at Guasave, Sinaloa, Mexico.* Anthropological Papers of the American Museum of Natural History No. 38(4). New York.
Ferdon, Edwin N., Jr.
  1967 The Hohokam "Ball Court": An Alternative View of Its Function. *Kiva* 33(1):1−14.
Flannery, Kent V.
  1972 The Origins of the Village as a Settlement Type in Mesoamerica and the Near East: A Comparative Study. In *Man, Settlement and Urbanism,* edited by Peter J. Ucko, Ruth Tringham, and A. W. Dimbleby, pp. 23−53. Duckworth, London.
Ford, Richard I.
  1981 Gardening and Farming Before A.D. 1000: Patterns of Prehistoric Cultivation North of Mexico. *Journal of Ethnobiology* 1(1):6−27.
Fowler, Catherine
  1980 Some Lexical Clues to Uto-Aztecan Prehistory. Paper presented at the Uto-Aztecan Historical Symposium, June 24, at the 1980 Linguistics Institute, University of New Mexico, Albuquerque.
Freidel, David A.
  1979 Culture Areas and Interaction Spheres: Contrasting Approaches to the Emergence of Civilization in the Maya Lowlands. *American Antiquity* 44:36−54.

Gladwin, Harold S., Emil W. Haury, E. B. Sayles, and Nora Gladwin
  1937 *Excavations at Snaketown I: Material Culture.* Medallion Papers No. 25. Globe, Ariz.
Greenberg, Joseph H.
  1963 *Essays in Linguistics.* Phoenix Books, Chicago.
Grove, David C.
  1981 The Formative Period and the Evolution of Complex Culture. In *Archaeology,* edited by Jeremy A. Sabloff, pp. 373–391. Supplement to the Handbook of Middle American Indians, vol. 1. Victoria Reifler Bricker, general editor, University of Texas Press, Austin.
Haas, Mary R.
  1969 *The Prehistory of Languages.* Mouton, The Hague.
Hammond, George P., and Agapito Rey
  1953 *Don Juan de Onate: Colonizer of New Mexico, 1596–1628.* University of New Mexico Press, Albuquerque.
Haury, Emil W.
  1945 The Problem of Contacts Between the Southwestern United States and Mexico. *Southwestern Journal of Anthropology* 1(1):55–74.
  1976 *The Hohokam: Desert Farmers and Craftsmen.* University of Arizona Press, Tucson.
Heartfield, Lorraine
  1975 Archeological Investigations of Four Sites in Southwestern Coahuila, Mexico. *Bulletin of the Texas Archaeological Society* 46:127–177.
Hellmuth, Nicholas M.
  1975 Pre-Columbian Ballgame, Archaeology and Architecture. *F.L.A.A.R. Progress Reports* 1(1):1–31.
Hester, Thomas R.
  1975 Late Prehistoric Cultural Patterns along the Lower Rio Grande of Texas. *Bulletin of the Texas Archeological Society* 46:107–126.
Jennings, Jesse D.
  1973 The Short Useful Life of a Simple Hypothesis. *Tebiwa* 16(1):1–9.
Johnson, Ann Stoffler
  1958 Similarities in Hohokam and Chalchihuites Artifacts. *American Antiquity* 24:126–130.
Kelley, Ellen Abbott, and J. Charles Kelley
  1980 Sipapu and Pyramid Too: The Temple of the Crypt at Alta Vistas, Chalchihuites. In *New Frontiers in the Archaeology and Ethnohistory of the Greater Southwest,* edited by Carroll L. Riley and Basil C. Hedrick, pp. 62–80. Transactions of the Illinois State Academy of Science No. 73(2).
Kelley, J. Charles
  1952 Factors Involved in the Abandonment of Certain Peripheral Southwestern Settlements. *American Anthropologist* 54(3):356–387.
  1953 Some Geographic and Cultural Factors Involved in Mexican-

Southeastern Contacts. In *Indian Tribes of Aboriginal America, Selected Papers of the 29th International Congress of Americanists*, edited by Sol Tax, pp. 139–144. University of Chicago Press.

1956 Settlement Patterns in North-Central Mexico. In *Settlement Patterns of the New World*, edited by Gordon R. Willey, pp. 128–139. Viking Fund Publications in Anthropology No. 23.

1966 Mesoamerica and the Southwestern United States. In *Archaeological Frontiers and External Connections*, edited by Gordon F. Ekholm and Gordon R. Willey, pp. 95–110. Handbook of Middle American Indians, vol. 4, Robert Wauchope, general editor. University of Texas Press, Austin.

1971 Archaeology of the Northern Frontier: Zacatecas and Durango. In *Archaeology of Northern Mesoamerica*, edited by Gordon F. Ekholm, pp. 768–804. Handbook of Middle American Indians, vol. 11(2), Robert Wauchope, general editor. University of Texas Press, Austin.

1980 Discussion of Papers by Plog, Doyel, and Riley. In *Current Issues in Hohokam Prehistory*, edited by David Doyel and Fred Plog, pp. 49–66. Arizona State University Anthropological Research Papers No. 23, Tempe.

Kelley, J. Charles, and Ellen Abbott
1966 The Cultural Sequence on the North Central Frontier of Mesoamerica. *XXXVI Congreso Internacional de Americanistas, Espana, 1964*, vol. 1.

Kelley, J. Charles and Ellen Abbott Kelley
1975 An Alternative Hypothesis for the Explanation of Anasazi Culture History. In *Collected Papers in Honor of Florence Hawley Ellis*, edited by Theodore R. Frisbie, pp. 178–223. Papers of the Archaeological Society of New Mexico No. 2. Hooper Publishing, Norman.

Kelley, J. Charles, and Howard D. Winters
1960 A Revision of the Archaeological Sequence in Sinaloa, Mexico. *American Antiquity* 25:547–561.

Kelly, Isabel T.
1944 West Mexico and the Hohokam. In *El Norte de México y el Sur de Estados Unidos*, pp. 206–222. Tercera Reunion de Mesa Redonda sobre Problemas Antropologicos de México y Centro America, vol. 3. Sociedad Mexico de Antropología, Mexico City.

Kidder, A. V.
1962 *An Introduction to the Study of Southwestern Archaeology*, edited by Irving Rouse. Yale University Press, New Haven.

Kirchoff, Paul
1954 Gatherers and Farmers in the Greater Southwest: A Problem in Classification. *American Anthropologist* 56(4:1):529–550.

LeBlanc, Steven A.
1980 The Dating of Casas Grandes. *American Antiquity* 45:799–806.

1982 The Advent of Pottery in the Southwest. In *Southwestern Ceramics: A Comparative Review*, edited by Albert H. Schroeder, pp. 27–52. The Arizona Archaeologist No. 15. Phoenix.

Leyenaar, Ted J. J.
1978 *Ulma, the Perpetuation in Mexico of the Pre-Spanish Ballgame Ulamatiztli*. Medeelingen van het Rijksmuseum voor Volkenkunde No. 23. Ministerie van Cultuur, Recreatie, en Maatschappelijk Werk, Leiden.

Lowe, Garth
1977 The Mixe-Zoque as Competing Neighbors of the Early Lowland Maya. In *The Origins of Maya Civilization*, edited by Richard E. W. Adams, pp. 197–248. University of New Mexico Press, Albuquerque.

McBride, Harold W.
1969 The Extent of the Chupicuaro Tradition. In *The Natalie Wood Collection of Pre-Columbian Ceramics from Chupicuaro, Guanajuato, Mexico at UCLA*, edited by J. D. Frierman, pp. 33–47. Museum and Laboratories of Ethnic Arts and Technology, University of California, Los Angeles.

McGuire, Randall H.
1980 The Mesoamerican Connection in the Southwest. *Kiva* 46(1–2): 3–38.

Martin, John F.
1973 On the Estimation of the Size of Local Groups in a Hunting-Gathering Environment. *American Anthropologist* 75(5): 1448–1468.

Martin, Paul S., and Fred Plog
1973 *The Archaeology of Arizona*. Doubleday/Natural History Press, Garden City, New York.

Meillassoux, Claude
1981 *Maidens, Meal and Money; Capitalism and the Domestic Community*. Cambridge University Press, Cambridge, England.

Miller, Wick R.
1983 Uto-Aztecan Languages. In *Southwest*, edited by Alfonso Ortiz, pp. 113–124. Handbook of North American Indians, vol. 10, William G. Sturtevant, general editor. Smithsonian Institution, Washington, D.C.

Moore, James A.
1981 The Effects of Information Networks in Hunter-Gatherer Societies. In *Hunter-Gatherer Foraging Strategies*, edited by Bruce Winterhalder and Eric Alden Smith, pp. 194–217. University of Chicago Press.
1983 The Trouble with Know-it-alls: Information as a Social and Ecological Resource. In *Archaeological Hammers and Theories*, edited by James A. Moore and Arthur S. Keene, pp. 173–192. Academic Press, New York.

Needham, Rodney
1975 Polythetic Classification: Convergence and Consequences. *Man* 10(3): 349–369.

Nelson, Richard S.
  1981 *The Role of a Pochteca System in Hohokam Exchange*. Ph.D. dissertation, New York University, New York. University Microfilms, Ann Arbor.
Olsen, Stanley J., and John W. Olsen
  1974 The Macaws of Grasshopper Ruin. *Kiva* 40(1–2):67–70.
Pailes, Richard A.
  1972 *An Archaeological Reconnaissance of Southern Sonora and Reconsideration of the Rio Sonora Culture*. Ph.D. dissertation, Southern Illinois University, Carbondale. University Microfilms, Ann Arbor.
  1976 Recientes Investigaciones Arqueologicas en el Sur de Sonora. In *Sonora: Antropología del Desierto*, edited by Beatriz Braniff and Richard Felger, pp. 137–156. Colección Cientifica No. 27. Instituto Nacional de Antropología y Historia, Mexico City.
  1980 The Upper Rio Sonora Valley in Prehistoric Trade. In *New Frontiers in the Archaeology and Ethnohistory of the Greater Southwest*, edited by Carroll L. Riley and Basil C. Hedrick, pp. 20–39. Transactions of the Illinois State Academy of Science No. 72(4).
Palerm, Angel, and Eric Wolf
  1957 Ecological Potential and Cultural Development in Mesoamerica. In *Studies in Human Ecology*, pp. 1–37. Anthropological Society of Washington and Pan American Union Social Science Monograph No. 3.
Pasztory, Esther
  1978 Artistic Traditions of the Middle Classic Period. In *Middle Classic Mesoamerica: A.D. 400–700*, edited by Esther Pasztory, pp. 108–142. Columbia University Press, New York.
Pennington, Campbell W.
  1969 *The Tepehuan of Chihuahua, Their Material Culture*. University of Utah Press, Salt Lake City.
Plog, Fred, Steadman Upham, and Phil C. Weigand
  1982 A Perspective on Mogollon-Mesoamerican Interaction. In *Mogollon Archaeology, Proceedings of the 1980 Mogollon Conference*, edited by Patrick H. Beckett and Kim Silverbird, pp. 227–238. Acoma Books, Ramon, Calif.
Plog, Stephen
  1980 Village Autonomy in the American Southwest: An Evaluation of the Evidence. In *Models and Methods in Regional Exchange*, edited by Robert E. Fry, pp. 135–146. SAA Papers No. 1. Society for American Archaeology, Washington, D.C.
Powers, Robert P., William B. Gillespie, and Stephen H. Lekson
  1983 *The Outlier Survey: A Regional View of Settlement in the San Juan Basin*. Reports of the Chaco Center No. 3. National Park Service, Albuquerque.

Riley, Carroll L.
1982 *The Frontier People: The Greater Southwest in the Protohistoric Period*. Center for Archaeological Investigations Occasional Paper No. 1. Southern Illinois University.

Riley, Carroll L., and Howard D. Winters
1963 The Prehistoric Tepehuan of Northern Mexico. *Southwestern Journal of Anthropology* 19(2):177–185.

Root, Dolores
1983 Information Exchange and the Spatial Configurations of Egalitarian Societies. In *Archaeological Hammers and Theories*, edited by James A. Moore and Arthur S. Keene, pp. 193–220. Academic Press, New York.

Salisbury, R. F.
1962 *From Stone to Steel: Economic Consequences of a Technological Change in New Guinea*. Cambridge University Press, Cambridge, England.

Sapir, Edward
1918 *Time Perspective in Aboriginal American Culture, A Study in Method*. Geological Survey of Canada Memoir No. 90, Anthropological Series No. 13.

Satterthwaite, Linton, Jr.
1944 Ball Courts. In *Piedras Negras Archaeology: Architecture*. University Museum, University of Pennsylvania, Philadelphia.

Sauer, Carl O.
1934 *The Distribution of Aboriginal Tribes and Languages in Northwestern Mexico*. Ibero-Americana No. 5. Berkeley.

Sauer, Carl O., and Donald Brand
1930 Pueblo Sites in Southeastern Arizona. *University of California Publications in Geography* 3(7):415–458.
1931 Prehistoric Settlements of Sonora with Special Reference to *Cerro de Trincheras*. *University of California Publications in Geography* 5(3): 67–148.

Sayles, E. B.
1945 *The San Simon Branch Excavations at Cave Creek and in the San Simon Valley I: Material Culture*. Medallion Papers No. 34. Globe, Ariz.

Scarborough, Vernon, Beverly Mitchum, Sorraya Carr, and David Friedel
1982 Two Late Preclassic Ballcourts at the Lowland Maya Center of Cerros, Northern Belize. *Journal of Field Archaeology* 9(1):21–34.

Spielmann, Katherine Ann
1982 *Inter-societal Food Acquisition among Egalitarian Societies: An Ecological Study of Plains/Pueblo Interaction in the American Southwest*. Ph.D. dissertation, University of Michigan, Ann Arbor. University Microfilms, Ann Arbor.

Spinden, Herbert J.
1928 *Ancient Civilizations of Mexico and Central America*, 3d rev.

ed. American Museum of Natural History Handbook Series No. 3. New York.

Steele, Susan

1979 Uto-Aztecan: An Assessment for Historical and Comparative Linguistics. In *The Languages of Native America: Historical and Comparative Assessment*, edited by Lyle Campbell and Marianne Mithun, pp. 444–544. University of Texas Press, Austin.

Stern, Theodore

1948 The Rubber Ball Games of the Americas. *Monographs of the American Ethnological Society* 17.

Taladoire, Eric

1981 Les Terrains de Jeu de Balle (Mésoameriqué et Sud-ouest des Etats-Unis). In *Etudes Mesoamericaines*, Serie No. 2(4). Mission Archeologique et Ethnologique Française au Mexique. Mexico.

Titiev, Mischa

1960 A Fresh Approach to the Problem of Magic and Religion. *Southwestern Journal of Anthropology* 16(3): 292–298.

Weigand, Phil C.

1968 The Mines and Mining Techniques of the Chalchihuites Culture. *American Antiquity* 33: 45–61.

1978 The Prehistory of the State of Zacatecas: An Interpretation (part 1). *Anthropology* 2(1): 67–87.

1979 The Prehistory of the State of Zacatecas: An Interpretation (part 2). *Anthropology* 2(2): 22–41.

Whalen, Michael E.

1981 Origin and Evolution of Ceramics in Western Texas. *Bulletin of the Texas Archaeological Society* 52: 215–229.

Wilcox, David R.

1979 The Hohokam Regional System. In *An Archaeological Test of Sites in the Gila Butte-Santan Region, South-Central Arizona*, by Glen Rice, et al., pp. 77–116. Arizona State University Anthropological Research Papers No. 18, Tempe.

1984 Multi-ethnic Division of Labor in the Protohistoric Southwest. In *Collected Papers in Honor of Harry L. Hadlock*, edited by Nancy L. Fox, pp. 141–154. Papers of the Archaeological Society of New Mexico No. 9. Albuquerque.

Wilcox, David R., and Charles Sternberg

1983 *Hohokam Ballcourts and their Interpretation*. Arizona State Museum Archaeological Series No. 160. University of Arizona, Tucson.

Wobst, H. Martin

1976 Locational Relationships in Paleolithic Society. *Journal of Human Evolution* 5: 49–58.

1977 Stylistic Behavior and Information Exchange. *Anthropological Pa-

pers 61:317–342. Museum of Anthropology, University of Michigan, Ann Arbor.

1978 The Archaeo-Ethnology of Hunter-Gatherers, or the Tyranny of the Ethnographic Record in Archaeology. *American Antiquity* 43: 303–309.

Wyshak, Lillian Worthing, Rainer Berger, John A. Graham, and Robert F. Heizer

1971 A Possible Ball Court at La Venta, Mexico. *Nature* 232:650–651.

Zingg, Robert Mowry

1939 *A Reconstruction of Uto-Aztekan History.* Contributions to Ethnography, vol. 2. University of Denver.

9

Pochtecas and Prestige: Mesoamerican Artifacts in Hohokam Sites

Richard S. Nelson

In recent years, the topic of prehistoric exchange has assumed increasing importance for archaeologists working in the American Southwest much as it has for archaeologists working elsewhere. No single aspect of this subject has attracted more attention or excited more controversy among southwesternists than the problem of exchange between the Southwest and Mesoamerica (e.g., Di Peso et al. 1974; McGuire 1980). Much argument has centered around the possible existence of *pochtecas*, organized trading groups from Mesoamerica similar to those characteristic of the Aztecs, and their possible role, if any, in exchange links between Mesoamerica and the Southwest. Some archaeologists (e.g., Di Peso 1974; Kelley and Kelley 1974) have argued that these groups not only existed but managed to obtain some degree of control or dominance over local southwestern societies, while others (Haury 1976; McGuire 1980) have taken essentially opposing positions.

In this paper it will be argued that another model, one which can be applied to both regional and long-distance (mesoamerican) exchange, without invoking any conquest or colonization explanation, offers a more rigorous and anthropological approach to the subject of exchange. This model utilizes the concept of spheres of exchange or conveyance, derived from social anthropological literature, and is applied to the problem of mesoamerican artifacts or materials occurring in a prehistoric southwestern culture. This study focuses upon the culture of the Hohokam, who occupied much of southern and southcentral Arizona for at least 12 centuries. The data used are summarized from the author's dissertation (Nelson 1981). The Hohokam are a particularly appropriate choice for this type of analysis. Not only have unusual numbers of probable mesoamerican artifacts been recovered at certain Hohokam sites, but other aspects of this culture, such as ballcourts, platform mounds, and a number of locally produced portable artifacts, also suggest unusually strong ties with Mesoamerica. These features and others have led several archaeologists (Di Peso 1968; Schroeder 1966) to suggest that this area came under the strong influence of *pochteca* groups from Mesoamerica.

The following procedure is followed. The concept of spheres of exchange or conveyance is defined and discussed, and then put into an archaeological context in the form of two hypotheses. These are tested using data on artifacts and materials and their quantities, ages, distributions, contexts, and associations. Relevant ancillary data on settlement systems are also discussed. Finally certain conclusions are reached concerning Hohokam spheres of exchange as they relate to the distribution of mesoamerican artifacts and materials and as they relate to Hohokam exchange and organization.

Theoretical Basis

The term *sphere of exchange* was used by Raymond Firth in his analysis of the economic system of the Polynesian outlier island of Tikopia to denote the existence of several series of exchanges in which the goods of one were not completely convertible into goods of the others (Firth 1965: 340). The term has also been used extensively by Paul Bohannon, who discusses the existence in premarket, often stateless societies of different types of exchanges involving different types of objects or services (Bohannon 1965:249). Thus, there can be a subsistence sphere, involving basic materials of subsistence, and a prestige sphere, involving objects related to wealth, status, role, or ritual. As Fried (1967:109–110) points out, the objects that move through different spheres or sectors of such economies are generally not mutually exchangeable; prestige objects cannot be used to procure food or productive resources.

There are some stateless societies in which prestige or wealth objects do move through the same channels as subsistence materials. This is true, for example, in such egalitarian Melanesian societies as the Tsembaga of the Central Highlands of New Guinea whose economy has been described by Roy Rappaport. According to him these groups trade such nonutilitarian wealth objects as shell ornaments, bird of paradise feathers, and specialized axe blades that they use in certain types of transaction such as bride price payments (Rappaport 1968:103). These objects are obtained from other groups, on the coast or elsewhere, through the same channels as those used to obtain basic necessities such as salt. In fact, prestige objects are freely exchanged for subsistence goods, a circumstance which Rappaport (1968: 106) believes both stimulates and facilitates the distribution of utilitarian goods. It seems obvious that, in the case of the Tsembaga at least, distinct prestige and subsistence spheres do not exist.

It should be reiterated here that the anthropological term *wealth* does not have the same connotation that it does in our own society, so that the wealth objects described above are really more closely related to prestige than to wealth in the colloquial sense. Wealth objects circulate most freely in specialized transactions such as bride wealth payments. It may be that objects more closely linked to status may circulate in an even more restricted fashion, especially in societies which are ranked or stratified in Fried's (1967) sense of those terms. However, the two categories of wealth and status objects are probably not completely separable. The degree to which they circulate is probably dependent upon the degree of social complexity and the nature of the role or status that is symbolized by the object. In other words, objects which symbolize or communicate something about a status or role which is held by only a few individuals may not circulate very widely, especially if that status is ascribed rather than achieved. These concepts are incorporated into the following hypotheses.

Hypotheses

Hypothesis 1. Exchange or procurement relationships with Meso-america involved a Hohokam elite. One would expect that mesoamerican objects or materials would display a special and more restrictive distribution than other imported materials. These materials or objects should tend to occur or cluster archaeologically in especially rich mortuary areas or features, or in sites distinguished by specialized public or ceremonial structures, such as platform mounds, house mounds, ballcourts, plazas, or great houses.

In terms of exchange spheres, one might expect to find a relatively distinct prestige sphere perhaps restricted to a few specialized sites and including as integral parts not only mesoamerican artifacts but also regional (southwestern) or local materials or artifacts which display the type of distribution described in the paragraph above. These regional or local objects should also be very rare or absent farther along regional exchange networks, at greater distances from the sources. Also, since the major recipients would have been located in sites with special, perhaps central place, functions in local settlement systems, these sites should actually contain larger quantities or proportions of the exotic artifacts than other sites intermediate between them and the ultimate source of the artifacts, in accordance with the patterns to be expected from the type of directional trade (Renfrew 1977:85–86) associated with central-place sites.

Hypothesis 2. Hohokam society was relatively egalitarian. One might expect that mesoamerican artifacts would display an even and continuous distribution, occurring in many sites and in sites along regional trade routes or networks farther from the sources, along with local or regional artifacts or materials. In this case, mesoamerican artifacts might also exhibit a fairly wide and even distribution in sites located between the Hohokam region and Mesoamerica. Such results might indicate either the absence of a well-defined prestige sphere or the presence of a diffuse one in which prestige objects were not only widely accessible, but were also able to move through the same channels as subsistence goods.

Methodology

As already stated, the scope of this paper comprises the Hohokam of central and southern Arizona. Figure 11 shows the area and the sites to be covered. The present paper deals only with the Colonial, Sedentary, and Classic periods of the Hohokam chronology. For the purposes of analysis and comparison, this discussion is divided into two sections, the Colonial and the Sedentary periods being one, and the Classic period, the other. In other words, the two sections comprise two chronological segments, one from circa A.D. 550–650 to circa 1150, the other from about A.D. 1150 or 1200 to about 1450.

The materials to be covered include probable mesoamerican artifacts, primarily copper bells and pyrites mosaic mirrors. Macaw and parrot remains, very rare in Hohokam sites as compared to other contemporary southwestern sites, and intrusive sherds or vessels, constituting a few specimens from three sites, are discussed very briefly. Only specimens pertaining to the Colonial, Sedentary, or Classic periods are included. In addition, certain regional or local artifacts or materials which display patterns of distribution or context similar to those of mesoamerican artifacts (and are in some cases actually associated with the latter) are described in the analysis section.

Artifacts

Copper Bells

Since the earliest days of archaeological fieldwork in the Southwest, the discovery of copper bells in Hohokam and other southwestern sites has suggested the possibility of trade or other contact with Mesoamerica. Various functions including use as ceremonial paraphernalia, ornaments, or musical objects have been suggested. Several archaeologists, including Pendergast (1962), Sprague and Signori (1963), and Di Peso et al. (1974, vol. 8), developed typologies for bells from the Southwest and Mesoamerica. It is the Sprague and Signori typology which is used here. Descriptions of the types and of the criteria used to define them can be found in Sprague and Signori (1963; see also Sprague 1964).

For hypothesis 1 to be accepted, the data on bells should reveal a pattern of concentration in specialized contexts at specialized sites. Bells should also exhibit the type of specialized associations that are predicted, and likewise exhibit scarcity or absence in areas farther along regional exchange networks and thus presumably farther from the ultimate sources. In

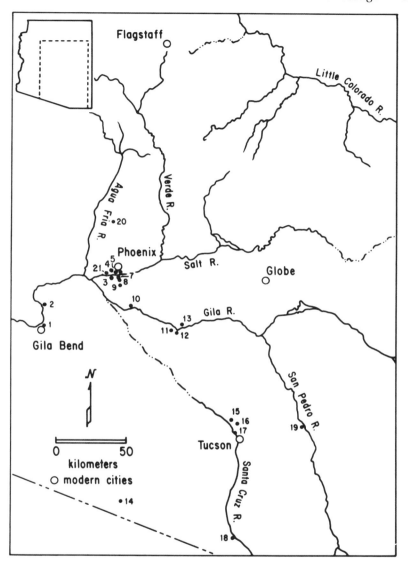

Figure 11. Hohokam sites mentioned in text

the present instance, the latter pattern might be exhibited in terms of different bell styles rather than simple presence or absence. For the second hypothesis to be accepted (and the first rejected) a more even and continuous pattern in terms of both intersite and intrasite distribution is predicted. Bells should occur in a variety of contexts and associations and should exhibit evidence, in terms of style distributions, of moving freely through regional exchange networks.

Unfortunately, as with other artifacts, the quality of data on bells varies greatly from site to site. While types and quantities are frequently recorded, data on contexts are much less likely to be available. Styles were frequently of long duration and were found over large geographical areas so that the exact source cannot be located at present even with the use of metallurgical techniques such as those of Root (1937). What can be done at present, however, is to describe the regional and temporal distribution of Hohokam bells and then attempt a comparison with the distribution of bells and bell styles from other southwestern cultures.

Table 4 lists Hohokam bells. It and Table 5 include separate counts of one widespread bell style, IA1a-i, for comparative purposes. As will be demonstrated in the analysis section, 6G, house #8 at Snaketown contained a variety and quantity of objects that would suggest a specialized function consistent with the predictions of hypothesis 1, an impression strengthened by its location in a part of the site (see Figure 12) characterized by a concentration of specialized features and artifacts. At the present time, there were no records of bells from Hohokam sites in the Papagueria, the Tonto Basin, or the Verde valley.

Since data on regional distributions of bell styles are also necessary for evaluating the hypotheses, data on other southwestern bells are presented in Table 5. These data indicate that in all non-Hohokam areas at all times and in Classic period Hohokam sites, from 50% to 100% of the typed bells were of one style, IA1a-i. It should be emphasized that the sample used here is rather small and that sampling error is a real possibility. Sources of error could exist in the large numbers of untyped bells not used in the analysis. Nevertheless, it is contended that the patterns exhibited by the data are valid, given their repeated occurrence among bells from different parts of the Southwest.

Data from the large late site of Casas Grandes, Chihuahua, Mexico, are also relevant to the present discussion. Of 115 crotals (bells) assigned to the Medio period, generally considered to be roughly contemporaneous with the Hohokam Classic period (Wilcox and Sternberg 1983:75), about 50 were of Di Peso's type IA1a, the equivalent of Sprague and Signori's type IA1a-i, while 13 others were of styles equivalent to eight of Pendergast's or Sprague's other styles. Forty-six others were of styles not reported by either Pendergast or Sprague (Di Peso et al. 1974, 7:608–529). It would appear that at Casas Grandes as elsewhere, IA1a-i bells comprised one of the dominant styles. This style in fact seems to have predominated everywhere in the

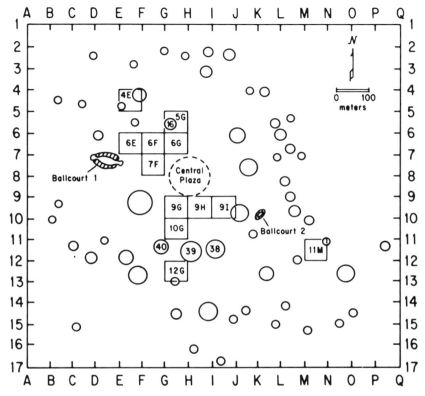

Figure 12. Map of Snaketown, Az : U : 13 : 1 (ASM)

Southwest after about A.D. 1150 or 1200. However, the most striking pattern in the bell distribution data is seen in bells dating between circa A.D. 900 or 1000 and 1150, at which time there seem to have been sharp contrasts between Sedentary period bells and bells from other contemporary southwestern ruins, primarily Chacoan and Classic Mimbres sites and perhaps Aztec Ruin. It is perhaps no coincidence that all these other sites are located in New Mexico. These data suggest that during the Sedentary period the Hohokam were obtaining their bells from different sources than those supplying bells to the rest of the Southwest at that time. More to the point, their bells were apparently not moving along regional exchange networks, and thus exhibited the type of distribution predicted by hypothesis 1. The appearance of what seem to be imitation bells made from black steatite at a few sites in the Vosberg area near Young, central Arizona, seems to confirm this inference, as does the absence of bells in the Verde valley (Fish et al. 1980 : 163).

TABLE 4. Hohokam Bells

Site	Location	Number of Specimens	Style	Context	Age
Snaketown	Phoenix Basin	28	ID1a	house 6G, #8 (storehouse)	Sacaton phase
Casa Grande, Compounds B, C, D or Clanhouse 1	Phoenix Basin	2	IA1a-i	no data	Soho phase?
Casa Grande, Compound B	Phoenix Basin	1	no data	no data	Soho phase?
Casa Grande, Compound B	Phoenix Basin	2	IA1a-i	one from ceremonial rooms, one from northwestern rooms	Civano phase
Casa Grande	Phoenix Basin	3	2 IA1a-i; 1 fragment (probably IC1a)	no data	Classic period
La Ciudad	Phoenix Basin	2	IA1a-i	child burial	Classic period
Pueblo Grande	Phoenix Basin	2	1 IA1a-i	no data	Probably Civano phase
Pueblo del Monte	Phoenix Basin	1	no data	no data	Civano phase
Los Hornos	Phoenix Basin	1	1 no data	from room Ruin 7	Classic period
Las Colinas	Phoenix Basin	10	1 IA1a-i	no data	Probably Classic period
Homestead	Phoenix Basin	1	no data	no data	no data
Salt River Valley	Phoenix Basin	1	IA1a-i	no data	no data
South of Phoenix	Phoenix Basin	3	IC6a	no data	no data
Near Casa Grande	Phoenix Basin	1	ID2a; ID4a; ID6a	no data	no data
Gatlin Site	Near Gila Bend	(a)	IA1a-i	(a)	(a)
		60–80 from private collections	(a) 43 IC2a; 9 IA1a-i; 4 IC7a; 1 IC1b	from very rich cremations east of platform mound in association with large numbers of arrow-points and some intrusive vessels	Sacaton phase

Site	Number of bells	Region	Typed Specimens	Context	Period/Phase
	(b) 3 found by Wasley		(b) 2 IC1a; 1 IA1a-i	(b) 2 from between linings of platform mound, 1 from nearby house	(b) Sacaton phase
Romo Cache	15 bells known plus indefinite number disposed of by collector	Tucson Basin	15 IA1a-i	as part of cache with about 100,000 stone beads with Tanque Verde Red-on-brown bowl	Classic period
Marana (private collection)	(a) 12 (b) 1	Tucson Basin	(a) 12 IA1a-i (b) IA1a-i	(a) with cremation (b) unknown	(a) no data (b) no data
Hodges	1	Tucson Basin	IA1a-i	unknown; no record of this bell either in catalogue or in final report	no data
Alder Wash	1	San Pedro Valley	no data available	from pithouse	unspecified but could be Sedentary period

Summary

Period	Number of Sites	Number of Typed Specimens	Number of Type IA1a-i	% of Total
Sedentary	2	88	10	11.4
Classic	2	26	25	96.2

Data compiled from Di Peso et al. (1974); Fewkes (1912); Hammack (1971); Haury and Gifford (1959); Sprague (1964); Sprague and Signori (1963); Turney (1929); Wasley (1960); and Withers (1946).

TABLE 5. Southwestern Bell Styles

Region	Sites	Total Number of Typed Bells	Number of Type IA1a-i Bells	%	Age
Flagstaff	Winona, Copper Bell Ruin, NA627, Canyon de Flag, Wupatki, Flagstaff area	13	11	84.7	Most probably 12th or 13th centuries
Little Colorado	Pollock Site; Chavez Pass; Four Mile Ruin; Showlow, Babbit Ranch	6	4	66.7	Pollock, Late 13th century; Chavez Pass, 14th century
Upper Salt River	Kinishba	1	1	100.0	Tree-ring dates: A.D. 1147–1361, but no clustering
Southeastern Arizona	Webb; Kuykendall; 76 Ranch; Mammoth	7	4	57.1	76 Ranch, ca. A.D. 1300–1400; Mammoth, A.D. 1200–1400; Kuykendall, archaeo-magnetic dates: A.D. 1385±23; A.D. 1375±18 yrs.
Prescott region	No specific sites	4	4	100.0	No data
Tonto Basin Miami area (data problematic)	Hilltop House; Gila Pueblo; Globe area; Young, Roosevelt Lake, and Roosevelt areas; Tonto Basin; Livingston	51?	27?	52.0	All dated post 1 A.D.

Point of Pines area					
Point of Pines area	Point of Pines; Turkey Creek	11	11	100.0	Both post A.D. 1200
Upper Gila-San Francisco River, New Mexico	Delgar Ruin; Apache Creek	2	1	50.0	No date
Mimbres area, S.W. New Mexico 1000–1150	Cameron Creek; Mattocks Ruin; Galaz; Old Town; McSherry?	16	13	81.3	Dated spp. maybe ca. A.D.
Near Mexican border, S.W. New Mexico	Osborne Ruin	11	11	100.0	No date
Southern and Southeastern New Mexico	Cox Ranch; Bloom Mound; Mt. Riley	9	8	88.9	No data
Chaco Canyon, New Mexico	Pueblo Bonito	20?	12	60.0	From ca. 900–1000 to ca. 1150
Four Corners San Juan; S.W. Colorado	Red Rock; Aztec Ruin and Vicinity Goodman's Point	4	3	75.0	For Aztec Ruin, ca. A.D. 1110–1121

Data compiled from Mills and Mills (1969); Sprague (1964); and Sprague and Signori (1963).

Some rather striking changes in Hohokam bell procurement and exchange may well have occurred during the Classic period, judging from bell style distributions. At this time, bells obtained by the Hohokam could have been passing from them to groups farther along regional exchange networks, a pattern predicted by hypothesis 2.

Regarding context, data already presented for Sedentary period bells from Snaketown and the Gatlin site give a hint of special distributional and contextual patterns. Data on context are lacking for many Classic period bells, so that one cannot say very much about possible patterns for these specimens. However, no concentration of bells similar to that found in the Gatlin site has yet been reported from any Classic period site. While sampling error is always a possibility, the available data when taken along with the style distributional data suggest the existence of a pattern very different from that of the Sedentary period, and one perhaps consistent with patterns predicted by hypothesis 2.

Pyrites Mosaic Mirrors

Among the most exotic objects found at a few Hohokam sites were pyrites mosaic mirrors. These were described by Woodbury as "some of the most remarkable products of prehistoric American workmanship" (1965 : 472), and they constitute some of the best evidence for a special exchange relationship with Mesoamerica. These are round or occasionally rectilinear plaques of stone or ceramics, covered or partly covered on at least one face by a mosaic of thin polygonal plates of iron pyrites or marcasite. The mosaic plates were rounded to shape, beveled, and placed on the base with some sort of cementing agent. The difficulty of cutting and grinding pyrites, which is both hard and brittle, has frequently been emphasized by archaeologists who have examined these artifacts (e.g., Gladwin et al. 1937; Smith and Kidder 1951).

The backs were made of slate, sandstone, shale, tuff, and occasionally pottery and were in some cases decorated by carving, by stucco, or by a technique called pseudo-cloisonné. In most cases, they had several perforations, presumably for attachment or suspension, either near the edge or near the center. While groups of mirrors have been found in the Southwest and as far south as Panama, their major concentration was in Mesoamerica, especially highland Guatemala, western Mexico, Yucatan, and possibly Vera Cruz. Chronologically they range from the late Formative to the Postclassic. Hohokam mirrors were apparently restricted to the Colonial and Sedentary periods and have so far been reported in publications from just six sites, including three sites in the Phoenix Basin (Snaketown, the Grewe site, and a cave near Tempe); two sites in the Santa Cruz valley (the Hodges Ruin and Paloparado); and one site (Valshni Village) in the Papagueria. Previously unpublished specimens have now been reported from the site of Cremation Hill in south Phoenix (David Wilcox, personal communication, 1982).

It is now generally accepted that southwestern mirrors were imports from Mesoamerica. Mirrors occurred in early Classic and Formative sites in Mesoamerica, thus establishing considerable temporal precedence there. Also, the technique of pseudo-cloisonné decoration has no obvious antecedents in the Southwest, but is both older and was more widespread in Mesoamerica (Holien 1974 : 164). Highland Guatemala is a possible source for Hohokam mirrors while more northerly sources such as western Mexico cannot be ruled out either. Objects covered with pseudo-cloisonné were common in western Mexico as early as A.D. 300 (Holien 1974 : 164) but do not seem to have included mirror backs.

Hohokam Mirrors

At least two classificatory systems have been developed for Hohokam mirrors, that which appeared in the original Snaketown report (Gladwin et al. 1937) and another which is contained in unpublished archival materials from the 1934–1935 Snaketown excavations. These latter materials are located in the archives of the Arizona State Museum, but a description of the mirror types described therein can be found in the author's dissertation (Nelson 1981 : 426).

As with copper bells, a distribution consistent with the postulates of hypothesis 1 would be characterized by concentration in restricted or specialized contexts in specialized sites and possibly by concentration in certain parts of those sites. In addition, mirrors would tend to be absent from sites farther along regional exchange networks. Hypothesis 2 would be accepted and hypothesis 1 rejected if mirrors exhibited a wider and less specialized regional intrasite and contextual distribution.

As the context and distribution of these artifacts are crucial to this discussion, every provenience record from Snaketown is listed in Table 6 along with the number of mirrors (at least approximated) from each locus. This is done for the Snaketown material because it comprises about 80 percent of all mirrors in the sample.

Examination of these data reveals that most specimens came from definite or probable mortuary or offertory features, and it is possible that at least the specimens from 9H, blocks 12, and 16 may have originally come from such contexts since this square contained a very large number of cremations. At least two major concentrations seem to have existed. One was in squares 8H, 9G, 9H, and 9I in which all dated mirrors belonged to the Colonial period. The other was in squares 6F, 6G, and 7F and apparently contained the bulk of the Sedentary period specimens as well as some late Colonial and undated mirrors as well.

One final characteristic of the Snaketown material is the presence

TABLE 6. Snaketown Mirrors

Square Number	Provenience	Number of Mirrors
1934–1935 Materials:		
Colonial Period		
7 F, cremation	# 1	3
7 F, cremation	# 2	1
8 H, cremation	# 5	6
9 G, cremation	# 4	2
9 G, cremation	#13	1
9 H, cremation	#37	4 (1 is fragmentary)
9 H, cremation	#49	2
9 H, cremation	#66	2
9 I, cremation	#10	1
9 I, cremation	#18	4
12 G, cremation	# 1	1
Sedentary Period		
4 E, mound	#11	1
6 E, house	# 1 (subfloor)	1
6 F, cremation	# 2	2
6 G, block 12 (6G:12), probably the cremation mound at least in part, one or two mirrors, plus more than 100 fragments representing at least 25 additional mirrors. This estimate of 25 mirrors from the fragments is derived from the archival materials. These are likely the fragments recorded in the report (Gladwin et al. 1937:130) as coming from the cremation mound in 6G:12.		
Undated Specimens		
6 F, cremation	#12	1
9 G, cremation	#14	1
9 H, blocks 12 and 16		At least 6 mirrors or mirror fragments
10 I, general		1
11 M, cremations	# 1	3
11 M, broadside		1
Specimens from 1964–1965		
Colonial Period		
10 G, cache	# 1	3
Undated? Specimen		
9E–10E, stripping operations	# 1	1

there of a few imitation mirrors, made from local potsherds but exhibiting the appropriate beveling and performation. A total of five of these came from both excavations. Dated examples belonged to the Colonial and Sedentary periods. Unlike the real mirrors, none of these came from cremations or caches, a contrast which is probably not coincidental.

Mirrors from other sites are listed in Table 7. While other mirrors may exist in private collections, the examples listed comprise not only the inventory of documented and reported Hohokam mirrors, but also almost the entire known population of southwestern mirrors. Two fragments encrusted with psuedo-cloisonné were found at Pueblo Bonito by Pepper (1920 : 51– 53), while one specimen was found in a Perros Bravos Phase (circa A.D. 950–1060) grave at Casas Grandes (Di Peso 1974 : 210–211). All these specimens were probably contemporaneous with the Hohokam Sedentary period.

TABLE 7. Mosaic Mirrors from Other Sites

Site	Number of Specimens	Context
Grewe Site (Woodward 1931, 1941)	14 (Presumably all are Colonial or Sedentary)	From cremations and the offertory area, according to Woodward (1931:13) or just from the offertory area (Woodward 1941:10).
Cave near Tempe (Gladwin et al. 1937:131)	1	No data
Cremation Hill (David Wilcox, personal communication)	Perhaps a half dozen	Data not available
Hodges Ruin (Kelly 1978:108)	Tucson Basin: 5 and a possible sixth specimen; all are undated; all considered to be of early type at Snaketown (Kelly 1978:108)	One from an unplaced floor, four from four undated cremations in which they were associated with shell beads (three cremations), arrowpoints (two cremations), bracelets (two cremations), and plainware vessels.
Paloparado (Di Peso 1956:110)	2 broken specimens	Found in Cremation Area 1 of the early Village by an amateur. This cemetery does seem to have had richer and more varied offerings than other cemeteries at the site.
Valshni Village	Papagueria 1, dated to Vamori phase which is at least partly contemporaneous with the Sedentary period.	In a pithouse

Function

One can now consider the question of function. In general archaeologists have believed these mirrors to be high value, perhaps ceremonial, objects used by individuals of high rank or priests. Such a function seems plausible, given the patterns of distribution and context in which these artifacts are found.

In Mesoamerica, where these objects ranged from the terminal Formative to the Postclassic, they tended to occur in specialized contexts, frequently the richest and most elaborate burials and caches, as at Kaminaljuyú (Kidder et al. 1946 : 126).

The data on Hohokam mirrors indicate a situation at least analogous with that in Mesoamerica. They also were concentrated in mortuary or offertory features, often very rich ones. Also, while a very few sites had numbers of these objects, many sites, even those with large numbers of burials, had none. Aside from two fragments from Chaco Canyon, they have not been recorded from other parts in the American Southwest, unlike macaws or copper bells.

One of the salient aspects of this distribution is that at Snaketown and the Grewe site at least, these artifacts represented repeated episodes or procurement, a situation which probably did not exist at most southwestern sites. Mosaic mirrors exhibit a pattern of distribution which is almost diametrically opposed to that of some other imported materials or objects, such as Glycymeris bracelets, which were locally produced from imported materials. This pattern could be related to restricted access. The occurrence of a few local imitations may also be an indication of restricted access to the genuine specimens, as Flannery (1976 : 343) suggested regarding the presence of both real and imitation stingray spines in Formative villages in Oaxaca. It is thus not unreasonable to suggest that the mosaic mirrors made up part of an elite exchange system linking the Hohokam to elites in Mesoamerica, a system that would fit the prediction contained in hypothesis 1.

Mesoamerican Intrusive Ceramics

Several sherds found at Snaketown in the course of the 1964–1965 excavations were apparently mesoamerican intrusives (Haury 1976:345). These included two red-on-brown sherds, three redware sherds, four brownware sherds, and one black slipped sherd.

Five sherds were from Sacaton phase associations, one each from Santa Cruz and Gila Butte deposits, and three were unplaced. On the basis of examination by archaeologists familiar with Mexican ceramics, these sherds were assigned possible or tentative sources in the highlands of Mexico, or from around Cojumatlan, Michoacan, Totoate, Jalisco, or Guanajuato. Some were said to be suggestive of Coyotlatelco (Haury 1976:345). Two sherds from late Classic period contexts at Las Colinas were identified as being from Sinaloa or Nayarit (Hammack and Sullivan 1981:144).

Finally, a tripod vessel of what was called Northern Mexican plainware was found associated with a very rich Sacaton phase cremation (#52) at Cashion (Antieau 1981:158). What is of special interest in this case is not only the association of this vessel with one of the richest cremations found at the site, but also its occurrence in the same cremation area as another very rich cremation containing *Pecten vogdesi* pendants, a type of artifact apparently associated with special status and one which itself has exhibited repeated associations with Mexican artifacts.

Because of the scarcity of these objects, it is difficult to evaluate their role in terms of the hypotheses proposed in this paper. However, it is worth noting that none of the Snaketown sherds were from cremations or caches, being mainly from trash, as was the case with southwestern intrusive sherds in this and other Phoenix Basin sites. Data were unavailable on contexts of the Las Colinas sherds. The context and location of the Cashion specimen, however, exhibit some analogies to those noted for Sacaton phase bells and mirrors.

Macaws and Parrots

If the role of intrusive sherds is difficult to evaluate in terms of hypotheses 1 and 2, then that of macaw and parrot remains is even more so, for they are even scarcer in Hohokam sites, a rather curious situation given their relative abundance in other southwestern sites (e.g., Hargrave 1970; Olsen and Olsen 1974). While Hargrave (1970:52) records more than 150 macaw remains from Southwestern sites, the known Hohokam inventory at this time comprises a single relatively complete bird from the Gatlin site platform mound; a fragment from Az.T:4:8 ASM, a hilltop site in the northern periphery of Hohokam territory (Gumerman and Spoerl 1980:144); plus a few fragments from Pioneer and Pioneer-Colonial trash at Snaketown (McKusick 1976:375). These specimens are so few and so scattered that no pattern of context or distribution can be detected, although the location of the Gatlin site macaw within the platform mound, from which two bells also came, may be significant. Even the reasons for this apparent scarcity seem unclear. They could include sampling error or inadequate recovery techniques, the destructive effects of crematory fires, or trade competition with Casas Grandes. Conversely it may simply be that macaws were not used to any great extent by the Hohokam, or that they were being brought into the Southwest by a trade network different from that which linked the Hohokam to Mesoamerica. These various possibilities are discussed in greater detail in the author's dissertation (Nelson 1981:3921–398). It is not feasible at this time to use these remains to test the hypotheses of this paper.

Analysis

Characteristics of Context and Association

From data already presented, there emerge different patterns of context for the different artifacts described, and for the same artifacts at different times. This aspect of distribution deserves more detailed discussion. Special emphasis is placed upon the following problems, which are intimately related to the patterns predicted by the two hypotheses: (1) whether or not the artifacts were associated with particularly rich cemeteries at certain sites; (2) whether or not there was localization of the artifacts at such sites; (3) whether or not they occurred as part of a pattern of cacheing, which might be related to aspects of ritual; (4) whether or not they occurred in direct association with, or in the same areas as, specialized materials or artifacts locally made of regional (Southwestern) materials; and (5) whether they were associated with unusually large or complex storage facilities possibly indicative of special concentrations of or special access to various resources.

The presence or absence of possible public ceremonial structures at these sites is also examined. These variables are examined in two sections, one for Colonial and Sedentary period material, the other for the Classic period. These discussions apply primarily to the major classes of mesoamerican artifacts found in Hohokam sites, namely bells and mosaic mirrors, although sherds and macaws are also very briefly mentioned.

Colonial-Sedentary Periods

Hypothesis 1 predicts that Mexican artifacts should occur in differentially rich cemeteries. There is evidence of especially rich cremation areas at three sites which have yielded the bulk of mesoamerican artifacts of the Colonial and Sedentary periods: the Grewe site, Snaketown, and the Gatlin site. At the Grewe site, cremation area II was marked by wealthier offerings than were found in the other two cremation areas located at the site (Woodward 1931:13). Similar specimens came from the offertory areas located about 80 or 90 ft from cremation area II. It is, of course, from the offertory areas that the bulk of the mosaic mirrors came, although in the original report it was implied that some came from the cremation areas as well (Woodward 1931:13).

At the Gatlin site, most of the bells came from a series of cremations located to the east of the platform mound. Hundreds of elaborate arrowpoints of styles largely restricted to cremations and caches in the Gila Bend area, and quite different from most of the points recovered in other contexts, were also found by amateurs in these cremations, as were several intrusive ceramic vessels from northern Arizona.

The best data on mortuary patterns come from the 1934–1935 excavations at Snaketown and are presented in detail in the author's dissertation (Nelson 1981), along with a discussion of the methodology utilized.

These data will be summarized here, however. First of all, the unit of analysis utilized was the occurrence defined as equivalent to an individual catalogue entry in most cases. The objects used in that analysis included artifacts that were considered nonutilitarian. Local ceramic vessels (that is, Hohokam buffwares and plainwares) were not included. A more recent analysis, the results of which should appear in a future publication, divides the grave goods into two broad categories: local ceramic vessels and all other artifacts. The results of this second analysis are essentially similar to those of the first.

In terms of artifacts other than local ceramic vessels, the following characteristics are evident. First there are a series of unusually rich cemeteries, with much higher means for numbers of occurrences per cremation than other cemeteries. These cemeteries are located in grid squares 6F and 6G in the northern part of the site (Figure 12). This area is the part of the site that produced all the copper bells and most of the Sacaton phase mosaic mirrors. All dated cremations from these grid units are either late Colonial or Sedentary period in age. A second characteristic of the data is the fact that the contrast between different cremation areas in terms of richness of offerings appears to be greatest during the Sacaton phase. Some probably earlier cremation areas had both rich and poor cremations. Third, the type of differential richness found in 6F and 6G is as true of the variety and types of goods deposited with the cremations and also in some crematoria as it is of the numbers of goods or occurrences. Finally, data on local ceramic vessels exhibit essentially parallel patterns, with 6F and 6G again being the richest cemeteries.

Another feature of the 6F-6G area, which was probably mortuary in function was the cremation mound in 6G:12. Two such features were found, one in 6G:12, the other in square 10F, both assigned to the Sacaton phase. These were described as being mounds largely composed of the types of materials more frequently found in cremations (Gladwin et al. 1937:95). One wonders if these might not have been some sort of charnel structures for the secondary or tertiary deposition of the remains and associated grave goods of high status individuals. The mound in 6G:12 was particularly rich and was, in fact, the locus of the very many fragments of mosaic mirror from 6G:12. Other unusual artifacts were concentrated in 6G:12 and may or may not be from the cremation mound. Some of these are mentioned in the following section.

The phenomena found at Snaketown and at the Grewe site were apparently absent at many contemporary sites in the Phoenix Basin and elsewhere. The situation at Hodges Ruin, the largest excavated and published site in the Tucson Basin, is unclear. While some rich cremations were recovered, the cremations there were numbered consecutively rather than by grid unit, so that it is not possible to say, on the basis of evidence presently available to the author, whether or not such concentrations as occurred at Snaketown or the Grewe site also occurred at the Hodges Ruin.

Localization of Artifacts

Hypothesis 1 proposes that not only would mesoamerican artifacts display a pattern of concentration within specialized contexts, sites, and parts of sites, but that in such loci they would also be associated with other artifacts or materials of local or regional origin which exhibited similar patterns. Such associations along with the distribution would suggest a linkage which is related to the existence of a distinct prestige sphere. In fact, such artifacts do exist and have been described elsewhere as being part of a prestige sphere (Nelson 1981), and some of the more important of these artifacts are discussed below.

Pecten vogdesi pendants. Among the local or regional artifacts are whole shell pendants made from the concave (lower) valve of *Pecten vogdesi*. At the Grewe site, hundreds of these, mostly fragments, were found in the offertory areas, where they were associated with mosaic mirrors, and in cremation area II (Woodward 1931 : 19). At Snaketown, many fragmentary specimens were found, with a concentration in squares 6F and 6G; in 6G:12 and the large storehouse, 6G #8, and in a second house; and in a crematory pit and in some cremations in square 6F. Judging from currently available data, these artifacts, while widespread in sites south of the Phoenix Basin and so closer to the ultimate source of the raw shell, were virtually absent from sites located to the north, northeast, or east of the Phoenix Basin and thus, as predicted by hypothesis 1, were not being passed along through regional exchange networks.

Shell overlay. Most overlay recorded during research for the author's dissertation was found to come from squares 6F and 6G at Snaketown, mostly in the cremation mound in 6G:12, but also from two cremations and several other loci in square 6F.

Shell trumpets. Both shell trumpets from the 1934–35 work at Snaketown came from square 6F, one from a Sacaton phase cremation, the other from trash.

Black steatite objects. At Snaketown most of the black steatite objects found in 1934 came from various contexts and loci in squares 6F and 6G. All dated pieces from this area are assigned to the Sacaton phase.

Asbestos. Most of the asbestos found in Snaketown in 1934–1935 came from the large storehouse, 6G #8.

Arrowpoints. At a few Colonial or Sedentary sites, some caches, cremations, or cremation mounds contained a hundred or more arrowpoints, often distinguished by a high level of workmanship as well as standardization in style and material, thus suggesting not only a deliberately high investment of production but also the deliberate procurement and selection of materials for such purposes. This, in fact, is what one might expect to find in a prestige exchange procurement system associated with an elite, the existence of which is predicted by hypothesis 1. Such deposits are repeatedly associated with bells at Gatlin and mosaic mirrors at Snaketown.

Human head figurines. The human head figurines, so characteristic of the Sacaton phase at Snaketown, and probably elsewhere as well, were concentrated in several contexts, including several cremations, a cache, and the large storehouse at Snaketown, in squares 5F, 6F, and 6G. Significantly, these materials included most of the specimens from both excavations there.

Carved bone hairpieces or daggerlike objects. At both the Grewe site, where these objects were common in the offertory area, and at Snaketown, where the material from 1934–1935 was especially common in cremations in squares 6F and 6G, and in 6G:12, there seems to have been a concentration in the same parts of the respective sites and even in the same features in some cases, as those where many mosaic mirrors were recovered.

Legged vessels of local wares. These vessels, whose shape is of obvious Mexican origin, were found mainly at Snaketown and the Grewe site. At Snaketown, at least 10 of around 17 catalogued specimens were from squares 6G and 5F; nine from a cache and the large storehouse in 6G, and one from a Sacaton phase house in square 5F. At least seven such vessels are listed in the Grewe site catalogues, but their provenience is unknown.

The data on these locally or regionally derived artifacts and materials indicate that they shared many aspects of distribution and context with the mesoamerican artifacts, and at least strongly suggest that they were functionally related. They form the type of pattern that is predicted by hypothesis 1.

Caches

Association with specialized caches was another attribute of Mesoamerican artifacts postulated by hypothesis 1. Such caches did occur at Colonial or Sedentary sites such as Snaketown, where they consisted of stone bowls or ceramic vessels often of specialized shapes, such as censers, legged vessels, or effigies. At Snaketown several mosaic mirrors were found in definite or possible caches.

Differentially Large Storage Facilities

The association of mesoamerican artifacts with differentially large storage structures is predicted by hypothesis 1. This linkage is important, for it suggests not only an association with differential wealth but also the possible existence of redistribution or mobilization. Such evidence, taken in conjunction with the existence of prestige objects, may well indicate the presence of an elite group which was receiving these goods. There is one such structure which seems to fit these requirements, square 6G, house #8, at Snaketown, a large Sacaton phase structure from which the copper bells at that site were recovered. This house not only contained about 61 vessels, 43 of them jars, but also had at least one shelf set into the floor, something which suggests use for long-term storage of very large quantities of materials. Aside from the bells, it contained such things as *Pecten vogdesi* pendants, head figurines, a steatite bowl, and asbestos, all items concentrated in squares 6G and 6F. These materials alone suggest that the house should be viewed as part of a complex which also included the rich cemeteries and cremation mound. In addition, several vessels contained wild or domesticated seeds, while at least seven others contained large amounts of yucca or sotol yarn rolled up in hanks. This structure, with its large accumulation of materials plus its concentration of prestige or ritual objects, could in fact have been used for redistribution or mobilization. In every way, this situation fits the test implications for hypothesis 1.

Ceremonial or Public Architecture

Hypothesis 1 predicts that Mexican artifacts should be concentrated in sites with specialized ceremonial or public structures. Excellent summaries and discussions of the evolution of ballcourts or platform mounds can be found in several sources (Doyel 1974; Ferdon 1967; Haury 1976; Wilcox and Sternberg 1983). What is relevant here is whether or not sites with large numbers of Mexican artifacts also had such structures, possibly located in the same parts of those sites.

There were at least two ceremonial structures at all three sites—Snaketown, Gatlin, and Grewe—which had the greatest number of mesoamerican artifacts, as well as at Hodges Ruin, at which were found most of the mirror backs reported from the Tucson Basin. All had at least two ballcourts, while two had platform mounds and two had definite or possible plazas. At both Snaketown and Gatlin, a platform mound was located close to the areas where many of the mesoamerican artifacts were found. Wilcox and Sternberg (1983 : 203) consider Snaketown, Gatlin, and Hodges to have been leading centers of their respective local settlement systems. This would not be discordant with the test implications of the first hypothesis.

Classic Period

The Classic period exhibited characteristics very different from those just outlined in regard to several variables, including mortuary practices. It was at this time that inhumation at least coexisted with cremation as a major form of mortuary practice in many parts of the Hohokam territory. Another pattern which now seemed to prevail, in the Phoenix Basin at least, was that there were rich burials, but apparently no rich cemeteries. This seems to be indicated by an admittedly superficial preliminary examination of burial data from the large sites of Los Muertos and Las Acequias. Moreover, while artifacts made locally of imported materials generally occurred in inhumations rather than cremations, most inhumations, at least at Los Muertos and Los Acequias, contained only ceramic vessels, most commonly the redwares which also predominated in cremations. Finally, it should be pointed out that of Sprague and Signori's sample of definite Classic period copper bells only two came from well-documented mortuary contexts. Outside the Phoenix Basin, Classic period burial areas frequently contained offerings such as shell and stone ornaments, of types widespread both within and among sites.

Similarly, there is less evidence of any clear pattern of localization of mesoamerican artifacts of the type described earlier. Two bells were recovered from Compound A, Casa Grande, the compound in which the Great House is located, while one bell was found in Compound B, Casa Grande, a ruin which enclosed two platform mounds and inside which numbers of shell trumpets were recovered. Very few burials have been located at Casa Grande and it is not inconceivable that additional excavations within these compounds might turn up rich burial areas with large numbers of bells or other Mexican imports. However, Cushing found no bells at all at either Los Muertos or Las Acequias where many burials were recovered. This is especially interesting since it is possible that one structure, Ruin I, at Los Muertos could have been a platform mound (Haury 1945 : 35). Likewise Escalante (Az. U:15 : 3 ASM), another Classic period site with a definite platform mound, did not yield even a single bell or macaw. One group of Classic period bells did occur as part of the Romo Cache, but unlike many Colonial or Sedentary period caches, this one was apparently not associated with any particular village site. Finally, concerning large-scale storage facilities, there is evidence of such a feature at Las Acequias, in the form of a huge deposit of charred plant food remains found on the floor of a room in one of the ruins and reported in Cushing's daily logs (1888). While this is of great interest in its own right, no Mexican artifacts were recorded from it. On the whole, the data for the Classic period, flawed as they undoubtedly are, do not suggest the existence of the distinctive pattern of context, distribution, and associations which encompassed so many Colonial or Sedentary period mesoamerican origins, and which seemed to fit very well with the test implications of hypothesis 1.

Conclusions

I have argued that the data on the Colonial and Sedentary period artifacts from the Phoenix Basin and Gila Bend exhibit patterns of distribution, context, and association which are in essential conformity with those predicted by hypothesis 1 and differ from those predicted in hypothesis 2. On the other hand, the Classic period data conform better to the predicted patterns associated with the type of system postulated in hypothesis 2. The appearance of certain types of mesoamerican artifacts in a few Colonial or Sedentary period sites in the areas described can be considered part of a pattern of distribution, context, and association which was the manifestation of a distinct and probably restricted prestige sphere of exchange or conveyance associated with a Hohokam elite present at certain sites. These sites were characterized by the presence of certain ceremonial or public structures, themselves probably inspired to some degree from Mesoamerica. Certain aspects of these patterns, namely intrasite localization of these artifacts and their association with differentially rich mortuary areas seem to have been especially well developed in, or possibly exclusive to, the Sedentary period, suggesting that the degree of social differentiation represented by the prestige sphere had increased relative to the Colonial period. Similar conclusions regarding increased social complexity from the Colonial to the Sedentary period have been reached by Doyel (1980 : 31), Wilcox (Wilcox et al. 1981 : 209), and Teague (1981 : 12). Some aspects of the pattern, however, such as specialized cacheing, were already well developed during the Colonial period, so that it does not seem necessary to invoke the *deus ex machina* of direct outside intervention to account for the Sedentary period phenomena. They were most likely the result of long-term indigenous developments.

Just how the type of prestige sphere described in this paper might have functioned is problematical. It has been suggested elsewhere (Nelson 1981 : 525−526) that some sort of redistribution or mobilization formed the basis for large accumulations of regional resources by certain groups or individuals who used them, in part, at least for exchanges with Mesoamerica. However, the highly localized distribution of some of the imported artifacts, especially the mirrors, suggests that access to them may have been restricted by factors other than wealth alone, perhaps status, role, or rank. We might speculate that some type of alliance or other specialized relationship between certain Hohokam and certain individuals or groups in Mesoamerica was involved. At any rate it seems safe to suggest that this was a form of exchange relationship that was qualitatively different from those which linked the Hohokam to other southwestern societies and which seem to have primarily involved widely distributed artifacts such as *Glycymeris* bracelets. Such a complex system need not have encompassed all exchanges with Mesoamerica. Simpler networks may have existed during parts of the Colonial period. Whether the intrusive sherds, most of which were found scattered in trash deposits, came through such a system or indeed represented exchange at all, is another area of uncertainty. Nevertheless, the fact that most of these have been found at Snaketown is itself suggestive.

Ultimately, the reasons for the initial development of this system and for its apparent decline are separate problems which remain to be fully understood. Demographic pressure, subsistence stress, and trade competition with the large center of Casas Grandes have all been suggested as possible factors in Classic period exchanges. The concept of spheres of exchange, which can be used to delineate possible relationships between regional and local settlement systems and long-distance trade, could constitute a powerful tool for increasing our understanding of those changes.

Acknowledgments

I would like to express my gratitude to Dr. David Wilcox, whose comments and criticisms of an early draft of this paper were extremely helpful, and to Dr. Howard Winters, who has always offered his encouragement.

References Cited

Antieau, John M.
  1981 *The Palo Verde Archaeological Investigations*. Research Paper No. 20. Museum of Northern Arizona, Flagstaff.
Bohannan, Paul
  1965 *Social Anthropology*. Holt and Rinehart, New York.
Cushing, Frank Hamilton
  1888 Daily Reports in Detail. Ms. on file, Huntington Free Library, Bronx, New York.
Di Peso, Charles C.
  1956 *The Upper Pima of San Cayetano del Tumacacori*. Amerind Foundation Series No. 7. Dragoon, Ariz.
  1968 Casas Grandes and the Gran Chichimeca. *El Palacio* 75(4):45–61.
  1974 *Casas Grandes: A Fallen Trading Center of the Gran Chichimeca*, vols. 1–3. Amerind Foundation Series No. 9. Dragoon, Ariz.
Di Peso, Charles C., John B. Rinaldo, and Gloria Fenner
  1974 *Casas Grandes: A Fallen Trading Center of the Gran Chichimeca*, vols. 4–8. Amerind Foundation Series No. 9. Dragoon, Ariz.
Doyel, David E.
  1974 *Excavations in the Escalante Ruin Group, Southern Arizona*. Arizona State Museum Archaeological Series No. 37. Tucson.
  1980 Hohokam Social Organization and the Sedentary to Classic Transition. In *Current Issues in Hohokam Prehistory, Proceedings of a Symposium*, edited by David E. Doyel and Fred Plog, pp. 23–40. Arizona State University Anthropological Research Paper No. 23. Tempe.
Ferdon, Edwin J., Jr.
  1967 The Hohokam "Ball Court": An Alternative View of Its Function. *Kiva* 33(1):1–14.
Fewkes, J. W.
  1912 Casa Grande, Arizona. *Annual Report of the Bureau of American Ethnology* 28:25–179. Washington, D.C.
Firth, Raymond
  1965 *Primitive Polynesian Economy*. W. W. Norton, New York.
Fish, Paul, Peter Pilles, and Suzanne Fish
  1980 Colonies, Traders and Traits: The Hohokam in the North. In *Current Issues in Hohokam Prehistory, Proceedings of a Symposium*, edited by

David E. Doyel and Fred Plog, pp. 151–175. Arizona State University Anthropological Research Paper No. 23. Tempe.

Flannery, Kent V.
1976 Contextual Analysis of Ritual Paraphernalia from Formative Oaxaca. In *The Early Mesoamerican Village*, edited by Kent V. Flannery, pp. 333–345. Academic Press, New York.

Fried, Morton H.
1967 *The Evolution of Political Society*. Random House, New York.

Gladwin, Harold S., Emil W. Haury, E. B. Sayles, and Nora Gladwin
1937 *Excavations at Snaketown: Material Culture*. Gila Pueblo Medallion Paper No. 25. Globe, Ariz.

Gumerman, George, and Patricia Spoerl
1980 The Hohokam and the Northern Periphery. In *Current Issues in Hohokam Prehistory, Proceedings of a Symposium*, edited by David E. Doyel and Fred Plog, pp. 134–150. Arizona State University Anthropological Research Paper No. 23. Tempe.

Hammack, Laurens C.
1971 *The Peppersauce Wash Project*. Arizona State Museum, Tucson.

Hammack, Laurens C., and Alan P. Sullivan (editors).
1981 *The 1968 Excavations at Mound 8, Las Colinas Ruins Group, Phoenix, Arizona*. Archaeological Research Series No. 154. Arizona State Museum, Tucson.

Hargrave, Lyondon L.
1970 *Mexican Macaws: Comparative Osteology and Survey of Remains from the Southwest*. University of Arizona Anthropological Paper No. 20. Tucson.

Haury, Emil W.
1945 *The Excavation of Los Muertos and Neighboring Ruins in the Salt River Valley*. Papers of The Peabody Museum of Archaeology and Ethnology No. 24(1). Harvard University, Cambridge, Mass.
1976 *The Hohokam: Desert Farmers and Craftsmen*. University of Arizona Press, Tucson.

Haury, Emil W., and Carol A. Gifford
1959 A Thirteenth Century Strongbox. *Kiva* 24(4):1–11.

Holien, Thomas
1974 Pseudo-Cloisonné in the Southwest and Mexico. In *Collected Papers in Honor of Florence Hawley Ellis*, edited by Theodore R. Frisbie, pp. 157–177. Papers of the Archaeological Society of New Mexico No. 2. Hooper, Norman, Okla.

Kelley, J. Charles, and Ellen Abbott Kelly
1974 An Alternative Hypothesis for the Explanation of Anasazi Culture History. In *Collected Papers in Honor of Florence Hawley Ellis*, edited by Theodore R. Frisbie, pp. 178–223. Papers of the Archaeological Society of New Mexico No. 2. Hooper, Norman, Okla.

Kelly, Isabel
1978 *The Hodges Ruin: A Hohokam Community in the Tucson Basin.*
University of Arizona Anthropological Paper No. 30. Tucson.
Kidder, Alfred V., Jesse Jennings, and Edward M. Shook
1946 *Excavations at Kaminaljuyú, Guatemala.* Carnegie Institute of Washington Publications No. 561. Washington, D. C.
McGuire, Randall H.
1980 The Mesoamerican Connection in the Southwest. *Kiva* 46(1 – 2):3 – 38.
McKusick, Charmion
1976 Avifauna. In *The Hohokam: Desert Farmers and Craftsmen*, by Emil W. Haury, pp. 374 – 377. University of Arizona Press, Tucson.
Mills, Jack P., and Vera M. Mills
1969 *The Kuykendall Site.* Special Report of the El Paso Archaeological Society No. 6. El Paso.
Nelson, Richard S.
1981 *The Role of a Puchteca System in Hohokam Exchange.* Ph.D. dissertation, New York University. University Microfilms, Ann Arbor.
Olsen, Stanley J., and John W. Olsen
1974 The Macaws of Grasshopper Ruin. *Kiva* 40(1 – 2):67 – 70.
Pendergast, David M.
1962 Metal Artifacts in Prehispanic Mesoamerica. *American Antiquity* 27:520 – 545.
Pepper, George H.
1920 *Pueblo Bonito.* Anthropological Paper of the American Museum of Natural History No. 27. New York.
Rappaport, Roy A.
1968 *Pigs for the Ancestors.* Yale University Press, New Haven.
Renfrew, Colin
1977 Alternative Models for Exchange and Spatial Distribution. In *Exchange Systems in Prehistory*, edited by Timothy K. Earle and Jonathan E. Ericson, pp. 71 – 90. Academic Press, New York.
Root, W. C.
1937 The Metallurgy of Arizona and New Mexico. In *Excavations at Snaketown: Material Culture*, by Harold S. Gladwin, Emil W. Haury, E. B. Sayles, and Nora Gladwin, pp. 276 – 277. Gila Pueblo Medallion Paper No. 25. Globe, Ariz.
Schroeder, Albert H.
1966 Pattern Diffusion from Mexico into the Southwest after A.D. 600. *American Antiquity* 31 : 638 – 709.
Smith, A. Ledyard, and Alfred V. Kidder
1951 *Excavations at Nebaj, Guatemala.* Carnegie Institute of Washington Publications No. 594. Washington, D.C.

Sprague Roderick
    1964 Inventory of Prehistoric Copper Bells: Additions and Corrections: 1. *Kiva* 30(1):18–24.
Srague, Roderick, and Aldo Signori
    1963 Inventory of Prehistoric Southwestern Copper Bells. *Kiva* 28(4): 1–20.
Teague, Lynn S.
    1981 *Test Excavations at Painted Rock Reservoir: Sites Az.A:1:7, Az.A:1:8, and Az.S:16:36.* Arizona State Museum Archaeologial Series No. 143. Tucson.
Turney, Omar
    1929 *Prehistoric Agriculture in Arizona.* Phoenix.
Wasley, William W.
    1960 A Hohokam Platform Mound at the Gatlin Site, Gila Bend, Arizona. *American Antiquity* 26:244–262.
Wilcox, David R., Thomas R. McGuire, and Charles Sternberg
    1981 *Snaketown Revisited.* Arizona State Museum Archaeological Series No. 155. Tucson.
Wilcox, David R., and Charles Sternberg
    1983 *Hohokam Ballcourts and Their Interpretation.* Arizona State Museum Archaeological Series No. 160. Tucson.
Withers, Allison
    1946 *Copper in the Prehistoric Southwest.* Unpublished M.A. thesis, Department of Anthropology, University of Arizona, Tucson.
Woodbury, Richard B.
    1965 Artifacts of the Guatemala Highlands. In *Archaeology of Southern Mesoamerica*, edited by Gordon R. Willey, pp. 462–468. Handbook of Middle American Indians, vol. 2, Robert Wauchope, general editor. University of Texas Press, Austin.
Woodward, Arthur
    1931 *The Grewe Site, Gila Valley, Arizona.* Occasional Papers of the Los Angeles Museum of History, Science and Art No. 1. Los Angeles.
    1941 Hohokam Mosaic Mirrors. *Quarterly of the Museum Patrons Association of the Los Angeles City Museum* 4:7–11.

10

New World Precolumbian World Systems

Joseph W. Whitecotton and Richard A. Pailes

In 1975 we proposed that world system theory offers an alternative to the local development-diffusion dichotomy used to discuss potential mesoamerican-southwestern relationships (Pailes and Whitecotton 1975, 1979). We later proposed further that world system theory was an alternative to traditional conceptualizations of mesoamerican culture history in which evolutionary stages and environmentally adaptive sociocultural types often substitute for period analysis based on the "influence" of one cultural region upon another (Whitecotton and Pailes 1979). In short, we posited that Mesoamerica as an historical unit was more than the sum of its many trait complexes and local adaptations; it was a system bound together by the competition among core states for control of peripheries and semiperipheries.

In the latter paper we also emphasized that, while world system theory had its explicit development in social history and sociology, many of the implications of this approach also had roots in anthropology. To a considerable extent world system theory is not new; it is a logical outgrowth of earlier anthropological studies which stress that local cultures and societies are but reflections of larger social fields. In a sense, world system theory is more like Stewardian "multilinear evolution" than it is like the "unilinear evolutionism" of White (1959), Sahlins (1958), Sahlins and Service (1966), and Service (1968). Steward (Steward and Faron 1959 : 178) argued that circum-Caribbean chiefdoms developed from an interaction with state systems and did not necessarily precede them; they were thus part of a larger social field. This theme was also emphasized in the Stewardian approach to community studies, in which communities were seen as complex adaptations to larger societies, as opposed to another tradition which viewed communities as microcosms of larger cultural wholes (Steward 1950). This distinction bears importantly upon archaeological studies, particularly those dealing with mesoamerican-southwestern relationships. Social field theory, world system theory, or Stewardian ecological theory would not predict southwestern archaeological cultures to be miniature clones of mesoamerican ones if they were included in a mesoamerican social field; only the totally discredited approach of the "national character" school and the community as "micro-cosm" school would predict such a situation.

The issue, then, seems to be not whether subcultures adapt to larger systems, but rather how extensive are the systems? To world system theorists, minisystems (those with a self-contained polity, culture, and division of labor) are extremely rare and probably have existed nowhere in the world since the earliest time, when world systems (those whose polity and division of labor are not coterminous) emerged. As a case in point, we now realize that many systems formerly conceptualized as closed, such as the Nuer segmentary lineage and the Trobriand kula ring (Kuper 1973), are responses to larger colonial regimes.

How many world systems there are at any given point in time and what their specific relationships are to one another thus constitute the most important questions relating to larger system adaptation. Braudel (1977) and Wallerstein (1974a) differ, for example, on how many world economies there were in Europe prior to 1850; Wallerstein (1974b) and Chirot and Hall (1982) differ on the specific modern characterization of the Soviet Union in the present age. Wallerstein sees the Soviet Union as a competing core state in the modern capitalist world system; Chirot and Hall see it as an old-fashioned world empire.

Similarly, there appears to be a disagreement between the present authors and Blanton, Kowaleski, Feinman, and Appel (Blanton et al. 1981) regarding the character of the mesoamerican world system. Although, curiously, Blanton et al. interpret us as arguing that Mesoamerica evolved into a world empire (when in fact we argue just the opposite), they nevertheless characterize Mesoamerica as a world system that: "was neither a world-empire nor a world economy. The relationships holding it together were neither those of a single empire nor those of separate economic institutions.
. . . What made Mesoamerica an encompassing social system was its structure of elite prestige" (Blanton et al. 1981 : 246). On the other hand, they state: "The elite prestige system did not comprise all of the interregional exchange in Mesoamerica. In addition to the rich trade, some consumer goods flowed among regions. Obsidian, for example, was mined in only two main mining areas . . . and carried to all parts of Mesoamerica" (Blanton et al. 1981 : 248).

In addition: "In the Late Post Classic Period . . . seemingly innovative economic linkages were beginning to threaten the politically based dominance of traditionally reckoned prestige. It seems likely that whole regional communities specialized in the production of particular basic commodities in response to extraregional demands and opportunities" (Blanton et al. 1981 : 250). Finally: "Nothing like the international markets for basic commodities and capital that characterized Europe were developed in Mesoamerica *until its last two pre-Columbian centuries*" (Blanton et al. 1981 : 246; emphasis added). Thus, Blanton et al. seem to be arguing that Mesoamerica was not a world economy until its last two centuries of development; prior to that time it was a world system but neither a world economy nor a world empire.

In our opinion, this argument obscures some crucial issues. One of these relates to the problem of characterizing mesoamerican development in terms of discrete stages and looking at only part of its historical trajectory. Another concerns certain fundamental issues in economic anthropology, namely the relationships between political forms and economic institutions and a distinction between *preciosities* and *essential goods*.

First of all, a world system perspective looks at the history of a system in the long term or over *"la longue durée" to use Braudel's phrase. To argue that Mesoamerica was a world economy only* in the long term (as they do) is synonymous with stating that the European world economy developed *only* in its last three centuries. This is a circular nonstatement.

Further, Blanton et al. characterize the earlier periods of meso-american history differently because they fail to embrace certain other perspectives that are crucial to world system analysis, fall back upon other models which are based on the evolutionary perspective of Sahlins and Service (along with many mesoamerican Formative archaeologists and southwestern archaeologists), and employ a Polanyi-Dalton substantivist view of economic systems. It is also interesting that when confronted with ethnohistorical data they see a world economy (in the late Postclassic), but when restricted to archaeological data (as in the Classic) they dismiss such a notion.

The Sahlins-Service-Polanyi-Dalton view of political economic systems is that they can be arranged in stages, each of which is dominated by a single exchange type: reciprocity, redistribution, or market. The first two types, derived from a non-world system ethnographic perspective, are typical of the primitive world and archaic states. The third type is modern—thus the view is extremely historiocentric (a charge that is often made of Wallerstein's view).

The evolutionary stage model also argues that, in primitive and archaic states, economies are embedded in political and social concerns and are thus "undifferentiated." As a result, these state systems cannot have markets which are "free," unencumbered by political concerns.

Another component of this view is that archaic states—perceived as fundamentally redistributive economies—are characterized by long distance trade in preciosities, which does not stimulate trade in basic commodities. Trade is primarily social; it creates inequalities of prestige.

However, as Braudel (1977, 1981, 1982) has pointed out, these three types of economy (reciprocity, redistribution, and market) are not necessarily stages of development, but may be levels within a single economy. Most economic systems of the state variety (and certainly Blanton et al. would not argue that Mesoamerica lacked states in the Classic period) contain all three levels—they are in fact layers (for a discussion of "layering" in the Aztec political economy, see Berdan 1977). To Polanyi's levels, Braudel

(1977, 1982) adds "capitalism," a layer characterized by a predominance of long-distance trade involving exchanges which are not of "transparent" value. Because of the great distance involved in the circulation of commodities, enormous profits are to be made because the value of the goods is not apparent to both partners in the exchange.

Thus, the presence of long-distance trade based exclusively on luxury or prestige exchange cannot be correlated only with archaic systems as is implied by some authors (see, for example, Chapman 1957; Carrasco 1978). It is also an important component of "market" and "capitalistic" systems (for a criticism of the Chapman-Polanyi approach with regard to Mesoamerica, see Berdan 1978; Kurtz 1974; Zeitlan 1982).

Further, a basic tenet of a world system perspective (shared by both Braudel and Wallerstein) is that the notion of a "free market" unencumbered by social and political concerns is an ideological myth perpetuated by economists and politicians to support the dominance of certain core states in the modern industrial world. They argue that there has never been anything like a "free market," even under capitalism, not to mention the fact that there is no universally agreed upon definition of capitalism. Anyone familiar with the economic literature of the last 200 years will readily admit this (for a discussion, see Braudel 1982:232–248).

In short, many of the distinctions made by mesoamerican anthropologists in their characterizations of the mesoamerican political economy will not stand in the light of world system theory. The many debates, for example, over the nature of the Aztec economic system (Berdan 1980; Brumfiel 1980; Carrasco 1981; Offner 1981a, 1981b) focus on the question of whether or not markets and profits are embedded in systems of political control. Now Wallerstein and Braudel show that even capitalism is embedded; thus the application of the term "imperialism" to capitalist exploitation.

The crucial problem then becomes not whether economies are embedded but how they are embedded. In short, was Mesoamerica a world economy (with core states competing for access to economic goods) or a world empire (with the dominance of a single core state). All mesoamericanists seem to agree that at no point in time was Mesoamerica a single world empire dominated by a single center.

An additional major point regarding the nature of exchange systems concerns the distinction between "preciosities" and "essentials" made by many mesoamericanists. As Schneider (1977) has pointed out, even Wallerstein has great difficulty in separating preciosities from essentials because of an over-rigid distinction between precapitalist and capitalist systems. In a carefully reasoned argument, she shows that the distinction between luxuries and essentials is more apparent than real. Regarding Wallerstein, for example:

> Committed to the proposition that "in the long run, staples account for more of men's economic trusts than luxuries," he [Wallerstein]

wants to find staples in the cargoes of Portuguese ships. There was indeed a modest quantity of cereals, imported from the Atlantic islands off the Portuguese coast, but this represented only a minor segment of the total trade and only one component of the island trade as well. Sugar imports were more substantial, but was sugar essential? Wallerstein argues that it provided calories . . . but so did honey which was widely available in Europe. . . . Sugar went to make rum and later chocolate, but by what criteria were they staple foods? He also mentions dyestuffs and wine which other authorities would similarly classify as luxuries (Schneider 1977 : 22–23).

Further, Schneider questions the lumping of all preciosities into one category:

> Pre-capitalist tribute systems at first glance give the impression that reliance upon luxury goods for the creation and maintenance of allies was indiscriminate. Anything which a potential ally might consider valuable or, through court ceremonial and ritual, might be influenced to consider valuable, could constitute a gift capable of obligating him to the donor. In fact, however, the various preciosities which circulated in long distance trade differed in the degree to which they could readily be converted into other resources. The greater an object's perceived value over both time and space, the greater its potential to bind allegiances, and thereby to promote energy capture [Schneider 1977 : 24].

And, as if to turn Wallerstein's own analysis in upon itself, she observes: "Wallerstein's categorical claim that luxuries are non-essential— read dangerous and corrupting—originated as the ideological aspect of a secular movement from import restriction and import substitution to eventual industrial development" (Schneider 1977 : 27). Thus, even Wallerstein's analyses reflect the basic ideological stances of "capitalist" development.

Richard M. Adams (1974) also finds that the distinction between "preciosities" and "essentials" obscures the basic importance of exchange and trade in precapitalist world economies. He challenges the idea that luxury goods merely served to satisfy the whims of elites, enabling them to maintain a social distance from commoners. Instead, luxury trade also induced massive changes in technology, leadership, class structure, and ideology. Braudel also questions Wallerstein's approach, if only by implication, when he stresses the importance of long-distance luxury trade "as an essential factor in the creation of merchant capitalism" (1982 : 403–408).

The above argument seems to parallel that of Berdan (1980) and Brumfiel (1980, 1983), who argue that tribute and trade in preciosities in central Mexico actually promoted trade in other commodities. Berdan shows how regions within the mesoamerican world (or, more properly, structural positions within it) were stimulated by the trade and tribute system of the Triple Alliance. She describes in considerable detail the extent to which regional merchants (non-*pochteca*) in areas outside of the Central Basin of Mexico dealt in commodities such as salt, cotton, cacao, maize, beans, chile, chia, fish, vegetables, fruits, honey, pinole, gourd bowls, mats, mantas, cochineal, and amole so that they might obtain more exotic goods like feathers, gold, silver, precious stones, and ocelot skins. Further, regularly scheduled markets in areas beyond the control of the central Mexican Triple Alliance dealt with an abundance of subsistence and utilitarian goods and with items that required a high degree of craft specialization. Raw materials were transported from their sources over long distances to towns that specialized in the production of finished goods, which were then exported back to the source areas to other consumers. As an example, the market at Tepeaca specialized in woven products that were locally made from raw cotton obtained in the *tierra caliente* (Berdan 1980 : 39).

Ball and Brockington (1978) have argued that at least three systems designed for long-distance exchange existed in the Postclassic, as seen from the perspective of Oaxaca. Apparently the Aztecs (or more specifically Aztec merchants who came from twelve cities or city-states) had at least two routes linking them to southern Mesoamerica. First, circumventing the competing states of Huexotzingo, Cholula, and Tlaxcala (which may have been tied to an eastern and northern network), they operated a trade center at Tuxtepec (Tochtepec) that is described by Sahagún (1959). From here merchants fanned out to Xicalango in the southeast and to Soconusco in the southwest. The route to Xicalango tied the Aztec to the Maya *ppolom*, who in turn were tied to Cozumel and ultimately to other Maya zones. The Soconusco route passed through the Mixteca Alta to Tuxtepec and from there across the isthmus to Tehuantepec (where the Aztecs had arranged an alliance with the Zapotecs) and ultimately to Soconusco. This route may also have passed into the Valley of Oaxaca, where at times the Aztecs had some semblance of political control.

Goods which Aztec merchants carried to the provinces of Xicalango and Soconusco (collectively called Anahuac) were obsidian knives, needles, rattles, alum stone, grain, red ochre, and rabbit hair fur (Sahagún 1959 : 30–31), as well as such consumer goods as a green or purple lake scum used as a kind of cheese, tortillas of worms or grubs, water bug eggs pressed into small cakes, and barbecued ducks (Durán 1951). In return, they received textiles, gold dust, amber, precious and semiprecious stones, cacao, worked gold, and a variety of feathers. It appears that while the Aztecs sought items which could largely be defined as preciosities, they brought general consumption goods to trade for them.

This Aztec system intersected and competed with a second exchange network, which Ball and Brockington call the Oaxacan Inland Highland-Lowland Symbiosis. This network probably dates from the late Preclassic, continued into the Classic (perhaps with Monte Albán as a crucial center), and collapsed in the late Classic (possibly after the fall of Teotihuacan), to be revived again in the late Postclassic. It joined the states of Tututepec, Mia-huatlan, and Coixtlahuaca—found respectively in the Mixteca Costa, the Valley of Oaxaca, and the Mixteca Alta—with the Zapotec state of Tehuantepec (which was at times allied with the Mixtecs and at other times with the Aztecs). Miahuatlan had multiple alliances and may have been a free port; Coixtlahuaca was in the Aztec orbit at times; Tututepec seems always to have been independent of the Aztecs, although it may have had alliances with Valley of Oaxaca towns and towns in the Mixteca Alta.

Cotton, quetzal feathers, and slaves were the major commodities traded in this system. Raw cotton apparently came from Tututepec and Tehuantepec and was manufactured into textiles in the highland towns of Tlaxiaco and Coixtlahuaca in the Mixteca Alta, perhaps in the Valley of Oaxaca town of Cuilapan, and in the highland town of Teotitlan del Camino, which may at one time have been allied to the Aztecs. As with many mesoamerican principalities, the political alliances were complex and often fleeting, depending on the strength of the various core states involved in these economic networks.

Quetzal feathers, which came from Chiapas and Guatemala (given as tribute by Coixtlahuaca and Tlaxiaco to the Aztecs) tied this economic network both to the Mexica Aztecs and to a third economic interaction sphere which Ball and Brockington call the West Mexican-South Coast Combine. Although this third network probably predates the Aztec sphere, it intersected and competed both with it and the Oaxacan Inland Highland-Lowland Symbiosis region in late Postclassic times. This combine included the so-called Tarascan empire, the Yope state, Tututepec (also important in the Highland-Lowland system), Tehuantepec (a part of all three systems), and the Chiapanec principalities (which had important trading relations with Soconusco). Miahuatlan in the Valley of Oaxaca was apparently also an important participant in this combine as well as in the Oaxaca Highland-Lowland system.

The West Mexican-South Coast Combine specialized in the production and trade of polychrome pottery of the Mixteca-Puebla variety, utilitarian bronze and copper bells, copper money axes, macaws and feathers, quetzal birds and feathers, hallucinogenic drugs, and textiles. It was clearly linked to regions further up the coast in Guerrero, Colima, and Nayarit, extending as far north as Guasave in northern Sinaloa, where it has been identified as the Mixteca-Puebla route associated with the Aztatlán complex in pre-Aztec times (Ekholm 1942; Kelley 1980; Kelley and Kelley 1975). Still further north, it probably linked with Casas Grandes (Di Peso 1974; Kelley 1980). The West Mexican-South Coast Combine was also linked to the Zoque-Acalan region (and thus to Xicalango on the Gulf Coast through the Chiapanec principalities, as well as to the north (perhaps as far away as Ecuador).

These three systems form but part of what was a mesoamerican world economy, and our few examples show that the "systemness" of its trade structure consisted of a series of intersecting trade networks dominated by various competing core states. A further extension of these links included regions in northern and western Mexico. Such provincial, regional, and extraregional exchange systems, often extending over considerable distances, are known to have existed outside the Aztec empire, independent of Aztec control (e.g., Berdan 1980) and even prior to the late Postclassic, certainly as early as Teotihuacan, if not earlier (Parsons and Price 1971; Price 1978).

Space does not allow us to cite the abundance of evidence from disparate sources to support the contention that tribute and trade in "preciosities" also stimulated exchanges of "more basic" commodities. However, one further example will serve to illustrate both the time depth of this system as well as the relationship between trade in one commodity and the exchange of others. One of the best studied trade items in mesoamerican history is obsidian. Obsidian figured importantly in all the major periods of mesoamerican culture history, especially in the Classic and early Postclassic.

Robert N. Zeitlin (1979, 1982) has studied the role of obsidian as viewed from the Oaxacan Isthmus of Tehuantepec and how trade in this commodity reflects this region's relationship to others in Mesoamerica. He concludes that politics and competition between core states (not necessarily the relationship of this trade item to local availability or down-the-line trade) conditioned the availability of sources of obsidian for the local population. In the Preclassic, obsidian came from the closest available sources. However, in the Classic (beginning around A.D. 1) the source was a new area near Zaragoza in Puebla. This is significant since much of the obsidian in Classic Mesoamerica previously had been thought to come from either Pachuca in central Mexico or El Chayal in Guatemala. These sources were controlled by the great central Mexican city of Teotihuacan, a major center of obsidian manufacture in the Classic, and its ally Kaminaljuyú in the Guatemalan highlands, where the Mexican and Mayan portions of Mesoamerica were linked.

While Zeitlin feels that the presence of obsidian from Puebla in his sample may seem an anomaly to those scholars (such as Sanders) who posit Teotihuacan's dominance in the Classic obsidian trade, he argues that Cholula in Puebla and El Tajín in Veracruz may have been competing with Teotihuacan. These cities supplied the trans-Isthmian region not only with obsidian but also with goods such as cacao, cotton, sea shells, and other lowland commodities. This would make sense "if there were two separate exchange mechanisms operating simultaneously" (Zeitlin 1982:269). Further: "as a rival of Teotihuacan, the Classic Cholula state may have established more amicable relationships with El Tajín. Indeed, a Late Classic alliance of Tajín and Cholula, along with two other regional states, Xochicalco and Tula, may have helped to undermine Teotihuacan sovereignty, contributing to its ultimate political and economic decline" (Zeitlin 1982).

Thus, as among core states in the burgeoning European world economy of the sixteenth century, competition among core states—and alliances among core states rivaling the Teotihuacan-Monte Albán-Kaminaljuyú network—not only promoted a world economy in Mesoamerica but also stimulated further changes in it. These changes are reflected in the character of the obsidian trade in the Postclassic:

> After A.D. 900 El Tajín civilization began to slide from dominance as it vied unsuccessfully for power with Cholula, Xochicalco, and Tula in the political fragmentation which resulted from the loss of Teotihuacan suzerainty. The decline of El Tajín, in turn, corresponds with a reduction of obsidian supply to the southern isthmus from the Altotonga and the possible Zaragoza sources. No obsidian whatsoever is attributable to those sources in samples from contexts dating later than A.D. 1200. Supplanting them are new sets of Postclassic obsidian sources whose linkages to the southern Isthmus correlate with the shifting fortunes of such political powers as Toltec Tula and Aztec Tenochtitlan (Zeitlin 1982 : 270).

As we do, Zeitlin sees obsidian as stimulating exchange in other commodities and redirecting the nature of regional economies. Further, unlike some mesoamerican anthropologists who view the obsidian trade as primarily a trade in luxury items (see, for example, Kowaleski and Finsten 1983; Marcus 1983), he presents evidence that the distinction between luxury and prestige exchange cannot be maintained in the case of obsidian. In a review of Spencer's (1982) work on the Cuicatlan Cañada and Monte Albán, he writes:

> Compared to obsidian, a Middle Formative increase in the density of Oaxaca valley export pottery at La Coyotera is taken as an indication of stepped-up prestige good export on the part of Monte Alban, as the Zapotecs there attempted to acquire more high status items for themselves by trading ever greater quantities of their own elite commodities. The problem with this interpretation stems from Spencer's classification of obsidian as a prestige commodity. While we have ethnohistorical evidence from other areas of ancient Mesoamerica confirming the surgical use of such blades in ritual auto sacrifice, it does not necessarily follow that obsidian was considered a prestige good. On the contrary, we know from Sahagún's description of Aztec commerce that obsidian, at least in late Post Classic times, was widely traded as a non-prestige item (Zeitlin 1983 : 647).

That obsidian was part of a large commercial enterprise beyond luxury exchange is also confirmed by the many workshops in Teotihuacan devoted to tool manufacture, only some of which were under direct state or elite control (Spence 1981). Santley (1980) has further argued that the

Teotihuacan obsidian industry was characterized by a highly discriminatory pricing policy, a policy not likely to be invoked under systems comprised only of prestige exchange among elites.

Thus, there is increasing evidence that (1) commercial systems involving considerably more than "prestige" exchange existed in Mesoamerica in the Classic and early Postclassic periods, and that (2) Mesoamerica constituted a world economy, not simply a world system with luxury exchange among elites, well before the elaborate market and exchange systems known from ethnohistorical accounts of the late Postclassic.

Mesoamerica and the Southwest

There can be no doubt that this mesoamerican world economy impinged upon the Southwest. In recent years even so-called isolationists have come to accept that some kind of on-going interaction took place between Mesoamerica and southwestern cultures (e.g., McGuire 1980; Plog et al. 1982). The issue is not whether such interaction took place, but its nature and intensity.

We note with satisfaction the attempts of a number of southwesternists to employ world system theory as a model for explaining such interaction. At least one southwesternist, Steadman Upham (1982), has cited the world system model in his purely internal analysis of the late prehistoric Western Pueblo. Yet the results of such analyses continue to deemphasize the role of Mesoamerica, picturing the Southwest in terms of a number of local exchange systems linked to each other and ultimately linked only indirectly to Mesoamerica by means of exchanges between independent local elites. The interpretation which has been emerging among southwesternists in recent years states that a number of local centers developed in the Southwest in response to local ecological and population factors. These centers were characterized by ranked social systems and redistributive economies. The local elites maintained their status and control through the exchange of exotics with other similarly evolved elites (e.g., Doyel 1980; McGuire 1980; Plog et al. 1982; Upham 1982). Mesoamerica was involved only to the extent that the elites of some of the more southerly situated "chiefdoms," such as Casas Grandes, were in contact with elites in northern Mesoamerica as well as with their counterparts in the Southwest (McGuire 1980). Hence, it is claimed that mesoamerican preciosities and, to a minor extent, ideas were indirectly introduced into the Southwest, while turquoise was moved southward in a down-the-line type of exchange. This interpretation neatly avoids the necessity of allowing any mesoamerican foreigners to enter the Southwest proper.

Central to such an interpretation is the recognition of the existence of complex social systems in the prehistoric Southwest, in contrast to the ethnographic Pueblos. Such systems are commonly referred to as chiefdoms, and equally common is the proposition that they were associated with re-distributive economies as described above; hence, the notion of elites ex-changing preciosities among themselves. In postulating chiefdoms, the au-thorities consistently cited are again the works of Service and Sahlins in Polynesia. However, unlike Polynesian islands, the Southwest is inland on a large continent, and it is bordered on the south by an area of state level civilization.

Further, the very concept of a chiefdom may be based on an inap-propriate "ethnographic analogy," as that of a tribe has been shown to be (Fried 1975). We know of no cases, for example, in which a tribe has evolved into a chiefdom or a chiefdom evolved into a state without external contact with a state. As a result, some investigators (e.g., Lewis 1978; Webb 1973) now question the status of a chiefdom as a general stage in cultural evolution. Its existence has been posited by archaeologists primarily on the basis of ethnographic studies in Polynesian and African cultures which, in fact, exist as parts of a much larger system, although this latter aspect has been slighted or ignored altogether.

In addition, Price points out in regard to chiefdoms and redistributive economies that "positions (of rank) do not create the exchange system, but are created by it" (1982:240). Elite exchange is related to other aspects of the economy; it serves to maintain relationships, thus facilitating utilitarian exchange in a manner similar to the *kula-gimwali* system (Harris 1968: 562–567; Parsons and Price 1971:189). We suggest that a better model than Sahlin's (1958) and Service's (1968) would be Steward's description of South and Central American chiefdoms as responses to neighboring states.

From our perspective, the Southwest would represent a peripheral area in a mesoamerican world economy. It is curious that Plog et al. (1982), in their recent paper suggesting such a world system, fail to make any men-tion of the parts of the system as defined by Wallerstein: the core, semi-periphery, and periphery. Rather, the impression they communicate is of local and regional elites exchanging preciosities with their equal counter-parts throughout the system, the only inequality being on the local level be-tween elites and nonelites. This notion is carried so far as to allow Plog et al. to assert that "regional centers in the Southwest and Mesoamerica were linked by their *relative political parity*" (Plog et al. 1982:233; emphasis added). Curiously, this parallels the characterization of Formative and Clas-sic Mesoamerica by Blanton et al. (1982).

The model of Plog et al. (1982) is developed further by McGuire (1983), whose concept of a "prestige goods economy" in the periphery is skewed in the same manner as similar models of prestige exchange already discussed. To understand this, we need only ask what happens to all that surplus production. According to McGuire, the elites are siphoning it off, noting at the same time that the surplus production is not in the form of "prestige goods," at least as defined by the periphery. Furthermore, the no-tion that the relationship between elites in the periphery and core allows for profits to be realized by the periphery elites draws attention to one of the means by which the core is able to exploit the periphery. By drawing the periphery elites into a dependency relationship (and, it might be argued, even creating periphery elites in the process), the core states are able to manipulate them, while periphery elites are powerless to manipulate core states. Once periphery elites are dependent on prestige goods (including ritual knowledge) from the core, the core state is in a position to play peripheral elites against each other, to withhold prestige goods, and to control the value of the exchange, limited only by the activities of competitor core states.

Further confusing the issue is Upham's (1982) argument that there are two ways of employing the world system concept. One he describes as a strictly spatial approach, noting Wallerstein's use of the concepts core, semiperiphery, and periphery. This approach, he argues, "tends to de-emphasize the important structural elements of world systems that explain how polities of varying organizational complexity are politically and economically linked in a single system. The emphasis on spatial structure thus evades the more important systemic question of world-system integration" (1982:5). The second approach, he argues, "relates directly to the issues of connectivity between polities, world-system integration, and world-system organization" (1982:5).

In the case of Plog et al. (1982), we are presented simply with a system of exchange between local elites in the Southwest, with the world system concept merely tacked on. Upham, on the other hand, erroneously equates the terms denoting parts of the system with literal spatial meaning. This is further illustrated when he explains the Hopi, Zuni, and Acoma survival of the Pueblo collapse by saying that because they "were spatially peripheral to the core of the fourteenth century regional system, they were removed from most of the direct interaction in the system's core" (Upham 1982:200). The confusion becomes apparent when it is realized that in his preceding excellent analysis he clearly identifies the Hopi, Zuni, and Acoma settlement clusters as part of the core of his regional system, not peripheral to it.

The terms core, semiperiphery, and periphery have nothing to do with space *per se*, except in the very real sense that societies are made up of people, and people occupy space. A better definition of these terms would be that they denote the status and role of a culture in a stratified economic system made up of multiple cultures. In this sense, they are somewhat analogous to concepts of lower, middle, and upper class in single societies. An important characteristic of a world system is that it is nonegalitarian. The core, semiperiphery, and periphery are unlike and unequal parts which are linked politically and economically to form a single system. The emphasis is on the relationships between the parts, or between the societies in different parts.

In such a system, the core states, in competition with each other, dominate the system and exploit the periphery and, to a lesser extent, the semiperiphery. What happens in the southwest, a periphery in the system, is in part the result of such unequal, exploitive relationships with core states. This need not involve direct relationships with core states themselves, since semiperipheral states are also in an advantageous position relative to the periphery and are themselves politically and economically related to core states.

One frequently voiced objection to this approach is that it overlooks local ecological factors that condition the evolution of society, so that it depicts the Southwest as a passive recipient of external culture. However, the proposition that the Southwest participated as a peripheral area in a mesoamerican world economy does not ignore southwestern ecology. On the contrary, local ecological factors are highly significant since world systems by definition encompass large areas which are ecologically diverse, and all societies exist in ecological space which plays an important role in determining the position a given society will occupy in the larger system at any given time.

A second, and perhaps related objection, is that the Southwest was composed of non-state societies while Mesoamerica had states. This is related to the chiefdom question mentioned above and also involves the misconception that world system analysis relates only to the analysis of states (i.e., that all parts in the system must be composed of state-level societies). Such a view has many components, not to mention a somewhat romantic view among anthropologists of the notion of the "primitive" and a substantivist notion of the state among most archaeologists (archaeologists are "minimalists" according to Balandier's 1970 classification). Another is a confusion between culture (or social structure) and social system, and a third is a misuse of ethnographic analogy by many archaeologists.

We need not address the first point, but the second and third points are crucial to understanding. In the first place, the society referred to by world system theory is the *total* society; and in the total society, the parts are unequal. Second, to argue that "primitives" may not be included in a world system fails to recognize the fact that we have no notions of primitive societies that are not parts of larger world systems. It is simply that ethnographers who have studied such societies treat culture and social system as synonymous and fail to note the larger system. Malinowski's study of the Trobriand kula ring is a study of Trobriand culture but not a study of the total social system of which it is a part, which included British colonials. Evans-Pritchard's study of the Nuer segmentary lineage system was a study of Nuer culture but not of total Nuer society, which also included both British colonials and neighboring African native groups, some of which were colonized at one time or another by other European core states.

Another more familiar case might better serve to illustrate this point. Murphy and Steward (1956) showed how the adaptation of the Mundurucú of Brazil and the Northeastern Algonkians in Canada (certainly not state-level entities in and of themselves) in response to the demand for rubber and fur respectively on international markets, resulted in a basic change in the "levels of sociocultural integration" of these groups, eventuating in both cases in a "nuclear family" type. The difficulty with such analysis is that it did not go far enough, but looked at the problem only from the point of view of Mundurucú and Algonkian culture or "levels of sociocultural integration." From the perspective of the world system, the process was one whereby the Munduruú and Algonkians became part of a much larger system; they changed from being part of a residual external arena within the world system to a peripheral status within the world economy.

Thus, in world system theory, if state level political economies significantly alter other cultures, then there are states everywhere. Further, it would not enhance our analysis if, instead, we were to study the Mundurucú and Algonkians after their adaptation to the world system and argue that they represented a "nuclear family" level of sociocultural integration that constituted a stage in evolution prior to the emergence of tribes and chiefdoms, categories also derived in large part from inappropriate ethnographic analogy as mentioned above (for other discussions concerning the relationship between non-states and world systems, see Baugh 1982; Hall 1983).

A third, and perhaps more frequently voiced, objection to the notion of the Southwest as a periphery of Mesoamerica concerns the "*pochteca* model" often cited by those who support the proposition. This objection generally takes one of the following forms: specific reference to sources concerning *pochteca* guilds in order to show that they were specifically Aztec (and hence too late to have affected the Southwest) and to show that the areas to which *pochteca* travelled did not include northwest Mexico; the observation that southwestern trade goods, with the exception of turquoise, do not appear in Mesoamerica; and a detailed comparison of putative mesoamerican traits in the Southwest with their mesoamerican counterparts, with an emphasis on differences, together with a search for southwestern antecedents. McGuire (1980) adds a fourth approach: from the *pochteca* model he deduces what we would expect to find in the Southwest and then demonstrates that his test expectations are not met. Clearly, space does not permit us to deal with all of these objections in detail, particularly those of McGuire, which are the most thoroughly presented. Only a few examples will be presented here by way of illustration.

The argument that the Aztec *pochteca* operated only to the south and east of the Basin of Mexico is simply not relevant to the question of mesoamerican-southwestern interaction. The argument pertains only to the Aztec in the late Postclassic. It is known that the Aztecs were cut off on the west by the emerging Tarascan "empire." Since what we know of *pochteca* is from Aztec sources, it perforce does not include the west. However, archaeological data clearly indicate that the antecedents of the West Mexican-South Coast Combine linked with an extensive trade network northward through

Jalisco, Nayarit, and Sinaloa on the west coast, forming the Mixteca-Puebla route at a time when the Aztecs were still uncivilized *chichimecs* (Kelley 1980; Kelley and Kelley 1975). In addition, there were obvious trade connections northward on the east side of the Sierras, through the Chalchihuites in Zacatecas and Durango. Also, we have already noted that a well-developed and extensive mercantile system existed in Mesoamerica at least as early as Classic times.

The remaining objections to the *pochteca* model are based on faulty expectations. From the perspective of a world economy, we would not expect to find finished southwestern trade goods in Mesoamerica, except perhaps for specialized material such as turquoise mosaics. Certainly, we would not expect to find southwestern pottery in Mesoamerica. Historically, the periphery is exploited by the core and semiperiphery for raw materials and scarce resources, not for finished products. When finished products are obtained from the periphery, they consist of products that are labor intensive relative to value, such as woven goods. Unfortunately the source of raw material is extremely difficult, if not impossible, to identify archaeologically, if for no other reason than that it is transformed into finished products somewhere down the line (in this case perhaps in Sinaloa or Durango) or because the material is perishable.

What, then, would we expect to find? From our perspective, precisely what we do find. It is not the evidence that is lacking, but our interpretive models. As an example, McGuire (1980) interprets Casas Grandes as a local chiefdom. As part of his analysis, he cites the distribution of specific trade items from Casas Grandes, such as Chihuahuan polychromes and copper bells, and the northern source of imported pottery found at Casas. On the basis of these data he argues that the elites at Casas Grandes were trading northward into the Southwest. Conversely, the relative lack of specific trade items from Mesoamerica and the lack of Chihuahuan polychromes in Mesoamerica he takes as clear evidence that there was little or no contact with the south and, hence, the site was not a mesoamerican trading outpost as Di Peso (1974) has postulated.

Elsewhere, Pailes and Reff (1980) have argued that because of the distance involved and the lack of advanced transport technology, mesoamerican merchants at Casas Grandes would have found it uneconomical to import trade goods from their patron state in the south. Thus, they would have been forced to produce trade goods locally for exchange with the northern inhabitants. Such trade goods might have taken the form of exotic items not otherwise available in the north, such as elaborate and superior polychrome pottery, copper items, and macaw feathers; also goods which otherwise were available in the north, but which, with their superior technology and organization, they could mass produce more efficiently than native craftsmen, such as shell crafts (which the evidence at Casas Grandes indicates was produced with slave labor); and, finally, ritual knowledge, the iconography of which incidentally was incorporated in the polychrome pottery. Thus, the items which McGuire cites are precisely those we would expect as the locally produced stock-in-trade of the mesoamerican merchants, and their distribution is exactly as we would expect. McGuire's citing the lack of Chihuahuan polychromes in mesoamerican sites is analogous to making a similar argument regarding French fur trappers who did not ship glass beads back to Paris. Additionally, his dismissal of mesoamerican cult symbolism in the Southwest because of differences in detail between mesoamerican and southwestern symbolic meaning is based on a comparison with ethnographically recorded Pueblo ceremonialism and fails to take into account well-known anthropological phenomena such as religious syncretism. Given that a mesoamerican presence in the Southwest probably terminated with the collapse of Casas Grandes, it would be surprising if ethnographically-recorded Pueblo symbolism were identical to mesoamerican symbolism of several centuries earlier. The ethnographically recorded Pueblos have changed remarkably since Coronado's time, let alone since A.D. 1340 (Wilcox 1981).

Thus, a world system perspective requires attention to history, a respect for chronology, and an insistence that human societies must be examined in their total relational context. It can be, however, evolutionary in the sense that it deals with the adaptations of subsystems through the long term and seeks general principles.

On the other hand, there are a number of possible dangers with this perspective. First, there is always the danger that the perspective will become too tied to history. This is perhaps a major criticism of Wallerstein—but less so of Braudel—for by overemphasizing the uniqueness of capitalism, he loses sight of some of the general implications of the approach. Wallerstein's "model" must not be applied too literally, but must be culled for its more general dimensions.

Second, there is also the danger that a world system perspective will simply be "tacked on" to an already existing unilineal evolutionary model which, to the extent that it uses inappropriate ethnographic analogy (ignores historical and chronological context), is antihistorical and, although supposedly universal in scope, contains certain built-in parochial biases among anthropologists. This, for example, seems to have been the fate of Julian Steward's multilineal evolution when his perspectives were "unilinealized" by Sahlins, Service, and Harris. Steward, like Wallerstein, emphasized that "minisystems" were rare after the emergence of the state and that larger social fields were part of the ecologies of specific cultures regardless of the level of sociocultural integration. Thus, evolution is not solely synonymous with endogenic change in cultural entities. Rather, cultural evolution is part of a much larger process, since cultures and their larger social fields (i.e., their "worlds") are not coterminous (see Wolf 1982, 1984).

Ignoring the relationship between cultures and their social fields obscures historical context and leads to historical particularism and parochialism. It makes no sense to argue that because a culture displays a certain character at one point in time that it will be the same at another point in time. Thus, sixteenth century Pueblo culture is not inherently the same as twentieth century Pueblo culture. The relationship between the two remains problematic, something to be investigated with historical research, not something to be asserted on the basis of a presumed cultural continuity. It is odd that southwesternists reject ethnographic analogy with the Pueblos when arguing for the existence of complex societies in prehistoric times and invoke that very same ethnography to argue that those same complex societies were unrelated to a larger mesoamerican world economy.

Similarly, notions that stress a strict distinction between "archaic" and "modern," or non-European and European, are anthropologically parochial and too historically particularistic. On the one hand, they imply that no "archaic" or non-European system could have achieved the complexity of a European world economy such as existed in the sixteenth century— after all, most "primitives" and "archaics" are also non-European. On the other hand, they ignore the basic continuity in all social life and imply that some models must be used for some human societies while other models must be used for other human societies. This latter view is a shaky foundation on which to build a general science of human sociocultural systems.

References Cited

Adams, Richard M.
    1974 Anthropological Perspectives on Ancient Trade. *Current Anthropology* 15:211–239.
Balandier, Georges
    1970 *Political Anthropology*. Pantheon Books, New York.
Ball, Hugh C., and Donald L. Brockington
    1978 Trade and Travel in Prehispanic Oaxaca. In *Mesoamerican Communication Routes and Culture Contacts*, edited by Thomas A. Lee, Jr. and Carlos Navarette, pp. 107–114. Papers of the New World Archaeological Foundation No. 40. Brigham Young University, Provo, Utah.
Baugh, Timothy G.
    1982 *Edwards I: Southern Plains Adaptations in the Protohistoric Period*. Studies in Oklahoma's Past No. 8. Oklahoma Archaeological Survey, Norman.
Berdan, Francis F.
    1977 Distributive Mechanisms in the Aztec Economy. In *Peasant Livelihood*, edited by Rhoda Halperin and James Dow, pp. 91–101. St. Martin's Press, New York.
    1978 Ports of Trade in Mesoamerica: A Reappraisal. In *Mesoamerican Communication Routes and Cultural Contacts*, edited by Thomas A.

Lee, Jr. and Carlos Navarette, pp. 187–198. Papers at the New World Archaeological Foundation No. 40. Brigham Young University, Provo, Utah.

1980 Aztec Merchants and Markets. *Mexicon* 2:37–41.

Blanton, Richard E., Stephen A. Kowalewski, Gary Feinman, and Jill Appel
1981 *Ancient Mesoamerica*. Cambridge University Press, Cambridge, England.

Braudel, Fernand
1977 *Afterthoughts on Material Civilization and Capitalism*. Johns Hopkins University Press, Baltimore.
1981 *The Structures of Everyday Life*. Civilization and Capitalism, 15th-18th Century, vol. 1. Harper and Row, New York.
1982 *The Wheels of Commerce*. Civilization and Capitalism, 15th-18th Century, vol. 2. Harper and Row, New York.

Brumfiel, Elizabeth
1980 Specialization, Market Exchange, and the Aztec State: A View From Huexotla. *Current Anthropology* 21:459–478.
1983 Aztec State Making: Ecology, Structure, and the Origin of the State. *American Anthropologist* 85:261–284.

Carrasco, Pedro
1978 La Economía del México Prehispanico. In *Economía Política e Ideología en el México Prehispánico*, edited by Pedro Carrasco and Johanna Broda, pp. 13–76. Imagen, Mexico, D.F.
1981 Comment on Offner. *American Antiquity* 46:62–68.

Chapman, Anne M.
1957 Port of Trade Enclaves in Aztec and Maya Civilization. In *Trade and Market in the Early Empires*, edited by K. Polanyi, C. M. Arensberg, and H. W. Pearson, pp. 114–153. Free Press, New York.

Chirot, Daniel, and Thomas D. Hall
1982 World-System Theory. *Annual Review of Sociology* 8:81–106.

Di Peso, Charles C.
1974 *Casas Grandes: A Fallen Trading Center of the Gran Chichimeca*, vols. 1–3. Amerind Foundation Series No. 9. Dragoon, Ariz.

Doyel, David
1980 Hohokam Social Organization and the Sedentary to Classic Transition. In *Current Issues in Hohokam Prehistory: Proceedings of a Symposium*, edited by David Doyel and Fred Plog, pp. 23–40. Arizona State University Anthropological Research Papers No. 23. Tempe.

Durán, Fray Diego
1951 *Historia de las Indias de Nueva España*, vol. 1. Editora Nacional, S.A., Mexico, D.F.

Ekholm, Gordon F.
1942 *Excavations at Guasave, Sinaloa, Mexico*. Anthropological Papers of the American Museum of Natural History, vol. 38(2). New York.

Fried, Morton
1975 *The Notion of Tribe*. Cummings, Menlo Park, Calif.
Hall, Thomas D.
1983 Peripheries, Regions of Refuge, and Non-State Societies. *Social Science Quarterly* 64:582–597.
Harris, Marvin
1968 *The Rise of Anthropological Theory*. Thomas Y. Crowell Co., New York.
Kelley, J. Charles
1980 Discussion of Papers by Plog, Doyel, and Riley. In *Current Issues in Hohokam Prehistory: Proceedings of a Symposium*, edited by David Doyel and Fred Plog, pp. 49–66. Arizona State University Anthropological Research Paper No. 23. Tempe.
Kelley, J. Charles, and Ellen Abbott Kelley
1975 An Alternative Hypothesis for the Explanation of Anasazi Culture History. In *Collected Papers in Honor of Florence Hawley Ellis*, edited by Theodore R. Frisbie, pp. 178–223. Papers of the Archaeological Society of New Mexico No. 2. Hooper, Norman, Okla.
Kowaleski, Stephen A., and Laura Finsten
1983 The Economic Systems of Ancient Oaxaca: A Regional Perspective. *Current Anthropology* 24:413–441.
Kuper, Adam
1973 *Anthropology and Anthropologists: The British School*. Pica Press, New York.
Kurtz, Donald V.
1974 Peripheral and Transitional Markets: The Aztec Case. *American Ethnologist* 1:685–706.
Lewis, Herbert S.
1978 Warfare and the Origin of the State: Another Formulation. Paper presented at the Post-Plenary Session: The Study of the State. Tenth International Congress of Anthropological and Ethnological Sciences, New Delhi, India, Dec. 21.
McGuire, Randall H.
1980 The Mesoamerican Connection in the Southwest. *Kiva* 46(1–2): 3–38.
1983 Prestige Economies in the Prehistoric Southwestern Periphery. Paper presented at the 48th Annual Meeting of the Society for American Archaeology, Pittsburgh.
Marcus, Joyce
1983 Lowland Maya Archaeology at the Crossroads. *American Antiquity* 48:454–488.
Murphy, Robert F., and Julian H. Steward
1956 Tappers and Trappers: Parallel Process in Acculturation. In *Economic Development and Culture Change* 4:335–355.

Offner, Jerome A.
1981a On the Inapplicability of "Oriental Despotism" and the "Asiatic Mode" of Production to the Aztecs of Texcoco. *American Antiquity* 46:43–61.
1981b On Carrasco's Use of Theoretical First Principles. *American Antiquity* 46:69–74.

Pailes, Richard A., and Daniel T. Reff
1980 Colonial Exchange Systems and the Decline of Paquime. Paper presented at the 45th Annual Meeting of the Society for American Archaeology, Philadelphia.

Pailes, Richard A., and Joseph W. Whitecotton
1975 Greater Southwest and Mesoamerican "World" Systems, An Exploratory Model. Paper presented at the Southwestern Anthropological Association Annual Meeting, Santa Fe, March.
1979 The Greater Southwest and the Mesoamerican "World" System: An Exploratory Model of Frontier Relationships. In *The Frontier: Comparative Studies II*, edited by William W. Savage, Jr. and Stephen I. Thompson, pp. 105–121. University of Oklahoma Press, Norman.

Parsons, Lee A., and Barbara J. Price
1971 Mesoamerican Trade and Its Role in the Emergence of Civilization. In *Observations on the Emergence of Civilization in Mesoamerica*, edited by Robert F. Heizer and John A. Graham, pp. 169–195. Contributions of the University of California Archaeological Research Facility No. 11. Berkeley.

Plog, Fred, Steadman Upham, and Phil C. Weigand
1982 A Perspective on Mogollon-Mesoamerican Interaction. In *Mogollon Archaeology: Proceedings of the 1980 Mogollon Conference*, edited by Patrick H. Beckett, pp. 227–238. Acoma Books, Ramona, Calif.

Price, Barbara
1978 Commerce and Cultural Process in Mesoamerica. In *Mesoamerican Communication Routes and Cultural Contacts*, edited by Thomas A. Lee, Jr. and Carlos Navarette, pp. 231–246. Papers of the New World Archaeological Foundation No. 40. Brigham Young University, Provo, Utah.

Sahagún, Fray Bernardino de
1959 *The Merchants*. The Florentine Codex, Part 10, edited by Charles E. Dibble and Arthur J. O. Anderson. University of Utah and the School of American Research, Santa Fe.

Sahlins, Marshall
1958 *Social Stratification in Polynesia*. University of Washington Press, Seattle.

Sahlins, Marshall, and Elman R. Service
1966 *Evolution and Culture*. University of Michigan Press, Ann Arbor.

Santley, Robert S.
  1980 Pricing Policies, Obsidian Exchange and the Decline of Teotihuacan Civilization. *Mexicon* 2:77–81.
Schneider, Jane
  1977 Was There a Pre-Capitalist World-System? *Peasant Studies* 6: 20–28.
Service, Elman R.
  1968 *Primitive Social Organization*. Random House, New York.
Spence, Michael W.
  1981 Obsidian Production at Teotihuacan. *American Antiquity* 46: 769–788.
Spencer, Charles S.
  1982 *The Cuitlan Cañada and Monte Albán: A Study of Primary State Formation*. Academic Press, New York.
Steward, Julian H.
  1950 *Area Research: Theory and Practice*. Social Science Research Council, New York.
Steward, Julian H., and Louis C. Faron
  1959 *Native Peoples of South America*. McGraw-Hill, New York.
Upham, Steadman
  1982 *Polities and Power: An Economic and Political History of the Western Pueblo*. Academic Press, New York.
Wallerstein, Immanuel
  1974a *The Modern World-System: Capitalist Agriculture and the Origins of the European World Economy in the Sixteenth Century*. Academic Press, New York.
  1974b The Rise and Future Demise of the World Capitalist System. *Comparative Studies in Society and History* 16:387–415.
Webb, Malcolm C.
  1973 The Peten Maya Decline Viewed in the Perspective of State Formation. In *The Classic Maya Collapse*, edited by T. Patrick Culbert, pp. 367–404. University of New Mexico Press, Albuquerque.
White, Leslie A.
  1959 *The Evolution of Culture*. McGraw-Hill, New York.
Whitecotton, Joseph W., and Richard A. Pailes
  1979 Mesoamerica as an Historical Unit: A World-System Model. Paper presented at the 43rd International Congress of Americanists, Vancouver, B.C.
Wilcox, David R.
  1981 Changing Perspectives on the Protohistoric Pueblos, A.D. 1450–1700. In *The Protohistoric Period in the American Southwest, A.D. 1450–1700*, edited by David R. Wilcox and W. Bruce Masse, pp. 378–409. Arizona State University Anthropological Research Paper No. 24, Tempe.

Wolf, Eric R.

1982 *Europe and the People Without History.* University of California Press, Berkeley.

1984 Culture: Panacea or Problem? *American Antiquity* 49:393–400.

Zeitlin, R. N.

1979 *Prehistoric Long-Distance Exchange on the Southern Isthmus of Tehuantepec, Mexico.* Ph.D. dissertation, Yale University, New Haven. University Microfilms, Ann Arbor.

1982 Toward a More Comprehensive Model of Interregional Commodity Distribution: Political Variables and Prehistoric Obsidian Procurement in Mesoamerica. *American Antiquity* 47:260–275.

1983 Review of Charles S. Spencer, The Cuicatlan Cañada and Monte Albán. *American Antiquity* 48:646–647.

Imperialists, Isolationists, World Systems and Political Realities: Perspectives on Mesoamerican-Southwestern Interaction

Steadman Upham

During the past several decades the topic of mesoamerican-southwestern interaction has been a major issue among researchers in these two culture areas (e.g., Beals 1943; Brew 1943; Ferdon 1955; Haury 1945; Kelley 1966; Schroeder 1965, 1966; and others). Within the last few years, however, this research has been infused with a new vitality and enthusiasm (e.g., McGuire 1980; Pailes and Reff 1980; Pailes and Whitecotton 1979; Plog et al. 1982; Riley 1982; Whitecotton and Pailes 1979). I believe the expression of this renewed enthusiasm has much to do with the recognition by many southwestern archaeologists that some prehistoric groups occupying the Southwest exhibited greater degrees of sociopolitical complexity than has been traditionally realized (Cordell and Plog 1979; Hantman 1983; Judge 1978; Lightfoot 1981; Upham 1980, 1982; Upham et al. 1981).

Many of these recent studies suggest that during some time periods groups occupying parts of the Southwest were participating in well-developed regional political and economic systems that were primarily southwestern both in character and orientation. In the past, for example, many archaeologists believed that during periods of increased sociopolitical complexity that "mesoamerican influence" played a major role in structuring southwestern developmental trajectories. In addition, it was nearly uniformly believed that if contact with groups in Mesoamerica occurred, it must have been a more or less one-way interaction with the more politically complex groups to the south dominating whatever exchanges of material, information, and people took place. In part, this position is supported prior to A.D. 500 given the apparently clearcut finding that agriculture and pottery manufacture diffused from south to north. With the new awareness of southwestern developmental complexity, however, the scale, directionality, and magnitude of mesoamerican-southwestern interaction must necessarily be reevaluated. The interpretation of this interaction, particularly after A.D. 500, assumes an even greater importance to our understanding of cultural sequences in both areas. In this paper I examine the issue of mesoamerican-southwestern interaction in relation to these new interpretations of southwestern prehistory by focusing on an increasingly used set of theoretical models drawn from the literature on world systems.

In the past it was perhaps more convenient than correct to label the various attempts to account for mesoamerican-southwestern interaction as either "isolationist" or "imperialist" explanations. The former position is said to be reflected in studies that have interpreted the prehistory of particular areas in terms of purely local developmental sequences, without regard to extralocal events. The latter is argued to refer to studies that posit largely extralocal events and processes as shaping to a substantial degree the evolution of cultures in hinterland areas. Both are labels that impel archaeologists to, in effect, choose sides over the issue of mesoamerican-southwestern interaction. As labels, these terms are categorizations that fail to account adequately for the variety of discrete positions that are represented by researchers of varying persuasions. Although some would argue that confrontation and controversy are an important structural component in the resolution of problems, more often than not they encourage intellectual positions to become polarized, foster the development of "camps," and result in a situation in which researchers talk past one another.

Some time ago, Plog, Weigand, and I attempted to suggest that it was unproductive to discuss the issue of mesoamerican-southwestern interaction in terms of these polarized positions (Plog et al. 1982). Rather, we suggested that what was needed was a theoretical framework which could structure the investigations of researchers working on both sides of the controversy. We also suggested that such a framework was already in existence, that a body of literature focusing on the development of economic and political systems of considerable scale was being applied by a few archaeologists working in the so-called frontier area on the interface between mesoamerican and southwestern culture areas (Di Peso 1980; Pailes and Reff 1980; Pailes and Whitecotton 1979; Weigand 1982; Whitecotton and Pailes 1979). This literature, the world systems literature, has now become relatively widely used, both as a vehicle to interpret mesoamerican-southwestern interaction and as a heuristic device to structure the interpretation of specific regions within these broad culture areas (e.g., Upham 1982).

World Systems Models: Stricture and Structure

During the last two years it has been difficult to escape reading how inappropriate world systems models are when applied to the interpretation of southwestern prehistory. Of course, the operational word here is "applied." To read the criticisms, one would think that explicit analyses were undertaken and were intended to demonstrate that prehistoric southwestern societies constituted a "world system." These criticisms are based on the mistaken belief that attempts to introduce world systems concepts to the interpretation of southwestern prehistory are predicated on a "direct" comparison of Medieval and Renaissance Europe with the Southwest. Such beliefs could only result from a hasty reading of the pertinent arguments or a purposeful misconstruction of them.

Nevertheless, these criticisms of the world systems approach have focused on the differences in geographic and economic scale between Medieval and Renaissance Europe and the Southwest, as well as on differences in technological development, population size and density, and social differentiation between the two regions. Given these misunderstandings, I believe it is necessary to restate my initial purpose in using the world systems framework and to emphasize the context in which this framework was employed.

World systems models are concerned explicitly with political processes, particularly those that are associated with commodity exchange and alliance formation. As such, the world systems approach of Wallerstein and Braudel is intended to illuminate the internal and external structure of social systems operating at a very large scale. The formation of large scale systems such as the Mediteranean world system are unique historical events; but the sociopolitical and economic processes that were critical to the formation of such systems are general processes operating in all human societies above the level of bands. Consequently, both the general structure and the processes of world systems formation are relevant to understanding and explaining the formation of any regional or panregional social system.

It was in this sense that I employed the world systems framework with the explicit caveat that such models were "heuristic devices that can aid rather than structure the interpretation of archaeological data" (Upham 1982 : 6). Since my own studies of southwestern prehistory based on a world systems perspective and those of others have entered the literature, there has been a growing chorus of discord over the use of this approach. I still believe that the world systems framework has utility in the interpretation of prehistory, particularly with respect to problems like mesoamerican-southwestern interaction. I have, however, developed some reservations about their wholesale and uncritical use.

There are difficulties that can arise in using models developed for capitalist, state-organized societies and applying them to prestate, precapitalist groups. Consequently, emphasis needs to be placed on the underlying economic and political structure that can be adduced from such models. In my examination of world systems structure, I explored the conceptual differences between what Wallerstein has identified as two types of world systems: world empires and world economies (Wallerstein 1974 : 16). I chose to focus my attention on the latter since world economies were part of the precapitalist world and the processual basis of world economies was relevant to both state level and prestate societies. I equated world economies with world systems (Upham 1982:5) and adopted world systems models as heuristic devices in a number of trial formulations.

There has been some concern about the fact that the application of world systems models emphasizes the exchange of what Wallerstein identifies as "preciosities." Although Henri Pirenne and Paul Sweezy have both argued that the exchange of preciosities is important from an integrative standpoint, since such exchanges link the elites from different regional centers, Wallerstein has expressed doubt that the exchange of preciosities could have "sustained the expansion of the Atlantic world" (Wallerstein 1974:41). He argues instead that exchanges of utilitarian commodities—food and fuel—were much more important economically to the organization and expansion of the world system. Both Schneider (1977) and Blanton and Feinman (1983) have suggested a broader conceptualization that encompasses precapitalist world economies that are based principally on the exchange of preciosities. Given the importance of long-distance exchange of luxury goods within the mesoamerican world system, as well as in peripheral areas like the Southwest, this aspect of Wallerstein's model may require reexamination (see Blanton and Feinman 1983). Conceptualizations that broaden the world systems framework to include precapitalist economies, like Schneider's and Blanton and Feinman's, are thus beginning points in refining Wallerstein's model.

Elsewhere I have criticized the way in which world systems models have been applied to the question of mesoamerican-southwestern interaction (Upham 1982:5). Essentially, my critique is one that acknowledges the conceptual utility of world systems models, but eschews their use as "spatial" models of political and economic systems. I believe that we have overdrawn the spatial distinctions made by Wallerstein (1974, 1979), using them uncritically as a simplified overlay on mesoamerican and southwestern culture areas. Because the spatial structure of the Mediterranean world system was composed of a core, semiperiphery, periphery, and external area—each functioning in a particular manner in its role of support for the "metropolis"—does not mean that all systems of similar scale will exhibit similar spatial domains. In fact, one might expect exactly the opposite, that certain historical factors of development (such as, the location and distribution of populations and population centers or the quality, character, and location of important rare resources) would militate against such isomorphic structures. Further, New World applications of the model fail to attend to the complex shifts in the precise location of centers.

More recently, Pailes (personal communication, 1983) has indicated that the structure of the Mediterranean world system suggested by Wallerstein does not necessarily pertain to spatial structure, but to differences in the distribution of status and prestige within the system. I agree with Pailes but also feel that status differences are linked to even more important structural distinctions that can be measured by archaeologists. I believe that a more profitable way world systems models can be used is as illustrations of the way in which systems at a very large scale are integrated and structure the character of their internal and external relationships. I believe that three general points emerge from the historical analysis of world systems that are relevant to the issues of political and economic connectivity and integration:

1. World systems are characterized by a number of large population centers that are participating in the production-distribution of subsistence, utilitarian, and nonutilitarian (exotic) goods. These centers are generally involved in a cooperative-competitive relationship, may be very differently organized, and assume dominant or subordinant roles at particular times.

2. The linkage between population centers is both political and economic and generally involves the transmission (via long-distance exchange) of scarce resources directly between ruling elites. The overwhelming majority of products, particularly subsistence and utilitarian goods, are locally exchanged, with the exchange managed and controlled by a centralized decision-making structure. Long-distance exchange of scarce resources, *including ritual knowledge and esoteric information*, between the elite of widely separated polities is both a vehicle for establishing political bonds (alliances) and a device for maintaining control over the local economic and political system.

3. World system economies often encompass groups of differing ethnic, cultural, or religious persuasions and tend to flourish when such diversity is greatest.

In the remainder of this paper I will discuss each of these points in greater detail. My purpose in this discussion is to suggest that we have overdrawn the material expectations of mesoamerican-southwestern interaction and to provide an alternative framework to evaluate connectivity between Mesoamerica and the Southwest.

Population Centers, Scale, and Change Through Time

There is simply no question that almost every area in the greater mesoamerican-southwestern region after A.D. 500 had at least a few sites that were substantially larger than those in the immediate area. Of course, in Mesoamerica large sites are present in many areas well before this time. The issue of large population centers, however, must be considered in relative terms. Certainly Nuvaqueotaka (Chavez Pass Ruin), a large Sinaguan pueblo in central Arizona, cannot be compared to Tenochtitlan in terms of size, total population, architectural elaboration, or almost any other criteria. Nevertheless, in relation to the Colorado Plateau and Mogollon Rim regions at the time the site was occupied, Nuvaqueotaka must be considered one of the most important localities from an economic, political, religious, and social perspective. The point of approaching this fact from a world systems perspective is not to argue that because of the obvious qualitative and quantitative differences between the two sites and their inhabitants that one, the larger and more elaborated, was in a position to dominate the other. Rather, from a theoretical perspective the issue is one of articulation.

Nuvaqueotaka was the nexus of a fairly extensive regional system between A.D. 1300 and 1450, if the quantity of nonlocal commodities such as ceramics, obsidian, shell, turquoise, and other materials are any indication (Upham 1980, 1982). As such, a few individuals at Nuvaqueotaka may have exerted substantial influence not only over those people living in the immediate vicinity, but also over individuals residing at other large sites across the plateau and Mogollon Rim region. A few studies that have now been completed using southwestern data have described the spatial dimensions and informational and material content of such regional systems (see particularly Hantman 1983). What has not been done is to examine the potential relationships of sites like Nuvaqueotaka to sites located in an intermediate position between the southwestern area and what I refer to here as the "metropolis," the largest and most powerful urban center of a world system.

It is also clear that through time various areas of Mesoamerica and the Southwest were proportionately more or less important politically and economically. This waxing and waning of local, regional, and panregional power centers is perhaps the most interesting aspect of mesoamerican-southwestern interaction and has clear implications for the evolution of the mesoamerican world system. Because of the broad theoretical applicability of the world systems literature, we often overlook the fact that we are dealing with possibly three separate epochs of world system formation, with the metropolis shifting successively from Teotihuacan to Tula to Tenochtitlan. Much the same can be said for the shifting character of organization in the Southwest. At some points in time the San Juan Basin may have been the principal point of contact for groups in the south; at others, the Salt-Gila drainage or the Mogollon Rim country were more important. In addition, consideration must be given to the relatively asynchronous character of cultural developments in much of the Southwest, which mainly follow or precede rather than parallel developments in the metropolis. The development of the Chacoan system, for example, follows the collapse of Teotihuacan and outlasts the Coyotlatelco-Tula horizon, although the latter and the Chacoan system are definitely contemporaneous for a period of roughly 150 years. The Jeddito Alliance (Upham 1982) predates the appearance of the Aztec empire and declines well before Spanish contact. In addition, mesoamericanists still must resolve how the major contemporaneous centers of Oaxaca, Veracruz, Tabasco, the Maya Lowlands, and Chiapas were articulated with the metropolis at different points in time.

The world systems literature suggests that systems operating at a very large scale are "layered," not necessarily in terms of core, semiperiphery, periphery, and external areas, but in terms of information. At this time we still have a poor understanding of how information emanating from the metropolis was incorporated into local settlement-subsistence systems at a distance. There are tantalizing indications that certain mesoamerican politico-religious concepts may have formed a central theme in some southwestern ideologies. The apparent presence of Quetzalcoatl motifs in rock art at Nuvaqueotaka and the arguable similarities between Tlaloc and the kachina cults (Brew 1943) are cases in point. However, until archaeologists are in a position to understand how intervening areas incorporate such information, particularly at sites like Schroeder, Zape, La Quemada, and the numerous centers in the Teuchtitlan region, we can only speculate on the structural implications of a mesoamerican world economy.

Commodity Exchange and Information Flow

Much has been made in the past regarding the exchange of exotic goods between the Southwest and Mesoamerica. Turquoise has been cited most often as the southwestern commodity that was in demand in the metropolis. Weigand et al. (1977) have suggested that southwestern turquoise was traded south and was relatively widely distributed to many areas of Mesoamerica. The exchange of other goods between Mesoamerica and the Southwest is less certain. Copper bells, for example, are demonstrably southwestern in origin (Di Peso 1974; Plog et al. 1982). Similarly, several varieties of parrots (e.g., *Amazona viridigenalis*, *Amazona albifrons*, *Amazona finschi*, and *Rhynchopsitta pachyrhyncha*) and the military macaw (*Ara militaris*) are known to have a recorded distribution in the past far to the north of their present range and, in fact, ranged over much of the Greater Southwest (Peterson and Chalif 1973). A few examples of the scarlet macaw (*Ara macao*), a tropical lowland bird, are known from the Southwest, but these are at best a low frequency occurrence. Only a handful of mesoamerican ceramics have been recovered from southwestern sites and most of these are from historic contexts (Di Peso 1974; McGuire 1980). Finally, enough is now becoming known about the structure and complexity of southwestern political and economic organization so that "high status burials" are no longer accounted for in terms of the intrusive *pochteca*. In fact, I know of only one object from a site in the northern Southwest that is clearly mesoamerican in origin: a carved piece of Oaxacan jade found in an historic context beneath the floor of the mission at Awatovi (Montgomery et al. 1949). How, then, are we to conceive of mesoamerican-southwestern interaction when it appears that very few commodities were in circulation and those goods that were being exchanged were only being traded in one direction?

Some archaeologists have sought to resolve this issue by focusing on the number of trading expeditions that would be required to transport a large quantity of a commodity between locations in the Southwest and Mesoamerica (e.g., Mathien 1981; Plog et al. 1982). Turquoise is often used in these exercises since the total quantity of southwestern turquoise from mesoamerican sites has been estimated. Weigand (personal communication, 1979) estimates that roughly 500,000 individual pieces of turquoise (tessera, pendants, and beads) are known from sites in Mesoamerica. Taking into consideration both weight and volume of the material, transport of the entire half million pieces of southwestern turquoise could be accounted for by less than two dozen trading expeditions, if each expedition included 10 burden carriers transporting a 50 pound load. Less than two dozen trading ventures spread over a millenium would suggest that interaction between the two regions was both infrequent and unimportant. As Weigand has pointed out, however, all of the diamonds that have been mined and shipped for exchange to countries around the world during the twentieth century could be loaded into a single jumbo jet and, consequently, could be accounted for by a single trading expedition. As we all know, diamonds do not travel in this manner.

It is perhaps a mistake to think that interaction between groups occupying different areas must be manifest materially by the exchange of goods. Certainly, there are many situations in the modern world in which interaction, particularly interaction at the highest political levels, does not involve the exchange of goods. Soviet-American relations are a case in point. There is rarely a policy decision made in which either or both powers are not cognizant of its effect on the other country. In fact, many such decisions are calculated precisely to achieve a desired effect. The effect of a decision may have a material correlate: an invasion of a third country may result in an embargo on the sale of grain. But the policy apparatuses, the decision-making structures, only have information content. Negotiators from both powers are involved in high level talks on the limitation of nuclear weapons; the growth and direction of technological development is structured, in large part, by the competitive nature of the Soviet-American relationship; the political and economic structure of both countries is reactive. But even given the serious and concrete linkage of the decision-making structures, the only Soviet commodity widely available in the United States is Stolichnaya vodka. Clearly, were we to analyze the content of Soviet-American interaction in terms of commodity exchange we would be forced to conclude that very little connectivity actually existed. In fact, the opposite is true but the connectivity is structured in terms of information exchange at the highest political levels.

In contrast to the linkage based on the exchange of information at the highest political levels, were we to examine commodity exchange in both countries we would find that the overwhelming majority of goods are locally exchanged. I believe that this situation is, in many respects, a parallel to the issue of commodity exchange in the mesoamerican world system. If we examine data from the fourteenth-century plateau Southwest, for example, we can identify local, regional, and panregional exchange systems that were all operating concurrently. I identify a local exchange system as one that operates within the confines of a single, spatially restricted settlement system. Elsewhere, I have termed such systems settlement clusters (Upham 1982). Regional and panregional exchange systems are those that involve the exchange of goods between discrete settlement clusters in one region and between groups of settlement clusters in different regions, respectively. During the fourteenth century, the majority of goods, particularly utilitarian commodities like lithic resources and cooking vessels, as well as wild and domesticated subsistence products, appear to have been locally exchanged. Regional exchange typically involved more labor intensive or scarce goods like polychrome pottery and varieties of exotic materials, such as turquoise and certain minerals and pigments. With the exception of marine shell, which could have been traded in a down-the-line fashion, panregional exchange in the Southwest during the fourteenth century is barely visible archaeologically. Based on these data are we to conclude that panregional exchange was simply a low frequency occurrence when a century later, during the protohistoric and early historic periods, contact between southwestern groups and groups occupying distant areas was common (see Riley 1982)? I believe that the most parsimonious way to account for panregional exchange and, by extension, contact between Mesoamerica and the Southwest is to focus on defining the extent of information flow and symbolic interaction between the two areas. Marcus (1973, 1976, 1978) has provided us with elegant models on how this work might proceed.

Cultural and Ethnic Diversity

There can be little doubt that cultural, ethnic, and religious diversity over an area as large as the mesoamerican world system was great. The wealth of contact period documents and detailed ethnographies that exist record, in part, the nature and spatial characteristics of this diversity. Compare, for example, the distribution of ethnographically known tribal territories (Jorgensen 1980; Ortiz 1983, vol. 10 : ix) and recorded linguistic distributions (Campbell 1983; Kendall 1983; Miller 1983) across Mesoamerica and the Southwest for a sampling of this diversity. But given what we now know about the catastrophic effects of European contact on aboriginal New World groups (see Dobyns 1983), there is every reason to believe that cultural, ethnic, and religious diversity was even greater prior to the coming of the Europeans.

Systems that thrive on diversity are paradoxical in the sense that the diversity that powers the system can also generate conflict. Consequently, system diversity necessarily requires articulation. The articulation of cultural diversity (see Cordell and Plog 1979) seems to be positively correlated with the process of political and economic centralization (Flannery 1972). In other words, increasing subsystem diversity generates a positive force toward centralization while, at the same time, it provides a basis for conflict, disunity, and disorganization. The mesoamerican world system, particularly during the fourteenth and fifteenth centuries, was an extremely large, diverse, and centralized system. The metropolis of Tenochtitlan controlled millions of square kilometers of territory. But there is a factor of critical mass: because cultural diversity in any given system is positively related to its size and spatial extent, the system must constantly consolidate its holdings. Failure to do so can threaten the stability of the system. In the case of a world system, the metropolis is continuously attempting to bring new regions, resources, and peoples under its dominion. On the one hand, the system is constantly expanding in the direction of its greatest potential. On the other hand, the metropolis is attempting to consolidate under its control these new regions while maintaining control over areas already under its power. Thus, diversity is at once the foundation of the system's growth and development and potentially at the root of the system's demise. Because of this fact, I suggest that world systems are inherently unstable structures. The failure of the Aztecs to completely incorporate their near neighbors—the Tarascans, Mixtecs, and Tlaxcalans—illustrates the internal vulnerability of a system that was attempting to expand its frontiers.

Conclusion

It is useful to remember that the issue of scale is of primary importance in approaching mesoamerican-southwestern interaction from a world systems perspective. McGuire (1980) has argued cogently that very little direct connectivity, in a material sense, existed between southwestern groups and the area of the changing metropolis in Central Mexico. Instead, he suggests that the link to Mesoamerica was indirect, that primary contact in the form of exchange was with groups occupying North and West Mexico. I believe that this argument is essentially correct, but that McGuire has only partially completed the formulation. Exchange is only one part of the mesoamerican-southwestern connection. Earlier in this paper I suggested that exchange could be conceptualized on three levels: local, regional, and panregional. One might argue further that local exchange is a continuous process, one that proceeds regardless of influences from a larger political or economic system. At some points in time, political or economic alliances, like the Jeddito Alliance, arise and regional exchange assumes greater importance. If several alliances exist concurrently, they may begin to impinge on one another. I believe it is this latter phenomenon, the articulation of a number of regional alliances, that ultimately leads to world system linkages. Recently, several archaeologists (Carmichael 1983; Plog 1983, 1984; Plog and Green 1983; Stuart and Gauthier 1981; Upham 1984) have suggested that instead of viewing southwestern developmental trajectories strictly in terms of phase sequences, that it may be more profitable to understand the dynamic interplay between two fundamentally different adaptive patterns: resilient and stable adaptations. As Plog and Green point out, "Resilient adaptations adapt by changing, by movement, by altering the mix of subsistence strategies, by modifying organizational patterns. Stable societies adapt by increasing the social, political and economic devices that promote the stability of whatever cultural or behavioral patterns underlie the societies" (1983:3).

These archaeologists have correctly argued that phase sequences, particularly in the northern Southwest, have been written as if they were the record of stable societies. Instead, data suggest that groups continually oscillated between patterns of stability and resiliency. At some points in time sedentism, a reliance on agriculture and exchange, and population growth were more characteristic patterns. At others, increased mobility, increased use of nondomesticated foods, low levels of exchange, and population equilibrium were common. Plog (1984) has characterized the former as periods when alliances likely formed. If Plog is correct, world systems necessarily must have formed during epochs when many such alliances, both in the Southwest and in Mesoamerica, were organized and articulated. This does not preclude the incorporation in the world system of groups in a resilient pattern. More mobile groups could, in fact, facilitate the exchange of goods and information. It does mean, however, that if we are to understand the changing structure of the mesoamerican world system we must have far more accurate and reliable information on groups who occupied the vast intervening area between the Southwest and the metropolis.

References Cited

Beals, R. L.
    1943 Relations Between Mesoamerica and the Southwest. In *Tercera Reunion de Mesa Redonda sobre Problemas Antropologicos de México y Centro America*, pp. 245–252. Sociedad Mexicana de Antropología, Mexico, D.F.
Blanton, Richard, and Gary Feinman
    1983 The Mesoamerican World System: A Comparative Perspective. *American Anthropologist* 86:673–682.
Brew, J. O.
    1943 On the Pueblo IV and the Katchina-Tlaloc Relations. In *Tercera Reunion de Mesa Redonda sobre Problemas Antropologicos de México y Centro America*, pp. 241–245. Sociedad Mexicana de Antropología, Mexico, D.F.
Campbell, T. N.
    1983 Coahuiltecans and Their Neighbors. In *Southwest*, edited by Alfonso Ortiz, pp. 343–358. The Handbook of North American Indians, William C. Sturtevant, general editor. Smithsonian Institution, Washington, D.C.

Carmichael, David
  1983 Possible Archaeological Evidence for Non-linear Culture Change in the Southern Tularosa Basin. Paper presented at the Second Mogollon Conference, Las Cruces, New Mexico.
Cordell, Linda S., and Fred Plog
  1979 Escaping the Confines of Normative Thought: A Reevaluation of Puebloan Prehistory. *American Antiquity* 44:405–429.
Di Peso, C.
  1974 *Casas Grandes: A Fallen Trading Center of the Gran Chichimeca*, vols. 1–3. Amerind Foundation Series No. 9. Dragoon, Ariz.
  1980 The Northern Sector of the Mesoamerican World System. Paper presented at the Meetings of the Society for Historical Archaeology and Conference of Underwater Archaeology, Albuquerque.
Dobyns, Henry
  1983 *Their Number Become Thinned.* University of Tennessee Press, Knoxville.
Ferdon, E.
  1955 *A Trial Survey of Mexican-Southwestern Architectural Parallels.* School of American Research, Museum of New Mexico, Monograph No. 21. Santa Fe.
Flannery, Kent V.
  1972 The Cultural Evolution of Civilizations. *Annual Review of Ecology and Systematics* 3:399–426.
Hantman, J. L.
  1983 *Social Networks and Stylistic Distributions in the Prehistoric Plateau Southwest.* Unpublished Ph.D. dissertation, Department of Anthropology, Arizona State University, Tempe.
Haury, E.
  1945 The Problem of Contacts between the Southwestern United States and Mexico. *Southwestern Journal of Anthropology* 1:55–74.
Jorgensen, J. G.
  1980 *Western Indians.* W. H. Freeman, San Francisco.
Judge, W. J.
  1978 The Development of a Complex Cultural Ecosystem in the Chaco Basin, New Mexico. Ms. on file, Division of Cultural Research, National Park Service, Albuquerque.
Kelley, J. Charles
  1966 Mesoamerican and the Southwestern United States. In *Archaeological Frontiers and External Connections*, edited by Gordon F. Ekholm and Gordon R. Willey, pp. 95–110. Handbook of Middle American Indians, vol. 4, Robert Wauchope, general editor. University of Texas Press, Austin.
Kendall, M. B.
  1983 Yuman Languages. In *Southwest*, edited by Alfonso Ortiz, pp. 4–

12. The Handbook of North American Indians, vol. 10, William C. Sturtevant, general editor. Smithsonian Institution, Washington, D.C.
Lightfoot, Kent
1981 *Prehistoric Sociopolitical Development in the Little Colorado Region, East-Central Arizona.* Unpublished Ph.D. dissertation, Department of Anthropology, Arizona State University, Tempe.
McGuire, Randall H.
1980 The Mesoamerican Connection in the Southwest. *Kiva* 46(1–2): 3–38.
Marcus, Joyce
1973 Territorial Organization of the Lowland Classic Maya. *Science* 180:911–916.
1976 *Emblem and State in the Classic Maya Lowlands: An Epigraphic Approach to Territorial Organization.* Dumbarton Oaks, Washington, D.C.
1978 Archaeology and Religion: A Comparison of the Zapotec and Maya. *World Archaeology* 10:172–191.
Mathien, Frances Joan
1981 *Economic Exchange Systems in the San Juan Basin.* Ph.D. dissertation, Department of Anthropology, University of New Mexico, Albuquerque.
Miller, W. R.
1983 Uto-Aztecan languages. In *Southwest*, edited by Alfonso Ortiz, pp. 113–124, The Handbook of North American Indians, vol 10, William C. Sturtevant, general editor. Smithsonian Institution, Washington, D.C.
Montgomery, Ross G., W. Smith, and J. O. Brew
1949 *Franciscan Awatovi: The Excavation and Conjectural Reconstruction of a 17th Century Spanish Mission Establishment at a Hopi Indian Town in Northeastern Arizona.* Papers of the Peabody Museum of American Archaeology and Ethnology No. 36. Harvard University, Cambridge, Mass.
Ortiz, Alfonso (editor)
1983 *The Southwest.* The Handbook of North American Indians, vol. 10, William C. Sturtevant, general editor. Smithsonian Institution, Washington, D.C.
Pailes, Richard A., and D. T. Reff
1980 Colonial Exchange Systems and the Decline of Paquime. Paper presented at the 45th Annual Meetings of the Society for American Archaeology, Philadelphia.
Pailes, Richard A., and Joseph W. Whitecotton
1979 The Greater Southwest and the Mesoamerican "World" System: An Exploratory Model of Frontier Relationships. In *The Frontier: Comparative Studies*, edited by W. W. Savage and S. I. Thompson, pp. 105–121. University of Oklahoma Press, Norman.

Peterson, R. T., and E. L. Chalif
1973 *A Field Guide to Mexican Birds*. Houghton Mifflin, Boston.
Plog, Fred
1983 Human Responses to Environmental Variation: The Anasazi Case. Paper presented at the Second Annual Anasazi Conference, Farmington, New Mexico.
1984 Political and Economic Alliances on the Colorado Plateau, A.D. 600–1450. In *Advances in World Archaeology*, vol. 2, edited by Fred Wendorf, pp. 289–330. Academic Press, New York.
Plog, Fred, and D. F. Green
1983 SARG: A Test of Locational Diversity. Paper presented at the 48th Annual Meeting of the Society for American Archaeology, Pittsburgh.
Plog, Fred, Steadman Upham, and Phil C. Weigand
1982 A Perspective on Mogollon-Mesoamerican Interaction. In *Mogollon Archaeology*, edited by P. Beckett, pp. 227–238. Acoma Books, Ramona, Calif.
Riley, Carroll L.
1982 *The Frontier People: The Greater Southwest in the Protohistoric Period*. Center for Archaeological Investigations Occasional Paper No. 1. Southern Illinois University at Carbondale.
Schneider, Jane
1977 Was There a Pre-capitalist World System? *Peasant Studies* 6: 20–29.
Schroeder, Albert H.
1965 Unregulated Diffusion from Mexico into the Southwest prior to A.D. 700. *American Antiquity* 30:297–309.
1966 Pattern Diffusion from Mexico into the Southwest after A.D. 600. *American Antiquity* 31:683–704.
Stuart, David, and Rory Gauthier
1981 *Prehistoric New Mexico*. Historic Preservation Bureau, Santa Fe.
Upham, Steadman
1980 *Political Continuity and Change in the Prehistoric Plateau Southwest*. Unpublished Ph.D. dissertation, Department of Anthropology, Arizona State University, Tempe.
1982 *Polities and Power: An Economic and Political History of the Western Pueblo*. Academic Press, New York.
1984 *Adaptive Diversity and Southwestern Abandonment*. Journal of Anthropological Research No. 40(2).
Upham, Steadman, Kent G. Lightfoot, and Gary Feinman
1981 Explaining Socially Determined Ceramic Distributions in the Prehistoric Plateau Southwest. *American Antiquity* 46:822–833.
Wallerstein, Immanuel
1974 *The Modern World System*. Academic Press, New York.
1979 *The Capitalist World Economy*. Cambridge University Press, Cambridge, England.

Weigand, Phil. C.
1982 Mining and Mineral Trade in Prehispanic Zacatecas. In *Mining and Mining Techniques in Ancient Mesoamerica*, edited by Phil C. Weigand and Gretchen Gwynne. Anthropology 6(1-2):87–134.
Weigand, Phil C., Garman Harbottle, and Edward V. Sayre
1977 Turquoise Sources and Source Analysis: Mesoamerica and the Southwestern U.S.A. In *Exchange Systems in Prehistory*, edited by T. K. Earle and J. E. Ericson, pp. 15–34. Academic Press, New York.
Whitecotton, Joseph W., and Richard A. Pailes
1979 Mesoamerica as a Historical Unit: A World System Model. Paper presented to the 40th International Congress of Americanists, Vancouver, B.C.

12

External Contact and the
Chaco Anasazi

Frances Joan Mathien

Recent investigations into the question of mesoamerican influence on pre-historic southwestern United States culture groups have included references to the Chaco Anasazi. In particular, Kelley and Kelley (1975) presented a detailed model as to how mesoamerican culture could have spread into the Chaco area over the centuries and how major sociopolitical changes in Mesoamerica could have affected the Chaco inhabitants. Briefly, their model suggests that a group of long-distance traders, modeled after the Aztec *pochteca*, and later called *trocadores* (Kelley 1979a), took control of Chaco between A.D. 1030 and 1040. Prior to this time, either itinerant traders or small groups of mesoamericans had been in contact with the Chacoans. After this date and until approximately A.D. 1250–1300, when abandon-ment of the Four Corners area occurred, the long-distance trade group greatly modified "the local Anasazi socio-economic organization, religion, ritual and perhaps, material culture" (Kelley and Kelley 1975:185). The mesoamerican group that initially interacted through the Loma-San Gabriel/Mogollon culture early in this exchange was identified as the Chalchihuites culture, located in Zacatecas and Durango. Once among the Anasazi, these traders established their headquarters in great kivas. Later, circa A.D. 1000, Kelley and Kelley felt that mesoamericans from the center at La Quemada, Zacatecas, could have worked through either the Casas Grandes or Guasave areas. While the number of traits carried from Mesoamerica to Chaco was considerable, only turquoise was listed as the major item sought in return.

Kelley and Kelley are not alone in their belief that mesoamericans influenced the Chacoans to a considerable degree. Di Peso (1968a, 1968b, 1974) also tied the rise and fall of Chaco to events further south, particularly among the Toltec. He, too, postulated a *pochteca*-like trade network, as well as religious influence, such as the cult of Quetzalcoatl that was intro-duced during early Pueblo III.

Frisbie (1978, 1980) and Reyman (1978) examined burial data from the southwestern United States and felt that there was evidence to support a *pochteca*-like trade network. Other trait studies, such as those on architec-ture by Ferdon (1955) and sandal types and cylinder jars by Washburn

(1978, 1980), suggested that there was some contact between mesoamerican groups and Chaco.

There can be no denial that certain artifacts, such as copper bells, marine shells, and macaws, must have been carried from the areas of their origin in the south to Chacoan sites, where they have been found during excavation. Other traits, however, such as architectural features, similarities in ceramic designs and decorative techniques, use of certain types of wooden objects, turquoise, water control devices, communication systems, and astronomical observations "do not necessarily reflect actual influences or contacts" (Lister 1978 : 240).

Vivian (1970 : 227 – 247) addressed the problem of *pochteca* within Chaco Canyon proper. His examination was limited to a specific time period, Pueblo III, and did not focus on turquoise as the major export. He was more concerned with the testing of several possible alternatives to explain the diversity of architectural features and artifact distributions as they relate to socioeconomic stratification. He concluded that there were no *pochteca* present in Chaco Canyon.

McGuire (1980) examined the concept of a *pochteca*-like long-distance trade network in the southwestern United States. After reviewing the numerous traits listed as coming from Mesoamerica, he concluded that there were insufficient data to support the presence of such a group in any southwestern area, including Chaco. Rather, the evidence suggested that Chaco was a cultural center with an elite class. The few goods that were found and the mesoamerican-derived characteristics present in Chaco could have been the result of trade between elite members of Chacoan and other northwest Mexican societies. He suggested periodic trade between the southwestern United States and northwest Mexico but not a highly formalized system.

Schroeder (1981) also discussed the effects of a *pochteca*- like group upon the Chaco Anasazi. He felt that a group of mesoamericans colonized the native Hakataya, who lived in the Gila-Salt drainage during the transition between the Pioneer and Colonial periods at about A.D. 600. These Hohokam then became the center from which mesoamerican culture traits spread among the Anasazi. According to Schroeder, there was no need for traders from Mexico; a trade network linking a number of cultural centers with their neighbors could account for the movement of goods and ideas into the Chaco area. Traders with Chaco could have been Hohokam who brought concepts and items from the Gila-Salt area, as well as those from further south. In this way, material expressions and concepts could have changed as they were utilized by the various intermediate groups. Schroeder (1981 : 55) tied the collapse of the Hohokam-Chaco to that of the Chalchihuites culture in the mid to late 1100s. A new corridor to the east via Casas Grandes and Zuni-Hopi was proposed from the 1100s through 1300s.

During the past several years, I have been concerned with the possible role of long-distance traders, particularly those seeking turquoise, and their effect upon the Chaco Anasazi (Mathien 1981a). Here I would like to examine the evidence available using the world-system model of Wallerstein (1974a, 1974b). This model was selected because it has been used by several investigators working in the southwestern United States and northwest Mexico as a framework against which to examine the data and discuss prehistoric trade networks among these areas (Di Peso 1980; Pailes 1978; Pailes and Whitecotton 1979; Weigand 1982). The use of this model by archaeologists does not imply that it has been adequately evaluated by economists to determine its validity under a number of different cultural contexts. However, use by archaeologists does provide a framework and testable propositions that are needed in order to analyze prehistoric behavioral systems.

The Wallerstein Model

Wallerstein (1974a) used the modern capitalistic system as his data base. He did not retrodict back into "primitive" prehistoric societies; that he left to the reader. He did note, however, that Chinese, Persian, and Roman, as well as the Ottoman and Russian empires of the 1500–1600s were earlier world systems which disappeared due to a top-heavy bureaucracy that could not be sustained. Wallerstein summarized his world system as: "an extensive division of labor, not merely in a functional (or occupational sense) but geographically, partly due to ecological factors and the social organization of work, which magnifies and legitimizes the ability to exploit the labor of others, that is to receive a larger share of the surplus" (Wallerstein 1974a:349). His approach encompasses more than just an analysis of an isolated economic system. It involves an examination of the sociopolitical interactions as well, particularly with regard to long-distance trade.

The Wallerstein model contains three structural components: (1) the core area or core state that contains a group of people who have strong political control, considerable military stength, and accidental advantages (such as location of natural resources); (2) a peripheral area, or exploited producers; and (3) a semiperiphery composed of middlemen who believe in and support the system. These are usually long-distance merchants or controllers of luxury trade.

Not all long-distance trade is classified as part of the world system. There are some external areas that provide "preciosities" or luxury goods, yet they remain outside of the system. Production for a market, even a luxury market, was contrasted with nonessential luxuries that can appear in a system. Only when a core area depended on a producer and the goods became necessary to the operation of the system as a whole was the hinterland considered part of the world system (Wallerstein 1974b:401).

Wallerstein (1974a:19) suggested that a world system could be bounded by travel time—the 40–60 day distance from a core area (actual distance varies with method of transportation). Travel costs would not warrant shipment of less than high-priced items over long distances. Communities further than 40–60 days' distance either are self-sufficient with regard to basic needs or make substitutions. Thus, he suggested that while luxuries from areas further away may appear in the core area, the source area for these items was not part of the world system. With regard to the identity of the traders, Wallerstein suggested these were usually foreigners from the semiperiphery who shared profits with core area leaders.

Wallerstein's model can be supplemented by the work of other investigators. Smith (1976b:52–53) was aware of Wallerstein's work and suggested that his world system may be similar to what occurred in other systems—her partially commercialized market or dendritic and solar systems. Accumulation of wealth and division of labor occur in these two types of exchange systems. Therefore, several of the variables she defines are useful to the archaeologist in an evaluation of a long-distance trade model.

Mobile Traders

Because the model and the data set under consideration necessitate an evaluation of long-distance traders, it is important to understand the principles pertaining to this type of trade, particularly those relative to mobile traders. Plattner (1976) studied the development of periodic markets cross-culturally, and he presented a detailed examination that focused on their role in developing areas without markets. Because he was concerned with variables that would create a need for mobile traders in any area, not just within modern market systems, his discussion and generalizations are appropriate in all situations, historic and prehistoric, as they explain when and why such an occupational niche would occur, who would occupy the position, and when and why such an occupational niche would disappear. Briefly, Plattner stated that a mobile long-distance trader takes over when the price of a good makes it too dear for the consumer to make the individual effort to travel to a central fixed location to obtain it, but where periodic demand in a locality is sufficient for the vendor to transact enough exchanges to cover the additional transportation costs to move his location and still obtain a profit high enough to insure a satisfactory living. The peddler becomes a facilitator for the integration of new areas into a system. He also provides information and unusual goods to all groups involved. However, as a region develops, transportation improves, and commercialization expands outward from the center, the mobile trader as such disappears. He often settles down as a fixed storekeeper or moves outward into new frontier zones. Whether or not exploration into a new area develops into a regular pattern depends on continued demand for items acquired and the size of the market for these goods, the ability of mobile traders to secure good relationships with the suppliers to warrant continued risk taking, availability of the good in other areas where competition is not as difficult, as well as other economic considerations. Wallerstein's (1974a) descriptions of long-distance traders who seek luxury items in areas external to a world system and take them back to the core area are examples of mobile traders.

I have suggested elsewhere (Mathien 1981a:51–58) that the Aztec *pochteca* operated under these same principles. One main problem in distinguishing among the various types of *pochteca* described by Chapman (1957) is the lack of evaluation of the *pochteca* concept against the ideas put forth by Plattner. If the term *pochteca* included a group that was distinguished as a social class and did not necessarily include other members of a society who did not belong to that particular social class, but yet were practicing traders, then it is easier to understand the confusion we have in our discussion of this Aztec group. Only some members of the Aztec *pochteca* traveled; these should operate under Plattner's concepts regarding the mobile trader.

The models for incorporation of the Greater Southwest into a mesoamerican sphere proposed by Di Peso (1968b) and Kelley and Kelley (1975), while differing in details, both suggest the presence of long-distance mobile traders who entered the American Southwest during the first millenium after Christ (circa A.D. 400–600) on an occasional basis. They found luxuries and other items that could be exchanged profitably in mesoamerican core areas, and eventually the system expanded as permanent settlers lived in the various centers in the Southwest. Missionaries, colonists, soldiers, and other seasonal migrants were suggested by A.D. 600–800. These people required nonluxury items and the southwestern items sent south could then have become "necessities" if supplied on a regular basis to the core area. The Southwest, over time, was incorporated into the mesoamerican world system. Therefore, one expects to find archaeological evidence of these colonists in Chaco after A.D. 1030, when hard diffusion or group migration on a permanent basis had taken place.

Evaluation of Mesoamerican-Chacoan Trade

The area encompassed by the Chaco Phenomenon is now known to extend beyond Chaco Canyon. During the past decade, investigators have realized that the large structures found in Chaco Canyon are not an isolated style. While the similarities of these structures to those found at Aztec or the Village of the Great Kivas were known at an earlier date (Morris 1928; Roberts 1932), the immensity of the system has only recently been defined to encompass the entire San Juan Basin (Marshall et al. 1979; Powers et al. 1983). This area may be expanded further as others examine the archaeological record from different perspectives, as Steve LeBlanc does in this volume (Chapter 7). The outlines provided by Di Peso and Kelley and Kelley suggest Chaco Canyon as the data base to be used for testing; Vivian (1970) analyzed the data from the canyon with regard to the presence of *pochteca* and concluded there was no basis to support the model. I have used the San Juan Basin as my region and have reached a similar conclusion based on the following criteria (Mathien 1981a):

1. There should be a core-area state-level system in existence in Mesoamerica/Mexico during the time period(s) the Chaco Anasazi were affected by major changes in their lifestyle and participated in the supposed trade network.

All scholars agree that the Valley of Mexico had achieved a state-level system by A.D. 300, as had several other areas of Mesoamerica such as the Valley of Oaxaca/Monte Albán, and the Maya Lowlands (Weaver 1972). To the north of the Valley of Mexico, however, archaeological knowledge is less complete. The Chalchihuites culture extended as far north as Zape, Durango, the area included in the Loma-San Gabriel cultural manifestation (Kelley 1979b). Kelley described the settlements in the Suchil valley as a local chiefdom with Alta Vista as the ceremonial center between approximately A.D. 300 and 900. He described the Schroeder site near Durango in the Guadiana valley as a "port of entry" second only to Casas Grandes. According to Di Peso (1974), Casas Grandes did not exceed a population of 2,500 (see below), nor was it considered a state. Thus, the Schroeder site was probably not a highly complex social center. Therefore, the Chalchihuites area probably was never a core area in Wallerstein's terms.

La Quemada, the center proposed as the possible mesoamerican source of influence on Chaco after A.D. 1000, is considered to be part of the high culture of Mesoamerica during its florescence. Kelley (1956:132) felt the closest ties of the La Quemada-Chalchihuites culture area were to Tula-Mazapan; Diehl (1981:290—291) also included La Quemada as part of the northern section of the Toltec state. Kelley later described La Quemada as "an imperium related to, if not actually part of, the Tarascan political domain" (1971:774). Thus, this area must be accepted as a possible core area.

To the north, in Chihuahua, was the Casas Grandes culture. Di Peso (1968a, 1968b) did not see the evolution of a complex social system equal to a state in this area. At A.D. 1060, he attributed the distinct change in patterning in the archaeological record to the influx of a mesoamerican culture group from further south. Only 750 people were estimated during the Buena Fe phase, A.D. 1060—1205, but it was not until A.D. 1206 that the Casas Grandes area reached its most complex stage, with high-rise apartments and an estimated 2,242 people. While Di Peso considered this a highly sophisticated settlement, he did not consider it an independent state; instead he linked it to an ever-expanding mesoamerican system, particularly the Toltec empire with its center at Tula (Di Peso 1974).

As for the coastal Mexican settlements, such as Guasave, Kelley (1979a) did not feel these represented states. He sugggested that Riley's

(1976a) ethnohistoric description of Sonoran statlets cannot be supported by archaeological data recovered by other investigators (e.g., Di Peso, Pailes, or others) working in that area.

Therefore, the most northern candidate for a *core* area or state from which long-distance merchants may have ventured out to obtain either luxury goods or subsistence material is Tula or La Quemada between A.D. 1030 and 1150, the proposed time for the major takeover of Chaco.

2. The core area must be within the 40–60 day transport range of the Chacoans in the San Juan Basin. In this case, the method of transportation was foot travel, since there were no pack animals or wheeled vehicles in North America prior to the Spanish conquest. Use of boats for part of the distance cannot be ruled out; however, there is little evidence in the Spanish chronicles that this means of transportation was used commonly along the Pacific coast of Mexico.

Recently Di Peso (1980) made several estimates of 40–60 days' distances based on ethnographic and other evidence. For inland foot transportation, he proposed a person could cover 25 km/day. If one traveled for 50 days, 1,250 km could be traversed. This seems most reasonable. Using his estimated 1,250 km, he concluded that Tula (Tollan) could be the center point for an area that extended from southern Honduras to slightly north of Casas Grandes. It did not include Chaco Canyon, which was approximately 2,000 km distant. Using the Tropic of Cancer as a core, Chaco Canyon fell approximately 1,500 km away, or at the limits of the 60 day range. Using 35 km as the daily distance traveled, the San Juan Basin-Chaco system could be reached on the fifty-sixth day from Tula.

From Chaco Canyon, the 40 day or 1,000 km distance would include Casas Grandes, but not until a 50 day or 1,250 km distance was reached would Guasave be included. These estimates are all based on airline miles and do not take into account the various topographic features that would be encountered on the ground. Evidence that this 40–50 day distance is possible is found in the ethnographic accounts of pueblo trading expeditions. For example, Bandelier (1890:39, 63) recorded that the Seri traded shells for turquoise with the Zuni, while Opata traded parrot feathers and plumes with the Zuni in exchange for turquoise. Elsewhere (Mathien 1983), I have evaluated the distances from Chaco Canyon in more detail. While one cannot rule out the 50-day trip at 25 km/day, evidence from several archaeological studies suggested a 700–900 km radius (a 28–36 day trip at 25 km/day) as a more reasonable estimate.

Thus, it is highly unlikely that Chacoans participated in a world system that had a core area in Tula or some other city south of the Tropic of Cancer. This does not eliminate the possibility that traders would not travel from the core to the San Juan Basin on an intermittent basis, but it suggests that this distance is at the far end of the scale. It does not eliminate the possibility that traders would not use a center at Casas Grandes or Guasave as a contact point or that inhabitants of these centers may have acted as middlemen who exchanged goods from areas further north with others in the south. If this were the case, then there is a need to document direct exchange with either of these two centers in the interim locations and the presence of these foreigners in Chaco during the correct time period.

3. The exchange of bulk or subsistence items from the Chacoan Anasazi to Mesoamerica during the proposed period of major contact, A.D. 1030–1300, should be documented. While many of these items may have been perishable in nature, an evaluation of the zones where they occur can be made.

Review of the proposed items of exchange brought into a mesoamerican core area (Mathien 1981a) revealed that all items could have been obtained from areas closer to any mesoamerican center than was Chaco. Slaves, peyote, salt, skins, herbs, cotton, and selenite were all available within Mesoamerica (Driver 1969) and some items (e.g., peyote) were never documented to grow in the Chaco area. Therefore, they make poor candidates for bulk items traded from the Chacoan area to a mesoamerican core. Turquoise could have been obtained in any of several Mexican states (Baja California, Chihuahua, Coahuila, Guerrero, Jalisco, Sonora, and Zacatecas), as well as from numerous areas in the American Southwest. And based on a review of the distribution of turquoise in the archaeological record (Mathien 1981a:93, Appendices A and B), this item probably was more a luxury item in Mesoamerica than a bulk item used by the population in general. The most extensive use of turquoise in Mexico was either late (Mixtec/Aztec) or early (Chalchihuites). Neither of these cultures were contemporaneous with the use and florescence of the Chaco Phenomenon. There is no evidence of extensive use of turquoise at Tula (Diehl 1981) nor any large amounts from La Quemada.

4. There should be evidence of foreign traders among the Chacoans, as well as three distinct social classes (see Smith 1967a). The regional trade center (not necessarily the political or ceremonial center) should contain evidence of a foreign presence. These foreigners may be core mesoamericans or members of a peripheral area culture. Because these elite are foreign, this group must be documented, not just through similarities of items, but by items that are definitely foreign to the local area, such as pottery, funeral practices, and house construction.

Such evidence should be detectable archaeologically. In other regions, this was possible to discern: for example, (a) the Teotihuacan occupation at Kaminaljuyú (Kidder et al. 1946) where the architecture in one area of the site of Kaminaljuyú was distinctly different from the surrounding Mayan structures. It was stylistically the same as architecture at Teotihuacan; (b) the Oaxacan complex at Teotihuacan (Millon 1974) where foreign inhabitants lived in houses of local style and construction, but the number and style of artifacts were definitely inconsistent with local patterns and could be readily identified with those from the Valley of Oaxaca; and (c) the establishment of *presidios* along the north Mexican border by the Spanish settlers.

The mesoamerican core may have made contact with the external suppliers in the Chaco region via the itinerant mobile trader who visited on a periodic basis at an early date (circa A.D. 450-600/700) but at the time the area did not necessarily become part of the peripheral system. If the economy of the core area grew outward, however, and expanded to the point where this previous external area became a peripheral part of system controlled by the core, the foreign presence either from a core area or its semiperiphery would be permanent in the *regional center*.

Both Frisbie (1978) and Reyman (1978) have attributed high status burials in the American Southwest to *pochteca*-like traders from Mesoamerica. However, neither author has adequately demonstrated that these high status burials are anything more than just that. Frisbie saw some differentiation in burial goods as early as Basketmaker II that were suggestive of some form of medicoreligious practice. With increased dependence on agriculture, he suggested some type of sociopolitical leadership would have been necessary; the individual during Basketmaker III-Pueblo I was becoming more specialized and important. This is reflected in abundance and differentiation of grave goods. By Pueblo III increased sociopolitical interaction had taken place and Frisbie (1978:210) cited the Chaco Anasazi as one of the earliest examples of this in the American Southwest. To me, this suggests the evolution of more complex social organization, and it need not be related to mesoamerican trade. Reyman's models for a *pochteca* burial are more explicit but still questionable (McGuire 1980; Mathien 1981a: 101–102), and even he admitted that one burial from Aztec Ruin did not meet his criteria and may represent a local status differentiation.

Akins and Schelberg (1984) analyzed both the morphological aspects and the grave goods recovered from all known burials in Chaco Canyon. They found evidence of a stratified society with two tiers that can be divided into two subdivisions. The burials are all Anasazi in morhpology and one burial suite (Room 33) of Pueblo Bonito has the largest number of grave goods. This may represent clan hierarchy. Akins and Schelberg concluded that the Chacoans were hierarchically organized and represented a local elite.

The trait lists provided by Kelley and Kelley (1975) and by Lister (1978) can also be examined to address the issue of whether or not a mesoamerican enclave lived among the Chacoans. If actual traders maintained an outpost in Chaco Canyon after A.D. 1030, the architectural features should show an abrupt change from previous forms and not an evolution in style. Location of architectural features should correlate with mesoamerican artifact distributions.

Lekson (1984) has undertaken a comprehensive study of the large Bonito phase structures in Chaco Canyon. His investigations detail a slow evolution in house unit design throughout the Pueblo period in Chaco. The earliest units constructed in the Classic towns were nearly identical to some contemporaneous units in the village sites. Four sites (Pueblo Bonito, Una Vida, Hungo Pavi, and Penasco Blanco), all located near junctions of the Chaco Wash and its side tributaries, grew through the addition of regularly sized and patterned units. The major differences between towns and villages include the extent of preplanning, wall construction techniques, and size. Ferdon suggested that walls are thicker in lower stories, probably to support the higher stories (Ferdon 1955 : 3). Layout of the town (C, D, or E shape) is a local style and contrasts with the mesoamerican court with low mounds on four sides. Even the core and veneer techniques used in Mexico differ from those found in Chaco (Wills 1977).

Suggested mesoamerican architectural features in Chaco appear in various towns and not in one town or area as would be expected: square columns at Chetro Ketl and Bc 51; raised platform at Talus Unit 1; tri-wall at Pueblo del Arroyo; other circular structures, such as great kivas, at numerous towns and villages.

Using the Teotihuacan model one would predict the number of artifacts to be abundant in one area—the postulated headquarters of mesoamerican traders, particularly the great kivas (Kelley and Kelley 1975 : 202–204). The earliest great kivas appear in Chaco at about A.D. 500 at 29SJ 423 (Windes 1975); yet no *objects* of a mesoamerican nature appear in the Chaco until the Bonito phase. When they do appear, most are found in Pueblo Bonito in the suite of rooms used as burial chambers for the elite. Cylinder jars were also found in Pueblo del Arroyo, in Pueblo Alto, and as well as in House C, Group 1 of Village A and in Arrowmaker Burial in the Piedra District. These black-on-white jars were definitely produced in the Chaco region, as are human effigy vases from Pueblo Bonito and Peñasco Blanco and incense burners from Pueblo Bonito. Stamps and cylinders from Pueblo Bonito are southwestern looking. The two pseudo-cloisonné on sandstone, however, resemble those from Guasave and may be trade items from West Mexico.

Thirty-one macaws were recovered from various rooms in Pueblo Bonito, three from Pueblo del Arroyo, one at Kin Kletso (Hargrave 1970), and one from village site 29SJ 1360 (McKenna 1984). Copper bells were not distributed in patterns with other mesoamerican objects; 21 were from six rooms and several kivas in Pueblo Bonito, 6 from Pueblo del Arroyo, 2 from Pueblo Alto, 1 from 29SJ 633, 1 from the Talus Unit. Shells of various species are found in sites, large and small, from Basketmaker II through Pueblo III, but need not reflect the presence of mesoamerican core area traders as these networks were established early in time and linked non-state culture groups in the American Southwest and northwest Mexico.

Because there is no correlation of artifacts with any one site in the central area, and especially not with great kivas, it is difficult to confirm an enclave settlement similar to that at Teotihuacan in the Chaco. Even though the greater number of artifacts attributed to mesoamerican "influence" (but not necessarily mesoamerican import) were found in Pueblo Bonito, other criteria eliminate this site. The rest of the materials could have been distributed by the local elite to relatives or associates at other sites. However, the elite burials from Pueblo Bonito were Anasazi and not mesoamerican. Thus, it is more likely, especially given the few numbers of truly mesoamerican items for the time span covered, that these represent items obtained through trade with other southwestern culture groups by Chaco elite rather than evidence of a mesoamerican group.

The foreign trade center need not have been located in the geographic center of the Chaco region; it could have been located at one end of the Chaco trade system. This is based on Chapman's description of ports-of-trade (1957), Sabloff and Rathje's analysis of Cozumel (1973), and Arnold's description of Dahomey (1957a, 1957b). However, this center (or the nearby area) must have considerable storage facilities for the bulk items to be shipped to the core if it is the staging center for the region.

To date, no center for foreign trade outside Chaco Canyon has been identified, even though surveys for outliers have been undertaken and over 75 Chacoan great houses have been found in the San Juan Basin (Marshall et al. 1979; Powers et al. 1983). Neither artifacts nor storage facilities suggest mesoamerican presence or even transshipment areas. Rather the storage at Chaco outlying communities probably was used for locally produced agricultural products that may have been traded within the Chaco system, as Neller (1978) has suggested for Casamero.

5. Imports to the Southwest should be numerous, with finished luxury items found mainly in local elite centers.

If a porter can carry 50–100 pounds (McBryde 1945) and a caravan included several porters, implications are that many foreign items could arrive on a regular basis. While perishables would leave little trace archaeologically, some luxury imports should be numerous and should be found mainly in the trade center or great kivas. As noted above, only 31 copper bells and 36 macaws have been recovered from sites in Chaco. If only one bird or one bell came through a trade network per year along with other items that perished, then this trade network could not have lasted much over 60 years.

Shell and turquoise items are more numerous, but they are available from different areas and need not represent trade with non-southwesterners. Shell species found in Chacoan sites came from the Gulf of California and the Pacific coast. They were present by Basketmaker III in small amounts and are not necessarily an item that supports a Pueblo III mesoamerican trade network model.

Sources of Chacoan turquoise remain unknown (Mathien 1981b). Turquoise could have been obtained from prehistoric mines located in almost any direction (Mathien 1981a:Appendix C). Besides, turquoise is cited as the major export, not a mesoamerican import.

6. Assuming turquoise was the major item desired by mesoamerican

traders: (a) there should be numerous items in the core area. This is based on Smith's (1976a) description of the flow of goods between the core and the periphery; and (b) the pieces of turquoise retained in the source area should be of poorer quality because higher quality raw materials were traded to the core area. This is based on Chapman's (1957) description of Aztec stone workers and their supplies, as well as economic concepts of supply, demand, and price.

As noted above, the greatest numbers of turquoise artifacts were recovered in sites dating either too late (Mixtec/Aztec) or too early (Chalchihuites) to correlate well with the existence of the Chaco Phenomenon. While there is evidence of turquoise processing at Alta Vista (Kelley 1979b) and Casas Grandes (Di Peso 1974), neither of these sites were contemporaneous with the proposed A.D. 1030 trade network. Review of turquoise found at Toltec or other mesoamerican centers revealed a paucity of material during that time period. There does seem to be an influx of turquoise in Mayan sites after A.D. 900, but the amounts are minor, and where and how this material was obtained is not known.

Turquoise workshops have been documented at both town and village sites in Chaco Canyon (Mathien 1984). The material found in Pueblo Bonito (Pepper 1909) cannot be classified as poorer in quality than other turquoise found archaeologically. Inlay recovered during recent excavations at Pueblo Alto are also of high quality workmanship and excellent color (blue). Many other pieces from various Chacoan sites compare favorably with pieces on the market today.

If Chaco Canyon was the regional export center, then the Chacoans should be the sole supplier of turquoise to the mesoamericans. Review of the location of prehistoric mines and sites with turquoise artifacts does not support the proposition that Chaco controlled any turquoise source (Mathien 1981a). There is little evidence that Chaco controlled the Cerrillos mining district (Warren and Mathien 1984; Warren and Weber 1979). Thus, it is doubtful the Chacoans would have been the sole suppliers of this commodity; and, as there are no documented sources of turquoise in the San Juan Basin, it is more likely that Chacoans in the canyon were importers of this resource from neighboring culture areas.

7. A route or set of routes connecting the periphery with the core area should exist, and there should be way-stations along the route at regular intervals of approximately one-day's distance where porters could stop.

While Riley (1975, 1976b, 1982) studied sixteenth century routes in the Greater Southwest, it is not appropriate to retrodict these routes back into the tenth through twelfth centuries, since major population shifts occurred between A.D. 1150 and 1300 in various areas. Evidence for actual road systems has begun to accumulate in several cultural areas, but none of these areas are currently linked together. Also the road construction differs (Mathien 1982; Obenauf 1980).

While data on many intermediate areas between mesoamerica and the American Southwest are lacking, there are no reports in the literature that suggest a line of way stations linking any culture groups in either Mesoamerica or the Southwest in a manner similar to that found in Peru (Morris and Thompson 1970). Nor are there any forts similar to those found along the Aztec/Tarascan border (Weaver 1972).

In conclusion, it is highly unlikely that any mesoamerican group controlled or participated in a world system that was so extensive in area that it included the Chacoans. There is no real evidence of a mesoamerican enclave in Chaco Canyon or the San Juan Basin to date. This does not preclude one or two adventurous traders coming on an irregular basis and introducing foreign items. Their influence on the local inhabitants, however, would be limited and any correlation of events in Chaco with those in Mesoamerica would be limited rather than a cause-event relationship. One possible explanation for the appearance of mesoamerican traits and objects is a down-the-line trade network that included the Chacoans, who may have developed an indigenous stratified society at this time.

Alternative Models

The prehistoric development of indigenous ranked or stratified social system(s) independent of mesoamerican influences, either in the San Juan Basin or the Greater Southwest, could also account for the importation of numerous items from long distances. Ranked or stratified social systems, as described by Smith (1976a), are divided into two groups, producers and nonproducers. Incipient chiefdoms (or Smith's polyadic model) should be minimally distinguishable from egalitarian societies based on a two-class distinction (as described by Akins and Schelberg 1984 for the Chacoans). And since indigenous chiefdoms (and even tribes) can be linked together into long-distance trade networks, the presence of stratification and the concomitant patterns of product distribution which may include foreign items could be confused with long-distance trade systems resulting from contacts with a world system, even if the area or development under consideration were external to the larger exchange network.

The volume of imports and exports, however, would be smaller. Contact with neighboring ethnic groups in the Southwest could have easily existed among the elite. In this situation, there would be no evidence of foreign mesoamericans at any center in the Southwest. There may be evidence of mesoamerican traits copied into southwestern cultural manifestations if the local elite visited neighboring groups on occasion and adopted certain designs or aspects of their culture, or if they exchanged marriage partners with outsiders who had access to different ideas. Because these new members would have status in their group, their ideas may have been tried and accepted.

At the tribal level, trade partnerships between ethnic groups exist (Flannery 1972). These have been discussed for the modern Pueblo Indians (Ford 1972), among whom local part-time specialists produce trade items. By the time ranked societies develop, specialists exist and presumably craft areas could be anticipated in the major center and possibly in local regional centers. In an indigenous system, the consumers may not be just the local elite.

The possibility that such indigenous systems did develop in the American Southwest and that they could have reached levels of social complexity beyond the tribal organization described for ethnographic Puebloan populations has been considered by Cordell and Plog (1979:419—424). They suggest that the entire Anasazi area may have been integrated into a larger system with several regional centers, such as the Chacoan sphere in the San Juan Basin. The formation of social alliances around A.D. 1000 was suggested as a response to increased demographic pressures once expansion of storage facilities and community fissioning into marginally productive areas had been utilized to a point where further expansion was insufficient to sustain continual growth of the system. Extension of social alliances meant a noticeable change in social organization, and increased craft specialization and exchange of products were cited as manifestations of this revision.

The broadening of social alliances requires managerial personnel. These personnel are often marked ethnographically by certain items or insignia of rank. Imported long-distance items, such as copper bells or macaws, may have fulfilled these requirements. And if Puebloan Anasazi groups were organized along family lines, a possibility suggested by Cordell and Plog (1979:422—423), these items might pattern archaeologically in clan-related situations (for example, room clusters or burial clusters) as suggested for Chaco by Akins and Schelberg (1984).

Schelberg (1982) examined the data, including those recently obtained with regard to roads, water control features, and outlying community structures, and concluded that the Chacoan system was a bounded hierarchy (in Smith's terms—and not part of a world system) rather than either a primate or dendritic system. While he feels it was a complex chiefdom, it was not politically but only ceremonially oriented. There were a few elites, but they had little lifestyle differences from their neighbors. The social complexity that did develop in the Chaco area was a response to stress in a marginal environment. The stress occurred as larger populations expanded throughout the semiarid environment and filled the lands where the greatest potential for agriculture existed (see also Gillespie and Powers 1983). However, because there was no resource controlled by the elite or upper class in the canyon area, the society could not buffer indefinitely the climatic, ecological, and social strains placed upon the system. Therefore, when benefits from this more complex social organization could not be derived, the system collapsed and the population dispersed.

Turquoise, the proposed mesoamerican export from Chaco Canyon, could have fulfilled many different functions. Since it was also an import into Chaco Canyon (from the peripheries of this system) it may have been one of several status items. It may also have had pan-Anasazi or pansouthwestern functions as a ceremonial offering, as an ornament, or both. In the indigenous model, turquoise could also have been desired by mesoamerican groups and could have been transported through a looser exchange network that expanded as indigenous social alliances occurred. Turquoise may have been an important item within the Chacoan system and much more available if the bulk of the item were not a major export to foreigners outside the area. And since turquoise must have been imported into the Chacoan system, it could have been obtained from several different ethnic neighbors or sources in whatever amounts were available.

There is some evidence, albeit limited at present, to suggest that a down-the-line trade model, and its variation, the prestige-chain model, of Renfrew (1975) may account for the trade items found and information on styles of masonry, ceramics, and other materials that show mesoamerican influence. In these two patterns, A visits B at his home and exchanges an item (1) before he returns to his home. B eventually visits C (or vice versa) at his home and trades the item (1). C then continues in a similar pattern to exchange items (1) with D until this item eventually crosses several territories in a long-distance trip.

In Renfrew's down-the-line model, at a distance of 200–300 km from the source there should be a dropoff in the distribution pattern of the artifacts with 90 percent found within the 200 km radial zone around the source. By 600 km the number of artifacts found at a site should be about 0.1 percent.

While the available data are not presented in a way to properly test Renfrew's models, there are several studies that provide information to suggest a down-the-line trade system may be a useful scenario to explain the mesoamerican artifacts and concepts found in the Southwest, particularly Chaco. This 600 km distance compares favorably with distance to sources Di Peso (1980) records for Casas Grandes. (It is also much less than the distance traveled during a 50 day trip at 25 km/day or 1,250 km). At Casas Grandes, only obsidian and alibates flint were transported from 750 and 765 km to the sites where recovered. Di Peso also noted a distance of 900 km for Neolithic obsidian in the Near East that contrasted with data he cited on early and middle Formative mesoamerican obsidians and other materials found at Casas Grandes—all less than 600 km from their source.

Hudson (1978) examined luxury items in the Southwest and assumed all came from the nearest local source. For shell, there was a relatively gradual decrease in percent of sites with shell present until a distance of 640 km from the source was reached. Once past this point, this percentage decreased rapidly. This matches the pattern of fall-off one would expect in the prestige-chain model. For turquoise, there was a fairly random distribution pattern for its presence up to 200 km from the nearest sources. After that the percentage of sites with turquoise decreased rapidly. One major exception to this was Chaco Canyon; this may be because Chaco was the center of a stratified system and could command items not found among agriculturalists. This, too, was suggested by Renfrew (1975) when a higher center was located a distance from the source. Hudson's examination of obsidian revealed a distinct pattern where 160 km was the distance at which noticeable changes in fall-off rates occurred.

Some data from Chaco are available. Cameron and Sappington (1984) reported distances to obsidian sources. The furthest was 516 km, to the San Francisco Mountains in Arizona. The only other exotic lithics to appear in significant amounts in Chaco Canyon are Brushy Basin chert from southeast Utah, yellow-brown spotted chert from the Zuni Mountains, and Washington Pass chert from the Chuska Mountains—all areas within the San Juan Basin (Cameron 1984). With regard to ceramics, the only Mexican sherd located during the survey of Chaco was a Ramos redware (identified by Lister) at site 29SJ 352, the central and largest site in a small Pueblo II–III community located near the mouth of Padilla Wash (McKenna 1981b:4). This was one out of 71,500 sherds, or less than 0.00013 percent. Other imported wares that may have come from outside of the San Juan Basin or Anasazi area included Gila corrugated and a Mogollon brownware. These were found in limited numbers; however, the data for these types were lumped with other similar difficult-to-categorize sherds. The total for all questionable redwares was 409, or 0.6 percent; miscellaneous 26, or <0.1 percent. Data from excavated sites has revealed no Mexican sherds and only a few non-Anasazi sherds. At Bc 59 there were 0.1 percent Reserve black-on-white, 0.4 percent Forestdale Smudged, 0.5 percent Showlow Smudged, and 0.3 percent corrugated smudged (McKenna 1981a). At 29SJ 629 there were 0.1 percent brownwares and 1.0 percent smudged wares (Toll and McKenna 1981). At Pueblo Alto, the percentages of sherds imported from outside of the San Juan Basin were also low: exotic mineral-on-whites, 0.4 percent; Tusayan whitewares, 0.5 percent; redwares, 1.4 percent; polished smudged, 1.5 percent; brownware, 0.01 percent (Toll and McKenna 1983). All of these imports from excavated sites are within the area LeBlanc (Chapter 7 this volume) suggests should be included in the Chaco interaction sphere.

Studies of minerals, ornaments, and other exotics from Chaco reveal only copper bells, shells, macaws, and turquoise were not available within the San Juan Basin. Using only data from recent excavations and lumping these materials into one category as opposed to ceramics or lithics reveals the one macaw equals 0.02 percent of the total of over 4,000 objects. Three copper bells equal 0.07 percent. The 595 shells equal 15.0 percent; only the shells are above the 0.1 percent expected value at a distance of 600 km on the down-the-line model. Even when *Olivella dama*, Haliotus, and Glycymeris are not included (as they are found in greater amounts and are present from Basketmaker III and may not represent the same phenomenon as other species), the 67 other shell species comprise 1.7 percent of the imports—still above expected. Again these might relate to the prestige-chain version of the down-the-line model.

Unfortunately, Renfrew's model has not been properly evaluated using the Chaco data. But this look at available data does suggest it may provide an explanation that accounts for the presence of mesoamerican influence as part of the development of an indigenous population. Goods that appear, as well as ideas, do not represent participation in a world-system centered on a mesoamerican culture. At best Chaco may have been an external area perhaps visited by an itinerant merchant seeking new customers although not on a frequent basis. The down-the-line trade model, however, might better explain the transmission of goods and ideas that seem to be more variable as one moves further from the mesoamerican heartland.

References Cited

Akins, Nancy J., and John D. Schelberg
    1984 Evidence of Organizational Complexity as Seen from the Mortuary Practices in Chaco Canyon. In *Recent Research on Chacoan Prehistory*, edited by W. J. Judge and J. D. Schelberg, pp. 89–102. Reports of the Chaco Center No. 8. National Park Service, Albuquerque.
Arnold, R.
    1957a A Port of Trade: Whydah on the Guinea Coast. In *Trade and Market in the Early Empires*, edited by Karl Polanyi, Conrad M. Arensberg, and Harry W. Pearson, pp. 156–176. The Free Press, New York.
    1957b Separation of Trade and Market: Great Market of Whydah. In *Trade and Market in the Early Empires*, edited by Karl Polanyi, Conrad M. Arensberg, and Harry W. Pearson, pp. 177–187. The Free Press, New York.
Bandelier, Adolph F.
    1890 *Final Report of Investigations among the Indians of the Southwestern United States*. Papers of the Archaeological Institute of America Series No. 8.
Cameron, Catherine M.
    1984 A Regional View of Chipped Stone Raw Material Use in Chaco Canyon New Mexico. In *Recent Research on Chacoan Prehistory*, edited by W. J. Judge, and J. D. Schelberg, pp. 137–152. Reports of the Chaco Center No. 8. National Park Service, Albuquerque.
Cameron, Catherine M., and Robert L. Sappington
    1984 Obsidian Procurement at Chaco Canyon, New Mexico, A.D. 500–1200. In *Recent Research on Chacoan Prehistory*, edited by W. J. Judge and J. D. Schelberg, pp. 153–172. Reports of the Chaco Center No. 8. National Park Service, Albuquerque.

Chapman, Anne C.
1957 Port of Trade Enclaves in Aztec and Mayan Civilizations. In *Trade and Market in the Early Empires*, edited by Karl Polanyi, Conrad M. Arensberg, and Harry W. Pearson, pp. 114–153. The Free Press, New York.
Cordell, Linda S., and Fred Plog
1979 Escaping the Confines of Normative Thought: A Reevaluation of Puebloan Prehistory. *American Antiquity* 44:405–429.
Diehl, Richard A.
1981 Tula. In *Archaeology*, Jeremy A. Sabloff, volume editor, pp. 277–300. Supplement to the Handbook of Middle American Indians, vol. 1, Victoria Riefler Bricker, general editor. University of Texas Press, Austin.
Di Peso, Charles C.
1968a Casas Grandes and the Gran Chichimeca. *El Palacio* 75:47–61.
1968b Casas Grandes, A Fallen Trading Center of the Gran Chichimeca. *Masterkey* 42:20–37.
1974 *Casas Grandes: A Fallen Trading Center of the Gran Chichimeca*, vols. 1–3. Amerind Foundation Series No. 9. Dragoon, Ariz.
1980 The Northern Sector of the Mesoamerican World System. Paper presented at the 13th Annual Meeting of the Society for Historical Archaeology, Albuquerque.
Driver, Harold E.
1969 *Indians of North America*, 2d ed. University of Chicago Press, Chicago.
Ferdon, Edwin N., Jr.
1955 *A Trial Survey of Mexican-Southwestern Architectural Parallels*. School of American Research, Museum of New Mexico, Monograph No. 21. Santa Fe.
Flannery, Kent V.
1972 Summary Comments: Evolutionary Trends. In *Social Exchange and Interaction*, edited by Edwin N. Wilmsen, pp. 129–135. Anthropological Papers No. 46. Museum of Anthropology, University of Michigan, Ann Arbor.
Ford, Robert I.
1972 Barter, Gift, or Violence: An Analysis of Tewa Intertribal Exchange. In *Social Exchange and Interaction*, edited by Edwin N. Wilmsen, pp. 21–45. Anthropological Paper No. 46. Museum of Anthropology, University of Michigan, Ann Arbor.
Frisbie, Theodore R.
1978 High Status Burials in the Greater Southwest: An Interpretive Synthesis. In *Across the Chichimec Sea. Papers in Honor of J. Charles Kelley*, edited by Carroll L. Riley and Basil C. Hedrick, pp. 202–227. Southern Illinois University Press, Carbondale.
1980 Social Ranking in Chaco Canyon, New Mexico: A Mesoamerican

Reconstruction. *Transactions of the Illinois State Academy of Science* 72:60–64.

Gillespie, William B., and Robert P. Powers

1983 Regional Settlement Changes and Past Environment in the San Juan Basin, Northwestern New Mexico. Paper presented at the 1983 Anasazi Symposium on Anasazi, Aridity and Altitude: Cultural Experimentation in a Marginal Environment, Farmington, NM.

Hargrave, Lyndon L.

1970 *Mexican Macaws: Comparative Osteology and Survey of Remains from the Southwest.* Anthropological Paper No. 20. University of Arizona, Tucson.

Hudson, Luanne B.

1978 *A Quantitative Analysis of Prehistoric Exchange in the Southwestern United States.* Ph.D. dissertation, Department of Anthropology, University of California at Los Angeles.

Kelley, J. Charles

1956 Settlement Patterns in North-central Mexico. In *Prehistoric Settlement Patterns in the New World*, edited by Gordon R. Willey, pp. 128–139. Viking Fund Publications in Anthropology No. 23.

1971 Archaeology of the Northern Frontier: Zacatecas and Durango. In *Archaeology of Northern Mesoamerica*, edited by Ignacio Bernal and Gordon T. Ekholm, pp. 768–801. Handbook of Middle American Indians, vol. 11, Robert Wauchope, general editor. University of Texas Press, Austin.

1979a Discussion of Papers by Plog, Doyel and Riley. In *Current Issues in Hohokam Prehistory*, edited by David E. Doyel and Fred Plog, pp. 49–66. Arizona State University Anthropological Research Papers No. 23. Tempe.

1979b Alta Vista, Chalchihuites: "Port of Entry" on the Northwestern Frontier of Mesoamerica. Paper presented at the meeting of the Mesa Redonda on "Rutas de Intercambio," Saltillo, Mexico.

Kelley, J. Charles, and Ellen Abbott Kelley

1975 An Alternative Hypothesis for the Explanation of Anasazi Culture History. In *Collected Papers in Honor of Florence Hawley Ellis*, edited by Theodore R. Frisbie, pp. 178–233. Papers of the Archaeological Society of New Mexico No. 2.

Kidder, Alfred Vincent, Jesse D. Jennings, and Edwin M. Shook

1946 *Excavations at Kaminaljuyú, Guatemala.* Carnegie Institute of Washington Publication No. 561.

Lekson, Stephen H.

1984 Standing Architecture and the Interpretation of Local and Regional Organization of Chaco Canyon. In *Recent Research on Chaco Prehistory*, edited by W. J. Judge and J. D. Schelberg, pp. 55–74. Reports of the Chaco Center No. 8. National Park Service, Albuquerque.

Lister, Robert H.
  1978 Mesoamerican Influences at Chaco Canyon, New Mexico. In *Across the Chichimec Sea. Papers in Honor of J. Charles Kelley*, edited by Carroll L. Riley and Basil C. Hedrick, pp. 233–241. Southern Illinois University Press, Carbondale.
McBryde, F. W.
  1945 *Cultural and Historical Geography of Southwest Guatemala*. Institute of Social Anthropology Publication No. 4. Smithsonian Institution, Washington, D.C.
McGuire, Randall H.
  1980 The Mesoamerican Connection in the Southwest. *Kiva* 46(1–2): 3–38.
McKenna, Peter J.
  1981a Ceramics of Bc 59. Ms. on file, Division of Cultural Research, National Park Service, Albuquerque.
  1981b The Distribution of Chaco Canyon's Survey Ceramics. Ms. on file, Division of Cultural Research, National Park Service, Albuquerque.
  1984 *The Architecture and Material Culture of 29SJ1360, Chaco Canyon, New Mexico*. Reports of the Chaco Center No. 7. National Park Service, Albuquerque.
Marshall, Michael, John Stein, Richard W. Loose, and Judith Novotny
  1979 *Anasazi Communities of the San Juan Basin*. Albuquerque Photo Lab, Albuquerque.
Mathien, Frances Joan
  1981a *Economic Exchange Systems in the San Juan Basin*. Ph.D. dissertation, Department of Anthropology, University of New Mexico, Albuquerque.
  1981b Neutron Activation of Turquoise Artifacts from Chaco Canyon, New Mexico. *Current Anthropology* 22(30):293–294.
  1982 Political, Economic, and Demographic Implications of the Road Network. Paper presented at the 81st Annual Meeting of the American Anthropological Association, Washington, D.C., Dec. 4–7.
  1983 The Mobile Trader and the Chaco Anasazi. In *Proceedings of the Anasazi Symposium 1981*, compiled and edited by J. E. Smith, pp. 197–206. Mesa Verde Museum Association, Mesa Verde National Park.
  1984 Jewelry Items of the Chaco Anasazi. In *Recent Research on Chaco Prehistory*, edited by W. J. Judge and J. D. Schelberg, pp. 173–186. Reports of the Chaco Center No. 8. National Park Service, Albuquerque.
Millon, Rene F.
  1974 The Study of Urbanism at Teotihuacan. In *Mesoamerican Archaeology: New Approaches*, edited by Norman Hammond, pp. 335–362. Duckworth, London.

Morris, C., and D. E. Thompson
1970 Huanco Viejo: An Inca Administrative Center. In *The Rise and Fall of Civilizations. Modern Archaeological Approaches to Ancient Cultures*, edited by Jeremy A. Sabloff and C. C. Lamberg-Karlovsky, pp. 191–208. Cummings, Menlo Park, Calif.

Morris, Earl H.
1928 The Aztec Ruin 1919. *Anthropological Papers of the American Museum of Natural History* 26(1):1–108.

Neller, Earl
1978 Casamero Ruin, AN-NM-01-144, LA #8779, Archeological Report. Ms. on file, Division of Cultural Research, National Park Service, Albuquerque.

Obenauf, Margaret S.
1980 *The Chacoan Roadway System*. Unpublished M.A. thesis, Department of Anthropology, University of New Mexico, Albuquerque.

Pailes, Richard A.
1978 The Rio Sonora Culture in Prehistoric Trade Systems. In *Across the Chichimec Sea: Papers in Honor of J. Charles Kelley*, edited by Carroll L. Riley and Basil C. Hedrick, pp. 134–143. Southern Illinois University Press, Carbondale.

Pailes Richard A., and Joseph W. Whitecotton
1979 The Greater Southwest and Mesoamerican "World" System: An Exploratory Model. In *The Frontier. Comparative Studies*, vol. 2, edited by William W. Savage, Jr. and Stephen I. Thompson, pp. 105–121. University of Oklahoma Press, Norman.

Pepper, George H.
1909 The Exploration of a Burial Room in Pueblo Bonito, New Mexico. In *Anthropological Essays: Putnam Anniversary Volume*, pp. 196–252. G. E. Steckert, New York.

Plattner, Stuart M.
1976 Periodic Trade in Developing Areas without Markets. In *Regional Analysis, vol. 1. Economic Systems*, edited by Carol A. Smith, pp. 69–89. Academic Press, New York.

Powers, Robert P., Willim B. Gillespie, and Stephen Lekson
1983 *The Outlier Survey. A Regional View of Settlement in the San Juan Basin*. Reports of the Chaco Center No. 3. Division of Cultural Research, National Park Service, Albuquerque.

Renfrew, Colin
1975 Trade as Action at a Distance: Questions of Integration and Communication. In *Ancient Civilization and Trade*, edited by Jeremy A. Sabloff and C. C. Lamberg-Karlovsky, pp. 3–59. University of New Mexico Press, Albuquerque.

Reyman, Jonathan E.
1978 *Pochteca* Burials at Anasazi Sites? In *Across the Chichimec Sea. Pa-

pers in Honor of J. Charles Kelley, edited by Carroll L. Riley and Basil C. Hedrick, pp. 242–259. Southern Illinois University Press, Carbondale.
Riley, Carroll L.
1975 The Road to Hawikuh: Trade and Trade Routes to Cibola-Zuni during Late Prehistoric and Early Historic Times. *Kiva* 41 : 137–159.
1976a Las Casas and Golden Cities. *Ethnohistory* 23 : 19–30.
1976b *Sixteenth Century Trade in the Greater Southwest*. Mesoamerican Studies No. 10.
1982 *The Frontier People: The Greater Southwest in the Protohistoric Period*. Center for Archaeological Investigations Occasional Paper No. 1. Southern Illinois University at Carbondale.
Roberts, Frank H. H., Jr.
1932 *Village of the Great Kivas on the Zuni Reservation, New Mexico.* Bureau of American Ethnology Bulletin No. 111. Washington, D.C.
Sabloff, Jeremy A., and William L. Rathje
1973 A Study of Changing Precolumbian Commercial Patterns on the Island of Cozumel, Mexico. *Acta XL International Congress of Americanists, Rome* 1 : 455–463.
Schelberg, John D.
1982 *Economic and Social Development as an Adaptation to a Marginal Environment in Chaco Canyon, New Mexico.* Unpublished Ph.D. dissertation, Department of Anthropology, Northwestern University, Evanston, Illinois.
Schroeder, Albert H.
1981 How Far Can a *Pocheteca* Leap without Leaving Footprints? In *Collected Papers in Honor of Erik Kellerman Reed*, edited by Albert H. Schroeder, pp. 43–64. Papers of the Archaeological Society of New Mexico No. 6.
Smith, Carol A.
1976a Exchange Systems and the Spatial Distribution of Elites: The Organization of Stratification in Agrarian Societies. In *Regional Analysis, vol. 2: Social Systems*, edited by Carol A. Smith, pp. 309–374. Academic Press, New York.
1976b Regional Economic Systems: Linking Geographical Models and Socioeconomic Problems. In *Regional Analysis, vol. 2: Social Systems*, edited by Carol Smith, pp. 3–63. Academic Press, New York.
Toll, Wolky, and Peter McKenna
1981 The Testimony of the Spadefoot Ceramics. Description and Analysis of the 29SJ629 Sherds. Ms. on file, Division of Cultural Research, National Park Service, Albuquerque.
1983 The Ceramography of Pueblo Alto or Aria (Alto): Kyrie Keramikos. Ms. on file, Division of Cultural Research, National Park Service, Albuquerque.

Vivian, R. Gwinn
1970 *Aspects of Prehistoric Society in Chaco Canyon, New Mexico.* Ph.D. dissertation, Department of Anthropology, University of Arizona, Tucson.

Wallerstein, Immanuel
1974a *The Modern World System.* Studies in Political Discontinuity, Academic Press, New York.
1974b The Rise and Future Demise of the World Capitalist System: Concepts for Comparative Analysis. *Comparative Studies in Society and History* 16:387–415.

Warren, A. Helene, and Frances Joan Mathien
1984 Prehistoric and Historic Turquoise Mining in the Cerrillos District. In *Collected Papers in Honor of Albert H. Schroeder,* edited by Charles Lange, pp. 93–127. Papers of the Archaeological Society of New Mexico No. 10. Albuquerque Archaeological Society Press.

Warren, A. Helene, and Robert H. Weber
1979 Indian and Spanish Mining in the Galisteo and Hagan Basins. *New Mexico Geological Society Special Publication* 8:7–11.

Washburn, Dorothy K.
1978 A Reanalysis of the Grave Goods from Pueblo Bonito: Some Mexican Affiliations. Paper presented at the Annual Meeting of the Society for American Archaeology, Tucson.
1980 The Mexican Connection: Cylinder Jars from the Valley of Oaxaca. *Transactions of the Illinois Academy of Science* 72(4):70–82.

Weaver, Murial Porter
1972 *The Aztecs, Maya, and Their Predecessors.* Seminar Press, New York.

Weigand, Phil C.
1980 Mining and Mineral Trade in Prehispanic Zactecas. In *Mining and Mining Techniques in Ancient Mesoamerica,* edited by Phil C. Weigand and Gretchen Gwynne. Anthropology 6(1-2):87–134.

Wills, Wirt H.
1977 An Alternative Perspective on Core-Veneer Masonry in Chaco Canyon, New Mexico. Ms. on file, Division of Cultural Research, National Park Service, Albuquerque.

Windes, Thomas C.
1975 Excavation of 29SJ423, An Early Basketmaker III Site in Chaco Canyon. Preliminary Report on the Architecture and Stratigraphy. Ms. on file, Division of Cultural Research, National Park Service, Albuquerque.

13

Economies and Modes of Production in the Prehistoric Southwestern Periphery

Randall H. McGuire

> By endowing nations, societies, or cultures with the qualities of internally homogeneous and externally distinctive and bounded objects, we create a model of the world as a global pool hall in which the entities spin off each other like so many hard and round billiard balls.
>
> —Wolf 1982:6

To the extent that any society must interact with other societies in consumption and production, we must consider the larger system of relationships to account for its reproduction. Recognizing this fact raises both empirical and theoretical issues in the study of southwestern prehistory. How interdependent were societies in the Southwest at different points in time, and how extensive was the larger system of relationships into which these societies entered? Perhaps more importantly, what conceptual tools best allow us to understand and account for variability and change in these relationships? Consideration of each of these issues leads us away from models of southwestern prehistory which treat societies or cultures as hard bounded objects interacting like so many billiard balls.

I have previously addressed the empirical issue of interregional relationships (McGuire 1980) and this paper primarily considers the theoretical issue. My presentation follows in four parts. First, I consider the strengths and weaknesses of the Wallerstein (1974, 1980) model for the interpretation of southwestern prehistory. Second, I propose an alternate theory which attempts to integrate both regional production and interregional exchange in accounting for prehistory. From this position I emphasize the model of prestige-goods economies for the study of southwestern-mesoamerican interactions. Finally, I utilize these conceptual tools to interpret one of the major events of southwestern prehistory: the final abandonment of the San Juan Basin and the rise of the Anasazi katsina cult.

The World System Perspective

The work of Immanuel Wallerstein (1974, 1978, 1980) and his concepts of core and periphery have had a major impact on how archaeologists currently conceptualize southwestern-mesoamerican interactions. Wallerstein leads us to examine how the development of cores derives from the creation of peripheries, shifting our focus from diffusion or adaptation to interaction and dependencies. There are, however, a number of general shortcomings to Wallerstein's theory and these limit our insights concerning southwestern prehistory. Wallerstein directs us to the right questions but his work does not provide us with the conceptual tools to answer those questions in noncapitalist economies.

In many ways Wallerstein's theory represents a quantum leap in the study of southwestern-mesoamerican interactions and for southwestern prehistory in general. It allows us to look at regional relationships instead of focusing only on human-environmental relations in a single river valley or basin. Societies are no longer bounded objects but dynamic entities defined and transformed by unequal relationships in a larger system. Core areas dominate this system and forge the relationships which create the great diversity necessary for linking a region as a whole.

The theoretical value of the world systems perspective has attracted many archaeologists in the Southwest and other regions. Some, such as Whitecotton and Pailes (Chapter 10, this volume) and Ekholm and Friedman (1982), have attempted to map Wallerstein's theory directly onto prehistory. Other archaeologists have found the world systems model heuristically useful but analytically inappropriate to their prehistoric cases (Blanton et al. 1981; Plog 1983; Upham 1982).

In *The Modern World System*, Wallerstein (1974, 1980) does not present a general theory of cultural evolution but instead a historical theory for the rise of capitalism. Wallerstein writes modestly about the empires that preceded the capitalist world economy and extensively on the rise of the capitalist world economy. He has, however, only slight concern with the noncapitalist world economies which characterize most of human existence and nearly all of prehistory. More important, Wallerstein's theory is historical and not evolutionary. Wallerstein's concepts refer to specific developments in the history of the world and are not generalizable to all times and places.

Wallerstein (1978) identifies four possible modes of production in world history: reciprocal minisystems, redistributive empires, a capitalist world economy, and a hoped-for socialist world government. In reciprocal minisystems all able-bodied individuals engage in production, and processes of reciprocal exchange create inequalities favoring senior males. World empires contain a stratum of nonproducers who preempt the surplus of others through a tribute network controlled by a centralized political system. The nonproducing capitalist bourgeoisie secures surplus from the workers via market exchanges. In these formulations Wallerstein draws his understandings of noncapitalist economics almost exclusively from Polanyi.

Southwestern archaeologists have primarily utilized Wallerstein's concept of world economy as a mode of production (Plog 1983; Plog et al. 1982; Upham 1982; Whitecotton and Pailes Chapter 10, this volume). Wallerstein, however, has made no original contributions to the study of precapitalist world economies. When he discusses world economies he inevitably moves immediately to the discussion of the capitalist world economy. World economies derive from a functional and geographic division of labor but differ from world empires in their lack of an overarching centralized government. Wallerstein indicates that world economies are inherently unstable and short-lived entities; the capitalist world economy is anomalous because it has lasted 500 years. Clearly the dynamics of the capitalist world economy must be markedly different from those of earlier world economies. Wallerstein does not provide us with discussions of those earlier dynamics.

Wallerstein's approach emphasizes how the core subjugates the periphery, but it does not adequately deal with the unique aspects and developments of peripheries or how peripheries affect the core (Wolf 1982:23). Archaeological interpreters of Wallerstein identify regional interaction as important to uneven development, but accounting for how this interaction leads to particular prehistorical sequences is another matter. We must be able to interpret the variation in societies that are not cores. Simply identifying all such societies as peripheries obscures both the variability and the role of these societies in determining prehistoric developments.

The concepts "core" and "periphery" themselves present some operational problems for the prehistorian. They have great heuristic value, helping us to interpret prehistory as the result of unbalanced interaction within a region. But, how do we decide if a prehistoric area was a core, periphery, or semiperiphery? There also exists a problem of scale. In the context of Anasazi prehistory we may wish to speak of Chaco Canyon as a core; but in terms of the Southwest and Mesoamerica the entire Southwest must be considered a periphery. These concepts may function well at the macro level of explaining the rise of capitalism as a worldwide phenomenon, but they are too broad and imprecise for understanding the specifics of development in a region.

A consideration of southwestern prehistory clearly illustrates these problems. Several different cores existed in the prehistory of highland Mesoamerica; the northernmost lay at Tula on the upper edge of the Valley of Mexico. Little or no evidence exists for direct contact between the Southwest and any mesoamerican core (McGuire 1980). The Southwest did interact with the societies of West Mexico, such as the prehistoric cultures of Durango, Nayarit, Jalisco, and Sinaloa. Most archaeologists consider this area a part of Mesoamerica only between A.D. 1100 and 1300 (Weaver

1972). Even during this time period West Mexico was a periphery first of the Toltec and then of the world economy that followed. The Southwest, therefore, was the hinterland of a periphery.

When we step back from our examination of the southwestern situation to examine the larger mesoamerican scheme, we realize that the Southwest was never more than a very distant and minor part of the mesoamerican world system. Identifying the Southwest as a periphery does not fully describe its position in the system, nor does it reveal the dynamics which link particular changes in the Southwest to alterations in the larger world system.

In summary, Wallerstein's theory has great heuristic value and has had a positive impact of the study of prehistory. His formulations, however, do not explicate the dynamics of world systems other than the capitalist. He derives his insights on primitive economics primarily from Polyani, largely ignoring the work of economic anthropology during the last 20 years. His discussions focus almost entirely on the core and do not consider the unique aspects and developments of peripheries, nor how peripheries affect cores. Finally, his concepts of core, periphery, and semiperiphery are difficult to rigorously operationalize in prehistoric cases. Wallerstein guides our research in the right direction but does not provide us with the conceptual tools to answer the questions he leads us to ask.

Relations of Production and Exchange

Wallerstein's is not the only model that directs us to seek answers in the dependencies that exist between societies and individuals. A number of contemporary scholars have advanced equally insightful theories. The French Marxists have developed an approach to the study of primitive economics based on the concept of modes of production (Godelier 1982; Meillassoux 1981; Terray 1975). Archaeologists at the University of London have published extensively on the concept of a prestige-goods economy (Frankenstein and Rowlands 1978; Gledhill 1978). Eric Wolf's (1982) penetrating analysis of the rise of capitalism reveals the global interconnectedness of this phenomenon yet manages to do so without relying on the simplistic opposition of core and periphery. A new formulation can be drawn from a synthesis of these ideas plus insights derived from Laclau (1977) and Ollman (1976).

This formulation focuses primarily on relations of dependency and how these relations link and oppose social groups. As long as social units are independent and self-sustaining, there exists no social mechanism for domination and exploitation (Marx 1964 : 67–120). Changes in dependencies result from the competition among individuals or groups within and between societies. Changes in material conditions affecting production and exchange, such as population growth, environmental change, and technological change, will confer advantages on some groups or individuals at the expense of others. Change in the nature of dependencies and in the structure of societies, however, only occurs if individuals manipulate these advantages to their own gain. The results of such competition are not preordained, and failings of human judgement and action affect the outcome, as do the material conditions that structure the competition.

Two types of relations create dependencies: (1) relations of production and (2) relations of exchange and distribution. Production and exchange are interconnected and interdependent processes. Production in a social context requires the distribution of the product, and exchange cannot exist without a product to transfer. The existence of one of these sets of relations both determines and demands the existence of the other; paradoxically, however, focusing on one often leads to different perceptions of social life than focusing on the other.

Productive processes create dependencies insofar as individuals must depend on others for access to the technology, energy, or natural resources necessary for production. The exact nature of these relations and the magnitude of the dependencies they create varies greatly in human history.

Relations of exchange and distribution link productive activities to the biological and social reproduction of households. Reproduction requires both the biological necessities of human existence and goods essential for social existence. Relations of exchange determine a household's access to those biological and social necessities that the household does not produce. The greater the number of such essentials and the fewer the sources for them, the more dependent households will be on others for their reproduction.

Many researchers have emphasized either production or exchange, subsuming one relation under the other. While this avoids artificially separating these two aspects, it raises a false issue of which relation is primary in determining cultural change. Although it seems reasonable that in certain cases production or exchange may be primary, it seems equally unreasonable that one will always dominate the other as a determinant of social forms. I want to deal with both production and exchange without treating one as necessarily dominant over the other and yet maintaining a holistic understanding of their interrelationship.

Modes of Production

The concept "modes of production" originated in the work of Karl Marx, and modern scholars interpret it in various ways. Researchers generally include the means of production (i.e., the materials, energy, human labor, and knowledge necessary for production) and the relations of production (i.e., the reciprocal relations between people producing goods) within a mode of production. Marx and Engels used the concept in an ambiguous manner, sometimes suggesting modes occurred in an evolutionary sequence and at other times treating modes as generic types following no set pattern of evolution (Hobsbawm 1964; Wolf 1982 : 400−402). Soviet-block scholars and the so-called vulgar marxists have accepted modes as evolutionary stages (Friedman 1974), while French researchers analyze modes of production as systems in their own right rather than as evolutionary stages (Althusser and Balibar 1970; Godelier 1982; Meillassoux 1981; Seddon 1974; Terray 1975).

My use of modes of production follows Wolf's (1982 : 400−402) eclectic formulation, which incorporates the French view with Ollman's (1976) emphasis on modes of production as sets of relations, not sets of dependent variables. In this manner, a mode of production is "a specific, historically occurring set of social relations through which labor is deployed to wrest energy from the environment" (Wolf 1982 : 75). In each mode a distinctive ideology mystifies or obscures the true nature of these social relations from the participants in the mode.

The value of this concept lies not in the classification of cases but in its elucidation of the strategic relations which structure social life. Wolf (1982) defines three modes of production; Marx defined five at one time, seven at another (Marx 1968; Marx and Engels 1947). There exists no universal list of modes; the scale of an analysis or the problems being addressed will determine what distinctions are usefully drawn and how many modes are constituted.

Nor should modes be construed as evolutionary stages. Modes of production are historically and not evolutionarily related (Wolf 1982 : 76). There exists no inherent ordering to modes of production, and, more important, multiple modes may exist at any point of time. This does not mean that any mode may be transformed into any other but that such transformations do not follow a set developmental sequence.

It is important to realize that modes of production refer to social relations between individuals and groups and are not therefore characteristics of a social unit. Multiple modes of production may exist in a society, or several societies may be involved in a single mode of production (Wolf 1982 : 76). Modes of production create the social units we see; they are not products of these units.

Each mode of production contains within it internal contradictions which are the basis for transforming that mode into another. Productive relations change gradually in modes until these contradictions can no longer be obscured by the existing ideology. The ideological crisis ultimately moves people to action, and this action transforms the mode (Godelier 1982). Cultural change is, therefore, gradual and developmental within modes and revolutionary in the transformation of modes.

Wolf (1982 : 77−100) defines three modes of production: the capitalist, the tributary, and the kin-ordered. Only the last two are potentially

relevant to discussions of prehistoric southwestern-mesoamerican interactions.

In the tributary mode of production the primary producer retains access to the means of production while members of the elite extract surplus
from the producers through the use of political or military means (Wolf
1982:79–80). A ruling elite in this mode will be strongest when it controls
a key productive element, such as irrigation, and some means of coercion,
such as a standing army. Considerable variability exists in the degree of centralized power that can exist in modes of this type. At one extreme the local
elite holds power, producing what anthropologists have previously called
chiefdoms or feudalism. At the other extreme, power is centralized in one
ruling elite, a situation characteristic of the asiatic mode of production or
empires (Wolf 1982:80–81). Tributary modes of production likely characterized the high culture centers of Mesoamerica, from the Olmec to the
Aztec (Blanton et al. 1981:226).

In a kin mode of production, kinship relations define the relations of
production and are both the locus and the form of the economy (Godelier
1982:23; Wolf 1981:52, 1982:91). "Kinship can be understood as a way
of committing social labor to the transformation of nature through appeals to
filiation and marriage and consanguinity and affinity" (Wolf 1982:91). Individuals achieve power and prestige through the manipulation of their lineage's productive power and by establishing, through marriage, alliances
with other lineages. Over time gains in power can produce real and lasting
inequalities and the ideological ranking of lineages.

The very characteristics that define a kin mode of production also
limit the extent of inequalities that can exist and the scale of political control
possible. As a leader develops a following through the judicious management of redistribution and alliance, he reaches a limit in the extent of his
power and influence. This can only be transcended by developing access to
production independent of kinship (Wolf 1982:95–96). Cumulative conflict can often exceed the integrative abilities of kin-based mechanisms,
leading to a fragmentation of groups. With no control that transcends kinship, the kin mode of production organizes groups like stacks of blocks,
easily decomposable into lower level constituent kin groups (McGuire
1983a:117–119).

Even when kinship is the dominant means of establishing rights to
resources and labor, the way in which these rights are established and the
extent of inequalities can vary greatly between groups. Following Wolf
(1982:91), kinship itself works in two different ways depending on the
availability of resources and how people obtain these resources. When resources are generally available and access to them is unrestricted—a situation characteristic of many hunting and gathering groups—kinship serves
primarily to create relationships between people and distribute social labor.
Kinship in these situations is fluid, incorporating newcomers and excluding

existing members as the dynamics of production require. Real inequalities evolve based on seniority, sex, and pioneer status. When resources are limited and access to them is restricted—a situation characteristic of groups that transform nature through mechanisms such as agriculture—then kinship serves to define rights of access to resources. Kinship boundaries are drawn tightly around rights to production, including and excluding individuals from production. Mythological ancestors legitimize membership in groups, and inequalities arise as a result of the ranking of lineages or clans. Many of the societies that anthropologists call chiefdoms lie at the extreme of this type of relationship.

This conceptualization of modes of production does not parallel traditional evolutionary classifications used in archaeology. For example, societies that anthropologists have labeled as chiefdoms include cultural groups involved in kin modes of production, tributary modes of production, or some combination of modes. The emphasis in this analysis is on the productive relations between individuals and groups, not on the forms of political organization.

The prehistoric Southwest included both extremes of the kin mode. Cultures in the Phoenix Basin (Wilcox and Shenk 1977) and Chaco Canyon (Grebinger 1973; Judge 1979; Tainter and Gillio 1980) exhibited the levels of inequality and types of organization that characterize chiefdoms within a kin mode of production. At no point in the prehistoric Southwest is there evidence of standing armies or coercive force adequate to infer a tributary mode of production.

Economic Systems

Whereas modes of production refer to the relations that organize production, economic systems define the relations of exchange that link different sectors of a economy or different productive units (Laclau 1977 : 34 – 35). Such systems operate on a local, regional, and even a global scale, as in the case of the modern capitalist economic system. An economic system may link different modes of production and societies into a whole, thereby creating a unity without which those modes and societies would not exist (Laclau 1977 : 35).

Economic systems should not be confused with the archaeological concept of modes of exchange (Renfrew 1975). Archaeologists have utilized modes of exchange as a classificatory scheme in order to pigeonhole societies in an evolutionary sequence based on the organization of long-distance exchange (see especially Findlow 1982). Modes of exchange are the mechanisms by which goods are moved across a landscape and inform only indirectly on the relations that create dependencies between individuals and groups.

Just as production and exchange each determine and demand the existence of the other, so too are modes of production and economic systems related. Certain types of economic systems require the existence of certain modes of production. For example, a capitalist economic system would not be possible if the only existing modes of production were kin modes. A capitalist economic system, however, incorporates modes in addition to the capitalist mode of production, including both tributary and kin modes (Laclau 1977; Wolf 1982).

Economic systems should not be equated with evolutionary stages. Like modes of production, economic systems represent specific historically occurring relations (Laclau 1977 : 43). There does not exist and could not exist an exhaustive list of types of economic systems; the scale of the analysis and the problems at hand will determine what systems are constituted. Finally, human groups do not pass through any necessary developmental progression from one type of economic system to another.

A variety of different economic systems have been constituted in the past, including the capitalist (Laclau 1977; Marx 1967), the mercantile (Marx 1967 : 331; Wolf 1982 : 83–88), and the prestige-goods (Frankenstein and Rowlands 1978; Gledhill 1978). The last of these types is the most relevant to the discussion of southwest-mesoamerican interactions.

Prestige-goods economies are based on the association of political power with control of access to foreign goods, which assume meaning as social valuables. The concept of such economies is derived from recent work in primitive economics (Sahlins 1972; Schneider 1974; Strathern 1971), and from the archaeological work of Frankenstein and Rowlands (1978) and Gledhill (1978). Such economies are most commonly associated with kin modes of production and may link kin and tributary modes.

In a prestige-goods economy, elites—usually male lineage heads— obtain power by controlling access to goods obtainable only through external exchange. Individuals do not require these goods for their physical well-being but the items are social valuables essential for the reproduction of the group. Individuals in the society must have these valuables in order to validate the major social and religious transitions of their lives, including births, marriages, deaths, and other major life events. Subordinate individuals become dependent upon elites for access to these valuables. The elites in turn extract surplus production of both utilitarian goods and valuables in return for the provisioning of these social necessities. The elites use this surplus production in status competitions with other elites and to obtain more valuables from outside the society. The relationship is asymmetrical in that the individual has only one source of valuables, whereas the elite can draw surplus production from a variety of subordinates.

The elite must also enter into subordinate relationships in order to maintain its position in this system. When multiple levels of dependency exist, as they do in societies labeled as chiefdoms, lower level elites depend on higher level elites to provide them with the goods they need to maintain their social position. These include valuables for distribution to their followers and items which symbolically legitimize lower elite status vis à vis their superiors and subordinates. Elite goods and lesser valuables for distribution to subordinates are linked at this point in the exchange system so that any disruption in the supply or flow of one affects the other. Ultimately the paramount elites must depend on others, outside their society, for the goods that allow them to maintain the system of dependencies within their own society.

By controlling the valuables required for social reproduction, the elite preempts the surplus production of a society. This appropriation derives primarily from the social meaning of the artifacts involved and not from the use of force. This meaning is an intregal part of an ideology that serves to deny the exploitative role of the elite and to legitimize the broader system of inequalities that exist. The artifacts derive their power from ideology, and their exchange and distribution maintains the ideology. Goods that are rare, that require unusual skill to produce, or that are associated with more powerful social systems provide the best candidates for valuables (Flannery 1968).

Inequality increases in this kind of system when elites exploit small advantages in competition to increase the number of individuals dependent upon them. Descent groups that have inferior productive resources are disadvantaged in competition and may become dependent upon the elite of a different descent group for their valuables. In this case the dominant group may compel the poorer descent group to produce goods that serve the needs of the dominant group. Elites gain power relative to their subordinates when they come to control the production or source of the valuables used in the system. The greater this control the less dependent the elites are on foreign elites, and the more they are able to monopolize access to valuables. This means less redistribution to dependents and an increasingly restricted circulation of valuables, to only within the elite group (Frankenstein and Rowlands 1978).

The elite may exploit distinctions drawn between richer and poorer descent groups to create real differences in the access to the means of production. Poorer descent groups may become indebted to them for valuables and this may be used as a justification for the dominant group usurping the resources and labor power of the poorer. The elite may also manipulate the symbolic, mythological, and genealogical differences between richer and poorer descent groups to create ideologically sanctioned rankings of kin groups.

These processes can ultimately transform a kin mode of production to an even more exploitative form and also transform the economic system. As elites come to control access to production as well as the distribution of valuables, they obtain retainers dependent upon them not just for access to social necessities but also for their livelihoods. The elites acquire followers whose allegiance transcends kin obligations.

Both internal contradictions and external dependencies make prestige-goods economies inherently unstable. The elites' access to foreign valuables and their ability to compete with other elites ultimately depends on the productive capabilities of their dependents. Here we are concerned with the traditional variables of an ecological archaeology: population size, environment, and technology. The elites possess a potentially unlimited demand for surplus but material conditions ultimately limit the productive capabilities of the society. If the elite attempts to exceed this limitation or coerce greater labor investments than subordinates are willing to expend, either the economy must collapse or the producers will overthrow the elite. Only if the productive power of the society increases or the elites obtain a source for coercive force may this contradiction be overcome and the system transformed to a more exploitative mode of production.

The dependency of such economies on external elites contributes to their instability, since individuals within the society or from competing social groups may break the elite's monopoly on foreign valuables, thereby displacing the old elite. This may be done by establishing new sources of valuables or by renegotiating social meanings and introducing new valuables. The external trade connections of the elite provide an even greater source of instability. The supply of foreign valuables normally depends on trade connections which link the elites to faraway societies, over which they have no control. Environmental, political, or social perturbations several hundred miles away can disrupt the flow of valuables to the elite.

A prestige-goods economy existed in the Southwest among the Hohokam at least as early as A.D. 700 (McGuire 1983b), and such a system clearly existed in the Chaco by approximately A.D. 950 (Akins and Schelberg 1981; Gledhill 1978). Blanton et al. (1981:250) have argued that a prestige-goods economy existed in Mesoamerica from 1000 B.C. until the final two centuries before the Spanish conquest. This economic system was notably more elaborate than in the Southwest with the movement of many utilitarian commodities, such as obsidian. According to Blanton et al. (1981:248) a prestige-goods economy structured this exchange and there is no evidence of regular interregional dependencies for food before the fifteenth century.

The Pueblo III Collapse and the Anasazi Katsina Cult

The theory presented here attempts to delineate the significant elements at work in processes of cultural change. It does not seek to specify universal causes but rather to identify the key structural relations we should examine in any given instance of change. Explanation comes from the revelation of the relations and contradictions that produce change in a specific prehistoric case. To illustrate how this consideration of production and exchange allows us to understand particular events in the prehistory of the Southwest and informs on mesoamerican-southwestern interactions, I will employ the model to analyze the abandonment of the San Juan Basin and the subsequent appearance of the Anasazi katsina cult.

One of the most dramatic events in Anasazi prehistory was the abandonment of Mesa Verde and the San Juan Basin at about A.D. 1300 and the subsequent concentration of Anasazi populations in the Rio Grande valley, around Zuni, Acoma, and at scattered locales in northwestern Arizona. The abandonment of individual sites and river valleys was a common occurrence in Anasazi prehistory, but the emptying of an area the size of the San Juan Basin was a rare event (Cordell 1979:102– 103). The Pueblo III to Pueblo IV transition marked the greatest demographic shift in Anasazi prehistory, so it has been of major interest to southwestern archaeologists.

Interestingly, this demographic shift occurred at a time of extreme drought in the Colorado Plateaus (Dean and Robinson 1977; Euler et al. 1979). The congruence between this drought and the abandonments has not been lost on southwestern archaeologists, many of whom cite a general environmental deterioration resulting from the drought as the cause for abandonment (Bradfield 1971; Dean 1970; Hayes 1964; Lister 1966; Zubrow 1971). Numerous other researchers have indicated the inadequacy of simple environmental explanations that do not take into account the internal social dynamics of the societies involved (Cordell 1979:150; Martin and Plog 1973:318–333; Tainter and Gillio 1980). Kelley (1981) points to alternative events that correspond to this period of abandonment: the rise of the Tarascan empire in northern Mesoamerica, the collapse of Casas Grandes, and the subsequent exclusion of the Southwest from a mesoamerican world system. After A.D. 1350 mesoamerican goods, such as copper bells and macaws, become very scarce or disappear altogether from southwestern sites (McGuire 1980; Schroeder 1966).

If we are to explain the abandonment of the San Juan Basin, we must examine the effects of both environmental stress and the ending of long-distance trade on Anasazi kin modes of production and the prestige-goods economy linking societies in the Southwest to each other and to Mesoamerica. For production, this requires defining the means of production, the limitations to production inherent in the means of production, and the organization of production. For exchange, we must consider what was being exchanged, what were the values of goods, and what were the linkages in the exchange network. Finally, both kin modes of production and prestige-goods economies are not maintained by coercive force but by an ideology embodied in kin relations and material goods. Events which reveal the contradictions in this ideology move people to transform these relations and no such transformation could occur without a renegotiation of the ideology.

The relations of production and exchange in the late thirteenth century developed from patterns of organization inherited from the past, and some discussion of this past facilitates our understanding of the Pueblo III to Pueblo IV transition.

Production in Anasazi prehistory centered on the cultivation of corn, beans, and squash. Wild resources, both plants and animals, almost certainly provided a significant portion of the diet in all periods (Cordell 1979 : 67–68). Cordell and Plog's (1979) summary of puebloan prehistory suggests that the Anasazi dependence on agriculture increased through time, with a marked increase in agricultural intensification after about A.D. 1000. Despite the importance of wild resources for survival, only corn agriculture provided a basis for the population aggregation and societal complexity of the Pueblo III period. Increasing emphasis on corn agriculture, however, ultimately led to an environmental crisis (Plog 1983 : 325).

The modern San Juan Basin is environmentally marginal for corn agriculture. Over nearly all of the area, both the rate of summer precipitation and the number of frost-free days only slightly exceed the minimal requirements for corn growth (Cordell 1979 : 68; Hack 1942 : 20; Tainter and Gillio 1980 : 11; Vivian 1974). Modern climatic conditions do not characterize all of Anasazi prehistory, and the key climatic factors of precipitation and growing season varied through time (Euler et al. 1979). However, because of the marginality of the area, even slight fluctuations in climate could significantly expand or contract the number of areas suitable for corn agriculture, and Anasazi populations reacted to these variations by expanding and contracting their range (Euler et al. 1979).

These expansions and contractions would have had a profound influence on the productive relations in a kin mode of production. With low population densities such as those that characterize Anasazi populations in the Basketmaker II to Pueblo II periods (Cordell and Plog 1979), expansion would have made a prime productive resource—agricultural land—more generally available. This increase in access would have weakened lineage control of resources and, concurrently, the power of lineage heads. Contraction without population loss would have decreased access to the means of production, strengthening lineage control and the power of lineage heads. Furthermore, contraction would have revealed an internal contradiction in this type of mode. While strengthening the power of lineage heads, contraction also would have increased the chances of conflict, straining the ability of lineage heads to hold societies together.

The widespread appearance of water control features to concentrate and store water after around A.D. 1000 suggests a general intensification of agricultural production over much of the San Juan Basin (Vivian 1974). The intensification appears to have been related both to environmental change and to population growth (Cordell and Plog 1979; Euler et al. 1979; Vivian 1974). These changes would have strengthened lineage control of production. The technology required for production (water control features) would have become part of lineage lands and provided lineage heads greater control of the technology needed for production.

The grandest and perhaps most complex expression of Anasazi culture occurred in Chaco Canyon between about A.D. 1030 and 1150 (Judge 1979; Vivian and Mathews 1965). The Anasazi built at least 13 multistoried Chacoan structures in the canyon itself and a network of roads linking outlying settlements, scattered across the San Juan Basin and beyond to a Chacoan interaction sphere (Altschul 1978; Lyons and Hitchcock 1977; Obenauf 1983; Powers et al. 1983; Tainter and Gillio 1980:98–113). Most researchers now agree that Chaco society contained ranked lineages centered on the main towns in the canyon (Altschul 1978; Grebinger 1973; Judge 1979; Tainter and Gillio 1980). The collapse of the Chaco system around A.D. 1150 resulted in a reorganization of San Juan Basin Anasazi populations, with many large pueblos built or expanded and a shift in stylistic dominance from Chaco to Mesa Verde.

Production in the late Pueblo III period was organized around widely scattered large pueblos with associated water control features. This organization coalesced during the mid-1200s and lasted until about A.D. 1300 to 1325. In the Mesa Verde region the large cliff dwellings, including Long House, Cliff Palace, Mug House, and Spruce Tree House, reached their peak in this period and along the Mancos and other rivers below the mesa even larger pueblos arose (Cattanach 1980; Martin et al. 1936; Rohn 1971). On the San Juan River the Anasazi reoccupied former Chacoan outliers, including Aztec and the Salmon Ruin (Irwin-Williams 1972; Morris 1919). Near Zuni, at El Morro, seven pueblos of several hundred rooms each were constructed in the mid-1200s and abandoned by 1300 (LeBlanc 1978). In the Manuelito Canyon population increased and large pueblos were built in the mid-1200s and abandoned by A.D. 1325 (Weaver 1978). On the upper Puerco the Guadalupe site grew during the late 1200s, only to be abandoned by A.D. 1300 (Pippin 1979). Around Acoma, on the Cebolleta Mesa, the Kowina ruin grew to over 300 rooms in the late 1200s, but the Anasazi abandoned it by A.D. 1300 (Dittert 1959:558). At each of these sites water control features are found associated with the larger pueblos, as are small pueblos economically linked to the large centers.

A commanding center such as Chaco Canyon did not exist during the late Pueblo III period. Mesa Verde forms dominated ceramic and architectural styles but available evidence does not suggest that Mesa Verde controlled an economic network like Chaco's or that a single polity united Mesa Verde. Instead of one center, there existed numerous competing centers each with its own supporting area. The relations of exchange in the late Pueblo III period reflect these changes in the organization of production.

During the early Pueblo III Chaco Canyon linked an Anasazi prestige-goods economy to the prestige-goods economy of Mesoamerica. At Pueblo Bonito in Chaco Canyon, Pepper's (1920) and Judd's (1954) excavations recovered the largest number of mesoamerican items located from an Anasazi site: 38 macaws, 34 copper bells, and a handful of pseudo-cloisonné items. In addition to these goods they recovered large quantities of southwestern prestige goods, including marine shell, turquoise, painted wood, and ceramic cylinder jars.

In the Chaco interaction sphere mesoamerican goods have been recovered only from large canyon towns, while other indigenous prestige goods also occur at outliers (Tainter and Gillio 1980 : 100–113). This suggests that the mesoamerican goods were high value goods used in exchanges between the Chaco elite and other elites of the Southwest and West Mexico, and that they provided the material basis for linkages between these elite and were the legitimizing symbols for elite status. The linkages maintained by the elite exchange of mesoamerican goods structured the exchange of southwestern lower valued prestige goods, which the elite distributed as social valuables to their dependents. The Chacoans probably traded turquoise south for the mesoamerican items (Weigand et al. 1977).

Accepting LeBlanc's (1980) reanalysis of the dates for Casas Grandes, the collapse of the Chaco interaction sphere corresponds with Medio period developments at Casas Grandes. During the Medio period Casas Grandes became the premier southwestern trading center and the strongest link to mesoamerican prestige-goods economies in the prehistory of the Southwest (Di Peso 1974). Casas Grandes appears to have controlled the flow of mesoamerican prestige goods into New Mexico and indeed some of these goods, including copper bells and macaws, were produced and raised at the town (Di Peso 1974). The bulk of trade, however, was in southwestern prestige goods, including shell and ceramics, exchanged to elites north of Casas Grandes (McGuire 1980 : 19–22).

In the late Pueblo III period Casas Grandes controlled the flow of shell and mesoamerican goods north and the flow of turquoise south. It linked the competing Anasazi elites of the San Juan to Mesoamerica through the exchange of mesoamerican items and supplied them with the southwestern valuables necessary for distribution to subordinates, most likely in exchange for turquoise. This control heightened the power of Casas Grandes and as the power increased so did the control. Intensified Casas Grandes control of the flow of valuables into the Anasazi also increased the instability of the prestige-goods economy, because all preciosities passed through a single node. Interference with this node could cut off the elites supply of prestige goods, both those mesoamerican goods that legitimized their status and the southwestern items necessary for distribution to followers.

The relations of production and exchange in the prehistory of the San Juan Basin were quite dynamic, with several major shifts in the nature of these relations. This discussion only concerns the final and most dramatic shift, the one that led to the abandonment of the basin. Both events which have been advanced to account for this abandonment, environmental deterioration and the breakdown of linkages to Mesoamerica, might have led to the collapse of the late Pueblo II Anasazi economy. They would have strained the relations of production and exchange and revealed the contradictions in the ideology which supported these relations, resulting in a transformation of the mode of production and the economy.

Environmental deterioration in the absence of technological innovations to increase production or population decline might have created a crisis for a kin mode of production. Such deterioration would have deprived lineages with marginal lands of their means of production and would have decreased the volume of production even for more affluent lineages. These changes would have increased the level of conflict within societies, possibly in excess of the abilities of kinship relations to mediate. A decrease in production would have also threatened the prestige-goods economy linking the San Juan Basin Anasazi societies. Lower rates of production would have forced elites to moderate their expenditures and lose power or to become more demanding in their extraction of surplus from the primary producers. The existence of many competing elite in the Pueblo III San Juan Basin would have mitigated against the first option and the second could lead the populace to dispose of the elite.

The hiatus in mesoamerican trade resulting from the rise of the Tarascan empire and the decline of Casas Grandes might have created a crisis even in the absence of the productive crisis. The cutoff of mesoamerican goods would have deprived the highest level elite of the material symbols they needed to legitimize their status and the valuables they needed to maintain exchange relations with other elites. Since exchange in prestige-goods economies tends to be organized from the top to the bottom, this disruption in the flow of high level valuables would have disrupted the exchange of lower level valuables, effectively denying all elites the means of enforcing the contributions of their subordinates. Thus the elite's hold over the system of asymmetrical exchanges would have been weakened or destroyed, leaving the door open for an effective challenge to the existing order.

The crisis of the late thirteenth century was not only environmental and social but also ideological. The resolution of this ideological crisis set in motion the transformation of Pueblo III society to Pueblo IV forms and the abandonment of the San Juan Basin. The productive and distributional crises undermined the sustaining ideology of the San Juan Anasazi to an extreme that had not occurred in the past. The drought probably resulted in real material hardship for the Anasazi, perhaps because of population densities greater than any in the past. The loss of social valuables would have thrown the system of social reproduction into chaos, requiring people to renegotiate the symbolic exchanges which legitimized their social lives in terms of a new set of social meanings with a new set of artifacts. Individuals would have perceived both the material deprivation and the social chaos as a failure of the elites to fulfill their obligations, a view reinforced by the elites' loss of their symbols of power and legitimization. The contradictions in the existing moral order would have been laid bare for all to see.

The demystification of a legitimizing ideology creates the necessary prerequisite for social transformation, the motivation needed before social action can occur. In prestige-goods economies power derives from the social meaning of elite controlled valuables and in a kin mode of production the elite's control of production derives from ideologically sanctioned kin relations. The creation of a new ideology transforms social meanings, destroying the advantage of the old elite. The new elite would be made up of those who could manipulate the new ideology and transform the system of dependencies to serve their own ends. Anthropologists commonly refer to such ideological transformations as crisis cults (LaBarre 1971). I propose that the sudden appearance, rapid spread, and popularity of the katsina cult among the Anasazi following A.D. 1300 resulted from such a crisis cult.

All such cults include prophets who promise a return to the happiness of the past if people reject the ways of the present and perform certain rituals. The promised rewards may come in the near future or lay in a foreign land. The ideal moves people to action and this action transforms reality (Godelier 1982).

Drawing on the anthropological literature concerning crises cults, we can identify a number of archaeologically visible characteristics of such cults (Hobsbawm 1959; LaBarre 1971; Wallace 1956; Worsley 1957). Material deprivation and social disintegration precede the appearance of these cults. Crisis cults spread rapidly, especially within the boundaries of cultural systems. The cults integrate existing beliefs and symbolic forms in new ways and they borrow elements from other ideologies, especially those of dominant societies. They commonly incorporate imitative magic; individuals imitate in ritual and through objects the new and better world promised by the cult.

The Pueblo IV Anasazi katsina cult manifests all of these characteristics. I have already discussed in some detail the collapse of social order and material stress that preceded the cult and identified the contradictions in the late Pueblo III San Juan Anasazi world. The mural and rock art of the cult commonly includes warriors and shields, interpreted by many researchers as evidence of cultural disequilibrium associated with the cult (Adams 1983; Ellis and Hammack 1968; Hibben 1975:130–132; Peckham 1981:34). I will now consider each of the other characteristics in its turn.[1]

The katsina cult appeared suddenly among the early fourteenth century Anasazi of southern New Mexico and rapidly spreads throughout the Anasazi region, except for the Taos archaeological district. Rock art associated with the cult manifested itself abruptly in southern New Mexico by 1325 and radiated swiftly to all Anasazi areas except Taos (Schaafsma 1980:243–301; Schaafsma and Schaafsma 1974:543). Archaeologists have reported kiva murals at a number of widely dispersed Pueblo IV pueblos, including Awatovi (Smith 1952), Pottery Mound (Hibben 1967,

1975), Kuaua (Dutton 1963), Pueblo del Encierro (Schaafsma 1965), and Gran Quivira (Peckham 1981).

The Pueblo IV cult incorporates a number of existing ritual features combined with innovations derived ultimately from Mesoamerica (Adams 1983). Kivas remained the centers of ritual life and the cult incorporated traditional kiva features such as the *sipapu*. Most researchers accept the ultimate mesoamerican origin of the basic symbols and features of the cult, including masked rain dancers, the feathered serpent, macaws, and jaguars (Beals 1943; Brew 1943; Parsons 1939). The Anasazi knew of many of these features and symbols before A.D. 1300: Ferdon (1955:8−12) reported a plumed serpent from a Pueblo III tower in McElmo canyon; macaws occurred in larger Pueblo III sites (Hargrave 1970); and masked dancers appear in the Southwest both in the rock art of the Jornada Mogollon, as early as A.D. 1000, (Schaafsma 1980:235−242; Schaafsma and Schaafsma 1974) and on Classic Mimbres ceramics (Carlson 1982). The Pueblo IV cult was not a totally original phenomena but a unique recombination of existing symbols and features, many of which were derived from Mesoamerica.

Pueblo IV kiva murals depict the rituals of the cult. Masked figures dance with representations of the lost valuables of the past: macaws, sea shells, copper bells, and tropical bird feathers (Hibben 1975; Smith 1952). The murals themselves appear to have been part of renewal rituals. Kivas contain from 1 to 100 separate murals painted one on top of the other, as repetitive imitative magic (Hibben 1975:30−34; Peckham 1981:34; Smith 1952:19−20). In the pueblos, archaeologists find little or no marine shell (Hayes et al. 1981:163; Hibben 1975:60,89; Smith 1952), no copper bells, and rarely macaws (Hargrave 1970). Instead they recover clay copies of copper bells and representations of macaws and marine shells on murals and ceramics (Hayes et al. 1981:162; Hibben 1975:60, 89; Kidder 1932:138; Smith 1952). The wealth of the past no longer attainable because of the collapse of the earlier prestige-goods economy lives on kiva walls, on ceramic vessels, and in clay copies—imitative magic to recover the glories of the past and insure the cycle of the universe.

The katsina cult spread rapidly to all areas of the Anasazi except the northern Tiwa around Taos (Adams 1983; Schaafsma and Schaafsma 1974:536). The modern northern Tiwa lack the cult (Parsons 1939) and there are no historic accounts of the cult among the northern Tiwa (Smith 1952:75, 92). Prehistoric kiva murals do not appear in archaeological sites in the region, and Schaafsma (1980:285−286) explicitly reports that katsina cult rock art rarely occurs in the Taos region. If the cult did exist among the northern Tiwa it must have been far weaker and less elaborate than in the other pueblo groups.

According to most researchers the Tiwa were the original inhabitants of the Rio Grande valley and the split into northern and southern groups occurred long before the early 1300s (Ford et al. 1972:30). The northern Tiwa lived in the Taos area probably by A.D. 1000 and the archaeology of this region shows far greater continuity in occupation and style than any other region in the Rio Grande (Ford et al. 1972; Wetherington 1968). The only area in the Anasazi range where the Pueblo IV katsina cult was absent or very weak was also the area least affected by the stresses and migrations of the late thirteenth century. Considering that this was a crisis cult, it apparently failed to take hold in the area where a crisis had not occurred.

Conclusion

I have proposed a complex scenario integrating material, social, and ideological factors to account for the transformation of Pueblo III Anasazi society. First, drought strained the Anasazi's productive capabilities. Given the population densities of the late Pueblo III period this would have challenged the organizational capabilities of the Anasazi kin-based elite to mitigate conflicts between competing lineage groups. Though Anasazi societies had survived drought in the San Juan Basin before, this time the high level exchange networks linking the Anasazi to West Mexico also collapsed. The elites could no longer sustain the prestige-goods economy which maintained social reproduction in the region nor the ideology that supported it. Anasazi populations faced real material deprivation and cultural breakdown. The stage was set for the rise of a crisis cult to transform the social and ideological order. Prophets of a new religion, incorporating some features familiar to the people and new features derived ultimately from mesoamerican models and proximally from the masked dances of the Jornada, promised a better life. A utopia lay to the east with much rain and a fertile river valley; the people should go there and dance to insure the cycle of the world and perform magic to recover the wealth of the past.

My purpose in this paper has been to examine how we might come to a new understanding of southwestern prehistory; an understanding that does not treat social units as self-contained billiard balls spinning off of each other; an understanding that gives weight to both local adaptations and interactions in a field greater than a single river valley or even the Southwest; an understanding that does not invoke the specter of mesoamerican domination of the Southwest or deny the connectedness of the two regions. I have reviewed the application of Wallerstein's theory to this issue and found it limited in the insights it gives us. In its stead I propose that we integrate considerations of production and exchange by using both the concepts of mode of production and economic systems. An examination of the Pueblo III to Pueblo IV transition illustrates how this approach allows us to link changes in the Southwest to changes in Mesoamerica without overly simplistic appeals to mesoamerican domination of the Southwest. Equally important, it allows us to speak of prehistoric cultural change in terms of the interaction of material, social, and ideological forces without reducing any of these factors to epiphenomena.

Acknowledgments

This paper benefitted from the assistance of many people. Conversations with Immanuel Wallerstein, Edward Ferdon, R. Gwinn Vivian, and Catherine Lutz helped me in the formulation of my ideas. Michael Schiffer, Jane Collins, Vincas Steponiatis, Richard Nelson, J. Charles Kelley, Emlin Myers, and Margaret Conkey reviewed earlier drafts of the paper. It was Wes Jernigan who first suggested to me that the Pueblo IV katsina cult was a crisis cult; correspondence with Chuck Adams concerning the katsina cult was very helpful. Finally, I appreciated the friendship, help, and encouragement of the late Charles Di Peso, even though he disagreed with most of what I have said about Southwest-mesoamerican relations. His passing was a major loss to the profession and saddened all of us who had the privilege to know him.

Notes

1. Adams (1983) provides a detailed consideration of the spread and variability of the katsina cult in the ethnographic and prehistoric pueblos. His discussion differs from my own most notably in terms of its scope. Whereas Adams seeks to explain the variety and detail of the cult, my emphasis is on accounting for those similarities that unify the cult. I primarily wish to answer the questions of why the cult appeared when it did and why it gained popularity and spread so rapidly. Researchers seriously interested in the pueblo katsina cult should consult Adams' work for a more in-depth consideration than I have presented here.

References Cited

Adams, E. Charles
  1983 The Appearance, Evolution, and Meaning of the Katsina Cult to the Pre-Hispanic World of the Southwestern United States. Paper presented at the 11th International Congress of Anthropological and Ethnological Sciences, Vancouver.
Akins, Nancy J., and John D. Schelberg
  1981 Evidence for Organizational Complexity as Seen From the Mortuary Practices at Chaco Canyon. Paper presented at the Annual Meeting of the Society for American Archaeology, San Diego.
Althusser, Louis, and Etienne Balibar
  1970 *Reading Capital*. Pantheon Books, New York.
Altschul, Jeffrey H.
  1978 The Development of the Chacoan Interaction Sphere. *Journal of Anthropological Research* 34(1):109–146.

Beals, Ralph L.
1943 Relations Between Mesoamerica and the Southwest. In *El Norte de México y el Sur de los Estados Unidos. Tercera Reunion de Mesa Redonda sobre Problemas Antropologicos de México y Centro America*, pp. 245–252. Sociedad Mexicana de Antropología, Mexico, D.F.
Blanton, Richard E., Stephen A. Kowalewski, Gary Feinman, and Jill Appel
1981 *Ancient Mesoamerica*. Cambridge University Press, Cambridge.
Bradfield, Richard M.
1971 *The Changing Pattern of Hopi Agriculture*. Royal Anthropological Institute of Great Britain and Ireland Occasional Papers No. 30. London.
Brew, John O.
1943 On the Pueblo IV and on the Katchina-Tlaloc Relations. In *El Norte de México y el Sur de los Estados Unidos: Tercera Reunion de Mesa Redonda sobre Problemas Antropologicos de México y Centro America*, pp. 241–245. Sociedad Mexicana de Antropología, Mexico, D.F.
Carlson, Roy L.
1982 The Mimbres Katchina Cult. In *Mogollon Archaeology: Proceedings of the 1980 Mogollon Conference*, edited by Patrick H. Beckett, pp. 147–156. Acoma Books, Ramona, Calif.
Cattanach, George S., Jr.
1980 *Long House, Mesa Verde National Park, Colorado*. National Park Service Publications in Archeology No. 7H, Washington, D.C.
Cordell, Linda S.
1979 *Cultural Resources Overview: Middle Rio Grande Valley, New Mexico*. U.S.D.A. Forest Service, Albuquerque.
Cordell, Linda S., and Fred Plog
1979 Escaping the Confines of Normative Thought: A Reevaluation of Puebloan Prehistory. *American Antiquity* 44:405–429.
Dean, Jeffrey
1970 Aspects of Tsegi Phase Social Organization: A Trial Reconstruction. In *Reconstructing Prehistoric Pueblo Societies*, edited by William A. Longacre, pp. 140–174. University of New Mexico Press, Albuquerque.
Dean, Jeffrey, and William Robinson
1977 *Dendroclimatic Variability in the American Southwest, A.D. 680 to 1970*. Laboratory of Tree-Ring Research, University of Arizona, Tucson.
Di Peso, Charles C.
1974 *Casas Grandes, A Fallen Trading Center of the Gran Chichimeca*, vol. 2: The Medio Period. Amerind Foundation Series No. 9. Dragoon, Ariz.
Dittert, A. Edward
1959 *Culture Change in the Cebolleta Mesa Region, New Mexico*. Unpublished Ph.D. dissertation, Department of Anthropology, University of Arizona, Tucson.

Dutton, Bertha P.
   1963 *Sun Father's Way, the Kiva Murals of Kuaua*. University of New Mexico Press, Albuquerque.
Ekholm, Kajsa, and Jonathan Friedman
   1982 "Capital," Imperialism and Exploitation in Ancient World Systems. *Review* 4(1):87–109.
Ellis, Florence Hawley, and Laurens Hammack
   1968 The Inner Sanctum of Feather Cave, A Mogollon Sun and Earth Shrine Linking Mexico and the Southwest. *American Antiquity* 33: 25–44.
Euler, Robert C., George J. Gumerman, Thor N. V. Karlstrom, Jeffrey S. Dean, and Richard H. Hevly
   1979 The Colorado Plateaus: Cultural Dynamics and Paleoenvironments. *Science* 205:1089–1101.
Ferdon, Edwin N., Jr.
   1955 *A Trial Survey of Mexican-Southwestern Architectural Parallels.* School of American Research Monograph No. 11, Santa Fe.
Findlow, Frank J., and Marisa Bolognese
   1982 Regional Modeling of Obsidian Procurement in the American Southwest. In *Contexts for Prehistoric Exchange*, edited by Jonathan E. Ericson and Timothy K. Earle, pp. 53–82. Academic Press, New York.
Flannery, Kent V.
   1968 The Olmecs and the Valley of Oaxaca: A Model for Interaction in Formative Times. *Dumbarton Oaks Conference on the Olmec*, pp. 79–110. Washington, D.C.
Ford, Richard I., Albert H. Schroeder, and Stewart L. Peckham
   1972 Three Perspectives on Pueblo Prehistory. In *New Perspectives on the Pueblos*, edited by Alfonso Ortiz, pp. 19–39. University of New Mexico Press, Albuquerque.
Frankenstein, Susan, and M. J. Rowland
   1978 The Internal Structure and Regional Context of Early Iron Age Society in South-Western Germany. *London University Institute of Archaeology Bulletin* 15:73–112.
Friedman, Jonathan
   1974 Marxism, Structuralism and Vulgar Materialism. *Man* 9:444–469.
Gledhill, John
   1978 Formative Development in the North American Southwest. *British Archaeological Reports* 47:241–284.
Godelier, Maurice
   1982 The Ideal in the Real. In *Culture Ideology and Politics*, edited by Raphael Samuel and G. S. Jones, pp. 12–38. Routledge and Kegan Paul, London.
Grebinger, Paul
   1973 Prehistoric Social Organization in Chaco Canyon, New Mexico: An Alternative Reconstruction. *Kiva* 39:3–23.

Hack, John T.
1942 The Changing Physical Environment of the Hopi Indians of Arizona. *Papers of the Peabody Museum of American Archaeology and Ethnology* 35(1):1–85. Harvard University, Cambridge, Mass.
Hargrave, Lyndon
970 *Mexican Macaws*. Anthrpological Papers of the University of Arizona No. 20. Tucson.
Hayes, Alden C.
1964 *The Archaeological Survey of Wetherill Mesa, Mesa Verde National Park, Colorado*. U.S. National Park Service Archeological Series No. 7A. Washington, D.C.
Hayes, Alden C., John Nathan Young, and A. Helene Warren
1981 *Excavation of Mound 7, Gran Quivira National Monument, New Mexico*. National Park Service Publications in Archeology No. 16. Washington, D.C.
Hibben, Frank C.
1967 Mexican Features of Mural Paintings at Pottery Mound. *Archaeology* 20:84–87.
1975 *Kiva Art of the Anasazi at Pottery Mound*. KC Publications, Las Vegas.
Hobsbawm, E. J.
1959 *Primitive Rebels*. W. W. Norton, New York.
1964 Introduction to *Pre-Capitalist Economic Formations* by Karl Marx, pp. 1–67. International Publishers, New York.
Irwin-Williams, Cynthia (editor)
1972 *The Structure of Chacoan Society in the Northern Southwest: Investigations at the Salmon Site 1972*. Eastern New Mexico University Contributions in Anthropology No. 4. Portales.
Judd, Neil M.
1954 *The Material Culture of Pueblo Bonito*. Smithsonian Miscellaneous Collections No. 147(1). Washington, D.C.
Judge, W. James
1979 The Development of a Complex Cultural Ecosystem in the Chaco Basin, New Mexico. In *Proceedings of the First Conference on Scientific Research in the National Parks*, vol. 2, edited by R. Linn, pp. 901–905. National Park Service Transactions and Proceedings Series No. 5.
Kelley, J. Charles
1981 Discussion. In *The Proto-Historic Period in the North American Southwest, A.D. 1450–1700*, edited by David R. Wilcox and W. Bruce Masse, pp. 434–439. Arizona State University Anthropological Research Papers No. 24, Tempe.
Kidder, Alfred Vincent
1932 *The Artifacts of Pecos*. Robert S. Peabody Foundation for Archaeology, Andover.

LaBarre, Weston
    1971 Materials for a History of Studies of Crises Cults: A Bibliographic Essay. *Current Anthropology* 12:3–27.
Laclau, Ernesto
    1977 *Politics and Ideology in Marxist Theory.* NLB, London.
LeBlanc, Steven A.
    1978 Settlement Patterns in the El Morro Valley, New Mexico. In *Investigations of the Southwestern Anthropological Research Group: An Experiment in Archaeological Cooperation,* edited by Robert C. Euler and George J. Gumerman, pp. 45–51. Museum of Northern Arizona, Flagstaff.
    1980 The Dating of Casas Grandes. *American Antiquity* 45:799–806.
Lister, Robert H.
    1966 *Contributions to Mesa Verde Archeology III: Site 866, and the Cultural Sequence at Four Villages in the Far View Group, Mesa Verde National Park, Colorado.* University of Colorado Studies Series in Anthropology No. 12. Boulder.
Lyons, Thomas R., and Robert K. Hitchcock
    1977 Remote Sensing Interpretation of an Anasazi Land Route System. In *Aerial and Remote Sensing Techniques in Archaeology,* edited by Thomas R. Lyons and Robert K. Hitchcock, pp. 111–134. Reports of the Chaco Center No. 2. National Park Service, Albuquerque.
McGuire, Randall H.
    1980 The Mesoamerican Connection in the Southwest. *Kiva* 46(1–2): 3–38.
    1983a Breaking Down Cultural Complexity: Inequality and Heterogeneity. *Advances in Archaeological Method and Theory* 6:91–142.
    1983b The Role of Shell Trade in the Explanation of Hohokam Prehistory. Paper presented at the 1983 Hohokam Conference, Tempe.
Martin, Paul S., and Fred Plog
    1973 *The Archaeology of Arizona: A Study of the Southwest Region.* Doubleday Natural History Press, Garden City, New York.
Martin, Paul S., L. Roys, and G. Von Bonin
    1936 Lowry Ruin in Southwestern Colorado. *Field Museum of Natural History Anthropological Series* 23(1):1–216.
Marx, Karl
    1964 *Pre-Capitalist Economic Formations,* edited by E. J. Hobsbawm, translated by Jack Cohen. International Publishers, New York. Originally published 1952.
    1967 *Capital,* vol. 3, translated by Samuel Moore and Edward Aveling. International Publishers, New York. Originally published 1894.
    1968 Preface to a Contribution to the Critique of Political Economy. In *Selected Works,* by Karl Marx and Frederick Engels, translated by S. W. Ryazanskaya, pp. 123–132. Lawrence and Wishart, London, Originally published 1903.

Marx, Karl, and Frederick Engels
  1947 *The German Ideology*, translated by R. Pascal. International Publishers, New York.
Meillassoux, Claude
  1981 *Maidens, Meal and Money*. Cambridge University Press, London.
Morris, Earl H.
  1919 *The Aztec Ruin*. Anthropological Papers of the American Museum of Natural History No. 26(1). New York.
Obenauf, Margaret S.
  1983 The Prehistoric Roadway Network in the San Juan Basin. In *Remote Sensing in Cultural Resources Management: The San Juan Basin Project*, edited by Dwight L. Drager and Thomas R. Lyons, pp. 117–122. National Park Service, Albuquerque.
Ollman, Bertell
  1976 *Alienation*. Cambridge University Press, London.
Parsons, Elsie Clews
  1939 *Pueblo Indian Religion*. University of Chicago Press, Chicago.
Peckham, Barbara A.
  1981 Pueblo IV Murals at Mound 7. In *Contributions to Gran Quivira Archaeology*, edited by Alden C. Hayes, pp. 15–38. National Park Service Publications in Archeology No. 17, Washington, D.C.
Pepper, George H.
  1920 *Pueblo Bonito*. Anthropological Papers of the American Museum of Natural History No. 27. New York.
Pippin, Lonnie C.
  1979 *The Prehistory and Paleoecology of the Guadalupe Ruin, Sandoval County, New Mexico*. Unpublished Ph.D. dissertation, Department of Anthropology, Washington State University, Pullman.
Plog, Fred
  1983 Political and Economic Alliances on the Colorado Plateaus A.D. 400 to 1450. *Advances in World Archaeology*, vol. 2, edited by Fred Wendorf, pp. 289–330. Academic Press, New York.
Plog, Fred, Steadman Upham, and Phil C. Weigand
  1982 A Perspective on Mogollon-Mesoamerican Interaction. In *Mogollon Archaeology: Proceedings of the 1980 Conference*, edited by Patrick H. Beckett, pp. 227–238. Acoma Books, Ramona, Calif.
Powers, Robert P., William B. Gillespie, and Stephen H. Lekson
  1983 *The Outlier Survey*. Reports of the Chaco Center No. 3. National Park Service, Albuquerque.
Renfrew, Colin
  1975 Trade as Action at a Distance: Questions of Integration and Communication. In *Ancient Civilization and Trade*, edited by J. Sabloff and C. C. Lamberg-Karlovsky, pp. 3–59. University of New Mexico Press, Albuquerque.

Rohn, Arthur H.
1971 *Mug House, Mesa Verde National Park, Colorado.* National Park Service Publications in Archeology No. 7D. Washington, D.C.
Sahlins, Marshall D.
1972 *Stone Age Economics.* Aldine-Atherton, Chicago.
Schaafsma, Polly
1965 Kiva Murals from Pueblo de Encierro (LA70). *El Palacio* 72:6–16.
1980 *Indian Rock Art of the Southwest.* University of New Mexico Press, Albuquerque.
Schaafsma, Polly, and Curtis F. Schaafsma
1974 Evidence for the Origins of the Pueblo Katchina Cult as Suggested by Southwestern Rock Art. *American Antiquity* 39:535–545.
Schneider, Harold K.
1974 *Economic Man.* Free Press, New York.
Schroeder, Albert H.
1966 Pattern Diffusion from Mexico into the Southwest after A.D. 600. *American Antiquity* 31:18–24.
Seddon, David (editor)
1974 *Relations of Production: Marxist Approaches to the Study of Economic Anthropology.* Frank Cass, London.
Smith, Watson
1952 *Kiva Mural Decorations at Awatovi and Kawaika-a, with a Survey of Other Wall Paintings in the Pueblo Southwest.* Papers of the Peabody Museum of American Archaeology and Ethnology No. 37. Harvard University, Cambridge, Mass.
Strathern, Andrew J.
1971 *The Rope of Moka.* Cambridge University Press, Cambridge, England.
Tainter, Joseph A., and David A. Gillio
1980 *Cultural Resources Overview: Mt. Taylor Area, New Mexico.* U.S.D.A. Forest Service, Albuquerque.
Terray, Emmanuel
1975 Classes and Class Consciousness in the Abron Kingdom of Gyaman. In *Marxist Analyses and Social Anthropology,* edited by Maurice Bloch, pp. 85–135. Malaby Press, London.
Upham, Steadman
1982 *Polities and Power.* Academic Press, New York.
Vivian, R. Gordon, and Thomas W. Mathews
1965 *Kin Kletso: A Pueblo III Community in Chaco Canyon, New Mexico.* Southwestern Monuments Association Technical Series No. 5. Globe, Ariz.
Vivian, R. Gwinn
1974 Conservation and Diversion: Water-Control Systems in the Anasazi Southwest. In *Irrigation's Impact on Society,* edited by T. E. Downing

and M. Gibson, pp. 95−112. Anthropological Papers of the University of Arizona No. 25. Tucson.

Wallace, Anthony
1956 Revitalization Movements. *American Anthropologist* 58 : 264−281.

Wallerstein, Immanuel
1974 *The Modern World System I.* Academic Press, New York.
1978 Civilization and Modes of Production. *Theory and Society* 5 : 1−10.
1980 *The Modern World System II.* Academic Press, New York.

Weaver, Donald E.
1978 *Prehistoric Population Dynamics and Environmental Exploitation in the Manuelito Canyon District, Northwestern New Mexico.* Unpublished Ph.D. dissertation, Department of Anthropology, Arizona State University, Tempe.

Weaver, Muriel Porter
1972 *The Aztecs, Maya and Their Predecessors.* Academic Press, New York.

Weigand, Phil C., Garman Harbottle, and Edward V. Sayre
1977 Turquoise Sources and Source Analysis: Mesoamerica and the Southwestern U.S.A. In *Exchange Systems in Prehistory*, edited by Timothy K. Earle and Jonathan E. Ericson, pp. 15−34. Academic Press, New York.

Wetherington, Ronald K.
1968 *Excavations at Pot Creek Pueblo.* Fort Burgwin Research Center No. 6. Taos.

Wilcox, David R., and Lynette O. Shenk
1977 *The Architecture of the Casa Grande and Its Interpretation.* Arizona State Museum Archaeological Series No. 115, Tucson.

Wolf, Eric R.
1982 *Europe and the People Without History.* University of California Press, Berkeley.

Worsley, Peter
1957 *The Trumpet Shell Sound.* MacGibbon and Kee, London.

Zubrow, Ezra
1971 Carrying Capacity and Dynamic Equilibrium in the Prehistoric Southwest. *American Antiquity* 36 : 127−138.

14

Perspectives on the Peripheries of Mesoamerica

Barbara L. Stark

Commentaries on sets of papers often address each in turn, but sometimes they are cast around underlying issues. I emphasize the latter approach because my role as a discussant in this symposium was to be that of a mesoamericanist with an "outside" perspective on mesoamerican-northwestern ("northwestern" as seen from the perspective of Mesoamerica) relationships (Braniff 1978:67). This also unfortunately entails an evenhanded lack of familiarity with the substantive details of southwestern United States and northwestern Mexican research. I hope to contribute to a useful division of labor since the papers are by specialists who are better able themselves to evaluate the substantive data. I address two issues: the scope of the problem considered and the nature of the "Mesoamerica" with which northwestern interactions occurred, specifically the processes that conditioned these interactions. The varied views of mesoamerican-northwestern interaction are a fascinating window on our conceptions of mesoamerican complex society. Only the Whitecotton and Pailes paper tackles the nature of Mesoamerica in an extended way, and I intend to add to this discussion.

Scope of the Problem

Curiously, mesoamerican-northwestern relationships are not often explicitly analyzed under the broader rubric of the mesoamerican peripheries, although that perspective is implicit in Whitecotton and Pailes's paper (Chapter 10). The models for interaction and questions of degree, timing, and effects of interaction discussed for the northwest are part of the larger problem of understanding the effects of mesoamerican states on distant areas.

The Central American literature, which I mention by way of comparison, has not been characterized by the polarization of opinion into an "isolationist" versus a "derivationist" position—the latter posits significant local effects from interaction with mesoamerican states, direct or indirect. In Central America there has been research progress on both tracing autochthonous change and noting external factors, including in some cases fairly

conclusive evidence of contact with or settlement by some groups of mesoamericans (Lange and Stone 1984).

There are differences in the history of research in the two "peripheries" as well as in the records from each that help account for the differences in treatment of the mesoamerican issue—besides the underlying
lassitude among North American researchers in dealing with Spanish and
Spanish-linked literature. First, a marked degree of social hierarchy has always been accepted for the Central American area, founded in ethnohistoric
comparisons, while in the U.S. Southwest social organization generally has
not been viewed from this perspective, founded in ethnographic and some
ethnohistoric accounts. Only relatively recently has attention in the Southwest been focused on prehistoric social hierarchies and their economic and
political effects, as Wilcox (Chapter 8), McGuire (Chapter 13), and Upham
(Chapter 11) have noted here. Because researchers accepted the notion of
elaborated social hierarchies or "chiefdoms" in Central America (Steward
and Faron 1959), it was not considered too surprising that external interactions might occur on a noteworthy scale. Nevertheless, chronicling and
modeling these interactions did not achieve the sharp theoretical focus that
it has in the Southwest, where the very notion was considered problematic
on occasion.

In addition, southwestern researchers reacted more clearly to the
strong archaeological interest in ecology during the 1960s and 1970s. Agricultural problems in the Southwest were treated as significant ecological
factors that played crucial roles in conditioning prehistoric behavior. In
other words, an interest in local environmental factors predisposed a regional rather than panregional focus.

Finally, warranting the divergences in thinking about the two peripheries was the fact that there is more resemblance, structurally and culturally,
between Central American and mesoamerican patterns than between Mesoamerica and the Northwest. For example, the continued role of hunting and
gathering in parts of the northwest stands out. In other words, we see the
combined effects of some real differences in the prehistoric record combined with differences conditioned by research histories and ethnographic
models.

Despite the differences in the apparent strength of interaction with
the two peripheries and Mesoamerica, there may be comparable processes
at work, but differing in effects because of local conditions (in part environmental) or other external factors (such as the geographic location of Central
America between Mesoamerica and the Andes). To argue otherwise implies
that mesoamerican societies acted differently toward each periphery. No
doubt this will be found to be true to some extent, especially because of
striking environmental differences or because of differences in the organization of those mesoamerican societies nearer to the two peripheries; but we
can best perceive differences by first sorting out potential common factors.
In sum, I suggest that there is value in future research on mesoamerican-

southwestern relations in a comparative perspective that seeks to examine the geographically extended effects of mesoamerican societies.

Concepts of Mesoamerica

In this section I discuss ideas about mesoamerican processes that may have had substantial spatially extended consequences. I distinguish "spatially extended effects" from the geographic notion of "peripheries," with the latter meaning a zone on or near the boundaries of Mesoamerica, with the understanding that the boundary itself may be defined quite differently according to various theoretically motivated models. (Note that a different, nongeographic concept of periphery occurs in Wallerstein's 1974 discussion of a dependency zone.)

We could find, for example, that there are peripheral regions into which mesoamerican polities made political or economic incursions periodically or into which mesoamerican groups moved at times, but which have distinct local histories as well as important relations with areas beyond. Other processes than direct mesoamerican intrusion may then lead to the adoption of mesoamerican traits in still more distant areas. A chain of relationships may involve shifts in their character. We must be prepared to examine "clinal," that is, gradually declining, effects of mesoamerican societies as well as structural relations of the sort represented in "world system" models adopted from Wallerstein (1974). "Mesoamerica" itself is notoriously difficult to define—not a given, the limits of which can be readily identified.

There are various processes that affect peripheries and areas beyond. These can be articulated as quite distinct models, and more than one is represented among the papers here. We can also expect that different processes may have operated in conjunction or sequentially, posing the problem of identifying and weighting each or of understanding their developmental relationships. In these papers discussions of mesoamerican-northwestern relations can be dichotomized into elite exchange and entrepreneurial exchange models, each of them potentially linked to a different view of "Mesoamerica."

Historically, Kirchhoff's (1966) essay defining Mesoamerica was a cornerstone in the culture area approach continued in many later syntheses (e.g., Willey 1966:85–87). But a developmental trajectory became a feature of later concepts of Mesoamerica as well, and, increasingly, economic and social structural traits have been emphasized, with the result that one recent discussion (Adams 1977) identifies both characters and processes.

With distinct intellectual roots a second perspective on Mesoamerica has emphasized the evolution of "state" sociopolitical forms as the key feature separating Mesoamerica from neighboring areas. William Sanders (e.g., Sanders and Price 1968) has been the long-standing advocate of an ecological, evolutionary approach to this problem. One consequence of this approach is that Mesoamerica is treated as a complex political and economic landscape, more dynamic than a culturally focused overview of "common features" would indicate. For example, one recent treatment of mesoamerican social change argues for multilineal evolution *within* Mesoamerica (Sanders and Webster 1978), relying on the importance of regional environmental factors. Thus, in this view "Mesoamerica" becomes the history of a set of regions and their intrinsic potentials, affected (to an undisclosed degree) by interregional interaction.

Finally, quite recently, self-conscious reexaminations of the notion of Mesoamerica have appeared, providing a basis for contrasting views represented among these papers. Arguments have been made that Mesoamerica constituted a world system in the form of a world economy, and Whitecotton and Pailes continue to elaborate this view here. A world system model emphasizes strong state formation in the "core," which results in economic and political imperialism with dependency consequences for distant areas. Here Whitecotton and Pailes include luxury goods as an important element in regional dependencies, in a modification of Wallerstein's (1974) position, which emphasized movement of "basic" goods.

In contrast, another group of scholars has rejected the Wallerstein model and emphasized that mesoamerican commonalities reflect predominantly elite exchange, at least until around the time of the Spanish conquest (Blanton et al. 1981). McGuire's paper, for example, draws on this perspective. More recently Blanton and Feinman (1984) proposed that Mesoamerica was a "precapitalist world economy" tied together by the movement of luxury goods, but with market exchange as the principal mechanism rather than elite exchange. Thus, there are recent notions about the nature of Mesoamerica which are sufficiently opposed as to predispose one to emphasize entrepreneurial as opposed to elite or prestige exchange in models of mesoamerican-northwestern Mexican interactions.

Prestige Exchange in Mesoamerica

Both synchronic and developmental aspects of prestige exchange models in Mesoamerica warrant discussion in relation to issues in these papers. By prestige exchange I mean the movement of highly valued commodities and mates among societies and individuals, with the goods and persons expressing or representing elevated social status (or used in social transactions or rituals which reflect status). A principal mechanism for movement would be prestations, usually in an alliance situation, sometimes asymmetrical. The social links so established might also provide a context for barter. Whatever the position one takes concerning regional relationships *within* Mesoamerica, at the peripheries and beyond societies may have related to each other in part through prestige exchange.

Despite the quite justified concern expressed by Whitecotton and Pailes that ethnographic "chiefdoms," which supply key examples of such situations in recent times, may be social forms conditioned by interactions with states and inappropriate as developmental models, several of the characteristic features of these societies do appear early in the archaeological record of developing social complexity, not just in Mesoamerica but also in other regions (Flannery 1968; Peebles and Kus 1977; Renfrew 1982; Streuver and Houart 1972; Upham 1982).[1]

It is not surprising that prestige exchange, sometimes on a substantial geographic scale, often appears early in the record of increasing social complexity. The elaboration of authority and status differences soon is expressed materially (rare exotics and rare, labor-intensive goods function well in this fashion). But aside from the circulation of goods, social changes are involved. Protection of internal social distinctions may lead high ranking individuals to an "outward-looking" social and kin network as they strive to distinguish themselves via ties to neighboring high ranking persons (see, for example, Goldman 1970). Finally, well-developed ranking or authority distinctions in an environment of socially interlinked similar societies (perhaps especially under certain environmental and demographic conditions) can result in a socially competitive environment.

The factional rivalries and fissioning of high ranking genealogical groups can produce a centrifugal social effect. This is particularly true if high ranking leaders have polygynous maritally-based alliances which result in especially large numbers of potential heirs. The centrifugal effect is the movement outward of high ranking individuals through marriage (see Ekholm 1978; Friedman 1975:35; Leach 1964:130–131) or simply political arrangements and relocation in outlying communities (see Southall, 1953, re the "segmentary state"). In addition, an outward relocation of high status persons occurs because (relatively) weakly institutionalized internal authority and power cannot easily overcome factional rivalries and fissioning (Cohen 1978). Marital exchanges have been mentioned in the archaeological literature discussing prestige exchange (Flannery 1968), but the context has been one with status goods and esoteric lore as other features of on-going (if sporadic) exchange between two polities or communities. Outward movement of fissioning elites is analytically different.

The diverse patterns of Olmec "contact" or interaction with non-heartland sites and regions are provocative in regard to the notion of the fissioning and relocation of high ranking groups. There are regions, like Oaxaca, where Flannery's (1968) classic model of prestige exchange seems to fit the evidence concerning exchange of goods and Olmec style diffusion; but there are other locations, such as Chalcatzingo, where a body of Olmec sculpture and iconography suggests the presence of Olmecs in the community even though there was a strong local tradition in other cultural remains such as pottery (Grove et al. 1976). The latter situation continues to be viewed by many as indicating direct Olmec control of long-distance exchange (e.g., Charlton 1984 : 34) even though it could represent fissioning and outward relocation of Olmec elites.[2]

The Flannery model, which I suggest can be amplified to include centrifugal fissioning and relocation, is one of the strong competitors for explaining patterns of extended mesoamerican traits. Prestige exchange systems require attention both to internal (i.e., local) patterns of change and to external factors. The vigor and duration of these systems are inherently dependent on internal factors, although the ethnographic situations from which they have been modeled clearly indicate that trade and status patterns in neighboring long-lived complex societies can provide enduring economic opportunities that may encourage exchange as well as provide social and ideological templates.

The potential of prestige exchange models is not confined to the "description" of certain prehistoric phenomena. Recently some scholars have discussed dynamic properties of these systems. Spence (1982) notes that new valuables of highly restricted availability introduced into these systems may disequilibrate them, with the possible result that some individuals or families may exercise more exclusive or more centralized control over their distribution. Spencer (1982 : 62−68) has argued that if two participating regions develop dissimilar population sizes (or more exactly, differences in the potential consumers of status related goods), the larger region may undergo institutional change (in the case he discusses, toward a "state"). It may undertake political expansion into key resource zones.

Thus, there are signs that the intellectual potential of prestige economies is still being explored actively, both to account for changes in the prehistoric record and to "describe" parts of it. It is not surprising, then, to find that a number of papers in this collection examine aspects of the U.S. southwestern and northwestern Mexican record in terms of prestige economy models. This approach is applied among these papers in a largely descriptive vein, with some tendencies toward "just so" stories—where the anticipated elements of the models outstrip any firm anchor in the material record—not surprising when the alternatives to more traditional models are first articulated.

But how should we understand these models when, as in most of the papers here, they are applied to eras in which Mesoamerica contained states, including quite sizable ones? The classic application of a prestige exchange model *within* Mesoamerica, in Olmec times, antedates the periods of concern here. One view would be that less complexly organized peripheral and more distant societies embody processes more akin to earlier eras in Mesoamerica. But a cogent argument can be made that later prestige exchange is more than a "living fossil."

Although scholarly attention has been focused on the largest and most successful Mesoamerican states, such as Teotihuacan, Monte Albán, Tula, and Tenochtitlan, large states were episodic in the central and southern Mexican highlands. Even in the sixteenth century, many regions did not have such large states. Regions with small polities seem to have constituted two categories. Some represent a long history without large states (Tehuacán) and others are regions in which numerous small states (petty states) represent the "shatter products" of the dissolution of quite large polities (e.g., Oaxaca). Bray (1972) and Adams (1977 : 311) remark that the city-state became an enduring and basic sociopolitical unit in Mesoamerica (in a sense, a building block of large states). Clearly small states were often absorbed by expansionist polities, but all of Mesoamerica was never politically unified.

Whether eventually absorbed or not, there are indications that, from the perspective of their local elites, these small polities faced a generally uncertain political climate. Spores (1974) describes the importance of marital alliances for Mixtec states in the late part of the prehispanic sequence. The Quiché elite struggled to develop and maintain their political power (Carmack 1981 : 43–74, 120–147). Prior to the success of the Triple Alliance, Valley of Mexico polities had a tumultuous history (Brumfiel 1983; Offner 1979). Some of these petty states do not greatly differ from "chiefdoms" in a number of respects, such as settlement hierarchy, degree of occupational specialization, manpower, and competititve concern with status and alliance. They do differ in the degree of class distinction and in the political context in which they found themselves.

Some scholars are beginning to look at certain mesoamerican iconographic and style horizons as possible effects of elite or prestige interaction among regions which had small polities or which included a mixture of larger and smaller polities (Rice 1983; Smith and Heath-Smith 1980). In fact, although I have not located an example in the mesoamerican ethnohistoric literature, we cannot rule out asymmetrical elite or marital exchanges between more powerful states and distant neighbors who were situated at the far reaches of their capacity for direct political intervention or war. States do not always have tightly delimited territories and may have increasingly tenuous authority and power over more distant regions. Perhaps allegiances such as that of the Quiché to the Triple Alliance can be viewed in the light of asymmetrical status exchange, as two Mexica princesses were given in marriage and the Quiché provided luxury product tribute to the Aztecs (Carmack 1981 : 142–143). However, the degree of coercion suggests a regular tributory situation, one in accord with Hassig's (1984) interpretation of an Aztec "hegemonic" empire.

The anxious concern of the Quiché for "Toltec" legitimization (Carmack 1981 : 125–126) constitutes an example of the importance of ideologically grounded trappings of office to small or incipient state elites. Given the unstable history of petty states, prestige exchanges may have played a noteworthy role comparable to that proposed for chiefdoms. In states elites faced factional challenges, successional disputes (Goody 1966), and generally uncertain access to institutionalized rule.

Schneider (1977) and Blanton and Feinman (1984) have drawn attention to the importance of luxury goods for internal maintenance of clientship. They were undoubtedly important in this respect, although Webster (1975) notes the role of conquest in acquisition of external land. In general, as Eisenstadt (1963:esp. 25) has observed, "free-floating" resources are essential for the central authority to develop a stronger power base. Elsewhere I have commented that tribute demands from conquered provinces, which, over great land distances, were energetically feasible only for light weight, high value goods (Drennan 1984a, 1984b), have the effect of denying certain resources to potential rivals (Stark 1983). We have, then, an ample sociopolitical basis in Mesoamerica for the important role of exchanges of status-marking goods, status-oriented marriages, and elite fissioning and relocation in addition to tribute in luxury goods.

Blanton et al. (1981:245–251) stress the effective limits of imperial expansion and consolidation of power in Mesoamerica and, as a consequence, the role of prestige exchange in accounting for transregional and even panmesoamerican cultural traits. It does not tax the imagination to extend prestige exchange farther than the generally accepted boundaries of Mesoamerica. Peripheral societies as well as more distant ones could have participated in prestige economies via a series of links among polities—producing spatially extended effects of Mesoamerica in regard to ideologically defined status goods, rituals, and other items.

To recapitulate, the prestige exchange view sees broad mesoamerican cultural patterns established through some imperial expansion within Mesoamerica, some marketing effects (as will be discussed below), but with many enduring transregional effects ascribable to prestige exchange and fissioning among state (and less institutionalized) elites.

An alternative mechanism involves entrepreneurial exchange of luxury or status goods. In fact the mechanism of preciosity exchange is an important difference between Flannery's (1968) model, which it is convenient to refer to as prestige exchange, and Whitecotton and Pailes's (this volume) and Blanton and Feinman's (1984) view of luxury exchange, which places more emphasis on entrepreneurial action. The extent to which either prestige or luxury exchange represents an ideological complex focused on a particular region ("core" zone) at different times (as in the case of the Olmecs) is open to question. Such a focus would seem to be more important for a prestige sphere, but I doubt it is essential even in that case.

With respect to the northwest, in a prestige model long-distance exchanges would reflect principally elite or leadership relations among a series of adjacent polities and would constitute primarily prestige items, elite marriage partners, and ritual matters, with any exchanges of utilitarian goods dependent on the current status of political alignments as well as economic factors affecting the production and distribution of goods, as discussed below. Such a model would be compatible with a series of local exchanges among contrastive environmental zones in some basic resources—exchanges that I suggest would primarily flow across altitudinal gradients, for example, from coast to highlands (because of the redundancy along the coastal zone), or across adaptive patterns, such as between settled farmers and nomads (see Ford 1972; Wilcox, this volume). Elite fissioning and relocation would be a potential factor in the extension of prestige spheres in addition to exchange. Dynamic relationships among regions, such as Le-Blanc addresses in this volume, can be a feature in prestige exchange systems without appeals to core zones.

Entrepreneurial Exchange

There are reasons to be wary of too exclusive a focus on the prestige exchange approach, and a different model is represented in Whitecotton and Pailes's paper, as well as in Kelley's (Chapter 6), with its mercantile emphasis. As noted above, Blanton and Feinman (1984) recently have stressed entrepreneurial exchange over elite exchange by emphasizing markets as a mechanism for the movement of prestige goods. In sum, alternative processes to prestige exchange have been argued to account for spatially extended mesoamerican effects, ones which, in extreme form, ascribe to mesoamerican mercantilism and strong state authority responsibility for significant transformations of peripheral and even more distant societies. Because of the proposed strength of the effects, these societies can be viewed in a structurally dependent role. If Wallerstein's (1974) concepts are applied validly, the societies affected become part of the mesoamerican social system in a division of labor upon which their economy and social order become dependent. This is a proposition that goes far beyond simply identifying processes which spread mesoamerican "traits."

The key issue, then, is the structural transformation and dependency of peripheral zones upon actions emanating from a state or states in the core region. "The impact of long-distance trade on social organization of course depends upon the degree to which productive activity is diverted to serve the purposes of external demand" (Goody 1971 : 24). Wallerstein's emphasis on mercantile relations and "basic" goods rather than prestige goods is a logical consequence of the notion that key social transformations and structural dependencies are at stake. Certainly we cannot object to the critical role that basic goods play. Prestige goods may symbolize a social order, they may reinforce it, and changes in the prestige system may effect social changes, as McGuire argues here, but it is hard to argue that a prestige system per se creates a social form.

In her discussion of provincial markets in Oaxaca, Berdan (1980) outlined a manner in which large mesoamerican states may have catalyzed more mercantile exchange—perhaps both within "Mesoamerica" as well as beyond. Her paper has become a foundation for recent mercantile arguments. She suggested that tribute demands from conquered provinces provoked individuals to intensify exchange with neighbors beyond the Aztec imperium. One can then imagine a "ripple" effect with increasingly distant areas indirectly affected by this exchange. A well-extended net of marketing activity is the institutional backdrop against which propositions about specialist traders such as Kelley's (in this volume) must be seen.

I think it is safe to assume that mercantile exchange models with indirect links are more likely to be widely accepted than *pochteca* type models simply because Aztec long-distance traders typically went beyond their own political boundaries, but not far—to nearby "port-of-trade" locations or neighboring polities. Where very large distances are involved, such as with the southwestern United States, this type of exchange institution becomes problematic both from the point of view of distance and with respect to the initial absence of highly active mercantile centers. In sum, the mercantile model is powerful, well grounded in the prevalence of ethnohistoric market institutions in mesoamerican societies, and responsive to progressive commercialization in Mesoamerica linked to the cumulation of similar political and economic effects from earlier "core" states and to the substantial long-term population increases in Mesoamerica, which would enlarge consumer markets.

A seemingly different model concerning mesoamerican expansion is not represented among these papers but was discussed in the symposium from which these papers were drawn: efforts at rare resource extraction undertaken by mesoamerican states. Weigand (1982) has proposed that colonies or enclaves were established in some cases to assure the production and acquisition of particularly valued rare commodities, especially minerals. These would then have operated as mesoamerican outposts and, through their presence and interaction with local communities, further extended mesoamerican cultural traits. I suspect that Weigand would expect mercantile exchange to have been a major mechanism for this subsequent spread of mesoamerican goods and ideas (see Weigand et al. 1977:23), so that we could include this as another form of mercantile stimulus, although colonial rare resource extraction could certainly have provided mesoamerican "templates" for prestige goods as well. Since it remains to be seen to whom we can ascribe the inception and maintenance of mining and processing in many cases, I concentrate on the noncolonial, mercantile ripple model here.

The mercantile ripple model has much to recommend it when we look *within* the confines of Mesoamerica. Expansionist states have considerable antiquity in the Mexican highlands and various goods moved considerable distances. Some scholars have argued for a progressive commercialization of regions (Blanton et al. 1981:234–242; Sabloff and Rathje 1975). A key issue currently in mesoamerican research is how much was moved, how far, and over what time span (Drennan 1984a, 1984b; Sanders and Santley 1983; Santley 1984). Efforts at quantification have undercut some of the broader claims about the role and pervasiveness of long-distance exchange. Of great importance in these papers is the groundwork for a differentiation of the exchange potential of different goods. Importantly, this differentiation goes beyond simple dichotomies, such as "luxury" and "basic." Scarcity, weight, production effort, and use-life are some of the variables addressed.

Sanders and Santley (1983; Santley 1984) have stressed the special potential of obsidian in long-distance trade and have even proposed discriminatory pricing by states controlling the commodity. Discriminatory pricing is currently hypothetical. I see a stronger case for the importance of exchange in this commodity simply because of the lack of local siliceous stone in most of the coastal lowlands of Mesoamerica (with the exception of cherts in the Yucatan peninsula). Inventories from Pacific and Gulf coastal sites typically show obsidian as virtually the exclusive material for chipped stone. Thus, neolithic Mesoamerica does have considerable potential for economic exchange in basic commodities and structural dependencies among regions.

Nor is obsidian the only product that may have assumed a significant role. Drennan (1984b) has suggested that cotton and cotton cloth were other commodities of particular importance in long-distance movement. Cotton has restricted environmental requirements for growth. Andrews (1983) has discussed salt, also of restricted distribution, with marked contrasts in the productivity of different sources. Slaves warrant attention also because, in many cases, state urbanization and territorial expansion seem to have had a powerful centripetal effect on population (see Sanders et al. 1979); attendant warfare and agricultural intensification seem to have led to encouragement of manpower increases by a variety of means. Since local political organizations and population sizes vary over time and space, regions may vary in their susceptibility to manpower raids.

However, how far predominantly mercantile relations extended out from Mesoamerica (and were stimulated by events there) is less clear than might be supposed. The issue is not one of relatively localized exchanges between adjacent ecologically or economically complementary zones, but of commercial movement of goods over a larger sphere which we can appropriately view as exhibiting *structural dependencies*. A number of problems beset such arguments if applied to Mesoamerica and the Northwest. For example, calculation of the distances through which foods can be transported by human carrier suggests noteworthy constraints on this form of interdependency (Drennan 1984b; Lightfoot 1979), with effective limits of 50 to 275 km proposed for land transport. Blanton and Feinman's (1984) suggestion of the transformation of regions to cacao production involves examples *within* Mesoamerica. Schneider's (1977) discussion of medieval European exchange of preciosities makes the point that a two-way flow of resources is critical—yet to date we do not have good documentation of two-way exchange linking core states in Mesoamerica and the far northwest. Adams's (1974) ethnographic cases of marked impact from entrepreneurial exchange all involve situations where the value of a two-way flow was made particularly outstanding by introduction of new and potent "means of destruction" (Goody 1971), guns, or of means of transportation, horses. The argument for entrepreneurial action in creating northwestern-mesoamerican dependencies cannot draw strength from situations elsewhere if key economic incentives or patterns are not comparable.

In general, the costs of travel and transport have not been addressed very effectively in the literature on mesoamerican-northwestern relationships. Even Mathien's rebuttal of a world economy model for the Chacoan record (Chapter 12) would be strengthened by further consideration of this topic. Wallerstein (1974:16–17) identified a 40–60 day travel time as effectively limiting a world system because of travel and transport costs. But European travel could draw on draft herbivores, and sailing technology made more use of wind energy (see Sanders and Santley 1983). Drennan (1984b) notes a much higher effective distance in Mesoamerica for water transport of foods, 1300 km, than land transport, 275 km. The problematic late northward extension of "mesoamerican" stylistically influenced sites along the west coast of Mexico could be related to greater use of water transport. But if "basic" goods were involved, I suggest trade routes would have incorporated some land transport to draw in constrastive resources along an altitudinal gradient. Otherwise, resource redundancy along the coast would severely curtail the feasibility of extensive exchanges. The addition of water transport does not radically transform the situation if goods must be moved inland considerable distances as well (see Stark 1983).

In the regions for which a Wallerstein "peripheral" status is at stake, it is by no means clear to what extent exchange systems were independent of political and status manipulation. So many of the goods mentioned seem to be "preciosities" and, given the ethnohistoric indications of warfare and alliance formation (Riley 1982), one can also afford to be cautious about the meaning of exchanges in more "basic" commodities. There are ethnographic instances elsewhere of the use of exchange, including "everyday" items, to symbolize political links (Chagnon 1968:97–102). Future research that clarifies the role of exchange will have to pay meticulous attention to the functions of goods (Adams 1974:241); it will have to accomplish more quantification of production and exchange; and it will have to continue the current interest in determining the origin of goods. The latter has been a major preoccupation in economic research to this point, but the other two factors also are vital. Mathien's (and others, such as Plog et al. 1982) consideration of a combination of these matters is beneficial.

Although Whitecotton and Pailes (see Blanton and Feinman 1984) attempt to link the effects of luxury exchange to a situation with economic dependencies, the manner in which this link may be expected to have occurred in peripheral and more distant areas remains unclear, unless it is simply the "energizing" of exchange in basic goods to obtain luxury goods. But I would contend that this is subject to considerable decline in intensity as distance from the core states increases and as less complex, highly centralized polities occur. Over greater distances, there is increased potential for interference from political turmoil among small intervening polities. Warfare interrupts market exchange (e.g., Ford 1972).

A possible link between luxury exchange and local exchanges of basic goods could be established if augmentation of local political authority through use of status goods contributed to expansion of polity sizes and hence resource zones. As a consequence, internal exchange could be promoted (see Helms 1979, for Panama). Alternatively, political alliances arranged and expressed partly through use of prestige exchange might facilitate exchange in more diverse goods among neighboring societies. But again, the extent of these spheres of exchange faces cost factors, as discussed previously, and it is not clear in what manner the process is strictly dependent on Mesoamerica.

It would seem that a strong link between prestige or preciosity exchange and broader economic dependencies must rely on a view of luxury commodities as a kind of "lingua franca" of value, one established in the core or semiperiphery and upon which distant regions depended heavily. Yet certain highly decorated vessels in the Southwest seem to have been valued exchange items defined locally rather than in the core. If so, this undercuts dependency on the core.

It is not clear that the magnitude of exchanged goods flowing through consecutive polities was sufficient to establish structural dependencies.[3] It is not clear that any dependencies established were with the "core." Whitecotton and Pailes suggest that the semiperiphery concept helps account for peripheral dependencies since smaller states outside the orbit of core states may have mediated the expansion of mesoamerican dependencies. This is an interesting suggestion, but as yet it has not been effectively established. Use of the semiperiphery concept still requires substantiation of "threeway" structural dependencies. We have to be concerned not with the establishment of "mesoamerican" concepts of preciosities, but with the character of economic and political dependencies. Note that a prestige exchange model of consecutive society links is one which can account for a spread of ritual and cognitive constructs over sizable distances, but mercantile exchange does not. The modern world economy, for example, does not require any kind of ethnic or ritual commonalities among the societies involved, as Upham notes in this volume. In part, mesoamerican-northwestern (and Central American) resemblances are argued to be conceptual ones.

However, I do not argue for pessimism in trying to establish structural dependencies, although I see the need for a focus first on the peripheries of Mesoamerica to establish the case. We still know little concerning the production and exchange of certain goods. Schneider's (1978) analysis of changing European textile production suggests that asymmetrical luxury exchange may have catalyzing internal effects, as Wallerstein (1974 : 14) notes as well. Whitecotton and Pailes's emphasis in this volume on long-term change in the development of economic and political relations is valuable and points to the need to critically evaluate Mesoamerican economic and political changes of the sort they discuss (see Gledhill and Larsen 1982).

Summary

It has been my aim to draw out underlying implications of prestige versus entrepreneurial exchange for Mesoamerica, its peripheries, and even more distant areas. Enterpreneurial exchange can be treated two ways. Some consider that it reflects a fundamental dependency on mesoamerican "core" states. Others emphasize this type of exchange as providing a series of links to Mesoamerica, but without a clear idea of fundamental dependencies on the core (e.g., Riley 1982). Prestige exchange as discussed in these papers would also involve a series of links, although some episodes of more direct state contacts involving part of the northwest may have occurred from time to time. The editors' choice for the volume title is appropriate since all parties represented here see the processes of interaction as involving a series of polity relations in the northwest rather than very direct intervention by core states. Disagreements concern "ripples versus tsunamis" and, more fundamentally, which kinds of interlinked actions account for the material record.

My own view is that structural dependencies have not yet been demonstrated for the northwest and Mesoamerica. I consider it unlikely that a single dominant pattern of relationships will apply equally well to areas within Mesoamerica, on its peripheries, and to very distant zones such as the far northwest and Central America. Prestige exchange seems likely to have played an especially important role farther from Mesoamerica. However, allegiance to positions is not really the point of this volume, but, rather, fresh attempts to figure out mesoamerican-northwestern relations.

Migration dynamics deserve more attention than they have been accorded in this volume. Although I noted in passing that manpower demands in states might draw in human labor, it is also the case that ethnic or interest groups and political or elite factions may move outward seeking refuge from state demands or political competition. At least it is clear that this occurred *within* Mesoamerica (Offner 1979). If land (or other means of production) is sufficiently scarce near the limits of Mesoamerica, some population could relocate outward because of population-resource imbalances. Physical expansion of mesoamerican peoples could account for some extension of mesoamerican traits, although it does not necessarily establish structural dependencies among regions. Such a process may not be independent of mercantile expansion, as Hole (1974) notes that entrepreneurship may be a recourse for persons who lack adequate access to traditional means of production, such as land.

It would appear both from a prestige exchange focus or one that emphasizes mercantile structural dependencies that future research will need to focus on interregional relations—that is, on the successive ties among adjacent societies northwest of Mesoamerica. Wilcox (Chapter 8) and LeBlanc (Chapter 7) particularly exemplify this kind of concern here. It is also apparent that besides an economic and sociopolitical focus to research, better chronological data are needed to produce more agreement in the alignment of regional changes. Braniff's essay (Chapter 5) as well as LeBlanc's and Wilcox's appropriately target chronology. I would add that there is too much reliance in the mesoamerican-northwestern literature on the idea that links to Mesoamerica will be most noteworthy during periods of core state expansion. In fact, it may be that the collapse of core states provides added political and economic opportunities for geographically peripheral polities which then activate relations with more distant areas.

Acknowledgments

Lynette Heller provided helpful comments that improved this essay. I also thank the organizers and contributors for the opportunity to participate in the exchange of ideas and for their well-organized, prompt submissions of papers.

Notes

1. The original concept of a redistributive economy in chiefdoms has been revised (Earle 1977; Feinman and Neitzil 1984; Peebles and Kus 1977; Taylor 1975). Certainly problems arise if we try to apply the "chiefdom" concept to earlier times as a single package of characteristics. I do not take this to mean that none of their institutional features should be expected in the early record. We need not conceptualize developing social complexity and hierarchy as involving a tightly fixed set of characteristics since different social institutions or features may change at different rates and may exhibit differing degrees of systemic connectivity, as Feinman and Neitzil (1984) have discussed.

2. It seems reasonable that the centrifugal movement of high ranking factions would be partly dependent on the prior existence of some prestige exchange relations and that it would seldom involve such great distances as implied by Chalcatzingo because (1) the political ambitions of these factions might make proximity to their origin points desirable, and (2) geographic propinquity would improve the chances for prior prestige exchange relations in the first place. However, the patterns of centrifugal factionalism, like prestige exchange, are dependent on the existence of appropriate social

forms in both of the societies involved and are influenced by the geographic distribution of population nodes and of exotics for which ideology has fixed a social status relationship or which are defined as valuables in social transactions. Fissioning effects are unlikely to fit a simple model of concentric zonation, nor does the Olmec record suggest it.

3. In the future, it will be necessary to address the possibility of a chain of exchanges which contains shifts in commodities. On the assumption that commodities are reasonably plentiful in their region of origin, a shift or "substitution" for a good moving in a particular direction could infuse the circulation of goods with increased flow and thereby account for greater economic dependency on the chain of exchange at either terminus. Although this idea has not been proposed in the papers here, it is a model which could help overcome the attritional effects of distance costs on the magnitude of exchange and hence could increase its economic impact on distant regions.

References Cited

Adams, R. E. W.
   1977 *Prehistoric Mesoamerica*. Little, Brown, Boston.
Adams, Robert McC.
   1974 Anthropological Perspectives on Ancient Trade. *Current Anthropology* 15(3):239–258.
Andrews, Anthony P.
   1983 *Maya Salt Production and Trade*. University of Arizona Press, Tucson.
Berdan, Frances F.
   1980 Aztec Merchants and Markets: Local-Level Activity in a Non-Industrial Empire. *Mexicon* 2:37–41.
Blanton, Richard, and Gary Feinman
   1984 The Mesoamerican World System. *American Anthropologist* 86:673–682.
Blanton, Richard E., Stephen A. Kowalewski, Gary Feinman, and Jill Appel
   1981 *Ancient Mesoamerica: A Comparison of Change in Three Regions*. Cambridge University Press, Cambridge, England.
Braniff C., Beatriz
   1978 Preliminary Interpretations Regarding the Role of the San Miguel River, Sonora, Mexico. In *Across the Chichimec Sea: Papers in Honor of J. Charles Kelley*, edited by Caroll L. Riley and Basil C. Hedrick, pp. 67–82. Southern Illinois University Press, Carbondale.
Bray, Warwick
   1972 The City State in Central Mexico at the Time of the Spanish Conquest. *Journal of Latin American Research* 4(2):161–185.

Brumfiel, Elizabeth M.
    1983 Aztec State Making: Ecology, Structure, and the Origin of the State. *American Anthropologist* 85(2):261–284.
Carmack, Robert M.
    1981 *The Quiche Mayas of Utatlan: The Evolution of a Highland Guatemala Kingdom.* University of Oklahoma Press, Norman.
Chagnon, Napoleon
    1968 *Yanomamo: The Fierce People.* Holt, Rinehart and Winston, New York.
Charlton, Thomas H.
    1984 Production and Exchange: Variables in the Evolution of a Civilization. In *Trade and Exchange in Early Mesoamerica*, edited by Kenneth G. Hirth, pp. 17–42. University of New Mexico Press, Albuquerque.
Cohen, Ronald
    1978 State Origins: A Reappraisal. In *The Early State*, edited by Henri J. M. Claessen and Peter Skalnik, pp. 31–75. Mouton, The Hague.
Drennan, Robert D.
    1984a Long Distance Movement of Goods in the Mesoamerican Formative and Classic. *American Antiquity* 49:27–43.
    1984b Long-Distance Transport Costs in Pre-Hispanic Mesoamerica. *American Anthropologist* 86(1):105–112.
Earle, Timothy K.
    1977 A Reappraisal of Redistribution: Complex Hawaiian Chiefdoms. In *Exchange Systems in Prehistory*, edited by Timothy K. Earle and Jonathan E. Ericson, pp. 213–229. Academic Press, New York.
Eisenstadt, S. N.
    1963 *The Political Systems of Empires.* The Free Press of Glencoe, London.
Ekholm, Kajsa
    1978 External Exchange and the Transformation of Central African Social Systems. In *The Evolution of Social Systems*, edited by J. Friedman, and M. J. Rowlands, pp. 115–136. University of Pittsburgh Press, Pittsburgh.
Feinman, Gary, and Jill Neitzil
    1984 Too Many Types: An Overview of Prestate Societies in the Americas. In *Advances in Archaeological Method and Theory*, vol. 7, edited by Michael B. Schiffer, pp. 39–102. Academic Press, New York.
Flannery, Kent V.
    1968 The Olmec and the Valley of Oaxaca: A Model for Inter-regional Interaction in Formative Times. In *Dumbarton Oaks Conference on the Olmec*, edited by E. P. Benson, pp. 79–110. Dumbarton Oaks Research Library and Collection, Washington, D.C.
Ford, Richard I.
    1972 Barter, Gift or Violence: An Analysis of Tewa Intertribal Exchange. In *Social Exchange and Interaction*, edited by Edwin N. Wilmsen,

pp. 21–45. Anthropological Paper No. 46. Museum of Anthropology, University of Michigan, Ann Arbor.

Friedman, Jonathan
   1975 Tribes, States, and Transformations. In *Marxist Analyses and Social Anthropology*, edited by Maurice Bloch, pp. 161–202. John Wiley, New York.

Gledhill, John, and Mogens Larsen
   1982 The Polanyi Paradigm and a Dynamic Analysis of Archaic States. In *Theory and Explanation in Archaeology: The Southhampton Conference*, edited by Colin Renfrew, Michael J. Rowlands, and Barbara Abbott Segraves, pp. 197–229. Academic Press, New York.

Goldman, I.
   1970 *Ancient Polynesian Society*. The University of Chicago Press, Chicago.

Goody, Jack
   1966 Introduction. In *Succession to High Office*, edited by J. Goody, pp. 1–56. Cambridge Papers in Social Anthropology No. 4. Cambridge University Press, Cambridge, England.
   1971 *Technology, Tradition, and the State in Africa*. Cambridge University Press, Cambridge, England.

Grove, David C., Kenneth G. Hirth, David E. Buge, and Ann M. Cyphers
   1976 Settlement and Cultural Development at Chalcatzingo. *Science* 192:1203–1210.

Hassig, Ross
   1984 The Aztec Empire: A Reappraisal. In *Five Centuries of Law and Politics in Central Mexico*, edited by Ronald Spores and Ross Hassig, pp. 15–24. Vanderbilt University Publications in Anthropology No. 30.

Helms, Mary W.
   1979 *Ancient Panama: Chiefs in Search of Power*. University of Texas Press, Austin.

Hole, Frank
   1974 Comment on "Anthropological Perpsectives on Ancient Trade," by Robert McC. Adams. *Current Anthropology* 15(3):251.

Kirchhoff, Paul
   1966 Mesoamerica: Its Geographic Limits, Ethnic Composition and Cultural Characteristics. In *Ancient Mesoamerica: Selected Readings*, by John A. Graham, pp. 1–10. Peek Publications, Palo Alto, Calif. Originally published 1943.

Lange, Frederick W., and Doris Z. Stone (editors).
   1984 *The Archaeology of Lower Central America*. University of New Mexico Press, Albuquerque.

Leach, E. R.
   1964 *Political Systems of Highland Burma, A Study of Kachin Social Structure*. Reprinted Beacon Press, Boston. Originally published 1954.

Lightfoot, Kent G.
1979 Food Redistribution Among Prehistoric Pueblo Groups. *Kiva* 44: 319–339.
Offner, Jerome A.
1979 A Reassessment of the Extent and Structuring of the Empire of Techotlalatzin, Fourteenth Century Ruler of Texcoco. *Ethnohistory* 26(3): 231–241.
Peebles, Christopher, and Susan Kus
1977 Some Archaeological Correlates of Ranked Societies. *American Antiquity* 42:421–448.
Plog, Fred, Steadman Upham, and Phil C. Weigand
1982 A Perspective on Mogollon-Mesoamerican Interaction. In *Mogollon Archaeology: Proceedings of the 1980 Conference*, edited by Patrick H. Beckett, pp. 227–237. Acoma Books, Ramona, Calif.
Renfrew, Colin
1982 Socio-Economic Change in Ranked Societies. In *Ranking, Resource and Exchange, Aspects of the Archaeology of Early European Society*, pp. 1–8. Cambridge University Press, Cambridge, England.
Rice, Prudence M.
1983 Serpents and Styles in Peten Postclassic Pottery. *American Anthropologist* 85(4):866–880.
Riley, Carroll L.
1982 *The Frontier People: The Greater Southwest in the Protohistoric Period*. Center for Archaeological Investigations, Carbondale Occasional Paper No. 1. Southern Illinois University at Carbondale.
Sabloff, Jeremy A., and William L. Rathje
1975 The Rise of a Maya Merchant Class. *Scientific American* 233(4): 73–82.
Sanders, William T., Jeffrey R. Parsons, and Robert S. Santley
1979 *The Basin of Mexico: Ecological Processes in the Evolution of a Civilization*. Academic Press, New York.
Sanders, William T., and Barbara J. Price
1968 *Mesoamerica: The Evolution of a Civilization*. Random House, New York.
Sanders, William T., and Robert S. Santley
1983 A Tale of Three Cities: Energetics and Urbanization in Pre-Hispanic Central Mexico. In *Prehistoric Settlement Patterns: Essays in Honor of Gordon R. Willey*, pp. 243–291. University of New Mexico Press, Albuquerque, and Peabody Museum of Archaeology and Ethnology, Harvard University, Cambridge.
Sanders, William T., and David Webster
1978 Unilinealism, Multilinealism, and the Evolution of Complex Societies. In *Social Archaeology: Beyond Subsistence and Dating*, edited by Charles L. Redman et al., pp. 249–302. Academic Press, New York.

Santley, Robert S.
  1984 Obsidian Exchange, Economic Stratification, and the Evolution of Complex Society in the Basin of Mexico. In *Trade and Exchange in Early Mesoamerica*, edited by Kenneth G. Hirth, pp. 43–86. University of New Mexico Press, Albuquerque.

Schneider, Jane
  1977 Was There a Pre-Capitalist World-System? *Peasant Studies* 6(1): 20–29.
  1978 Peacocks and Penguins: The Political Economy of European Cloth and Colors. *American Ethnologist* 5(3):413–447.

Smith, Michael E., and Cynthia M. Heath-Smith
  1980 Waves of Influence in Postclassic Mesoamerica? A Critique of the Mixteca-Puebla Concept. *Anthropology* 4(2):15–50.

Southall, Aidan
  1953 *Alur Society: A Study in Processes and Types of Domination.* W. Heffer, Cambridge, England.

Spence, Michael W.
  1982 The Social Context of Production and Exchange. In *Contexts for Prehistoric Exchange*, edited by Jonathan E. Ericson and Timothy K. Earle, pp. 173–197. Academic Press, New York.

Spencer, Charles S.
  1982 *The Cuicatlan Cañada and Monte Albán: A Study of Primary State Formation.* Academic Press, New York.

Spores, Ronald
  1974 Marital Alliances in the Political Integration of Mixtec Kingdoms. *American Anthropologist* 76:297–311.

Stark, Barbara L.
  1983 Coastal Adaptations in the Gulf and Caribbean Coasts of Mesoamerica. Paper presented at the annual meeting of the Society for American Archaeology, Pittsburgh.

Steward, Julian H., and Louis C. Faron
  1959 *Native Peoples of South America.* McGraw-Hill, New York.

Struever, Stuart, and Gail L. Houart
  1972 An Analysis of the Hopewell Interaction Sphere. In *Social Exchange and Interaction*, edited by Edwin N. Wilmsen, pp. 47–79. Museum of Anthropology, Anthropological Paper No. 46. University of Michigan, Ann Arbor.

Taylor, Donna
  1975 *Some Locational Aspects of Middle-Range Hierarchical Societies.* Unpublished Ph.D. dissertation, Department of Anthropology, The City University of New York.

Upham, Steadman
  1982 *Polities and Power: An Economic and Political History of the Western Pueblo.* Academic Press, New York.

Wallerstein, Immanuel
1974 *The Modern World-System. I. Capitalist Agriculture and the Origins of the European World-Economy in the Sixteenth Century.* Academic Press, New York.

Webster, David
1975 Warfare and the Evolution of the State: A Reconsideration. *American Antiquity* 40:464–470.

Weigand, Phil C.
1982 Introduction. In *Mining and Mining Techniques in Ancient Mesoamerica*, Anthropology 6(1–2):1–6.

Weigand, Phil C., Garman Harbottle, and Edward V. Sayre
1977 Turquoise Sources and Source Analysis: Mesoamerica and the Southwestern U.S.A. In *Exchange Systems in Prehistory*, edited by Timothy K. Earle and Jonathan E. Ericson, pp. 15–34. Academic Press, New York.

Willey, Gordon R.
1966 *An Introduction to American Archaeology*, vol. 1. North and Middle America. Prentice-Hall, Englewood Cliffs, New Jersey.

15

Mesoamerican-Southwest Relationships: Issues and Future Directions

Stephen Plog

If there was once any question about the existence of contact between prehistoric cultural groups in Mexico and the southwestern United States, it is now clear that interaction did occur. Commodity exchange involving goods such as shell, copper bells, or macaws and the probability of information exchange because of ideological and political ties now seems clear. Perhaps equally important, if the articles in this volume are representative of the positions of most archaeologists working in either area, those archaeologists accept that evidence. For that reason, the extreme "isolationist" and "imperialist" perspectives espoused in the past no longer seem relevant; as Upham argues (Chapter 11), they fail to account for the variability in interpretations that now exist. There are few, if any, efforts in the volume to, in Kelley's terms, defend the boundary of the Chaco Canyon at all costs, and neither are there interpretations at the other extreme whereby every aspect of southwestern prehistory is explained by the growth and decline of mesoamerican social groups. Thus perhaps the most important contribution of these articles is that they collectively make an important step away from the polarization of the past by developing more realistic models of the nature of the interaction and the mechanisms that created the contact, by conducting some initial tests of aspects of those models, and by presenting evidence to resolve some related issues.

In discussing the reduction in polarity, as well as the increased variability in interpretations that now exists as illustrated by these articles, it is important to recognize that the differences in opinion concerning mesoamerican-southwestern interaction were and are a result of disagreements over a number of different issues. The polarization that once existed was not simply a product of the tendency on the part of one group of archaeologists to look for local causes of culture change and the tendency on the part of others to consider larger spatial scales and look for external causes of those same changes. In the same manner, the welcome trend toward greater variability in interpretive models and away from polarized extremes is not

simply a result of a sudden willingness on the part of southwestern archaeologists to accept evidence for contact with Mesoamerica, nor does it reflect
radical changes on the part of those who have held positions at the other
extreme. Rather, the trend toward more varied but less extreme interpretations results from several factors.

First, archaeologists working not only in the Southwest but also in
other parts of the world have tended to expand the spatial scale upon which
explanatory models have focused as it has become clear that even relatively
simple social systems sometimes encompassed large areas and that interaction over long distances can have important impacts on the structure and
evolution of local social networks in such societies. This is exemplified by
the now frequent discussions of Wallerstein's world systems framework
(Blanton and Feinman 1984, and many articles in this volume), by efforts to
examine regional social networks in the Southwest (e.g., Braun and Plog
1982; Hantman 1983; Plog 1983; Upham 1982; Wilcox and Sternberg
1983), and by studies of the interaction of southwestern groups with "outside" populations, including populations residing not only Mesoamerica but
also the Plains (Spielman 1982).

Second, chronological issues are always a source of disagreement
among archaeologists, particularly when correlations among the cultural sequences of different areas are argued to be due to a causal interrelationship.
Both within the Southwest and Mesoamerica and between the Southwest
and Mesoamerica, it has been suggested that some correlations occur between periods of population growth and decline or in other aspects of culture change. Chronological information in the past, however, often was not
precise enough to actually assess the degree of correlation. Some of these
issues now appear to be approaching resolution, and the articles by David
Wilcox, J. Charles Kelley, and Beatriz Braniff are noteworthy for that reason.
Some correlations that have been suggested no longer seem to be supported
by the chronological data, while others now appear to be very strong,
making it much less likely that they are accidental and much more likely
that they occur because of the types of cultural interrelationships discussed
in this volume. LeBlanc's model (Chapter 7) is particularly provocative in
this respect because it provides us with some interesting ideas about those
interrelationships and at the same time postulates some new correlations
among areas that will have to be assessed more thoroughly with improved
chronological data.

Another important factor reducing the degree of polarization has
been a shift in the area of Mexico on which some of the discussions have
concentrated. Although some type of at least indirect ties between the
Southwest and core mesoamerican states in central Mexico have been and
are still advocated by some, as Whitecotton and Pailes demonstrate in their
essay (Chapter 10), perhaps the most consistent similarity among the articles
in this volume is their emphasis on the importance of northern and western
Mexico, and thus the focus on the "Chichimec Sea" in the title of the vol-

ume. This may, to a large extent, be the result of an increasing awareness on the part of southwestern archaeologists of archaeological information from northern and western Mexico and increasing recognition of the importance of these data. Unfortunately, the prehistory of western and northern Mexico is often underemphasized in texts both on the Southwest and on Meso-america and, as Kelley argues, southwestern archaeologists have in the past failed to expend the necessary effort to acquire a detailed knowledge of the archaeology of the area, a charge to which I plead guilty myself. That effort is being expended now, however, and Wilcox's summary (Chapter 2) of the history of research on southwestern-mesoamerican connections (particularly his discussion of the northern and western Mexican data and chronology), his discussion of the Tepiman connection (Chapter 8), and Kelley's discussion of aspects of exchange systems in the area (Chapter 6) are important additions to the available literature.

Beneath the common focus on northern and western Mexico and the general retreat from extreme interpretations, however, lie definite differences in the interpretations of mesoamerican-southwestern relationships offered in this book. While Whitecotton and Pailes (Chapter 10) and Foster (Chapter 4), for example, speak of the "exploitation" or "manipulation" of the Southwest by mesoamerican groups, others such as McGuire (Chapter 13), Wilcox (Chapter 8), and Mathien (Chapter 12) see little of the direct control implied by such terms. As noted above, while the degree of difference between the most extreme general interpretations may have decreased over the past few years, some issues in the debate remain unresolved and are one source of the variability that still exists in these interpretations. In addition, new issues have developed as the variability in models has increased. Although some of those issues have been touched upon briefly in other articles, I think it is important to consider some of them in somewhat more detail in order to outline the range of issues that must continue to be addressed if we hope to resolve the questions that now exist.

An old problem that always has hindered discussions of mesoamerican-southwestern relationships, as well as group relationships in other areas, concerns the material indices that individuals are willing to accept as indicative of contact, or even the diffusion of information, among groups. That is, archaeology always has had difficulties identifying and measuring social interaction in the archaeological record. The increasing development and use of methods of characterizing the various chemical and mineralogical constituents of raw materials from which artifacts are manufactured has allowed more precise statements concerning the exchange of goods such as turquoise and copper bells. Information obtained in that way is one important reason why it is now difficult to deny the existence of interaction between the Southwest and a variety of mesoamerican groups.

Social interaction, however, includes more than commodity exchange, and agreement of how those other types of interaction can be measured or how particular types of evidence should be interpreted has been more difficult. What is the significance, for example, of similarities in color symbolism between the areas? Or, as Wilcox has asked, what is the significance of the presence of ballcourts in both areas? What kinds of social ties do such similarities indicate? Alternatively, if one wants to test the degree of information and symbolic interaction between two areas, what type of information in the archaeological record should research focus on to measure that interaction? And, does the appearance of new characteristics, such as head deformation and dental mutilation or "the mingling of ceramic traits," necessarily indicate the presence of or contact with foreigners, as Kelley argues, or can they be explained by other factors?

It is significant that several of the essays in this book develop models that address these issues either explicitly or implicitly. Particularly noteworthy are the articles by Wilcox, LeBlanc, and McGuire, which go beyond broad generalizations and begin to focus on some of the specific issues and specific evidence, particularly issues of how the dynamics of internal relationships in the Southwest are linked with mesoamerican-southwestern interaction. As McGuire argues, describing the Southwest as a peripheral region or Mesoamerica as a core region says very little about the cultural dynamics that link those areas. Continued progress is needed, however. Upham, for example, makes the needed point that we must focus on information flow and symbolic interaction in examining mesoamerican-southwestern interaction, given that linkages among population centers are often of a political or ideological nature. Although the work of Joyce Marcus is referred to as an excellent example of research in that area, it would have been valuable to have had a more detailed discussion of how the models developed by Marcus could be applied to mesoamerican-southwestern issues. This is particularly the case given Marcus's ability to analyze epigraphic evidence from the Maya area to obtain some of the difficult measurements of types of interaction other than commodity exchange, and the absence of such epigraphic evidence in northern Mexico and the Southwest. In short, we need continued efforts to provide more detailed models, more explicit discussions of how various types of interaction can be measured, and more rigorous examination of the significance of changes in ceramics and even skeletal characteristics.

A second general issue that continually has been important, yet implicit and often not addressed in discussions of mesoamerican-southwestern relationships, is the role of analogy, as Whitecotton and Pailes emphasize. Questions range from specific issues of the applicability of models based on characteristics of late prehistoric mesoamerican systems to systems of earlier periods, to more general issues concerning ethnographic analogies and models derived from crosscultural studies (e.g., Whitecotton and Pailes's discussion of the validity of the chiefdom concept), to the degree to which one is willing to infer that entire systems are homologous on the basis of known similarities in a limited number of characteristics of those systems. Some of the arguments for exploitation of the Southwest by Mesoamerica, for example, are based on the extrapolation of characteristics of interaction patterns in better known parts of Mesoamerica and in better known time periods to the more poorly known northern periphery or to time periods for which we have less information. In contrast, some of the proposals by those who see less direct mesoamerican exploitation are often based on more general ethnographic knowledge concerning the role of such critical variables as the exchange of valuables, as exemplified in McGuire's essay.

It is unfortunately the case that one can choose from an infinite number of interpretations of either ethnographic or archaeological evidence to draw analogies and develop models, and that one can usually find conflicting interpretations of the same data. A good example concerns one of the specific areas of disagreement among the interpretations presented in this volume. Some of the authors suggest that political and economic affairs can be separated or, alternatively, that economic and political spheres (Foster's spheres of conveyance) of exchange potentially can be independent. This assertion is one of the fundamental arguments of the prestige exchange model that has been discussed by many, but articulated most carefully by McGuire. Probably the explanation of mesoamerican-southwestern relationships most accepted by southwestern archaeologists, the model proposes that the mesoamerican goods that appear on southwestern sites can be largely explained as a result of the exchange of luxury goods-status symbols among elites in different regions.

In contrast, others have argued that the exchange of luxury or prestige goods cannot be separated from the exchange of basic economic commodities in the manner that McGuire, Foster, or others have proposed in their essays. Whitecotton and Pailes, for example, suggest on the basis of information on exchange in central and southern Mexico during the Classic period that commercial systems involved considerably more than mere "prestige" exchange, that the exchange of luxury goods and economic goods was interrelated. They therefore question the proposals of, for example, Nelson, McGuire, and many others who have argued that the presence of mesoamerican-derived artifacts such as macaws and copper bells in southwestern sites is a product of an exchange system that included little or no economic or subsistence goods but did include the exchange of luxury goods or status goods among elites.

As noted above, however, one can often find conflicting interpretations of the data from which analogies are drawn. Drennan, for example, has shown that arguments similar to those of Whitecotton and Pailes concerning the interrelationship of luxury and subsistence exchange in Mesoamerica are unlikely to be incorrect for the Formative period. While such proposals are more realistic for the Classic period because of demographic growth, his analyses "do not provide any actual support for models" suggesting the "direct economic importance for long-distance movement of goods," and thus, "a heavy burden of proof is still left on the proposer of such a model" (Drennan 1984 : 40). I do not cite Drennan's study to show that the argument of Whitecotton and Pailes is incorrect, however (in fact, there are other, similar proposals in both articles). Rather, I only wish to show that existing interpretations of data from the "core" areas of central Mesoamerica can be used to argue both sides of a given issue, in this case the degree to which economic and political exchange can be separated. That is why too much discussion based on analogy is dangerous. Analogy can provide models, but it is fruitless to try and evaluate the relevance of a model to a given area on the basis of the data from which the analogy is derived or on the basis of other analogies drawn from data in other areas.

Two needs must be met to improve the situation. First, some of the expectations that can be derived from the specific proposals that have been made must be tested in several areas. The studies of Nelson and Mathien are important in this respect. Although Drennan (1984) has shown that some mesoamerican goods commonly regarded as luxury items do not seem to occur in elite or high status contexts during the Formative period, Nelson has shown very nicely that similarly interpreted items in Hohokam areas do occur in contexts suggesting that they are status objects. Although Nelson's study supports the general prestige exchange model, Mathien's analysis raises questions about the structure and importance of such exchange. If Mesoamerican derived goods served the functions McGuire suggests, for example, why are the known trade items not more common in Chaco Canyon? Similarly, if the collapse of the trade network had the specific impact that McGuire suggests, why did such impacts occur in areas where meso-american items were absent, even during earlier periods?

Such questions lead to the second issue referred to above. In addition to empirical tests of various propositions, we also need more explicit and detailed discussion of the range of economic or luxury goods that could have been important in southwestern-mesoamerican exchange and the development of methods of measuring the importance of that exchange in the archaeological record. It is too often the case that, for example, some type of economic interaction has been postulated between Mesoamerica and the Southwest, but no real evidence has been produced to demonstrate that goods or that the exchange had a major impact. Drennan, for example, notes that:

> It has become almost a ritual in discussions of exchange to specu-late that many kinds of perishable goods were also moved long dis-tances, and that the materials of which we have direct evidence were only the tip of the trade iceberg. This is, of course, entirely possible. It is also entirely possible that long-distance movement of goods was accomplished by visitors from outer space. Voicing such specula-tions, however, does not advance our knowledge until, first, some-one articulates specific notions about just what perishable goods might have been moving between what places, in what quantities, by what mechanisms, and, second, someone takes such specific notions

and figures out just what kind of archaeological evidence would enable us to verify their accuracy (1984 : 35 – 36).

If progress is to be made toward documenting that prestige and economic exchange were interrelated, some of the needs outlined by Drennan will have to be met—models will have to be outlined in more detail and expectations will have to be derived that can realistically be tested in the archaeological record. One could, for example, expand upon Whitecotton and Pailes's interesting suggestion that raw materials or such labor intensive products as woven goods were obtained from the southwestern periphery. A variety of studies in other areas has shown the importance of woven goods in exchange between "cores" and "peripheries" (Murra 1962; Schneider 1975), and Drennan has noted that "the overwhelmingly important role of textiles in Aztec tribute collections suggests that much more attention should be given to the potential for recovering evidence from earlier periods for this particular category of perishable goods" (1984 : 39). Similarly, Blanton and Feinman, in their discussion of the Mesoamerican world economy, note that the demands of core state:

> ripple outward, beyond territories conquered by the emergent core, influencing production strategies over a broad area and thus incorporating more and more local groups into a Mesoamerican world economy (Berdan 1980 : 38, 39). As an example, Saindon (1977) points out that tributary provinces paying in cotton were not necessarily capable of producing these quantities of the good, and therefore were forced to obtain some, if not most, of what they had to pay from adjacent, nontributary cotton-growing areas. It seems logical to us that as researchers begin to unravel the structure and functioning of the Mesoamerican world economy they will find that the movement of cloth between regions will prove to be one of the most important categories of interaction, as it was in the development of the capitalist world economy (1984 : 678).

Finally, of particular relevance to Whitecotton and Pailes's suggestions concerning Mesoamerica and the Southwest, Schneider, citing evidence from the development of European civilizations and from other areas, argues that "the flow of cloth was a diagnostic predictor of competition for power among groups, of their symbiosis and interdependence, of the penetration of one group by the exports of another, and of the range of possible responses" (1975 : 416).

Beyond these analogies with other areas, several recent studies, both in this volume and elsewhere, mention either ethnohistoric evidence for the exchange of woven goods or raw materials in the northern Mesoamerica-Southwest area and archaeological evidence of tools or raw materials associated with textile production. Ethnohistoric data include the leagues of cotton fields and thousands of cotton blankets reported by Spanish explorers in the Hopi area and evidence of Hopi involvement in cotton trade throughout the upper Southwest (Riley 1982; Upham 1982). Archaeological data include the spindle whorls Kelley notes are abundant in Aztatlán components, the possible redistribution structure at Snaketown discussed by Nelson that had at least seven vessels with large amounts of yucca or sotol yarn, and abundant spindle whorls at other sites in the Hohokam region (Gumerman et al. 1976). These data are hardly sufficient to support a postulated relationship between prestige exchange and the movement of such goods as cloth or raw materials, but they do demonstrate that evidence may exist or could be collected to rigorously test such proposals.

This suggestion leads to the final point that has created problems in the discussion of mesoamerican-southwestern relationships—the fact that there has been much less fieldwork in northern and western Mexico than in the Southwest, particularly studies that concentrate on local cultural dynamics, as Wilcox notes (Chapter 2). This scarcity of information is particularly acute for many of the variables that are often emphasized in contemporary discussions of the Southwest, variables such as demographic change, environmental variation, settlement systems, subsistence change, or intra-regional exchange patterns. It is for those reasons, as well as the "isolationist" explanatory models, that northern and western Mexico always have been underemphasized in syntheses and texts on the Southwest, as noted above.

Testing the various models outlined in this volume, however, will require that we focus increasing amounts of our fieldwork on northern and western Mexico. Wilcox's discussion of the Tepiman connection (Chapter 8), for example, is an excellent example of a model that incorporates mechanisms for contact and information transmission that have been underemphasized or ignored in discussions of southwestern-mesoamerican ties. As Wilcox notes, however, the model only outlines future research directions because there is almost a total absence of archaeological data from the areas discussed. Data on the history of subsistence change and settlements systems thus is not available to test hypotheses concerning the dynamic relationships between hunter-gatherers and sedentary agriculturists, nor is settlement information nearly adequate enough to make the detailed demographic estimates needed to test hypotheses concerning the nature of mating networks. Such information is critical for studies (e.g., Hantman 1983) in even some of the less productive parts of the northern Southwest have shown that population densities were high enough that very small, localized, and potentially closed, endogamous mating networks could have been present well before the period discussed by Wilcox.

It is thus clear that increasing amounts of fieldwork are needed in northern and western Mexico, and it is also clear from this volume that good models to guide such fieldwork have or are being developed. If continued improvements can be made in those areas and progress can be made toward resolving many of the issues that have been highlighted by this volume, we will soon have a much improved understanding of the Southwest, of northern Mesoamerica, and of their interrelationship.

References Cited

Berdan, Frances F.
  1980 Aztec Merchants and Markets. *Mexicon* 2 : 37 – 41.
Blanton, Richard, and Gary Feinman
  1984 The Mesoamerican World System. *American Anthropologist* 86 : 673 – 682.
Braun, David P., and Stephen Plog
  1982 Evolution of "Tribal" Social Networks: Theory and Prehistoric North American Evidence. *American Antiquity* 47 : 504 – 525.
Drennan, Robert D.
  1984 Long-Distance Movement of Goods in the Mesoamerican Formative and Classic. *American Antiquity* 49 : 27 – 43.
Gumerman, George J., Carol Weed, and John Hanson
  1976 Adaptive Strategies in a Biological and Cultural Transition Zone: The Central Arizona Ecotone Project. Ms. on file, Department of Anthropology, Southern Illinois University, Carbondale.
Hantman, Jeffrey L.
  1983 *Stylistic Distributions and Social Networks in Prehistoric Plateau Southwest.* Ph.D. dissertation, Arizona State University, Tempe. University Microfilms, Ann Arbor.
Murra, John V.
  1962 Cloth and Its Functions in the Inca State. *American Anthropologist* 64 : 710 – 728.
Plog, Fred
  1983 Political and Economic Alliances on the Colorado Plateau, A.D. 600 to 1450. In *Advances in World Archaeology*, vol. 2, edited by Fred Wendorf, pp. 289 – 330. Academic Press, New York.
Riley, Carroll L.
  1983 An Overview of the Greater Southwest in the Protohistoric Period. Paper presented at the 48th annual meeting of the Society for American Archaeology, Pittsburgh.
Saindon, Jacqueline
  1977 Cotton Production and Exchange in Mexico, 1427 – 1580. Unpublished M.A. thesis, Hunter College, City University of New York.
Schneider, Jane
  1975 Peacocks and Penguins: The Political Economy of European Cloth and Colours. *American Ethnologist* 5 : 413 – 417.

Spielman, Katherine Ann
   1982 *Inter-Societal Food Acquisition Among Egalitarian Societies: An Ecological Study of Plains/Pueblo Interaction in the American Southwest*. Ph.D. dissertation, University of Michigan. University Microfilms, Ann Arbor.
Upham, Steadman
   1982 *Polities and Power: An Economic and Political History of the Western Pueblo*. Academic Press, New York.
Wilcox, David, and Charles Sternberg
   1983 *Hohokam Ballcourts and Their Interpretation*. Arizona State Museum Archaeological Series No. 115. Tucson.